WordPerfect® PC Tutor

Marianne B. Fox
Lawrence C. Metzelaar
Susan Hafer

WordPerfect® PC Tutor

ISBN 0-88022-619-6

93 92 91 90 6 5 4 3 2

Interpretation of the printing code: the rightmost double-digit number is the year of the book's printing; the rightmost single-digit number is the number of the book's printing. For example, a printing code of 90-1 shows that the first printing of the book occurred in 1990.

WordPerfect PC Tutor is based on WordPerfect 5.1.

Publishing Director
David P. Ewing

Product Development Manager
Charles O. Stewart III

Acquisitions Editor
Terrie Lynn Solomon

Acquisitions Editorial Assistant
Stacey Beheler

Production Editor
Tim Ryan

Editors
Don Eamon
Kathy Simpson

Technical Editors
Andy Young
Jerry Ellis

Editorial Secretary
Karen Opal

Technical Support
J. D. "Doc" Watson

Book Design and Production
Dan Armstrong
Brad Chinn
William Hartman
Chuck Hutchinson
Betty Kish
Bob LaRoche
Sarah Leatherman
Matthew Morrill
Dennis Sheehan

Indexer
Jill D. Bomaster

Composed in Garamond by
Que Corporation

Screen shots produced with InSet software from
INSET Systems Inc.

Contents at a Glance

Table of Contents

Lesson 6 Formatting and Enhancing Text 111

Lesson 7 Formatting Pages and Designing Documents 137

Lesson 16 Working with Text Columns......................357

Lesson 17 Working with Math Columns 377

Lesson 18 Working with Tables 395

Lesson 19 Integrating Text and Graphics 421

Trademark Acknowledgments

Que Corporation has made every effort to supply trademarks about company names, products, and services mentioned in this book. Trademarks indicated below were derived from various sources. Que Corporation cannot attest to the accuracy of this information.

ATI is a trademark of American Training International.

PageMaker is a registered trademark of Aldus Corporation.

AutoCAD is a registered trademark of Autodesk, Inc.

PC TOOLS is a trademark of Central Point Software, Inc.

GEM Paint is a trademark of Digital Research, Inc.

LaserJet is a trademark of Hewlett-Packard Company.

IBM is a registered trademark of International Business Machines Corporation.

1-2-3 is a registered trademark of Lotus Development Company.

Dr. HALO is a registered trademark of Media Cybernetics, Inc.

Microsoft Windows Paint and MS-DOS are registered trademarks of Microsoft Corporation.

Norton Utilities is a trademark of Peter Norton Computing.

Ventura Publisher is a registered trademark of Ventura Software, Inc.

WordPerfect is a registered trademark of WordPerfect Corporation.

PC Paintbrush is a registered trademark of ZSoft Corporation.

Conventions Used in This Book

A number of conventions are used in *WordPerfect PC Tutor*:

- References to keys are as they appear on the keyboard of the IBM PC AT.
- Direct quotation of WordPerfect screen prompts and messages are printed in a `special typeface`.
- Information you are asked to type is printed in **boldface**.
- The name of a WordPerfect menu option is presented first followed by the appropriate menu-number in parentheses—for instance, **F**ootnote (**1**). The letter (the *mnemonic*) or number you press appears in **boldface**. Pull-down menu options are treated in a similar manner: the **S**ave option on the **F**ile pull-down menu.
- Words printed in uppercase letters are used to distinguish file names, DOS (disk operating system) commands, macro commands({PAUSE}), and merge commands ({END FIELD}).
- Key combinations that must be pressed together are separated by a hyphen. For example, Ctrl-F2 means that you press and hold the Ctrl key as you press the F2 key.
- When a series of keys are separated by commas, press and release each key. For example, to move to the top of document in WordPerfect, you press and release Home, press Home again, then press the up arrow (Home, Home, up-arrow).

DISK TUTOR — This icon is used to point out an important connection between the interactive tutorial lessons and the book lessons.

LESSON FILES — This icon appears in the book whenever you are asked to access a lesson file.

Introduction

WordPerfect 5.1 is a powerful yet easy-to-use word processing program with which you can create a variety of documents, including these:

- ❑ Letters, memos, and reports
- ❑ Term papers, theses, dissertations, and manuscripts with tables of contents, footnotes and endnotes, tables of authorities, lists, and indexes
- ❑ Financial statements and invoices requiring mathematical calculations
- ❑ Labels, envelopes, and individualized letters for mass mailings

WordPerfect 5.1 also offers a full range of editing capabilities, as well as advanced printing and utility options. Using this program, you can do the following:

- ❑ Move and copy text within the same document or from one document to another
- ❑ Import or link data directly in a WordPerfect file
- ❑ Set and change text format and appearance
- ❑ Create mathematical or engineering formulas, and tables with graphic lines
- ❑ Number paragraphs, number footnotes and endnotes, and outline automatically
- ❑ Check spelling and refer to a thesaurus for synonyms
- ❑ Type or execute commands automatically from a macro
- ❑ Merge and then print quantities of individualized documents
- ❑ Restore inadvertently deleted text
- ❑ Integrate line drawings and graphics into text

WordPerfect 5.1 adds pull-down menus as an alternative to the regular menus that you activate by pressing function key combinations. All menus are accessible through the keyboard or a mouse.

Who Should Use This Book?

WordPerfect PC Tutor is a structured learning experience designed to lead you easily and logically through WordPerfect's many features. This book and the Disk Tutor complement each other and together provide comprehensive exercises with practical applications to help you quickly gain the skills to put WordPerfect 5.1 to work.

The book is written for a variety of users:

- ❏ Professionals and other users who want a self-instructional, hands-on guide to WordPerfect.
- ❏ Instructors in WordPerfect workshops, seminars, and courses can use the complete course package, which includes an independently-run tutorial program, a book with exercises and sample documents on disk, an instructor's manual, and pages for creating transparencies.
- ❏ Training personnel in business and industry can use the materials for group or individual instruction.

Providing a flexible, easy-to-use learning package was the primary goal in creating *WordPerfect PC Tutor*. The Disk Tutor is an example of CBT (computer-based training) and is an indispensable part of the learning experience. Reviewer Richard Shrout of *The WordPerfectionist* described the benefits of computer-based training (CBT) in the following excerpt:

> Computer-based training can be the most cost-effective method for self-motivated students because no instructor or additional equipment is necessary. Also, the software can be left on the trainee's computer for a period of time to allow for further review as needed.[1]

Other books in the *PC Tutor* series include:

- ❏ *MS-DOS PC Tutor*
- ❏ *dBASE IV PC Tutor*
- ❏ *1-2-3 Release 2.2 PC Tutor*

[1]*The WordPerfectionist*, Volume III, No. 9, p. 15, 1989.

What the PC Tutor Package Contains

The instructional package consists of the book, with its series of lessons, and the disk. The disk contains lesson files in WordPerfect. You will be asked to use these when you follow the lessons in the book. The disk also holds the tutorial program, which simulates WordPerfect's basic screens and functions.

The tutorial has several advantages for learning WordPerfect's basic features. Because the tutorial program simulates WordPerfect, you can use less sophisticated hardware to run it. You need not use a computer "loaded" with the WordPerfect program. Finally, because the tutorial is error-proof, it can instill more confidence in new users as they learn WordPerfect commands.

The book, the lesson files, and the tutorial were specifically designed to work together. Each lesson in the book cross-references both the tutorial (where applicable) and the lesson files. For example, the book's Lesson 5 covers working with blocks of text, and it refers to the tutorial's Lesson F which also covers blocks, among other topics.

Although each lesson is designed to be independent, you can make the most of your learning experience by working Lessons 1 through 9 in order. For more advanced features, you can easily do Lessons 10 through 19 in any order.

The 19 lessons are organized into three groups:

- ❑ Part I, "Learning WordPerfect with the Tutorial" (Lesson 1), focuses on the interactive tutorial, which introduces and demonstrates the fundamental features of WordPerfect 5.1: starting the program; entering text; editing text; naming, saving, and retrieving documents; changing formats; printing documents; and getting help. If you're new to WordPerfect, you'll want to begin with the tutorial in Part I.
- ❑ Part II, "Learning WordPerfect's Basic Features" (Lessons 2–9), utilizes the lesson files to provide more hands-on experience with sample text exercises. Lessons in this section refer to related lessons on the Disk Tutor and provide an in-depth treatment of the topics introduced in Part I. In addition, Part II addresses document-support capabilities such as spell-checking, printing on a laser printer, and file-maintenance routines. You are encouraged to work through these exercises in order.
- ❑ Part III, "Learning WordPerfect's Advanced Features" (Lessons 10–19), illustrates more advanced features such as List Files, Macros and Styles, graphics, text and math columns, footnotes, endnotes, outlines, and line numbers. You may complete Part III's lessons in any order.

The following table outlines how the tutorial and book lessons are integrated throughout the book.

Table I.1
ATI Training Disk Lessons and Their WordPerfect 5.1 Book Counterparts

ATI Training Disk Lessons	*Book Lesson(s)*
Lesson A (How to Use Your Training Program)	Introduction
Lesson B (Start Up WP)	Lesson 2
Lesson C (Enter Text)	Lessons 2 and 3
Lesson D (Save a Document)	Lesson 3
Lesson E (Move Cursor)	Lessons 2, 3, and 4
Lesson F (Edit a Document)	Lessons 3, 4, and 5
Lesson G (Change Format)	Lessons 6 and 7
Lesson H (Print a Document)	Lesson 3 and Lesson 9
Lesson I (Get Help)	Lesson 2
Lesson J (Pull Down Menus)	Lesson 2

Each Disk Tutor lesson or sub-lesson contains the following:

- An overview of the topics to be covered

  Each lesson first highlights the features to be covered, then gives background information needed to prepare the reader for the lesson.
- A sub-menu of topics

  If the general topic has a broad scope, it is broken down into individual tasks and features. For example, Lesson F covers editing documents, which is broken down into a sub-menu for inserting, deleting, moving, and copying text.

  When a sub-menu is selected, the reader is given background information about the functions covered, and then the sub-menu appears. From there the reader selects a specific function and additional background information for that topic is displayed. For example, when you select **F** from the Main Menu for text editing, a screen of information related to editing documents is displayed; then the sub-menu for inserting, deleting, moving, and copying text is shown. The reader might select from the sub-menu for the Move Text lesson and see a brief discussion of reorganizing text in a document.

- Directives to the reader to accomplish a certain task using that feature

  For example, in the lesson on moving text within a document, the user sees text in a WordPerfect document and a message saying which part of the text should be moved, and where.

- Step-by-step instructions on using the WordPerfect feature under study

  For example, when learning to move text, the reader sees that three steps are needed to accomplish the task: mark the text to be moved, mark the destination, and tell WordPerfect to move the text.

- A keystroke-by-keystroke example, demonstrating the feature

  To continue the "Move Text" example, several screens guide the reader through the moving of a particular group of words from the middle of the text to the end.

- A review of the concepts or procedures covered

  Lessons end with a summary of what was covered in the lesson or the keystrokes used to accomplish a given task.

Lessons 2 through 19 in the book each contain the following:

- Lesson objectives

  The objectives for each lesson are listed at the start. Studying the referenced material in the supplementary text will give the reader the full information needed to master the lesson.Tutorial Lessons will be referred to, if any cover the same features as the lesson in the book. Use or review the tutorial for basic, "self-correcting" practice.

- Explanations of WordPerfect features

  WordPerfect capabilities are described in general terms and then through step-by-step, hands-on illustrations. Each lesson contains figures and tables to help you learn the features.
  Note: Your screen displays may vary slightly from those shown in book figures, depending on WordPerfect settings on your system.

- Summary of concepts

  A list of features you worked through concludes each lesson.

- Review exercises

  You can reinforce the concepts in each lesson by working through suggested exercises in which step-by-step instructions are omitted.

- Reference to advanced-level commands and information

  Where to go after you have mastered the skills and concepts presented in this tutorial

What Learning Path Fits Your Needs

Repeat lessons as often as necessary until you feel comfortable using each WordPerfect feature. You'll find that there are a number of learning paths through *WordPerfect PC Tutor*. You can choose the path that best meets your needs and matches your level of comfort with WordPerfect:

- ❏ You might complete the interactive Disk Tutor, work through all the book lessons, and then use the book as a subsequent desk reference.
- ❏ You might complete the interactive Disk Tutor, move to specific book lessons, and then use the book as a subsequent desk reference.
- ❏ You might complete the interactive Disk Tutor, begin the book lessons, occasionally return to specific sections of the interactive tutorial, and then use the book as a subsequent desk reference.
- ❏ You might want to bypass the interactive tutorial entirely and go directly to the book lessons, then use the book as a subsequent desk reference.

If you're an instructor or a corporate trainer...

Have your students work through the tutorial on their own before class. This preparation will enable them to approach your training session with greater confidence and far less self-consciousness. In addition, the group will be entering the class at more or less the same level, and they will be able to progress through the book lessons more quickly.

How to Use the Tutorial

If you plan to complete the WordPerfect tutorial program included with this book, you need to install the appropriate Disk Tutor files either on a separate, "working" floppy or in a subdirectory on your hard disk. To install the tutorial, follow the instructions in Appendix A.

To use the tutorial once installed, change to the proper drive or directory, type **ATI**, and press Enter. For more information on starting and running the tutorial, see Lesson 1 in this book.

How to Use the Lesson Files

The disk that accompanies this book also contains sample documents to be retrieved as you progress through the lessons. Appendix B contains an alphabetical list of these Lesson files. To install these files either on a separate, "working" floppy or in a subdirectory on your hard disk, follow the instructions in Appendix A.

Caution: Be sure to install the files from the original disk as instructed in Appendix A and use that copy rather than using the original disk.

After you have completed installation of the lesson files, load WordPerfect 5.1. If the Lesson files do not display after a command to list files, failure to specify the location of the files is the probable cause. Change the default to the proper location by pressing List (F5) and then typing the equal sign (=) followed by the drive letter and a colon, and any subdirectories that are appropriate (for example, **=B:** or **=C:\ATIWP**). If copies of lesson files are stored on a disk, be sure that the disk is inserted properly and that the disk drive door is closed.

Sample documents included on the book disk eliminate typing most of the text that illustrates WordPerfect features. The book instructs you to revise these sample documents.

Caution: Do not save a document that you create or revise unless you are instructed to do so, or you may overwrite a file needed at another point in the book.

The names of the lesson files include a lesson number (see Appendix B). Files you are asked to create and save on your own do not include a lesson number.

What You Need to Get Started

If you plan to use only the tutorial program, which does not require WordPerfect 5.1, you need this equipment and software:

- ❑ An IBM PC or 100-percent-compatible microcomputer with 384K of random-access memory (RAM) and at least one floppy disk drive
- ❑ PC DOS or MS-DOS, version 2.0 or higher
- ❑ A copy of the original tutorial files (see Appendix A)
- ❑ A monochrome or color monitor

To run WordPerfect 5.1 and complete the book lessons, you need this equipment and software:

- ❑ An IBM PC or 100-percent-compatible microcomputer with 404K of random-access memory (RAM) and two high density floppy disk drives

- ❑ PC DOS or MS-DOS, version 2.0 or higher
- ❑ WordPerfect 5.1 program files installed on your hard disk or on high-density disks

  Note: Book illustrations reflect installation of the program in the \WP51 subdirectory on the C: disk drive.
- ❑ A copy of the original book lesson files (see Appendix A)

  Note: If you followed the installation procedure for copying the lesson files to your hard disk, these files will be found in an appropriate subdirectory, such as the \WP51\QUEDISK subdirectory appearing in book's illustrations. In hands-on steps, the assumption is that the directory containing the lesson files is the current directory.
- ❑ A printer
- ❑ A monochrome or color monitor

For information about starting WordPerfect 5.1 on a hard disk or two-disk system, refer to Lesson 2 of this book.

For information about saving and retrieving WordPerfect files, such as those on your copy of the lesson files, refer to Lesson 3 of this book.

For Further Reference

For further information about preparing your disks and installing WordPerfect 5.1, consult *Using WordPerfect 5.1,* Special Edition (Que Corporation, Carmel, IN, 1989), Appendix A.

Learning WordPerfect with the Disk Tutor

Part

I

The first lesson in this book introduces the interactive tutorial software included with *WordPerfect PC Tutor*.

- ❑ Lesson 1 presents the details of how to use the ATI Disk Tutor

Getting Started with the Tutorial

1

The following topics are covered in this lesson:

- ❑ How to start the tutorial on floppy and hard disk systems
- ❑ How to use your training program
- ❑ Keys you need to know to run the tutorial
- ❑ What features of WordPerfect are covered in the tutorial
- ❑ What to expect in a typical lesson module
- ❑ How to exit the tutorial and resume interactive training at a later time
- ❑ What to do after you've completed the tutorial

In this lesson, you use the tutorial included with this book to learn the basic word processing features of WordPerfect 5.1. Appendix A gives installation instructions for the program, which you should do before continuing here.

Note: You cannot use the tutorial until you have either prepared a disk for your floppy drive or installed the tutorial on your hard drive. Once you have completed the Appendix A installation instructions, return here to learn how to start the tutorial, how to navigate through it, what it covers, how to exit the tutorial and return to an interrupted session later, and what to do next.

Starting the Tutorial on Floppy and Hard Disk Systems

After following the instructions in Appendix A to install the tutorial, follow these steps to start up the tutorial.

On a floppy disk system:

Step 1: Turn on your computer and type the current date and time if prompted to do so. Note the A> prompt on screen.

Step 2: Insert the disk that you labeled Disk Tutor (do not use the original disk) into drive A.

Step 3: At the A> prompt, type **ATI** and press Enter. Proceed to Step 4.

On a hard disk system:

Step 1: Turn on your computer and type the current date and time if prompted to do so. Note the C> prompt on screen.

Step 2: Change to the subdirectory where you installed the tutorial files according to Appendix A.

Step 3: At the C> prompt, type **ATI** and press Enter.

Step 4: Type **Y** or **N** to the prompt: `DOES THIS TEXT APPEAR IN WHITE AND BLUE?` (See fig. 1.1). In other words, are you using a color monitor, yes or no?

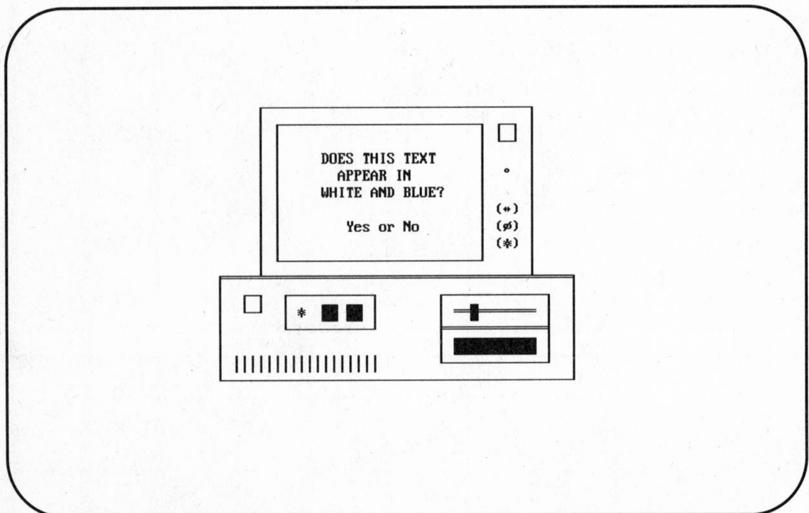

***Fig. 1.1.** Prompt for indicating a color or monochrome monitor.*

Step 5: Press the space bar after the tutorial's title screen appears and the bell sounds to begin (see fig. 1.2)

Step 6: Type in your first name and press Enter when prompted (see fig. 1.3).

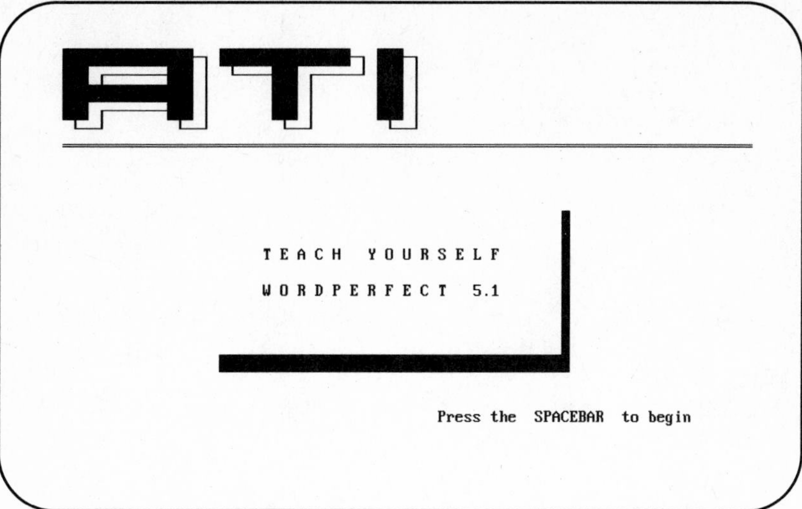

Fig. 1.2. The tutorial's title screen.

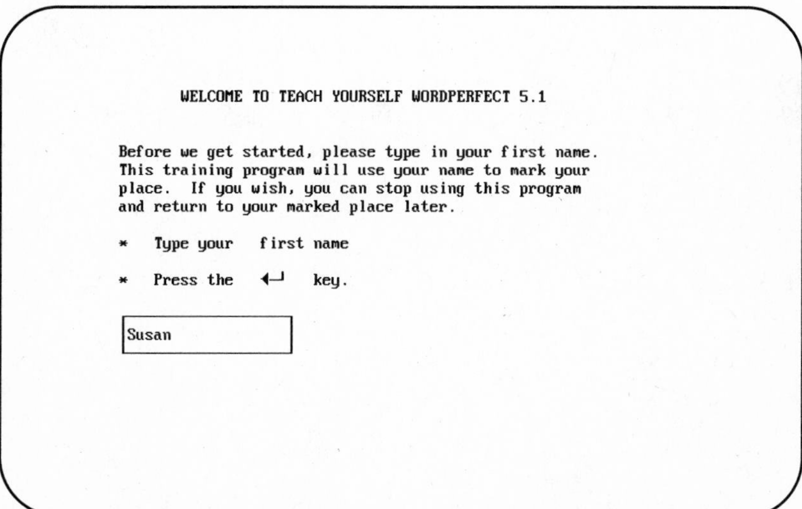

Fig. 1.3. The tutorial prompts you for your name.

If you have never used the tutorial, a screen appears entitled "Getting Started with WordPerfect" (see fig. 1.4) giving a brief overview of WordPerfect. Press the space bar to continue.

```
GETTING STARTED WITH WORDPERFECT

WordPerfect is a powerful word processing
program developed by the WordPerfect Corporation.
With it you can create, change, and reorganize a
document.  When the document is the way you
want it, you can print it onto paper.

Press SPACEBAR to go on; HOME for menu; END for help
```

Fig. 1.4. Screen shown if this is your first time using the tutorial.

If this is not your first session, and you type in your first name exactly the way you did in your last session, the screen shown in figure 1.5 appears instead of the one in figure 1.4. You can either return to where you were last session by pressing 1 or start the program from the Main Menu by pressing 2 (see fig. 1.5). Make your choice by pressing the appropriate key.

```
Hello, Susan, welcome back.

You can choose to return to the place in this program where
you left off, or you can start from the beginning.

To return to your previous place:     Press the  1  key.

To start from the beginning:          Press the  2  key.
```

Fig. 1.5. Screen shown if you have used the tutorial previously.

The next screen that appears is the Main Menu, as shown in figure 1.6. From here you choose the lesson you would like to do by typing the letter (A-J) next to it. You may type your choices in either uppercase or lowercase. Selecting **A** for How to Use Your Training Program gives you an overview of the main components of the tutorial, explained in the following section.

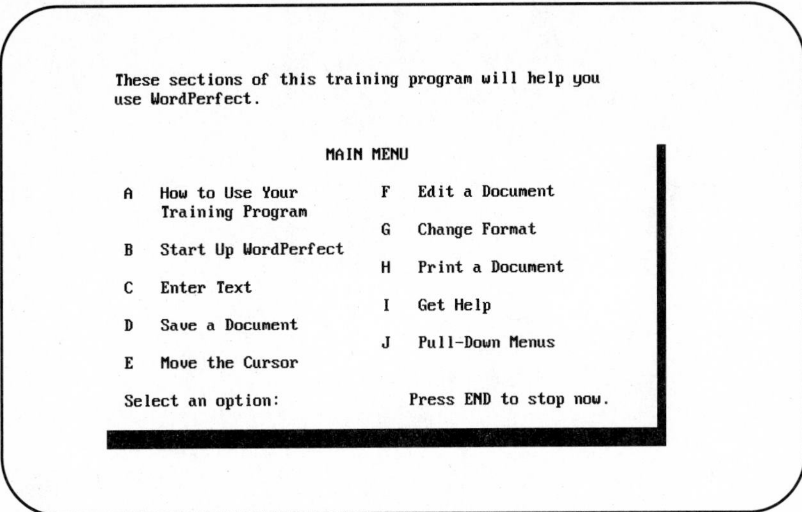

These sections of this training program will help you use WordPerfect.
MAIN MENU
A How to Use Your Training Program
B Start Up WordPerfect
C Enter Text
D Save a Document
E Move the Cursor
F Edit a Document
G Change Format
H Print a Document
I Get Help
J Pull-Down Menus
Select an option:
Press END to stop now.

Fig. 1.6. *The tutorial's Main Menu.*

How to Use the Training Program

After you select **A** from the Main menu, you will see a screen showing the Disk Tutor and the *WordPerfect 5.1 PC Tutor*; when you press the spacebar to continue, as instructed on the screen, you reach the menu shown in figure 1.7, which lets you choose between the following items to learn more about using the tutorial:

- ❑ Find out about interactive training
- ❑ Learn how to use the tutorial in conjunction with Parts II and III of *WordPerfect PC Tutor*
- ❑ Learn about the special keys used by the tutorial
- ❑ Return to the Main menu to begin the training sessions

Select any of those options that you would like to learn more about. Additional information about each is given in the following sections of this lesson.

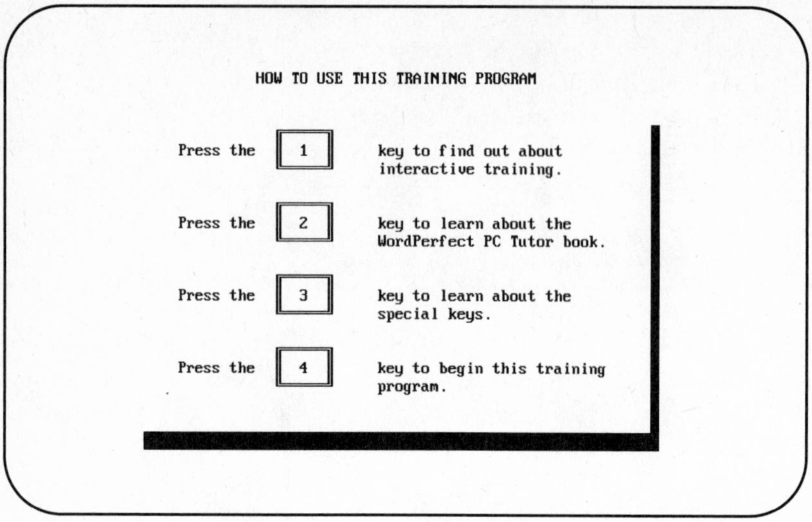

HOW TO USE THIS TRAINING PROGRAM

Press the [1] key to find out about interactive training.

Press the [2] key to learn about the WordPerfect PC Tutor book.

Press the [3] key to learn about the special keys.

Press the [4] key to begin this training program.

Fig. 1.7. The How to Use This Training Program menu.

Interactive Training

Pressing **1** from the How to Use This Training Program menu will give you some information about interactive training. This tutorial is an example of computer-based training (CBT), a style of training that uses the computer as a one-on-one interactive "trainer" giving you immediate feedback. Rather than sitting in a class with students competing for the guidance of one teacher, it's just you and the tutorial, and it lets you know when you have done correctly what is needed at each point in a lesson, or what key you should press if you do not press the correct one. You may learn at your own pace, and you can repeat any lesson as many times as you wish. This particular CBT tutorial uses a "split-screen" approach, showing you how the various WordPerfect screens will appear in one part of the screen, while giving you some explanatory information in another part of the screen (see fig. 1.8).

Unlike WordPerfect's own tutorial, this ATI Disk Tutor does not run a real copy of WordPerfect but simulates it instead. Each screen and prompt that would be displayed in WordPerfect is shown as though you were actually running the real program, much like a simulated flight program displays on your monitor what you would see if you were actually flying in an airplane. Also, as previously mentioned, this simulation aspect of the Disk Tutor has the advantage of allowing you to use the tutorial on computers that do not or cannot, because of hardware limitations, have WordPerfect 5.1 installed on them.

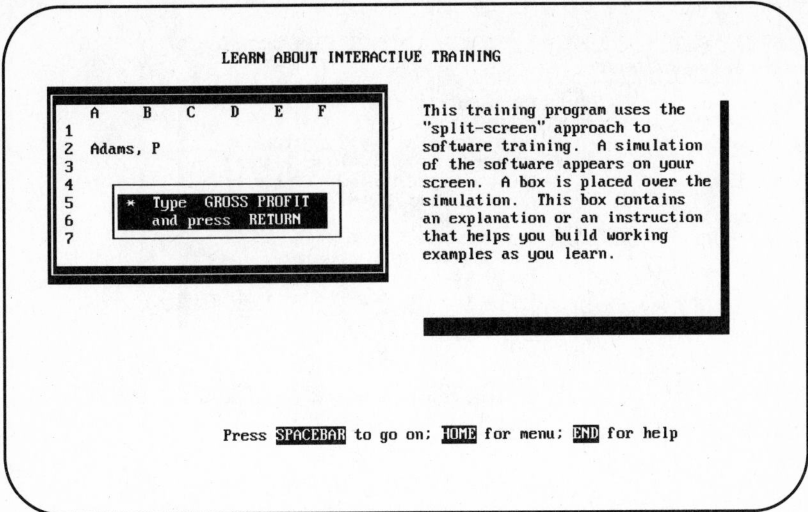

Fig. 1.8. Example from tutorial of the split-screen approach.

Tutorial and PC Tutor Book

If you select **2** from the How to Use This Training Program menu, you are reminded that this tutorial and the *WordPerfect PC Tutor* book were designed to work together. We suggest that beginners go through the entire tutorial first, then proceed either to a WordPerfect training class or, on your own, to the rest of the lessons in this book, using the tutorial again as needed for review. After completing all the lessons in the tutorial, you will then be able to refer back to the tutorial or to the book whenever you need a refresher lesson about a particular WordPerfect feature (see fig. 1.9).

Keys You Need to Know

The following table is provided to help you navigate through the tutorial. It shows the various keys to use with the Disk Tutor and is a more complete listing of keys than the one shown in the tutorial when you select item **3** from the How to Use This Training Program menu.

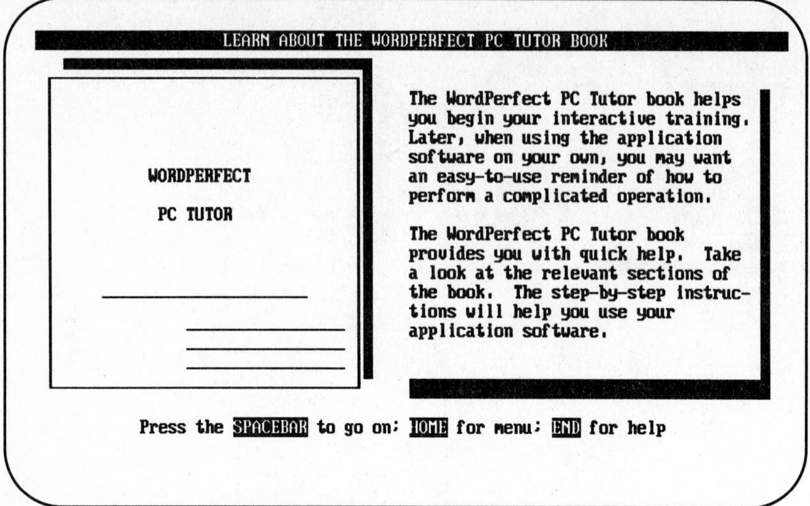

Fig. 1.9. Using the tutorial and the book together.

Table 1.1
The Disk Tutor Keys

Key	*When To Use It*	*Action*
Home	Any time during the tutorial	Displays the Main Menu
PgUp	Any time during the tutorial	Reviews the previous screen (up to three screens back)
PgDn	Any time during the tutorial	Proceeds to the next screen, bypassing any keystrokes needed to get to that screen
End	Any time during the tutorial	Displays the Help screen with the special keys listed; also used to exit the Disk Tutor
Esc	When prompted	Used to exit the Disk Tutor
Space bar	When prompted	Continues to the next screen
Enter	When prompted	Completes a command

These keys perform different functions in the WordPerfect program than they do here in the tutorial. For example, pressing PgUp in the tutorial goes back one screen within a lesson, but pressing PgUp in WordPerfect takes you to the top of the previous page of text in your document. These will be explained as you proceed through the lessons in the tutorial and in the book.

WordPerfect Operations Covered by the Tutorial

Choices B through J in the tutorial's Main Menu (see fig. 1.6) cover the basics of WordPerfect: starting up the program, entering and saving text, moving within the text, editing text, changing the format, printing, getting help, and using the pull-down menus.

The Edit a Document option (**F**), like the How to Use Your Training Program option (**A**), has its own submenu of choices, broken down into an edit menu with options to learn how to insert, delete, move, and copy text.

Option B—Start Up WordPerfect. This option covers the following topics:

- ❏ Starting WordPerfect from the DOS prompt
- ❏ Parts of the WordPerfect editing screen.

Notice that the tutorial shows a `C>` prompt; if you use WordPerfect from a floppy disk rather than from a hard disk, there are separate instructions in Lesson 2 of this book for starting up WordPerfect 5.1.

Option C—Enter Text. This lesson explains the following:

- ❏ What the cursor is
- ❏ How to enter text
- ❏ How WordPerfect uses *word wrap*
- ❏ How to type over existing text

Option D—Save a Document. This option covers the following topics:

- ❏ Use of the F7 key to name a document, save it to disk, and exit WordPerfect
- ❏ Getting back into WordPerfect
- ❏ Retrieving a document from disk with the Shift-F10 function key
- ❏ WordPerfect's color-coded function key template
- ❏ Use of the Cancel (F1) key to cancel an operation and the Save (F10) key to save a document while you continue to work on it

Option E—Move the Cursor. This lesson covers the many ways that WordPerfect lets you move the cursor:

- ❑ Using the left-arrow and right-arrow keys to move by one character
- ❑ Using the Ctrl key with these keys to move by one word
- ❑ Using the down- and up-arrow keys to move by one line
- ❑ Using the Home key twice with a down- or up-arrow to move to the top or bottom of your document

Option F—Edit a Document. This option offers a submenu for the following topics:

- ❑ Inserting text
- ❑ Deleting text
- ❑ Moving text
- ❑ Copying text

Option G—Change Format. This lesson demonstrates the following:

- ❑ How to change the standard line spacing, tab settings, and margins
- ❑ How to change justification, set line numbers, and use hyphenation

Option H—Print a Document. This option illustrates how to use the Print (Shift-F7) function key to do the following:

- ❑ Print a document that has been saved to disk
- ❑ Print all pages of a document or just specified pages
- ❑ Control the printer to start and stop print jobs
- ❑ Change print options

Option I—Get Help. This lesson demonstrates WordPerfect's general help facility.

Option J—Pull-Down Menus. This lesson introduces WordPerfect 5.1's pull-down menus and has you use them to do the following:

- ❑ Retrieve a document
- ❑ Display WordPerfect's hidden codes
- ❑ Use Help to display a template on the screen

Note: The Disk Tutor uses the function-key approach to accessing commands until this last lesson. Beginning with Lesson 2, however, the book emphasizes the use of pull-down menus. Because the pull-down menus are a feature new to WordPerfect 5.1, people who used earlier versions of the software are often more comfortable using the trusty old function keys, while beginners find it easier to learn to use the pull-down menus. You will use whichever method is best for yourself.

Basic Components of Each Training Module

In general, the tutorial lessons follow a pattern where you choose a brief lesson, get some background information on the lesson's topic, practice certain keystrokes, receive positive feedback, and are given a review of what you have just learned. This cycle is repeated for each action demonstrated in the lesson.

Each tutorial lesson prepares you for a particular action by saying something like "Let's try thus-and-such." When you are asked to make specific keystrokes to perform an action, a beep sounds if you press the wrong keys. At times when you reach the end of a lesson, you see not only a review of what you learned but some additional information about the concepts discussed in the lesson. Then you return to the Main Menu. At that point the tutorial highlights the lesson you have just completed and asks what you would like to do next.

To illustrate how a typical tutorial lesson is organized, we'll look at the Delete Text lesson from the Edit a Document menu. Following along using the tutorial, you select Edit a Document from the main menu. You see next the screen shown in figure 1.10, explaining what the Edit menu covers.

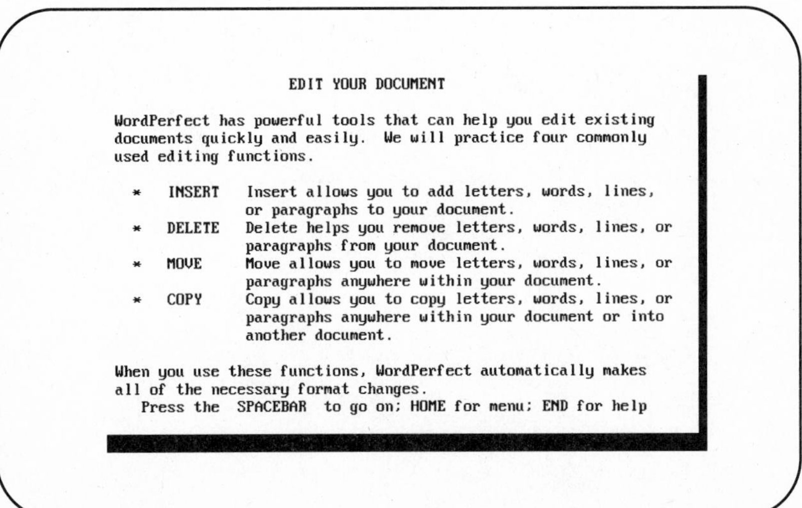

Fig. 1.10. *Explanation of the Edit Menu.*

Notice that the tutorial tells you to press the space bar to continue. Doing so brings you to the Edit menu. We have already said that for this example we want to practice deleting text, so choose the Delete Text option by pressing **B**.

This lesson first shows you an overview of what deleting text is all about as shown in figure 1.11. This is your background information, before you begin practicing the concept.

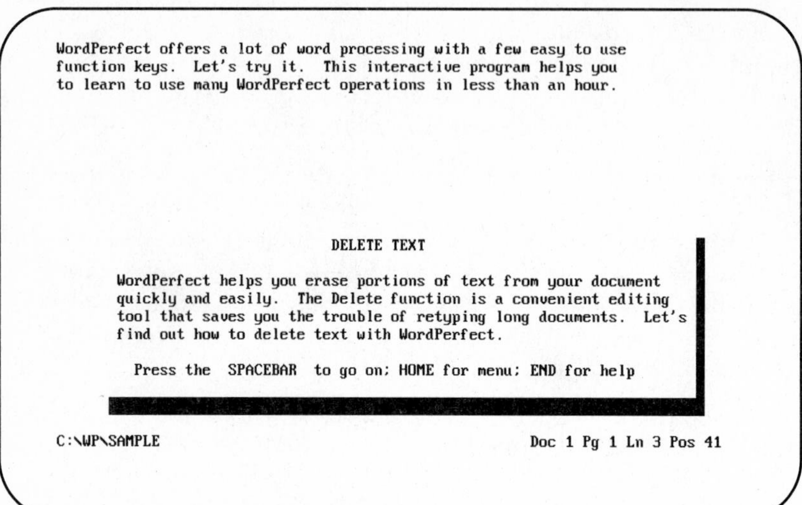
WordPerfect offers a lot of word processing with a few easy to use
function keys. Let's try it. This interactive program helps you
to learn to use many WordPerfect operations in less than an hour.
DELETE TEXT
WordPerfect helps you erase portions of text from your document
quickly and easily. The Delete function is a convenient editing
tool that saves you the trouble of retyping long documents. Let's
find out how to delete text with WordPerfect.
Press the SPACEBAR to go on; HOME for menu; END for help
C:\WP\SAMPLE
Doc 1 Pg 1 Ln 3 Pos 41

Fig. 1.11. *Overview of deleting text.*

After you press the space bar to continue, you see what general steps you will follow when you want to delete text in a document (see fig. 1.12).

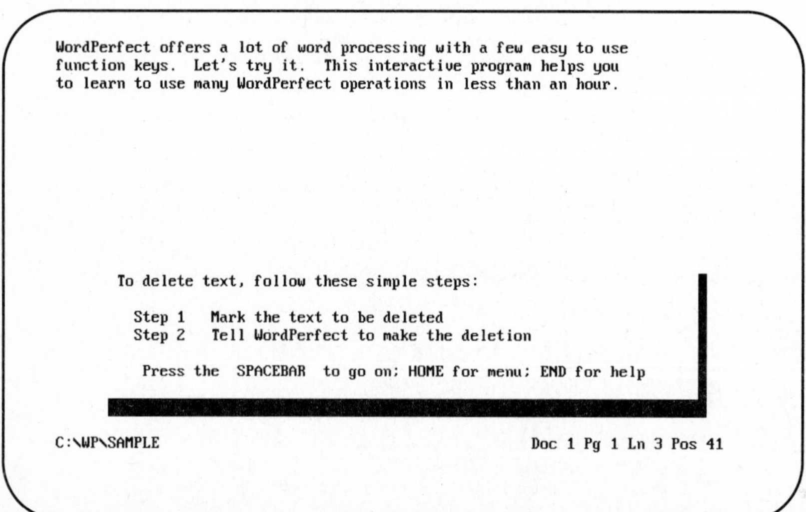
WordPerfect offers a lot of word processing with a few easy to use
function keys. Let's try it. This interactive program helps you
to learn to use many WordPerfect operations in less than an hour.
To delete text, follow these simple steps:
Step 1 Mark the text to be deleted
Step 2 Tell WordPerfect to make the deletion
Press the SPACEBAR to go on; HOME for menu; END for help
C:\WP\SAMPLE
Doc 1 Pg 1 Ln 3 Pos 41

Fig. 1.12. *General steps for deleting text.*

Next, the tutorial points out a particular application for deleting text in your sample document and walks you through the particular steps. In this case, first you move the cursor to the place in the text where there is text is to be deleted by pressing Ctrl-← four times to move to the left four words (see fig. 1.13). Then you delete the text by pressing the Delete key three times (see fig. 1.14).

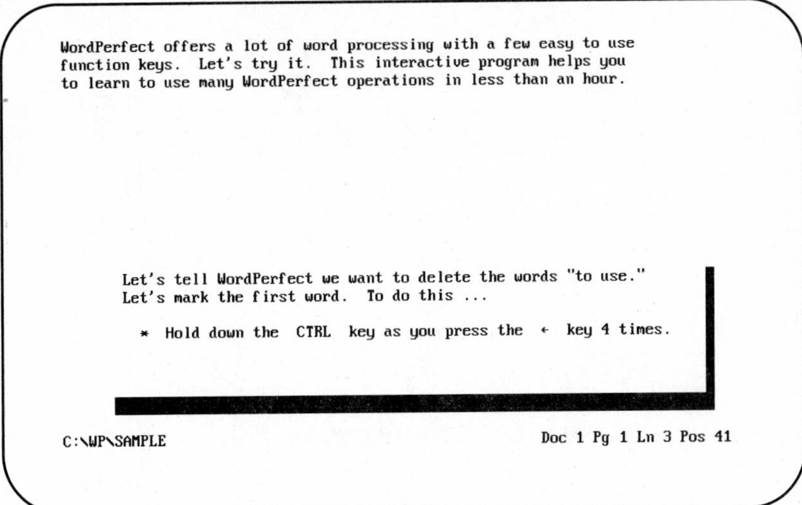
WordPerfect offers a lot of word processing with a few easy to use
function keys. Let's try it. This interactive program helps you
to learn to use many WordPerfect operations in less than an hour.
Let's tell WordPerfect we want to delete the words "to use."
Let's mark the first word. To do this ...
* Hold down the CTRL key as you press the ← key 4 times.
C:\WP\SAMPLE
Doc 1 Pg 1 Ln 3 Pos 41

Fig. 1.13. Moving to the sample text to be deleted.

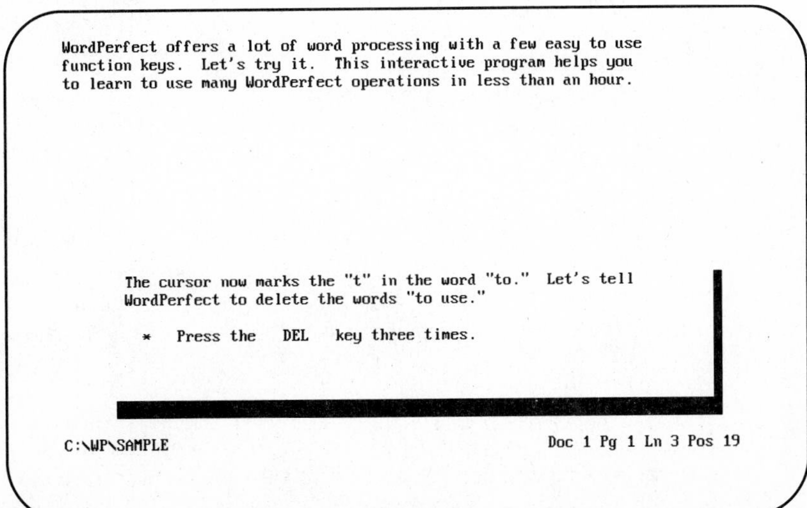
WordPerfect offers a lot of word processing with a few easy to use
function keys. Let's try it. This interactive program helps you
to learn to use many WordPerfect operations in less than an hour.
The cursor now marks the "t" in the word "to." Let's tell
WordPerfect to delete the words "to use."
* Press the DEL key three times.
C:\WP\SAMPLE
Doc 1 Pg 1 Ln 3 Pos 19

Fig. 1.14. Deleting text one character at a time using the Delete key.

Please note that while all beginners should practice WordPerfect's keystrokes by typing exactly what is requested, you may press the PgDn key to move on to the next tutorial screen and have the tutorial enter the particular keystrokes itself. This can save you time when you come back to review a lesson later.

After completing the required keystrokes, the next screen (see fig. 1.15) gives you some feedback, explaining what you have just done.

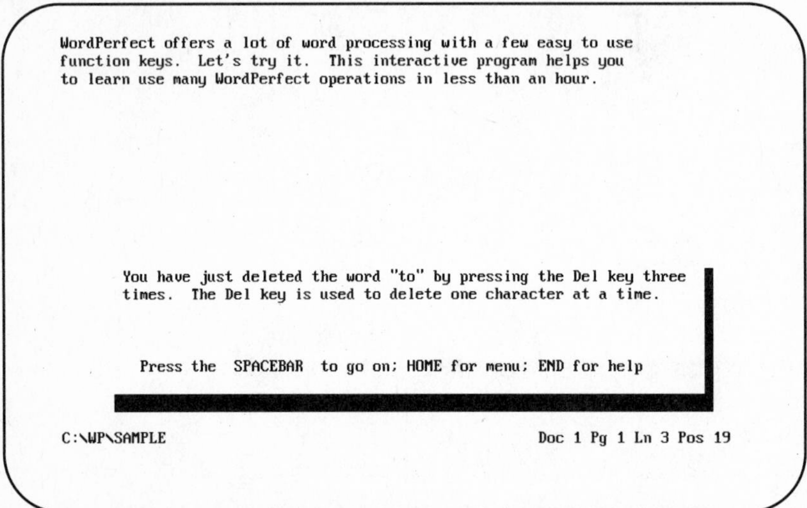
WordPerfect offers a lot of word processing with a few easy to use
function keys. Let's try it. This interactive program helps you
to learn use many WordPerfect operations in less than an hour.
You have just deleted the word "to" by pressing the Del key three
times. The Del key is used to delete one character at a time.
Press the SPACEBAR to go on; HOME for menu; END for help
C:\WP\SAMPLE
Doc 1 Pg 1 Ln 3 Pos 19

Fig. 1.15. *The tutorial gives you feedback and explains again what you just did.*

For this particular feature, there are many ways to delete text, and the tutorial lesson demonstrates several, going through the cycle of an overview, simple steps, action, feedback, and explanation for deleting one word at a time and deleting a block of text.

At the end of any given lesson, the tutorial reviews what has been covered. Some reviews also show one or more screens of concepts related to the lesson. Some of the concepts may not have been demonstrated during the interactive lesson, but it is information that you find useful. Our sample lesson for deleting text has a list of concepts shown in figure 1.16.

Once you press the space bar to go on, you will either see additional screens of concepts and review information, or you will be returned to the Main Menu. The tutorial highlights the lesson you have just completed and asks you what you would like to do next. This might be choosing the next lesson, going to another menu, or exiting the tutorial.

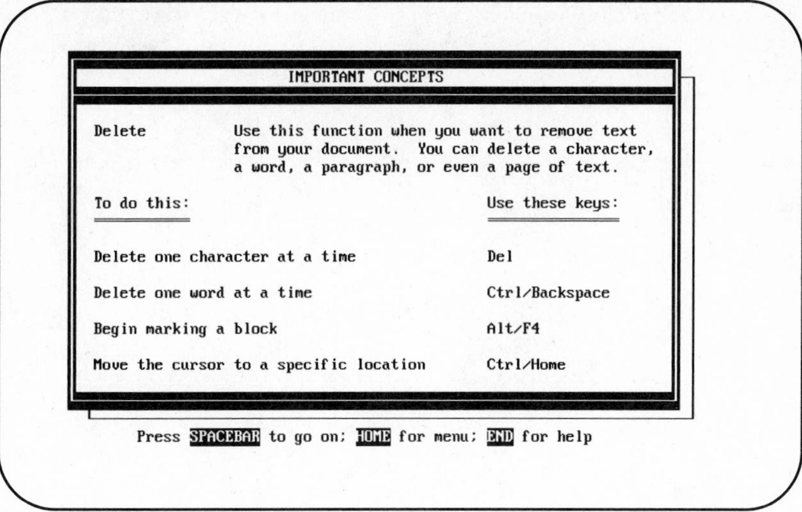

Fig. 1.16. *Concepts related to deleting text in WordPerfect.*

Ending Your Training Session

When you complete the lessons in the tutorial and wish to exit back to the DOS prompt, press the End key from anywhere within the tutorial. This produces the Help screen shown in figure 1.17, at which point you press the space bar to continue.

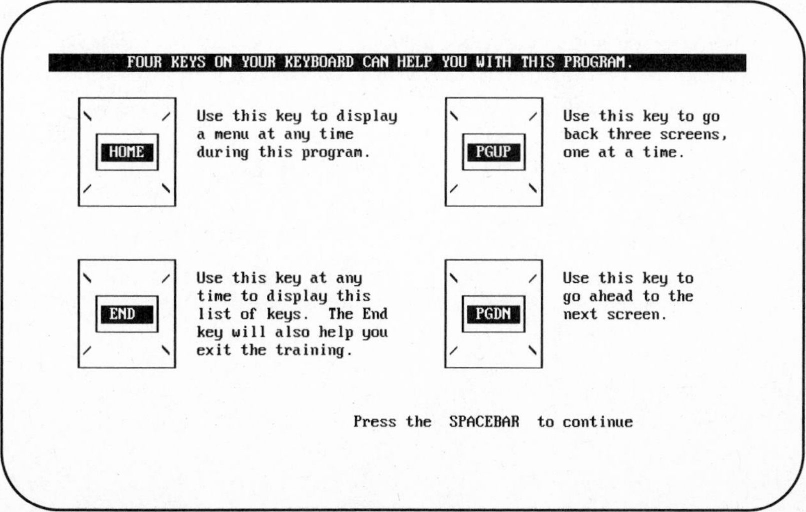

Fig. 1.17. *The help screen (first screen shown when exiting the tutorial).*

After pressing the space bar, the following screen gives you a menu of two choices, one to stop the tutorial and the other to continue where you were (see fig. 1.18)

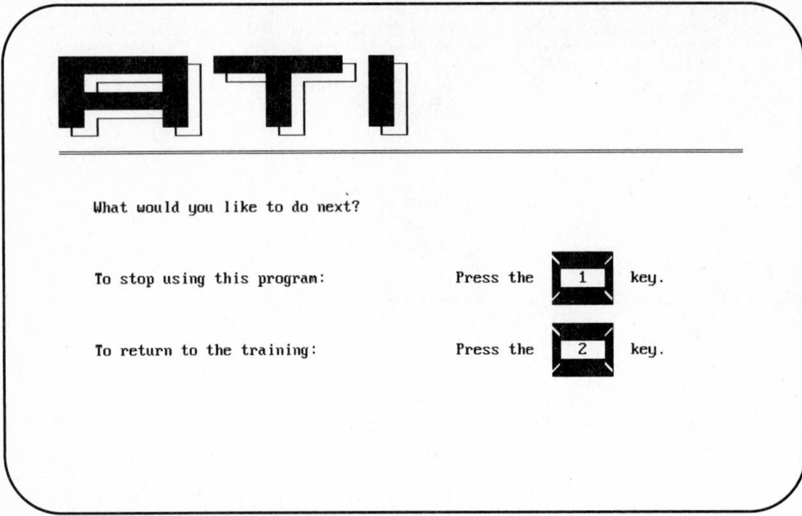

Fig. 1.18. *The tutorial double-checks to see if you want to stop.*

If you wish to exit, press **1**. The next screen shows some ordering information for other training products made by ATI, the company that created this tutorial (see fig. 1.19).

As it says at the bottom of the screen, pressing the Esc key will exit the tutorial. You will then be left back at the DOS prompt where you began the lesson in this book.

Resuming an Interrupted Session

If you must interrupt a lesson and would like to return to it later, use the End key to exit the tutorial, following the instructions in the previous section. Then, when you come back to finish the lesson, start up the tutorial and identify yourself; when you reach the screen shown in figure 1.5, choose **1** to return to your place in the lesson you interrupted.

```
              AMERICAN TRAINING INTERNATIONAL Product Line

 WORD PROCESSING:         SPREADSHEET:              OTHERS:
  DisplayWrite 4           Lotus 1-2-3 2.0           Basic
  Microsoft Word 5.0       Lotus 1-2-3 2.2           DOS 3.3
  MultiMate 3.3            1-2-3 Macros              DOS 4.0
  MultiMate Advantage      SuperCalc4                Enable
  MultiMate Advantage II   SuperCalc5                Freelance
  Samna Word IV                                      Open Access II
  WordPerfect 4.2                                    OS/2
  WordPerfect 5.0         DATABASE:                  PageMaker
  WordPerfect 5.0 Adv.     DataEase                  PC Tools Deluxe
  WordPerfect 5.1          dBASE III Plus            Symphony
  WordStar 2000 Plus       dBASE IV                  Typing Tutor
  WordStar Pro 4.0         ORACLE for 1-2-3          Ventura Publisher
                           Paradox 2.0              HOW TO USE:
 MACINTOSH:                Paradox 3.0               IBM PC/AT
  Excel                    R:BASE for DOS            IBM PC/XT
  MacCoach                 R:BASE 3.0                IBM PS/2

  To order, call a dealer or call ATI at 800-955-5ATI; in CA, 213-823-1129.
                 Press ESC to exit, HOME to view menu.
```

Fig. 1.19. The final screen before exiting the tutorial.

Where to Go from Here

Once you have completed all the lessons in the tutorial, you are ready either to move on to Lesson 2 in this book, which will have you using a real version of WordPerfect, or to go back and review any lessons in the tutorial that you feel would be helpful. Because you probably will not do all the lessons in the tutorial and the book in the same sitting, you might also wish to go back and review relevant tutorial lessons before tackling lessons in Part II of the book. The appropriate lessons are referenced throughout the book to help you with this task.

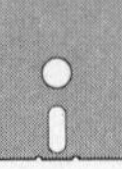

Summary of Concepts

Lesson 1 explains these concepts about the tutorial:

- ❑ **ATI**, when typed at the DOS prompt, starts the tutorial.
- ❑ CBT (Computer-Based Training) is the efficient one-on-one interactive training method used by this simulation program.
- ❑ All 10 tutorial lessons of the Disk Tutor should be attempted before going on to the lessons that follow in this book.
- ❑ Important keys to know in the tutorial are Home, which displays the most recent tutorial menu; PgUp, which allows you to go back up to three screens; PgDn, which moves you to the next screen; End, which displays these keys and their functions as well as helping you exit the tutorial; and Esc, space bar, and Enter, which you should press when prompted to do so.

Learning WordPerfect's Basic Features

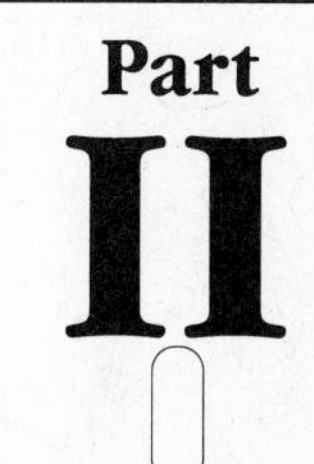

Now that the Disk Tutor has introduced you to WordPerfect, you are ready to work directly with the word processing software. The Lessons in Part II make extensive use of the Lesson files to teach you the basic, practical applications of WordPerfect.

- ❑ Prepare to use WordPerfect in Lesson 2
- ❑ Create, save, and print documents in Lesson 3
- ❑ Edit existing documents in Lesson 4
- ❑ Work with blocks of text in Lesson 5
- ❑ Format and enhance text in Lesson 6
- ❑ Design special documents in Lesson 7
- ❑ Learn about the built-in Speller and Thesaurus in Lesson 8
- ❑ Print your text in Lesson 9

Preparing To Use WordPerfect 5.1

2

DISK TUTOR

If you haven't yet explored the Disk Tutor, you might want to complete the appropriate tutorial lesson before continuing with this book lesson. If you have already run the tutorial, you might want to run it again and review the pertinent options. The parts of the tutorial relevant to this lesson are:

- ❑ Lesson B: Start Up WordPerfect
- ❑ Lesson C: Enter Text (introduces the cursor and explains the status line)
- ❑ Lesson D: Save a Document (introduces the function key template and saving and exiting WordPerfect)
- ❑ Lesson E: Move the Cursor (provides more information about moving the cursor and interpreting the status line)
- ❑ Lesson I: Get Help
- ❑ Lesson J: Pull-Down Menus

If you complete the options on the Disk Tutor, you will be more familiar with the techniques and commands found in this lesson. This lesson will cover the topics just mentioned in more detail and will walk you through other tasks, as summarized below.

In this lesson, you practice these tasks:

- ❑ Start WordPerfect
- ❑ Understand the WordPerfect screen and status line
- ❑ Understand the WordPerfect template
- ❑ Use pull-down menus and a mouse
- ❑ Use the help facility
- ❑ Specify automatic backups

- ❑ Change the unit of measure
- ❑ Establish the location of files
- ❑ Exit from WordPerfect

In this lesson, you learn how to load the previously installed WordPerfect program into your computer. You will find directions for a dual-floppy-disk system and for a hard disk system. After you view the WordPerfect editing screen and learn to access menus, you explore customizing the program according to your operating preferences and equipment setup. Finally, you learn how to access the help facility and exit from the program.

Starting the WordPerfect Program

Floppy disk system (high-density disks required): In the following instructions, the assumption is that you installed WordPerfect 5.1 on two 5 1/4-inch disks labeled *WordPerfect 1* and *WordPerfect 2*. If you use an IBM PS/2, the main program files should be installed on one high-density 3 1/2-inch disk labeled *WordPerfect 1/ WordPerfect 2*.

To start WordPerfect from a floppy drive, follow these steps:

Note to those of you who ran the tutorial: Lesson B had you start up WordPerfect from the C> prompt and did not address the issue of using the program from floppies. This is an example of how the tutorial keeps things very simple and the lessons in the book give you more practical, hands-on experience.

Step 1: Turn on your computer and type the current date and time if prompted to do so. Note the A> prompt on-screen.

Step 2: Insert the disk labeled WordPerfect 1 into disk drive A.

Step 3: Insert the copy (not the original) of the lesson files disk into disk drive B.

Step 4: At the A> prompt, type **B:** and press Enter.

Step 5: After the B> prompt appears, type **A:WP** and press Enter.

Step 6: Follow the screen prompts to complete the loading process. For example, if you use 5 1/4-inch disks, you see a message to insert the disk labeled *WordPerfect 2*. Change disks in the A: disk drive and press any key. In a few seconds, the WordPerfect program loads, and a blank document screen appears.

Hard disk system: These instructions assume that the WordPerfect program files and the files on the *WordPerfect PC Tutor Disk* are copied into appropriate subdirectories on the hard disk. The assumption is that you installed WordPerfect 5.1 program files in the WP51 subdirectory on the C: hard disk drive.

To start WordPerfect, follow these steps:

Step 1: Turn on your computer and access the C> prompt.

Step 2: Type **CD \WP51** and press Enter.

If the subdirectory containing your WordPerfect 5.1 program files is not named \WP51, replace \WP51 with the appropriate name.

Note to those of you who ran the tutorial: Lesson B did not have you change work areas on the hard disk. These instructions vary because it is simpler to begin a WordPerfect 5.1 session where the WordPerfect program is located on a hard disk (here, the C:\WP51); this directory may not be in the computer's path and it is easy to control where 5.1 retrieves and saves documents from within the program. This is an example of how the tutorial keeps things very simple and the lessons in the book give you more practical, hands-on experience.

Step 3: Type **WP** and press Enter. In a few seconds, the WordPerfect program loads, and a blank document screen appears.

Understanding the WordPerfect Screen and Status Line

Figure 2.1 shows the blank screen as it appears once you load WordPerfect into the computer.

The cursor, a blinking indicator, appears in the upper left corner of the screen. The only information you see on this initial screen is on the status line, across the bottom of the screen. The status line shows the current cursor position in the document and changes as you move the cursor. After you save or retrieve a document, the status line also displays the current document name (including the full path on a hard disk system). The status line across the bottom of the screen currently displays this information:

- ❑ `Doc`: WordPerfect permits you to have two documents at once and to switch between the two. This indicator tells which document is currently displayed.
- ❑ `Pg`: This indicator displays the current page number within the document.

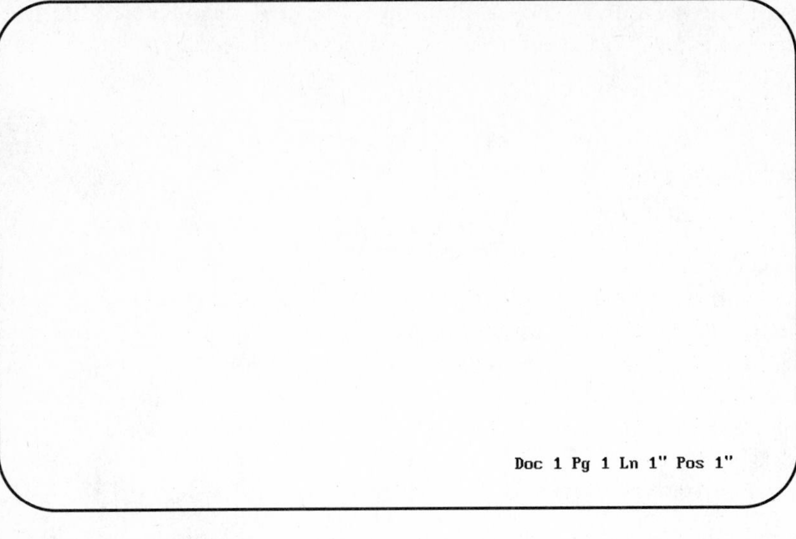

Fig. 2.1. The WordPerfect editing screen.

- Ln: This indicator displays information about the line where the cursor currently rests. In figure 2.1, Ln: 1" indicates that the cursor is one inch from the top of the page. You can change this setting to other units of measure.
- Pos: This indicator displays the exact location of the cursor within the line. In figure 2.1, Pos 1" indicates that the cursor is one inch from the left edge of the paper. You can change this setting to a different unit of measure.

  Note: The word Pos appears as POS if the Caps Lock key is on and blinks if Num Lock is on. If you use bold, underline, or some other function that affects the appearance of your text, the Pos number appears in bold or underline or whatever function you use.

In version 5.1, WordPerfect introduces pull-down menus (see "Using Pull-Down Menus" in a later section of this lesson). Figure 2.2 illustrates the WordPerfect editing screen if you choose to have the pull-down menu bar visible.

Using Function Keys

Use the keyboard to communicate with the computer by typing text and giving commands. The standard keyboard has 10 function keys, labeled F1 through F10, at the left side of the keyboard; the Enhanced Keyboard has 12 function keys, labeled

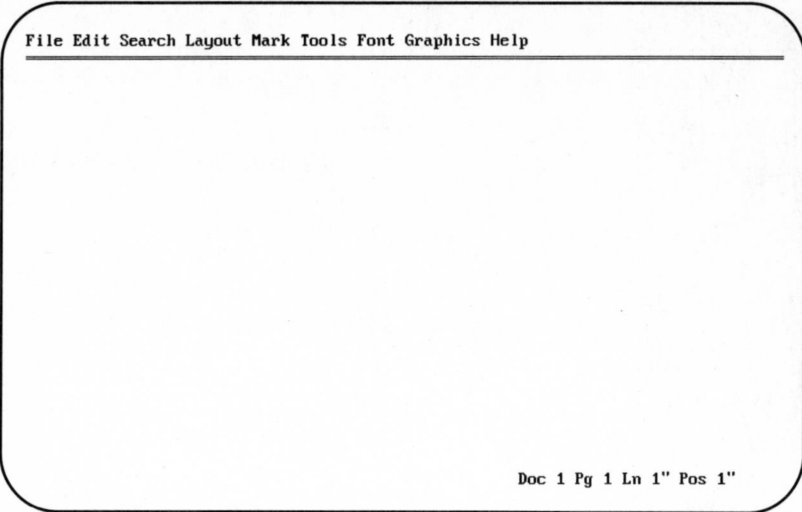

Fig. 2.2. *The WordPerfect editing screen with menu bar and separator line.*

F1 through F12, across the top of the keyboard. Because you use function keys to give commands, a large part of learning any program involves understanding what tasks each function key performs. You may prefer using the new pull-down menus, explained later in this lesson.

In WordPerfect, you may use each function key alone or in combination with the Ctrl, Alt, or Shift key. When you use the combination keys, first hold down the Ctrl, Alt, or Shift key and then press the function key you want.

Caution: Once you press the combination of keys, release both keys immediately. Most keys repeat if you hold them down—and this fact can cause unwanted results.

WordPerfect has 40 programmed functions that use the combination keys and function keys F1 through F10. If you use the Enhanced Keyboard, you will find that WordPerfect assigns only one function each to the extra keys F11 and F12, Reveal Codes, and Block. These often-used commands are also included in the original 40. The following are some examples of function-key assignments:

Key(s) To Press	*Result*
F3	Accesses the help facility
F6	Bolds text
Shift-F8	Accesses the format menu

Key(s) To Press	*Result*
Shift-F10	Retrieves a user-specified document
Alt-F3 or F11	Reveals codes hidden in a document
Alt-F4 or F12	Marks a block of text
Ctrl-F2	Accesses the spell-check feature
Ctrl-F4	Initiates move or copy operations

You will quickly memorize the key combinations that you invoke frequently. WordPerfect does, however, provide a keyboard template summarizing the function-key assignments to make it easier to use less ordinary options.

Understanding the WordPerfect Template

WordPerfect 5.1 provides templates (one for a standard keyboard and one for an Enhanced Keyboard) that fit over or above the function keys on the keyboard. Figure 2.3 illustrates the template for a standard PC-style or AT-style keyboard.

The templates are color-coded. To execute a red-coded, green-coded, or blue-coded action, hold down the Ctrl, Shift, or Alt key (respectively) and press the appropriate function key. Do not hold the function key down; simply press it and then let up on both keys. A black-coded action means to press only the function key indicated.

If you misplace your template, use the tear-out keyboard command map in *Using WordPerfect 5.1*, Special Edition. You also can look at the template by accessing Help, discussed in a later section.

Using Pull-Down Menus

Rather than selecting menu options by pressing a function key or function-key combination, you may prefer to select menu options from pull-down menus. To reach the pull-down menu, press the two-key combination Alt- =. The menu system includes an initial horizontal menu bar containing nine options: **F**ile, **E**dit, **S**earch, **L**ayout, **M**ark, **T**ools, F**o**nt, **G**raphics, and **H**elp. Additional levels of menus include pull-down and pop-out menus.

Figure 2.4 illustrates the menu bar and the pull-down F**o**nt menu. An arrowhead symbol right of a menu option indicates the existence of an additional pop-out menu. Figure 2.5 illustrates the pop-out menu that you see after you select

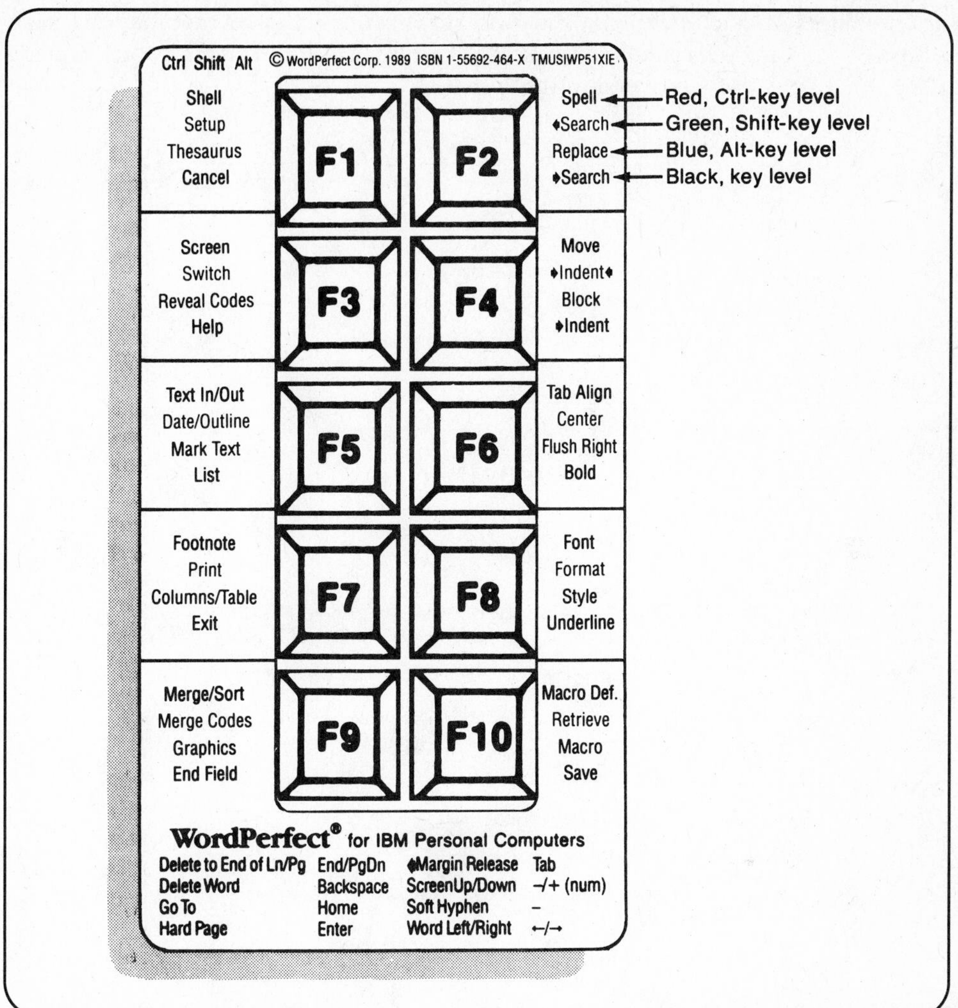

Fig. 2.3. *One of two WordPerfect 5.1 templates for IBM Personal Computers and compatibles.*

Appearance from the F**o**nt menu. To select a menu option, highlight your choice; then press Enter or type the highlighted letter of the option. Press the right arrow or left arrow to highlight an option on the horizontal menu bar; press the up arrow or down arrow to highlight an option on a pull-down or pop-out menu.

Note: Figures 2.4 and 2.5 display function keys or function-key combinations, such as Ctrl-F8 for **A**ppearance and F6 for **B**old. The function keys appear if you are using a March 30, 1990, or later version of WordPerfect 5.1.

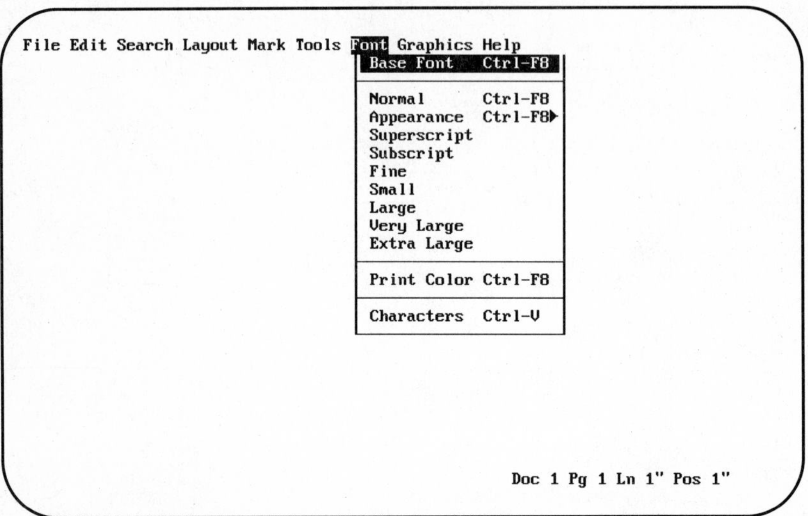

Fig. 2.4. A pull-down menu.

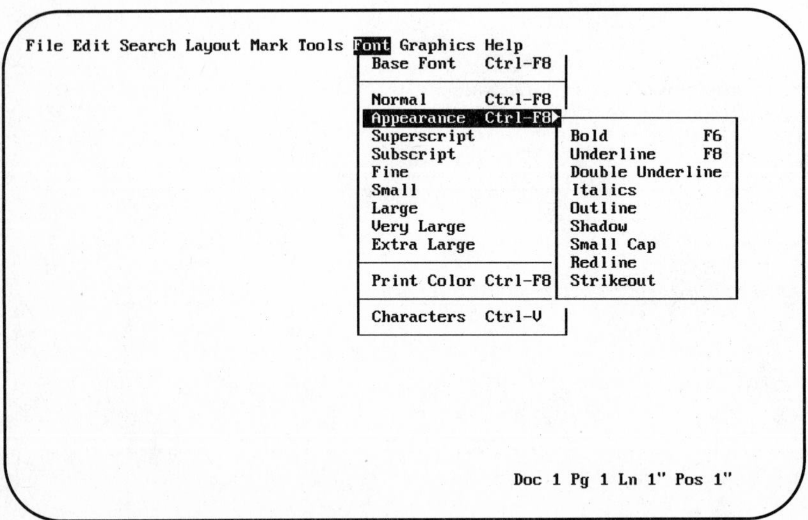

Fig. 2.5. A pull-down menu with an accompanying pop-out menu.

Accessing Menus from the Keyboard

Remember that from the keyboard you can initiate commands involving menu selections in one of two ways: by pressing a function-key combination or by accessing the pull-down menu. The following hands-on activities illustrate both methods.

To use a *function-key combination* to format a page and to then abort the command, follow these steps:

Step 1: Access a blank WordPerfect document screen.

Step 2: Press Shift-F8 (that is, press and hold down the Shift key, press the F8 key, and let up on both keys).

Step 3: Press **2** (Page) and notice the Format: Page full-screen menu.

Step 4: Press Exit (F7) to restore the WordPerfect editing screen without making formatting changes to the page.

To use the *pull-down menu* to format a page and to then abort the command, follow these steps:

Step 1: Access a blank WordPerfect document screen.

Step 2: Press Alt-= (that is, press and hold down the Alt key, press the = key, and let up on both keys).

Step 3: Select **L**ayout (that is, press **L** or the right arrow or left arrow to highlight **L**ayout on the horizontal menu bar, and press Enter).

Step 4: Select **P**age (that is, press the down or up arrow to highlight **P**age on the pull-down menu, and press Enter or **P**) and notice the Format: Page full-screen menu.

Step 5: Press Exit (F7) to restore the WordPerfect editing screen.

Note: Throughout *WordPerfect PC Tutor*, the instructions to access menus will be based on pull-down menu selections, with function-key directions in parentheses. For example, an instruction to access the Format: Page submenu will be written like this:

Step X: Access the **L**ayout pull-down menu and select **P**age (or press Shift-F8, **2**).

If you use the pull-down menu, complete only the menu-access instructions that appear *before* text in parentheses. In the current example, access the **L**ayout pull-down menu and select **P**age.

If you prefer to access menus using a function-key combination, complete only the instructions *within* parentheses. In the current example, press the Shift-F8 key combination; then press 2. Keys pressed in combination are separated by a hyphen; keys pressed sequentially are separated by a comma.

Using a Mouse

WordPerfect 5.1 supports a mouse, but you do not need the device in order to use the program. The mouse serves two main purposes: use it to make selections in most menus, including the new pull-down menus, or use it to mark text so that you can perform a block action (such as deleting or moving) or modify text (such as underlining or centering).

WordPerfect 5.1 supports virtually every type of mouse, whether two-button or three-button. You can use buttons in four ways:

click	Press and then quickly release a button.
double-click	Quickly press and release one button twice.
drag	Click and then hold a button down as you move the mouse.
multiclick	Click and release two (or more) buttons at the same time.

The results of clicking or dragging the mouse vary according to the button you press and the current WordPerfect operation. For example, pressing the *left* mouse button has these effects: when used with the editing screen, you can mark (highlight) text for a block operation if you drag the mouse; when used with pull-down menus, clicking on a menu item selects that item; and when used with lists, double-clicking on a file name in a List Files screen displays the file.

Pressing the *right* mouse button has two other effects: when used with the editing screen, clicking makes the menu bar appear; and when used with pull-down menus and lists, clicking is the same as pressing Exit (F7).

Follow one of two methods to execute a Cancel (F1) command: on a two-button mouse, hold down one button while clicking the other button; on a three-button mouse, click the middle button.

Using the Help Facility

WordPerfect offers a quick and easy-to-use help facility that contains information concerning all WordPerfect commands. You can access Help by pressing the function key F3.

If you prefer to use the pull-down menu to access Help, press Alt-= or click the right mouse button to access the menu bar. Access the **Help** pull-down menu by pressing **H**, by clicking the left button of a mouse on the menu bar option **Help**, or by highlighting the menu bar option **Help** and pressing Enter. Repeat one of the three procedures to select **Help** from the pop-out menu and see the initial help screen.

To access information from Help about the Format (Shift-F8) and Save (F10) commands, follow these steps:

Step 1: Access the **Help** pull-down menu and select **Help** (or press F3). The release date of your version of WordPerfect 5.1 appears in the upper right corner.

Note: Throughout *WordPerfect PC Tutor*, the instructions to access menus are based on pull-down menu selections first. Function-key directions are in parentheses. Also, pull-down menu instructions do not remind you to press Alt-= (or click a mouse) to access the menu bar.

Step 2: Press Shift-F8 to access the Format command help screen (see fig. 2.6).

```
Format

     Contains features which change the current document's format. Options on
     the Line, Page and Other menus change the setting from the cursor
     position forward. Document Format options change a setting for the entire
     document. To change the default settings permanently, use the Setup key.

     If Block is On, press Format to protect a block.  You can use Block
     Protect to keep a block of text and codes together on a page (such as a
     paragraph which may change in size during editing).

     1 - Line

     2 - Page

     3 - Document

     4 - Other

Note: In WordPerfect 5.1, you can enter measurements in fractions (e.g., 3/4")
     as well as decimals (e.g., .75").  WordPerfect will convert fractions to
     their decimal equivalent.

Selection: 0                                          (Press ENTER to exit Help)
```

Fig. 2.6. *A help screen.*

Step 3: Press the space bar or Enter to exit from Help.

Step 4: Access the **Help** pull-down menu and select **Help** (or press F3).

Step 5: Press **S** to access a list of commands that begin with the letter S.

Step 6: Find Save Text on the list in column 1. Note that the F10 key listed in column 3 corresponds to the key word *Save* in column 2.

Step 7: Press F10 to access the Save command help screen.

Step 8: Press the space bar or Enter to exit from Help.

Whether or not you remember the keystrokes that activate the feature with which you need help, WordPerfect's help facility is fast, easy, and friendly to use. You can activate Help any time during a work session, even in the middle of a command.

Customizing WordPerfect

Once you install WordPerfect programs, you can use WordPerfect's Setup menu to customize the system. Changing the default settings within this menu changes how many WordPerfect features work. The choices you make while in Setup affect all documents every time you use WordPerfect; you create changes that remain in effect until you reset the defaults.

To access Setup in WordPerfect 5.1, select Setup from the **F**ile pull-down menu (see fig. 2.7) or press Shift-F1. The initial Setup menu contains six options: **M**ouse, **D**isplay, **E**nvironment, **I**nitial Settings, **K**eyboard Layout, and **L**ocation of Files.

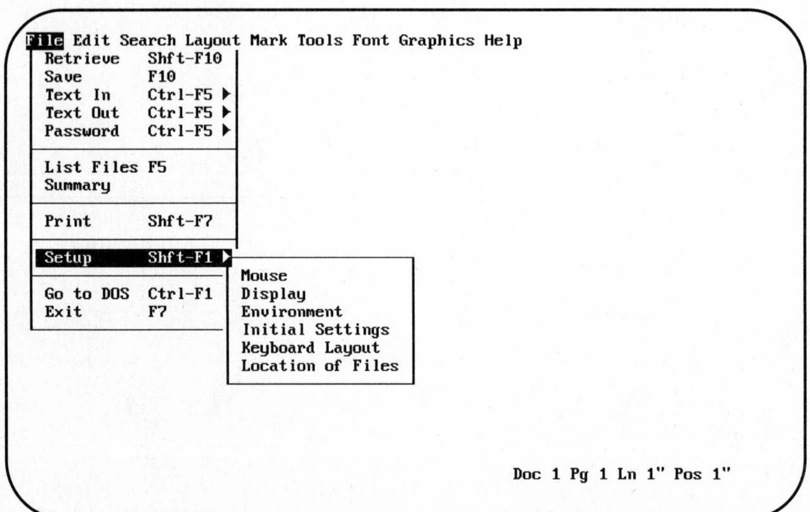

***Fig. 2.7.** The Setup pop-out menu.*

WordPerfect PC Tutor illustrations depict making changes in two Setup menu choices: **L**ocation of Files and **E**nvironment (establishing automatic backups of current documents and changing the unit of measure).

Specifying Automatic Backups

The **B**ackup Options selection on the Setup: Environment menu lets you request one or both types of backups: *timed* document backups that occur at a user-specified interval (such as every 5 minutes or 30 minutes) and *original* document backups created at the time you save documents.

If your work on a document (or documents) currently in memory is interrupted by a power loss or a similar problem, you can retrieve the most recent version of your document from the backup disk directory. WordPerfect creates timed backups by default, storing them under the names WP{WP}.BK1 (Document screen 1) and WP{WP}.BK2 (Document screen 2). You can disable this feature or alter the time interval between backups. The .BK1 and .BK2 extension files are deleted from disk if you exit normally from WordPerfect by using the Exit (F7) function key or the Ex**i**t option on the **F**ile pull-down menu.

If you specify **Y** from the `No (Yes)` **O**riginal Document Backup option, WordPerfect makes a backup of the old version every time you save. Your disk will thus have the two most recent versions of a document at any time, the older file designated with a .BK! extension. In other words, when using this option, you have both the most recent document (such as MYFILE) and its previous version (MYFILE.BK!) on disk.

To set timed backups to 15-minute intervals, follow these steps:

Step 1: Access the **F**ile pull-down menu and select Se**t**up (or press Shift-F1).

Step 2: Select **E**nvironment (**3**); select **B**ackup Options (**1**).

Note: The current settings displayed on your Setup screens may vary from those shown in *WordPerfect PC Tutor* figures. The defaults in your own copy of WordPerfect may already be changed.

Step 3: Select **T**imed Document Backup (**1**); press **Y** for Yes and type **15** for Minutes Between Backups, and press Enter (see fig. 2.8).

Step 4: Press Exit (F7) to restore the WordPerfect editing screen.

```
Setup: Backup

     Timed backup files are deleted when you exit WP normally.  If you
     have a power or machine failure, you will find the backup file in the
     backup directory indicated in Setup: Location of Files.

         Backup Directory                     C:\WP51\BACKUP

     1 - Timed Document Backup                Yes
         Minutes Between Backups              15


     Original backup will save the original document with a .BK! extension
     whenever you replace it during a Save or Exit.

     2 - Original Document Backup             No





Selection: 0
```

Fig. 2.8. *The Setup: Backup menu.*

Timed backups occur every 15 minutes. Shorten this time if you want backups made more frequently. As you work, you will notice a slight pause every 15 minutes and the `* Please wait *` message at the bottom of the screen as the computer makes a backup to disk.

Changing the Units of Measure

Measurement units, such as those that display the current cursor position within a document in the lower right corner of the screen, can be displayed in inches, centimeters, points, 1200ths of an inch, or the WordPerfect 4.2 default line/column presentation. Measurement units display in *inches* (the WordPerfect 5.1 default) in *WordPerfect PC Tutor* figures. To view (and change, if you want) the units of measure, follow these steps (see fig. 2.9):

Step 1: Access the **F**ile pull-down menu and select Set**u**p (or press Shift-F1).

Step 2: Select **E**nvironment (**3**); select **U**nits of Measure (**8**).

```
Setup: Units of Measure

     1 - Display and Entry of Numbers                    "
           for Margins, Tabs, etc.

     2 - Status Line Display                             "


Legend:

     " = inches
     i = inches
     c = centimeters
     p = points
     w = 1200ths of an inch
     u = WordPerfect 4.2 Units (Lines/Columns)








Selection: 0
```

Fig. 2.9. *The Setup: Units of Measure menu.*

Step 3: Choose **D**isplay and Entry of Numbers for Margins, Tabs, etc. (**1**). Then select from the legend options the letter of the unit you want for displaying margins, tabs, and other settings. Inches (") are used in *WordPerfect PC Tutor*.

Step 4: Choose **S**tatus Line Display (**2**) and then select from the legend options the letter of the unit you want for the status line display. Inches (") are used in *WordPerfect PC Tutor*.

Step 5: Press Exit (F7) to restore the WordPerfect editing screen.

Specifying the Location of Files

You can specify where you store a variety of WordPerfect files: backup, keyboard, macro, thesaurus, spelling, printer, style library, graphic, and document files. Create the directories before you assign files to the directories by using the Setup: Location of Files menu.

To view (and change, if you want) the location of WordPerfect files, follow these steps (see fig. 2.10):

Step 1: Access the **F**ile pull-down menu and select Set**u**p (or press Shift-F1).

Step 2: Select **L**ocation of Files (**6**).

```
Setup: Location of Files

     1 - Backup Files                     C:\WP51\BACKUP

     2 - Keyboard/Macro Files             C:\WP51\KBMAC51

     3 - Thesaurus/Spell/Hyphenation
                        Main              C:\WP51\DIC51
                        Supplementary     C:\WP51\DIC51

     4 - Printer Files                    C:\WP51

     5 - Style Files                      C:\WP51\STYLE51
                Library Filename          C:\WP51\STYLE51\BC.LIB

     6 - Graphic Files                    C:\WP51\GRAPG51

     7 - Documents                        C:\WP51\DATA51



Selection: 0
```

Fig. 2.10. *The Setup: Location of Files menu.*

Step 3: To specify one or more file locations, select the appropriate number (1 through 8) and enter the applicable location.

Select **D**ocuments (7) to specify the directory location that appears on-screen when you list files. (You learn to override the automatic display in *WordPerfect PC Tutor* Lesson 10.)

Step 4: Press Exit (F7) to restore the WordPerfect editing screen.

Exiting from WordPerfect

You can exit from WordPerfect 5.1 by using a pull-down menu selection or pressing a function key. Pressing the F7 exit key is probably the easiest for most people. Whichever method you choose, you can save the current document before you complete the exit process.

To exit from WordPerfect without saving the current document, follow these steps:

Step 1: Access the **F**ile pull-down menu and select E**x**it (or press F7).

Step 2: In response to the prompt `Save document? Yes (No)`, press **N**.

Step 3: In response to the prompt `Exit WP? No (Yes)`, press **Y**.

For Further Reference

If you would like to know more about the menu bar and how to customize a mouse, consult *Using WordPerfect 5.1*, Special Edition (Que Corporation, Carmel, IN, 1989), Chapters 1 and 20.

Summary of Concepts

Lesson 2 explains these concepts:

- ❑ You may access WordPerfect 5.1 on either a high-density two-disk system or a hard disk system. The assumption, of course, is that the software is properly installed.
- ❑ WordPerfect provides a nearly blank editing screen to maximize the document viewing area.
- ❑ The status line across the bottom of the WordPerfect editing screen provides information about the name and location of the current document (if previously saved) and the cursor position within the document.
- ❑ You access WordPerfect features and execute commands by pressing each function key alone or in combination with the Ctrl, Alt, or Shift keys. When you use the combination keys, first hold down the Ctrl, Alt, or Shift key; then press the function key you want.
- ❑ WordPerfect includes two versions of a color-coded template outlining function-key assignments (one for standard keyboards, the other for Enhanced Keyboards).
- ❑ WordPerfect 5.1 introduces a system of pull-down menus to use as an alternative to function-key combinations. The pull-down menu includes an initial horizontal menu bar, pull-down menus, and pop-out menus.
- ❑ You press Alt–= to activate the pull-down menu bar. To select options, type the first letter or highlight your choice and press Enter.
- ❑ WordPerfect 5.1 supports the use of a mouse for making selections in most menus and for marking text for block operations.
- ❑ You can access a comprehensive on-screen Help facility by pressing F3 or by accessing the **H**elp pull-down menu.
- ❑ You can customize WordPerfect features to suit your needs and equipment by using the Setup menu. Setup options include setting the interval for timed backups, changing the unit of measure, and specifying the location of a variety of files.

Review Exercises

Practice using the WordPerfect features in this lesson by completing these exercises. If you do not remember how to do something, review the preceding explanations and practice steps.

1. Load the WordPerfect software.
2. Select **T**emplate from the **H**elp pull-down menu, study the on-screen WordPerfect template, and exit from Help.
3. Select **I**ndex from the **H**elp pull-down menu. After you view the WordPerfect operations beginning with *A*, press a variety of letters one after another to view additional explanations of features before you exit from Help.
4. Press a function key to activate Help; then look up *Cursor Speed*.
5. Access the Setup: Environment menu and establish timed backups at 10-minute intervals.
6. Access the Setup: Environment menu and change the cursor speed to a speed slightly faster or slightly slower than its current setting.
7. Make pull-down menu selections to exit from the current document without saving it, but do not exit from WordPerfect.
8. Press a function key to exit from the current document. Exit from WordPerfect without saving the current document.

Creating, Saving, and Printing a Document

3

DISK TUTOR

If you haven't yet explored the Disk Tutor, you might want to complete the appropriate tutorial lesson before continuing with this book lesson. If you have already run the tutorial, you might want to run it again and review the pertinent options. The parts of the tutorial relevant to this lesson are:

- ❑ Lesson C: Enter Text
- ❑ Lesson D: Save a Document
- ❑ Lesson E: Move the Cursor
- ❑ Lesson F: Edit a Document
- ❑ Lesson H: Print a Document

If you complete the options on the Disk Tutor, you will be more familiar with the techniques and commands found in this lesson.

In this lesson, you practice these tasks:

- ❑ Create a document
- ❑ Move the cursor within a document
- ❑ Make simple editing changes
- ❑ Save a document to disk
- ❑ Retrieve a document from disk
- ❑ Combine documents
- ❑ Print the current document

Lesson 2 contained few hands-on activities; it laid the groundwork for using WordPerfect 5.1 software effectively. In Lesson 3, you practice all the basic document-processing operations: creating, saving, retrieving, and printing. Figure 3.1 illustrates the document you create and save in this lesson.

```
January 16, 1990


Mr. Fred S. Gefeldt
Artesian Systems, Inc.
560 West Esteban Circle
Amazon, OK  78118

Dear Fred:

Crimson Travel & Tours is introducing a new corporate
reservations department.  We promise a prompt response to your
questions about schedules and free delivery of tickets to your
office or home.

The agents assigned to this department know that you have a very
busy schedule.  Their goal is to ensure that your trip is worry
free and that you arrive on time at your destination.  Our cruise
specialists can assist with incentive as well as pleasure tours.

We guarantee you the best service.  Call us the next time your
itinerary takes you across the state or around the world.

Sincerely,


Aimee Lockyer
Senior Account Representative
```

Fig. 3.1. *The CRIMSON.V1 document.*

Creating a Document

To create a WordPerfect document, just load the program and start typing on the blank editing screen. As you follow instructions over the next few pages to create the letter illustrated in figure 3.1, ignore any typing errors until you learn editing techniques, illustrated later in this lesson.

For a variety of reasons, the spacing of words within your document may vary from that shown in figure 3.1. There may be, for example, different settings on your system for margins, fonts (print styles), and justification (alignment of text against left and/or right margins). *WordPerfect PC Tutor* figures reflect one-inch margins, Courier 10-pitch (10 characters per inch) font, and left justification.

For now, do not worry about formatting details, which you learn to set in other lessons. Concentrate on entering sentences and paragraphs, moving the cursor within the document, and making simple editing changes.

Entering Single Lines of Text

If the words in a line of a document occupy less than the entire line, press Enter after you type the text to move the cursor to the next line. To begin typing the letter in figure 3.1, follow these steps:

Step 1: Load the WordPerfect 5.1 software and access a blank editing screen. The document status line should read `Doc 1 Pg 1 Ln 1" Pos 1"` (assuming that the unit of measure is inches).

Step 2: Type the date shown in figure 3.1 and press Enter. The cursor should be at the beginning of the next line.

Step 3: Press Enter three times to insert three blank lines. The cursor should be at the beginning of line 5, currently displayed in the status line as `Ln:1.67"` (meaning 1 2/3 inches from the top of the page).

Step 4: Type the four lines of name-and-address information, enter a blank line, and type the greeting **Dear Fred:**. Press Enter at the end of each line.

Understanding Word Wrap

When you type paragraphs or blocks of text, do not press Enter when you reach the end of a line; simply keep typing. The cursor advances automatically to the beginning of the next line. Words that do not fit on the last complete line move to the next line. Press Enter only at the end of the last line of the paragraph.

To illustrate the word wrap feature, finish typing the letter shown in figure 3.1 by following these steps:

Step 1: Move the cursor to the beginning of the line, one blank line below the greeting `Dear Fred:`.

Step 2: Type the first paragraph. Remember, do not press the Enter key until you finish typing the sentence which ends with `to your office or home.`

Step 3: Type the remaining two paragraphs, entering blank lines between paragraphs.

Step 4: Type the single lines of the closing to complete the letter. The final document should appear as shown in figure 3.1.

Using Arrow Keys To Move the Cursor

To move the cursor through the document one character or line at a time, use the arrow keys on the numeric keypad on the right side of the keyboard. (If you have an Enhanced Keyboard, the arrow keys are on a separate cursor pad.) In the next lesson, you practice using other keys that move the cursor.

Practice moving the cursor by following these steps:

Step 1: Move the cursor around the document, using the up, down, left, and right arrows.

Step 2: Move the cursor to the colon after `Dear Fred:` in line 10 (2.5") of the letter you just typed.

Making Simple Changes to the Document with Insert and Typeover

You can make simple editing changes to a document by using the Ins (Insert), Backspace, and Del (Delete) keys and typeover mode.

Inserting text into a document requires that typeover mode be turned off. Pressing Ins toggles typeover mode on and off. If typeover mode is on, the word `Typeover` appears in the lower left corner of the screen. Any new characters typed overwrite existing text. If insert mode is turned on, new characters typed are inserted, and existing text shifts right. WordPerfect is ordinarily in insert mode.

Change the letter you just typed. Follow these steps:

Step 1: Move the cursor to the first letter in the word `Systems` in the second address line.

Step 2: Activate insert mode. If `Typeover` does not appear in the lower left corner of the screen, you are already in insert mode; otherwise, press Ins once so that the `Typeover` message disappears.

Step 3: Type **Drinking** and press the space bar once. Notice that the existing text moves right as you insert the new word. The line should now read `Artesian Drinking Systems, Inc.`

Step 4: Move the cursor to the street number `560` in the third address line.

Step 5: Press the Ins key so that the word `Typeover` appears in the lower left corner of the screen.

Step 6: Type **711** as the new street number. Notice how the new text types over the old text.

Step 7: Press Ins to turn off typeover mode.

To prevent accidentally typing over text, leave typeover mode off until you need it.

Using Backspace and Del (Delete)

Backspace erases the character left of the cursor; Del (Delete) erases the character at the cursor. One character is removed each time you press either key. If you use Backspace or Del to remove a character when you are in insert mode, any text right of the deleted character shifts left. If you use Backspace or Del to remove a character when you are in typeover mode, text right of the deleted character holds its original position.

Because Backspace and Del repeat themselves, use caution—you may remove more text than you intend to. Practice changing the current document by following these steps:

Step 1: Move the cursor to the space following the street number `711` in the third address line.

Step 2: Make sure that you are in the insert mode. Then press Backspace three times and type **560**. The line should be restored to its original contents, `560 West Esteban Circle`.

Step 3: Move the cursor to the first letter of `very` in line one of paragraph two.

Step 4: Press Del five times to remove `very` and one of the extra spaces. Notice that the document reformats, allowing the word `busy` to move up to the first line of this paragraph. If the first word on the next line fits, it moves up one line.

Use Ins, Del, Backspace, and typeover mode frequently to edit documents. WordPerfect provides several ways to do the same editing task, and with practice you will adopt the technique that suits you best.

Saving a Document to Disk

When you finish working on a document or want to quit and exit from WordPerfect, it is vital that you save your work onto a disk, using a Save or Exit command. Use Save to store your document on disk but continue to work on the document. Use Exit to store your document on disk and either exit from WordPerfect or work on another document.

Do not confuse saving a document to disk by using Save or Exit commands with timed backups, presented in Lesson 2. Timed backups are useful only in the event of a power outage or other event that causes you to exit from WordPerfect improperly (for example, your keyboard "freezes," forcing you to reboot the system). Timed backups are automatically erased if you select Exit from the File pull-down menu (or press F7) and respond to prompts to leave the program.

WordPerfect prompts you to provide a new name, or accept a previous name, when you save a document. The next section provides guidelines that help you choose a name for your document.

Naming Documents

Before you can save a document (file), you must name it. The following guidelines help when naming a document:

- The file name can be one to eight characters long. The characters can be letters or numbers. Some punctuation characters—for example, the hyphen—are acceptable. You can use either uppercase or lowercase letters, but the computer converts all the letters to uppercase. Consult your DOS reference manual for a complete discussion of standards for naming files.
- A period (also called a dot) can follow the file name. An extension—up to three additional characters—can follow the dot. You are not required to use an extension.
- You do not have to type eight characters in the file name before you type a dot and an extension.
- A space is an illegal character in a file name. If you press the space bar as you type the file name, WordPerfect assumes that the name is complete and immediately begins saving the file.
- Many WordPerfect operators use extension characters to indicate a document category—for example, .LTR for letters, .CON for contracts, .RPT for reports, .AGR for agreements, and .INV for invoices.
- You will find it helpful to give the document a name that provides a clue to its contents. For example, CRIMSON.LTR is clearer than LETTER13, and ANNUAL90.RPT is more specific than REPORT.J15.

Setting the Current Directory

Each time you save a WordPerfect document, you can specify the exact location of the saved file in addition to the file name. If you fail to specify a disk drive and path when you assign a name, WordPerfect stores the document in the current directory specified through the WordPerfect Setup menu (or established through the disk operating system when you first loaded WordPerfect).

To *view* the current directory, select List **F**iles from the **F**ile pull-down menu (or press F5, the List function key). WordPerfect displays the current default drive and directory in the lower left corner of the screen. To *change* the default drive at this point, press the equal sign key (=), type a new drive and path, and press Enter. Verify that the display in the lower-left corner changes to the new directory, and press Cancel (F1) to restore the editing screen.

To save newly typed *WordPerfect PC Tutor* files and lesson-disk files in the same place, change the current directory to the disk or directory containing the copy of the lesson-disk files. Follow these steps:

Step 1: Select List **F**iles from the **F**ile pull-down menu (or press F5). The current directory path appears in the lower-left corner of the screen.

Note: Remember that throughout *WordPerfect PC Tutor*, instructions to access menus are based on pull-down menu selections, with function-key directions in parentheses. Instructions do not remind users of pull-down menus to press Alt-= (or click a mouse) to access the menu bar.

Step 2: Press = (the equal sign key), type the complete path describing the location of the lesson files, and press Enter.

For example, type

=B:

and press Enter if your lesson files are stored on a disk in the B: drive; on the other hand, type

=C:\ATIWP

and press Enter if your lesson-disk files are stored within the ATIWP directory on the C: hard drive.

Step 3: Verify that the display in the lower left corner changes to the directory containing your lesson-disk files.

Step 4: Press Cancel (F1) to restore the editing screen containing the letter concerning Crimson Travel & Tours. Alternatively, you can press Exit (F7) to restore the editing screen.

Pressing Cancel (F1) does not cancel the directory change, which was established by pressing Enter after typing a new path. Instead, the action cancels the List Files operation and restores the editing screen. Lesson 10 illustrates a more formal method of changing the current directory: selecting **Other Directory** (7) from the List Files menu.

Using the Save Command To Save a Document

Use Save to save a document and continue to edit the same document. Initiate the Save process by selecting **Save** from the **File** pull-down menu (see fig. 3.2) or by pressing F10. To save your newly created letter under the name CRIMSON.V1 (V1 means *version one*), follow these steps:

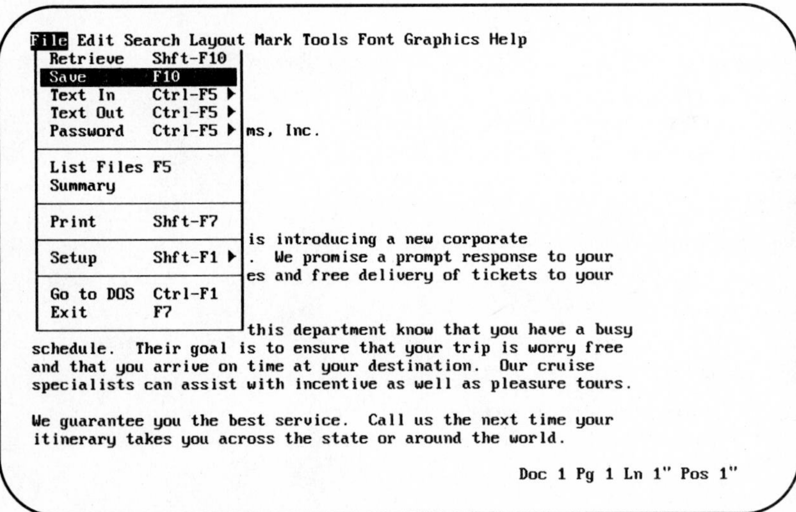
File Edit Search Layout Mark Tools Font Graphics Help
Retrieve Shft-F10
Save F10
Text In Ctrl-F5
Text Out Ctrl-F5
Password Ctrl-F5
ms, Inc.
List Files F5
Summary
Print Shft-F7
is introducing a new corporate
Setup Shft-F1
. We promise a prompt response to your
es and free delivery of tickets to your
Go to DOS Ctrl-F1
Exit F7
this department know that you have a busy
schedule. Their goal is to ensure that your trip is worry free
and that you arrive on time at your destination. Our cruise
specialists can assist with incentive as well as pleasure tours.
We guarantee you the best service. Call us the next time your
itinerary takes you across the state or around the world.
Doc 1 Pg 1 Ln 1" Pos 1"

Fig. 3.2. *The File pull-down menu.*

Step 1: Access the **File** pull-down menu and select **Save** (or press F10).

Step 2: At the prompt `Document to be saved:` in the lower left corner of the screen, type **CRIMSON.V1** and press Enter. You return to the document and may continue to edit.

Step 3: Access the **File** pull-down menu and select **Save** (or press F10) again. The message in the lower left corner of the screen now contains the file name. It should read `Document to be saved: C:\ATIWP\CRIMSON.V1`.

Note: Your drive and path name may be different, depending on the path you specified in the preceding section on changing the current directory.

Step 4: Press Enter to save the document. A new message appears in the lower left corner of the screen. It reads `Replace C:\ATIWP\CRIMSON.V1? No (Yes)`.

Note: Your choices are **Y** to replace the older version on disk with the current version on-screen and **N** to cancel the replace command.

Step 5: Press **Y** to replace the existing document on disk.

If you choose **N** to cancel the replace command, the cursor moves to the front of the path and prompts you to provide another name. Press Cancel (F1) to cancel the Save operation altogether. Regardless of whether you complete the save operation or not, the current document reappears on-screen.

Using the Exit Command To Save a Document

Use Exit either to exit from WordPerfect or to access a new blank document screen. In the process, you can choose to save the current document. Initiate the Exit process by selecting E**x**it from the **F**ile pull-down menu (see fig. 3.2) or by pressing the F7 key.

To exit from the CRIMSON.V1 document, follow these steps:

Step 1: Access the **F**ile pull-down menu and select E**x**it (or press F7). Notice the message in the lower left corner: `Save document? Yes (No)`.

Step 2: Press **Y** or Enter to save the document. The message `Document to be saved: C:\ATIWP\CRIMSON.V1` appears in the lower left corner of the screen.

Step 3: Press Enter to save the document under the name shown. Remember that if this were a new document, you would be asked for the name of the document. The message `Replace C:\ATIWP\CRIMSON.V1? No (Yes)` appears in the lower left corner of the screen.

Step 4: Press Y to replace the existing document on disk. The message `Exit WP? No (Yes)` appears in the lower left corner of the screen, and the message `(Cancel to return to document)` appears in the lower right corner of the screen.

Step 5: Press **N** or Enter to remain in WordPerfect with the cursor positioned in the upper left corner of a blank document screen.

Note: Press **Y** to exit from WordPerfect and restore DOS, or press Cancel (the F1 key) to restore the current document.

Retrieving Documents

Remember that when you load the WordPerfect program or exit from a document but remain in WordPerfect, a blank editing screen appears. If you don't want to create a new document, you can retrieve a document that you have saved on disk. You can execute a retrieve operation by using one of two commands: Retrieve or List Files. Use Retrieve to retrieve a document when you know its name. If you do not remember the name of the document, use List Files (F5) to recover the document.

Using the List Files Command To Retrieve a Document

When you select List **F**iles from the **F**ile pull-down menu (or press F5, the List function key), WordPerfect displays the current default drive and directory. At this point, take one of three actions:

- To see a list of the documents on the directory indicated in the current display, press Enter.
- To change the directory just for the duration of the current command, type the new path (for example, **A:**) and press Enter.

  Press Enter again to view a list of files on the new directory. The *original* directory is displayed the next time you access List Files.
- To change the directory to reflect the new directory each time you access List Files, type = (an equal sign) before the new path and press Enter.

  Press Enter again to view a list of files on the new directory. The *new* directory is displayed the next time you access List Files.

Figure 3.3 shows a sample List Files screen after the drive C:\ATIWP is specified.

Notice the two-line menu bar that appears at the bottom of figure 3.3. To retrieve a document shown on the List Files display, first use the arrow keys to move the highlight to the file name you want; then choose **R**etrieve (**1**) from the menu options at the bottom of the screen. If you press Enter by mistake, you select the default **L**ook (**6**) option, which lets you view, but not edit, the highlighted document. (Lesson 10 provides in-depth coverage of List Files menu options.)

To use List Files to retrieve the document that you previously saved as CRIMSON.V1, follow these steps:

Step 1: If your WordPerfect screen does not display a blank editing screen, clear the screen without saving the current document.

```
10-03-90  03:49a                Directory C:\ATIWP\*.*
Document size:          0  Free:    544,768 Used:    319,529     Files:       85

 .   Current     <Dir>                          ..   Parent     <Dir>
ANNOUNC6.DOC    1,847  03-13-90 08:04a  | ANNOUNC9.DOC    1,432  03-31-90 06:57p
ATI     .DIR    1,300  06-26-90 02:46p  | ATI     .EXE   50,192  05-10-89 11:10a
ATI     .FIL   85,636  06-26-90 02:46p  | BIRTH13 .LST    1,863  04-21-90 05:45a
BLKSRT13.DOC    1,648  04-13-90 10:40p  | CLIP19A .DOC    1,822  05-15-90 09:34a
CLIP19B .DOC    6,719  05-05-90 02:04a  | COL3-16 .DOC    2,234  04-29-90 04:12p
CONDEOP7.LST    3,357  05-15-90 09:35a  | COPYEX5 .       2,383  03-11-90 09:44a
COVER14 .MRK    3,601  04-22-90 07:49a  | COVER7  .DOC    2,653  03-16-90 10:02a
CRIM12A .PRI    1,475  05-15-90 09:37a  | CRIM12A .SEC    1,130  04-15-90 09:33a
CRIMSO10.LTR    1,879  05-15-90 09:42a  | CRIMSO11.LTR    1,346  04-14-90 10:25p
CRIMSO12.LTR    1,484  04-14-90 10:24p  | CRIMSON3.LTR    1,327  05-15-90 08:10a
CRIMSON3.TOP      609  05-15-90 09:39a  | CRIMSON4.LTR    1,335  05-15-90 08:11a
CRIMSON5.LTR    1,327  03-11-90 06:05a  | CRIMSON5.TOP      609  05-15-90 09:40a
CRIMSON6.LTR    1,085  03-13-90 05:20a  | CRIMSON6.TOP      609  03-14-90 11:50a
CRIMSON7.LTR    1,327  03-16-90 09:14a  | CRIMSON9.LTR    1,265  04-01-90 11:34a
CURSOR  .TBL    2,218  10-01-90 03:59p  | DELNO15 .DOC    4,529  04-23-90 02:57p
DOCREF14.EX     3,400  04-22-90 09:37a  | EDFOOT15.DOC    4,529  04-23-90 03:02p
EDIT19  .TBL    2,412  05-15-90 09:43a  | EDNO15  .DOC    4,485  04-28-90 05:30p
EXERCISE.15     4,043  04-25-90 10:48p  ▼ EXRCIS10.DOC    3,129  05-15-90 09:44a

1 Retrieve; 2 Delete; 3 Move/Rename; 4 Print; 5 Short/Long Display;
6 Look; 7 Other Directory; 8 Copy; 9 Find; N Name Search: 6
```

Fig. 3.3. A sample List Files screen.

Note: The instruction to clear the screen without saving the current document is used many times throughout *WordPerfect PC Tutor*. It means to access the **F**ile pull-down menu and select E**x**it (or press F7), press **N** when prompted `Save Document? Yes (No)`, and press **N** when prompted `Exit WP? No (Yes)`.

Step 2: Access the **F**ile pull-down menu and select List **F**iles (or press F5).

Step 3: Press Enter to accept the current directory as the location of the CRIMSON.V1 file (if necessary, specify the correct directory before pressing Enter).

Step 4: Move the highlight bar to the file name CRIMSON.V1, using the arrow keys.

Step 5: Choose **R**etrieve (**1**).

You should see the CRIMSON.V1 document on the screen.

Using the Retrieve Command To Retrieve a Document

Use Retrieve to retrieve a document when you know its name. WordPerfect prompts `Document to be retrieved:` in the lower left corner of the screen. At the prompt, type the name of the file and press Enter. The document then appears on-screen. If the document cannot be found, WordPerfect momentarily prompts `ERROR: File not found-filename`. The cursor rests on the first character of the file name, allowing you to edit the name. If you want to delete the entire name and start over, press Ctrl- End.

To retrieve a document when you know its name—for example, CRIMSON.V1—follow these steps:

Step 1: Clear the screen without saving the current document.

Step 2: Access the **F**ile pull-down menu and select **R**etrieve (or press Shift-F10).

Caution: If you select by the function-key approach rather than by pull-down menus, be careful not to press Save (F10) instead of Retrieve (Shift-F10). Pressing Save (F10) saves your current document instead of retrieving it.

Step 3: Type **CRIMSON.V1** at the prompt `Document to be retrieved:`; then press Enter.

The CRIMSON.V1 document should once again appear on-screen. The result is the same as if you had used the List Files (F5) command; this method requires that you type the name of the file to be retrieved rather than select the file name from a screen display.

Caution: If the document screen is not blank when you execute a Retrieve command, WordPerfect adds the retrieved document to the document on-screen, beginning at the cursor's position.

Combining Files by Using the List Files Command

LESSON FILES

Combining two files into one is a valuable feature. Consider a standard segment of text ("boilerplate") that you want to use in several documents. For example, if you create a special heading for letters to clients and store it in a file called CRIMSON3.TOP, you can then combine that letterhead with different bodies of letters such as the CRIMSON3.LTR document. Practice combining two documents by following these steps:

Step 1: Clear the screen without saving the current document.

Step 2: Access the **F**ile pull-down menu and select List **F**iles (or press F5); then press Enter to accept the lesson-files directory displayed in the lower left corner.

Step 3: Move the highlight bar to the file name CRIMSON3.TOP.

Step 4: Choose **R**etrieve (**1**).

Step 5: Move the cursor to the last line of the new document and Enter three blank lines. Leave the cursor on the last blank line.

Step 6: Access the **F**ile pull-down menu and select List **F**iles (or press F5); then press Enter to accept the lesson-files directory displayed in the lower left corner.

Step 7: Move the highlight bar to the file name CRIMSON3.LTR.

Step 8: Choose **R**etrieve (**1**).

Step 9: Press **Y** at the prompt `Retrieve into current document? No (Yes)`.

Your combined document (see fig. 3.4) should appear with a letterhead.

```
                CRIMSON TRAVEL & TOURS, INC.
           Serving American Corporations for 30 Years

                       Land - Sea - Air


January 16, 1990



Mr. Fred S. Gefeldt
Artesian Systems, Inc.
560 West Esteban Circle
Amazon, OK  78118

Dear Fred:

Crimson Travel & Tours is introducing a new corporate reservations
department.  We promise a prompt response to your questions about
schedules and free delivery of tickets to your office or home.

The agents assigned to this department know that you have a very
busy schedule.  Their goal is to ensure that your trip is worry
free and that you arrive on time at your destination.  Our cruise
C:\ATIWP\CRIMSON3.TOP                          Doc 1 Pg 1 Ln 2" Pos 1"
```

Fig. 3.4. *The result of combining documents.*

You also may combine documents by using Retrieve (Shift-F10) if you know the file names to be combined. Combining with Retrieve, however, does not provide the warning message (as illustrated in Step 9) that appears when you combine with List Files (F5).

Printing the Current Document

LESSON FILES

Printing completes the cycle of creating, editing, and saving a document. It puts the document on paper so that the document can be distributed to readers. Before you print a document, make sure that these conditions are met:

- ❑ A printer is attached to the computer with a cable, properly installed for use with WordPerfect, and selected for use.
- ❑ The printer is turned on.
- ❑ The printer is on-line, meaning that it is ready to accept instructions from the computer.
- ❑ Paper is in the printer. You may use single sheets of paper, continuous perforated sheets, or paper in a paper tray or bin, depending on your printer.

WordPerfect allows two modes of printing: printing from the screen and printing from disk. To print from the screen, access the main print menu by selecting **Print** from the **File** pull-down menu or pressing the Shift-F7 key combination.

To print the current document (the combination of lesson-disk files CRIMSON3.TOP and CRIMSON3.LTR) from the screen, follow these steps:

Step 1: Access the **File** pull-down menu and select **Print** (or press Shift-F7). The WordPerfect main print menu appears (see fig. 3.5).

```
Print

     1 - Full Document
     2 - Page
     3 - Document on Disk
     4 - Control Printer
     5 - Multiple Pages
     6 - View Document
     7 - Initialize Printer

Options

     S - Select Printer                 HP LaserJet Series II
     B - Binding Offset                 0"
     N - Number of Copies               1
     U - Multiple Copies Generated by   WordPerfect
     G - Graphics Quality               Medium
     T - Text Quality                   High
```

Fig. 3.5. *The main print menu.*

Step 2: Choose **Full Document** (**1**).

Choose **Page** (**2**) to print only the page marked by the current cursor position. Lesson 8 contains instructions for using the other print menu options and printing from the disk.

In this lesson you practiced the most basic aspects of creating and using a word-processed file. In Lessons 4 through 7 you learn a variety of techniques for editing and enhancing your WordPerfect documents.

For Further Reference

If you would like to know more about printing documents, consult *Using WordPerfect 5.1*, Special Edition (Que Corporation, Carmel, IN, 1989), Chapters 2, 3, 8, and 9.

Summary of Concepts

Lesson 3 explains these concepts:

- ❑ Load the program and start typing on the blank editing screen to create a WordPerfect document.
- ❑ Enter text, even if it exceeds the length of the line. Just type continuously and let WordPerfect automatically move the cursor, or word wrap the text, to a new line.
- ❑ Use the up arrow or down arrow to move the cursor up or down one line within a document; use the right arrow or left arrow to move the cursor one character right or left within a line in a document.
- ❑ Use one of four editing features to make minor changes: the insert mode to add text, the typeover mode to write over existing text, the Del key to remove the character under the cursor, and the Backspace key to remove the character left of the cursor.
- ❑ Save documents with names that conform to WordPerfect rules and organizational techniques. Names can be one to eight characters with an optional three-character extension. The name should reflect the content of the document.
- ❑ Select **S**ave from the **F**ile pull-down menu (or press F10) to save a document to disk and continue working on the same document.
- ❑ Select E**x**it from the **F**ile pull-down menu (or press F7) to leave a document with or without saving it. Then either exit from WordPerfect or access a blank document screen.
- ❑ Select List **F**iles from the **F**ile pull-down menu (or press F5) to select a document for retrieval from a list; select **R**etrieve from the **F**ile pull-down menu (or press Shift-F10) to specify a document for retrieval by typing its name.
- ❑ Combine two files, by retrieving the first file, positioning the cursor at the bottom of the first document, and retrieving the second file.
- ❑ Print the current document from the screen or print a saved document from disk. Select **P**rint from the **F**ile pull-down menu (or press Shift-F7) to access the main print menu.

Review Exercises

Practice using the WordPerfect features in this lesson by completing these exercises. If you do not remember how to do something, review the preceding explanations and practice steps.

1. Access a blank document screen and type a standard heading for a memo. Include **To:**, **From:**, and **Date:** at the top of the memo, with blank lines separating the three items.
2. Save the document containing memo header lines to disk, using the Exit command. Name the document MEMOTOP.V1. When you complete this exercise, you should see a blank document screen.
3. Type two short paragraphs to form the text within a standard memo, the first outlining the date, time, and purpose of a future meeting, the second describing the location and transportation arrangements for the future meeting.
4. Save the memo text about a future meeting to disk, using the Exit command. Name the document MEMOTXT.V1. When you complete this exercise, you should see a blank document screen.
5. Use Retrieve to retrieve the MEMOTOP.V1 document.
6. Use List Files to append the MEMOTXT.V1 file to the bottom of the MEMOTOP.V1 document.
7. Save the combined memo heading and memo text to disk, using Save. Name the document MTGMEMO.V1. When you complete this exercise, the combined memo should appear on-screen.
8. Practice moving the cursor around the combined memo with the arrow keys.
9. Edit the memo. Change both the date and the location of the meeting.
10. Print the current document from the screen.
11. Exit from the current document without saving the changes.
12. Exit from WordPerfect or continue with the next lesson.

Editing Documents

4

DISK TUTOR

If you haven't yet explored the Disk Tutor, you might want to complete the appropriate tutorial lesson before continuing with this book lesson. If you have already run the tutorial, you might want to run it again and review the pertinent options. The parts of the tutorial relevant to this lesson are:

- ❑ Lesson E: Move the Cursor
- ❑ Lesson F: Edit a Document
- ❑ Lesson J: Pull-Down Menus (shows Reveal Codes screen)

  If you complete the options on the Disk Tutor, you will be more familiar with the techniques and commands found in this lesson.

In this lesson, you practice these tasks:

- ❑ Move the cursor more than one character or line
- ❑ Delete characters, words, and lines
- ❑ Restore deleted text
- ❑ Center, underline, and boldface text
- ❑ Understand and use Reveal Codes
- ❑ Search forward and backward
- ❑ Search for whole words and embedded character strings
- ❑ Search using case significance
- ❑ Search for hidden codes
- ❑ Search and replace text and hidden codes
- ❑ Use global and confirmed replacement

This lesson begins by introducing you to additional cursor-movement commands and editing techniques that include enhancing the appearance of text and deleting text. You learn to view and edit WordPerfect's hidden codes in the middle section.

The lesson concludes with a variety of illustrations of the powerful search and search-and-replace commands.

Using Additional Cursor-Movement Commands

Moving the cursor quickly and easily is important. In Lesson 3, you used the arrow keys to move the cursor up and down one line or left and right one space. To work with larger documents, you need commands that move the cursor to a specific page, the top or bottom of a page or document, or a specific place within a document or line. Additional cursor-movement commands are listed in tables 4.1 and 4.2.

Table 4.1
Horizontal Cursor-Movement Commands

Action	*Keys To Use*
Character left	Left arrow (←) or right arrow (→)
Beginning of line	Home, Home, Home, left arrow (←) (before codes)
Beginning of line	Home, Home, left arrow (←) (after codes)
End of line	End or Home, Home, right arrow (→)
Word left or right	Ctrl-left arrow (←) or Ctrl-right arrow (→)

Table 4.2
Vertical Cursor-Movement Commands

Action	*Keys To Use*
Beginning of document	Home, Home, up arrow (↑)
End of document	Home, Home, down arrow (↓)
Up or down one line	Up (↑) or down (↓) arrow
Up or down **n** lines	Esc, [number], up arrow (↑) or down arrow (↓)
Top of current page	Ctrl-Home, up arrow (↑)
Bottom of current page	Ctrl-Home, down arrow (↓)
Top of preceding page	PgUp
Top of next page	PgDn
Specific page number	Ctrl-Home, [page number], Enter
Top of screen	Home, up arrow (↑) or minus (–)
Bottom of screen	Home, down arrow (↓) or plus (+)
Specific character	Ctrl-Home, [character]
Top of next paragraph	Ctrl-down arrow (↓)
Top of preceding paragraph	Ctrl-up arrow (↑)

Moving the Cursor within a Page

To use the cursor-movement tables, select the action you want and press the key sequence for that action. As you work with different cursor-movement commands, notice that you can accomplish the same action in more than one way. For example, you can combine the Esc key, used here to repeat commands or characters, with several cursor-movement commands (one of which is shown in Step 4 in the following exercise).

To practice a few cursor-movement actions, follow these steps:

Step 1: Clear the screen without saving the current document and retrieve CRIMSON4.LTR.

Note: The instruction to clear the screen without saving the current document is used many times throughout *WordPerfect PC Tutor*. It means to access the **File** pull-down menu and select Ex**i**t (or press F7), press **N** when prompted `Save Document? Yes (No)`, and press **N** when prompted `Exit WP? No (Yes)`.

Step 2: To move the cursor down 11 lines, press Esc, type the number **11** in response to the lower left corner prompt for the repeat value, and press the down arrow. The cursor should be on the first line of paragraph one.

Step 3: To move the cursor right five words, press Ctrl- right arrow five times. The cursor should be on the word `introducing`. Press Home, Home, left arrow to move the cursor to the beginning of the line.

Step 4: To move the cursor right five words by using an alternative method, press Esc, type **5**, and then press Ctrl-right arrow. The cursor should return to the word `introducing`.

Step 5: To move the cursor to the top of the screen, press the minus (-) key on the numeric keypad right of the keyboard.

Step 6: To move the cursor to the bottom of the screen, press Home and then the down arrow. In brief, you can move the cursor to the top or bottom of the screen by using the numeric keypad's minus or plus keys or the Home, up-arrow or down-arrow combination.

Step 7: To move the cursor up one paragraph at a time, press Ctrl-up arrow. Press Ctrl-up arrow several more times.

Moving the Cursor between Pages

WordPerfect inserts a *soft page break* at the end of a page of text (or when it encounters a protected block of text that won't fit on the current page). Text then continues on the following page. When text is added to a document or deleted from a document, soft page breaks are automatically recalculated so that pages always break correctly. On-screen, a soft page break appears as a single dashed line.

To force a page to break at a certain place—for example, at the beginning of a new section in a report—enter a *hard page break*. The page always breaks there, in spite of subsequent additions or deletions of text. To insert a hard page break, position the cursor at the place where you want the break to occur and press Ctrl-Enter. A double dashed line appears on-screen. To remove a hard page break, position the cursor at the beginning of the line above the double dashed line and press Del—or position the cursor immediately below the double dashed line and press Backspace.

Use the PgUp, PgDn, and Ctrl-Home commands described in table 4.2 to move the cursor throughout a long document. To create a multipage document and move the cursor between pages, follow these steps:

Step 1: Clear the screen without saving the current document and retrieve PAGES4.LST.

Step 2: Position the cursor at the beginning of the blank line between paragraphs one and two and press Ctrl-Enter. The status line indicates `Pg 2`.

Step 3: Position the cursor at the beginning of the blank line between paragraphs two and three and press Ctrl-Enter. The status line indicates `Pg 3`.

Step 4: Position the cursor at the top of the page by pressing Home, Home, up arrow.

Figure 4.1 displays PAGES4.LST on-screen with double dashed lines, which indicate hard page breaks.

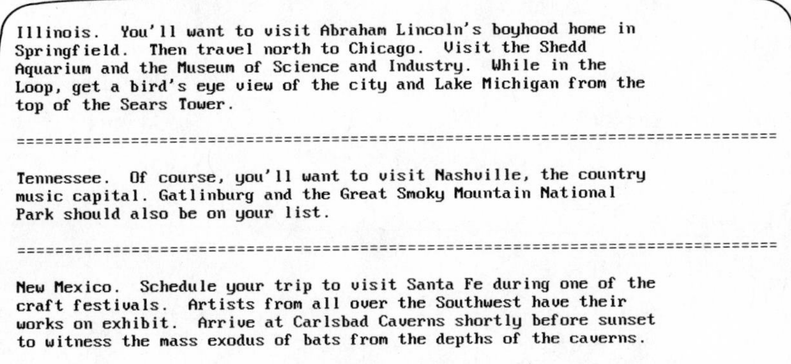

```
Illinois.  You'll want to visit Abraham Lincoln's boyhood home in
Springfield.  Then travel north to Chicago.  Visit the Shedd
Aquarium and the Museum of Science and Industry.  While in the
Loop, get a bird's eye view of the city and Lake Michigan from the
top of the Sears Tower.

===============================================================================

Tennessee.  Of course, you'll want to visit Nashville, the country
music capital. Gatlinburg and the Great Smoky Mountain National
Park should also be on your list.

===============================================================================

New Mexico.  Schedule your trip to visit Santa Fe during one of the
craft festivals.  Artists from all over the Southwest have their
works on exhibit.  Arrive at Carlsbad Caverns shortly before sunset
to witness the mass exodus of bats from the depths of the caverns.
```

Fig. 4.1. *Double-dashed lines, which indicate hard page breaks.*

Step 5: Press PgDn twice and watch the cursor move to the top of the next page each time, placing the new page at the top of the screen.

Step 6: Press PgUp two times, moving the cursor to the top of the first page.

Step 7: Press Ctrl-Home, type **3**, and press Enter to move the cursor to a specified page—in this case, page 3.

Deleting and Restoring Text

The Backspace and Del keys are useful for correcting minor typing errors. To remove larger sections of text, however, use the commands listed in table 4.3 or execute a menu-driven command sequence to remove a sentence, paragraph, or page. Lesson 5 shows you ways to delete text through the use of WordPerfect's block feature. Delete an entire document stored on disk by using option 2 from the List Files menu (see Lesson 10).

Table 4.3
Keys for Deleting Text

Action	*Key To Use*
Delete character at the cursor	Del key
Delete character left of cursor	Backspace
Delete word at the cursor	Ctrl-Backspace
Delete word left of cursor	Home, Backspace
Delete word to right of cursor	Home, Del
Delete to end of line (EOL)	Ctrl-End
Delete to end of page (EOP)	Ctrl-PgDn
Delete number (n) of lines	Esc, n, Ctrl-End
Delete a document	List Files, option 2

Deleting Characters, Words, and Lines

If you have a relatively small amount of text to delete, use keys to complete the operation. Follow these steps:

Step 1: Clear the screen without saving the current document and retrieve CRIMSON4.LTR.

Step 2: Move the cursor to the first line of paragraph two, position the cursor on the word `very`, and press Ctrl-Backspace. The word `very` is removed, and the text automatically repositions on-screen.

Step 3: To delete to the end of the line, move the cursor to the beginning of the next line and press Ctrl-End.

Step 4: To delete the next five lines, press Esc, type **5**, and then press Ctrl-End.

Step 5: To delete the remainder of the page, press Ctrl-PgDn and then press **Y** at the prompt `Delete remainder of page? No (Yes).`

Using Cancel (F1) To Restore Deleted Text

If you delete text accidentally, you may be able to restore it. WordPerfect retains the three most recently deleted portions of text. Therefore, text removed in the three most recent delete operations (including the removal with Backspace and Del keys) can be retrieved.

Suppose that you delete a word by positioning the cursor within the word and pressing Ctrl-Backspace. Now you decide that you want to restore the deleted text. If you place the cursor where you want to restore text and press Cancel (F1), WordPerfect displays the most recently removed text and the Undelete menu choices shown in figure 4.2. Choose **R**estore (**1**) to restore the displayed text. Choose **P**revious Deletion (**2**) to see the previous segment (if any) of deleted text.

Practice restoring text by following these steps:

Step 1: Clear the screen without saving the current document and retrieve CRIMSON4.LTR.

Step 2: Position the cursor at the beginning of the line `Dear Fred:` and then press Ctrl-End to delete the line.

Step 3: Position the cursor on the word `state` in the last line of the letter. Press Ctrl-Backspace to delete the word `state`.

Step 4: Position the cursor on the line that held the phrase `Dear Fred:` before it was deleted.

Step 5: Access the **E**dit pull-down menu and select **U**ndelete (or press F1). The Undelete menu appears at the bottom of the screen, and `state`, the most recent deletion, appears in the current cursor position above the body of the document (see fig. 4.2).

```
January 16, 1990


Mr. Fred S. Gefeldt
Artesian Systems, Inc.
560 West Esteban Circle
Amazon, OK  78118

state

Crimson Travel & Tours is introducing a new corporate reservations
department.  We promise a prompt response to your questions about
schedules and free delivery of tickets to your office or home.

The agents assigned to this department know that you have a very
busy schedule.  Their goal is to ensure that your trip is worry
free and that you arrive on time at your destination.  Our cruise
specialists can assist with incentive as well as pleasure tours.

We guarantee you the best service.  Call us the next time your
itinerary takes you across the or around the world.

Sincerely,
Undelete: 1 Restore; 2 Previous Deletion: 0
```

Fig. 4.2. *The display at the bottom of the screen of the two options that restore text.*

Step 6: To restore the proper salutation to the letter, select **P**revious Deletion (**2**) to see `Dear Fred:` and select **R**estore (**1**) to insert the text back into the document.

Deleting Sentences, Paragraphs, or Pages

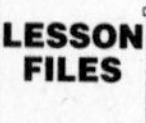

If the text you want to delete is exactly one sentence, one paragraph, or one page, you can execute the operation by using menus. Follow these steps to delete a paragraph:

Step 1: Clear the screen without saving the current document and retrieve CRIMSON4.LTR.

Step 2: Position the cursor anywhere in the first paragraph, such as within the word `reservations`.

Step 3: Access the **E**dit pull-down menu and choose Se**l**ect (or press Ctrl-F4).

Note: Figure 4.3 illustrates the next pop-out menu that appears if you use the pull-down menu system. If you press Ctrl-F4, you see the **S**entence, **P**aragraph, and Pa**g**e options across the bottom of the screen.

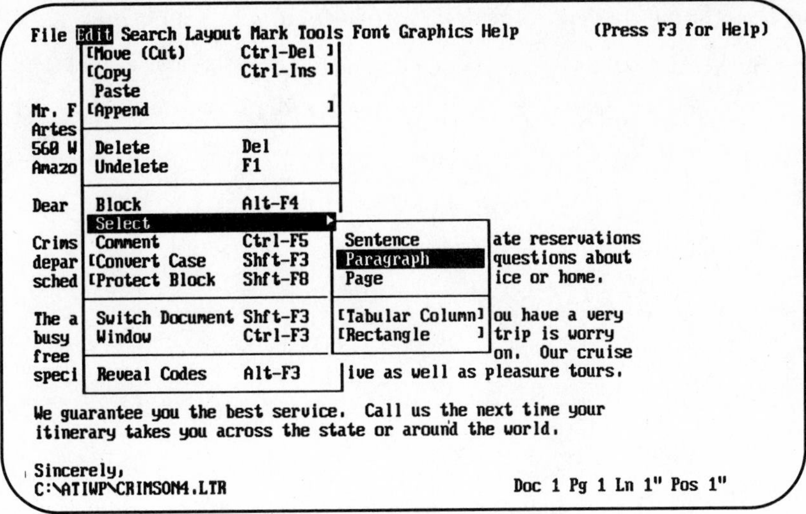

Fig. 4.3. The Select options on the Edit pull-down menu.

Step 4: Select **Paragraph**; the entire paragraph is highlighted.

Step 5: Select **Delete** (**3**).

Remember that in most cases it is faster to execute a command by using a function key or function-key combination than to select from the pull-down menu system (if you remember the appropriate function-key assignment).

Boldfacing, Underlining, and Centering Text as You Type

Boldfacing (F6), underlining (F8), and centering (Shift-F6) are ways to enhance and accent text to catch the reader's attention. You can use individual print-enhancement features or mix several features for added emphasis. Most printers and monitors produce these enhancements, and WordPerfect can support most hardware on the market today.

To boldface or underline text as you enter the text, simply press the command key (or pull-down menu selections) to turn the feature on; then type the text and press the command key (or pull-down menu selections) again to turn the feature off. To center text as you enter it, simply press the command key (or pull-down menu selections) to activate the feature, type the text, and then press Enter.

To center and underline as you enter the first line of a document, follow these steps:

Step 1: Clear the screen without saving the current document.

Step 2: Access the **L**ayout pull-down menu and select **A**lign (see fig. 4.4).

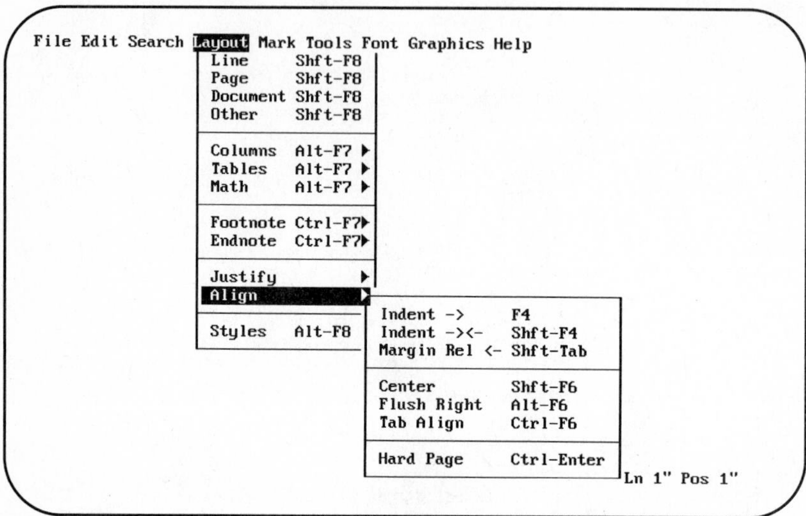

Fig. 4.4. *The Align options on the Layout pull-down menu.*

Step 3: Select **C**enter. The cursor moves to the center of the current line.

Note: As an alternative to Steps 2 and 3, you can simply press Shift-F6.

Step 4: Access the F**o**nt pull-down menu, select **A**ppearance, and then select **U**nderline (or press F8) to turn on underlining. Type

CRIMSON TRAVEL & TOURS, INC.

Step 5: Turn off underline by using one of these three methods:

❑ Access the F**o**nt pull-down menu and select **A**ppearance; then select **U**nderline.

❑ Press Underline (F8).

❑ Press the right arrow (→) once to move the cursor past the underline code.

Step 6: Press Enter twice: once to turn off centering and a second time to add a line for spacing.

To combine enhancing techniques for two more lines in the document, follow these steps:

Step 1: Turn on centering (if you do not remember the steps, refer to the previous hands-on illustration). Access the F**o**nt pull-down menu, select **A**ppearance, and then select **B**old (or press F6) to turn on boldface. Now type

Serving American Corporations for 30 Years

Step 2: Press Bold (F6) and then Enter to turn off bold print and end centering.

Note: You also can turn off boldface by using the F**o**nt pull-down menu or pressing the right-arrow key, the same way you turned off underline in the previous illustration.

Step 3: Press Enter twice to insert two blank lines.

Step 4: Press Center (Shift-F6) to turn on centering, press Bold (F6) to turn on boldface, press Underline (F8) to turn on underlining, and then type

Land - Sea - Air

Step 5: Press Bold (F6), press Underline (F8), and press Enter to turn all features off.

Note: If you do not turn off all three features at the same time, the text typed next displays a mixture of these features.

Understanding Hidden Codes

When you issue a format command, WordPerfect inserts a code into the document at the position of the cursor. These codes are not usually visible on-screen. You can see the codes, however, by accessing the **R**eveal Codes option on the **E**dit pull-down menu or by pressing Alt-F3 (F11 if you have an Enhanced Keyboard). Figure 4.5 shows the hidden codes for the "jazzed up" letterhead created in the previous illustration.

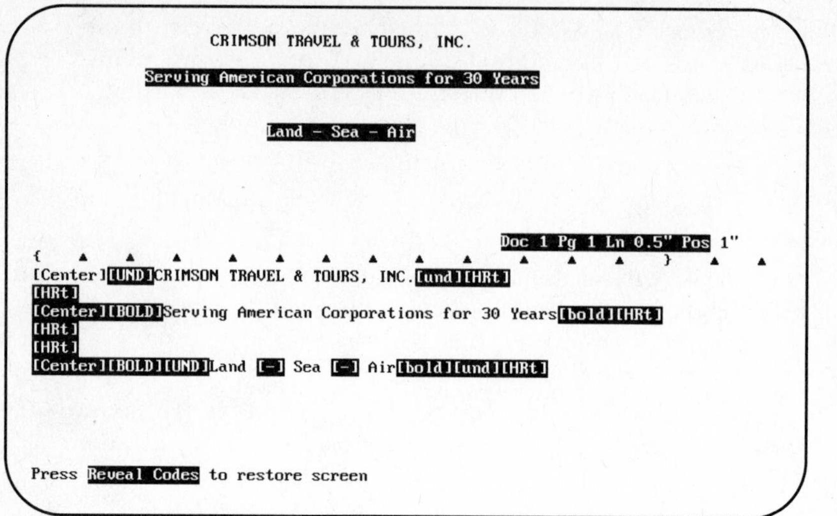

Upper half of the screen displays a portion of the current document.

Lower half of the screen displays the associated codes.

Fig 4.5. Using Reveal Codes to view the document.

The upper half of the screen displays the letterhead text as it was typed. The lower half of the screen shows the letterhead text with the embedded codes. Codes are always enclosed in square brackets, such as `[Center]` for center or `[UND]` for underline. Notice that some codes appear twice, such as `[UND]` and `[und]`. Referred to as *paired codes*, they define a block of data that is to be affected by the pair of codes. `[UND]` tells WordPerfect to begin underlining, and `[und]` terminates underlining. Other codes, such as `[Just:Left]`, work alone and are referred to as *open codes*. Open codes remain in effect from the point where you enter them in the document until you change them or until the end of the document. A few codes, such as `[HRt]` and `[SRt]`, cause an action to occur or mark a specific place in the text. They are neither open nor paired codes.

Two of the most common codes are `[SRt]` and `[HRt]`. The `[SRt]` code marks a soft return, a place where WordPerfect word-wrapped text and automatically started a new line. The `[HRt]` code indicates a hard return, marking a position where you pressed Enter to end a paragraph or text that did not fill a line.

When the screen displays the codes, you can move the Reveal Codes cursor (a solid square) by using any cursor-movement commands. You may edit text and codes in Reveal Codes mode. Edit codes by deleting them and inserting new ones as if you were not in Reveal Codes mode. Use Reveal Codes to troubleshoot a document that is not formatting or printing correctly. Look for these signs of trouble:

- ❑ The absence of a code that should be in the document

  For example, WordPerfect changes margins only if the command is given and the code is in the document. If the code is not there, WordPerfect does not have the necessary instructions to make a change.

- ❑ The presence of a code that should be removed

  WordPerfect reads commands in the order of their appearance. But if there are two margin-change codes, the program uses the second one. To prevent WordPerfect from using the wrong code, remove the one you do not need.

- ❑ A code in the wrong place

  If, for example, you want specific margins for the entire document, be sure that the code appears at the beginning of the document. If it does not, delete the misplaced code, reposition the cursor, and reissue the code. You may do this with Reveal Codes on or off, but it is easier to verify your position with Reveal Codes on.

When you remove embedded format codes, the text returns to its original appearance utilizing default WordPerfect format settings. Explore the hidden codes in the document you just created. Follow these steps:

Step 1: Place the cursor at the upper left corner of the newly created letterhead document.

Step 2: Access the **E**dit pull-down menu and select **R**eveal Codes (or press Alt-F3 or F11). You should see a screen display that resembles figure 4.5 (you may need to position the cursor to display the entire letterhead).

Step 3: Use arrow keys to move the square cursor in the lower half of the screen to the code `[BOLD]` in the last line of text.

Step 4: Press Del to remove the code. Notice that `[BOLD]` was part of a pair that ended with `[bold]` and that both codes are removed.

Step 5: Position the Reveal Codes cursor on the `[Center]` code on the last line of text.

Step 6: Press Del to remove centering. Notice the change in the upper portion of the screen.

Step 7: Now press Center (Shift-F6) to recenter this line. The line may appear off-center until you press the up arrow (↑) or down arrow (↓). Repeat Step 2 to turn off Reveal Codes.

When you edit codes with Reveal Codes mode off, WordPerfect warns you if you are about to remove a code. For example, if you try to delete an underline code when Reveal Codes mode is off, the prompt `Delete [UND]? No (Yes)` appears in the lower left corner of the screen. With Reveal Codes mode on, you do not see a warning.

LESSON FILES

If you work with multiple-page documents, you encounter soft page breaks (WordPerfect wraps text to the next page) or hard page breaks (you specify the last piece of text on a page by pressing Ctrl-Enter). To view codes associated with soft and hard page breaks, follow these steps:

Step 1: Clear the screen without saving the current document and retrieve MULTIPG4.LST.

Step 2: Access the **E**dit pull-down menu and select **R**eveal Codes (or press Alt-F3 or F11). Several `[HPg]` codes appear between paragraphs, indicating that each paragraph is on a separate page.

Step 3: Press Reveal Codes (Alt-F3 or F11) to restore the document to a full-screen display.

Step 4: Position the cursor at the bottom of the document.

Step 5: Press Enter several times until enough lines are inserted to create a soft page break, indicated by a single dashed line across the screen.

Step 6: Position the cursor just below the dashed line and press Reveal Codes (Alt-F3 or F11).

Note: The `[HRt-SPg]` code appears on the Reveal Codes screen, indicating a soft page break. Immediately below the page break code is a dormant hard return `[Dorm HRt]`. This code, one of WordPerfect 5.1's new features, prevents an unwanted blank line at the top of a page created by a soft page break.

Step 7: Press Reveal Codes (Alt-F3 or F11) to restore the full-screen display of the document.

Searching and Replacing

Two of the most powerful WordPerfect tools are the Search and Replace functions. If you have ever spent time looking through a long report for a particular phrase or name, you can appreciate the search-and-replace capabilities of WordPerfect.

WordPerfect's Search and Replace commands are easy to use and can improve the quality of documents. Here are some ways you can use Search and Replace:

- ❑ Searching for jargon the reader may not be familiar with (such as the computer term *byte*) and changing the term to a more easily understood one.
- ❑ Checking for poor writing habits such as the use of the vague pronouns *this* and *it*.
- ❑ Searching for clichés and replacing them with fresh images.

- Checking for matching punctuation such as open and closed parentheses or quotation marks.
- Checking for too many spaces. For example, laser printers and other printers that justify text produce better results if a single space is used after the period ending a sentence than if double spaces are used.

Searching for Text and Hidden Codes

You can search for text and hidden codes beginning at any point in a document—and you can search forward or backward. Searching is a simple three-step process:

- Access the **S**earch pull-down menu and select **F**orward or **B**ackward (or press F2 or Shift-F2, respectively).
- At the prompt, enter any hidden codes or text of up to 60 characters that you want to search for.
- Press Forward Search (F2) or Esc to begin the search (regardless of the direction you search).

You can search for whole words, for portions of words or phrases, and even for words you are not sure how to spell. Consider these examples for entering search criteria:

- If you type **and** as the text you are searching for, WordPerfect locates `and` as well as all words that have `and` in them. For example, WordPerfect finds `and`, `Band`, `Randy`, or `Andrew`.
- To find a whole word only, enter spaces before and after the word. For example, if you type [space]**and**[space] WordPerfect finds `And` or `and` but not `band`, `Randy`, or `Andrew`.
- To find text that has changing components or to find a word when you are unsure of its spelling, use the matching character (sometimes called a wild-card character) ^X (press Ctrl-V, Ctrl-X). If you type the search criteria **(^X)**, WordPerfect finds `(1)`, `(a)`, `(#)` or any other single character within parentheses.
- If you type criteria in lowercase only, the search is not case-sensitive. Typing **and** finds `and`, `And`, or `AND`. If you type in uppercase only, WordPerfect finds only uppercase matches. Typing **AND** finds only `AND`.
- If what you search for occurs in a header, footer, footnote, endnote, graphic-box caption, or text box, you must perform an extended search. Activate an extended search just as you do a regular search, except press Home before you press the Search key.

Searching Forward

Searching can begin at any point in the document and proceed forward to the end of the document. If text is found, the cursor stops immediately following it. You can repeat the search by pressing F2 twice. If no text is found, the message `*Not found*` flashes on the status line.

To search STATES4.LST for `Painted Desert`, follow these steps:

Step 1: Clear the screen without saving the current document and retrieve STATES4.LST.

Step 2: Access the **Search** pull-down menu and select **Forward** (or press F2).

Step 3: At the prompt `->Srch:` on the status line in the lower-left corner of the screen, type **painted desert** (do not press Enter).

Step 4: Press Search Forward (F2) or Esc. The cursor moves to the position immediately following the first location in the document of the search condition `painted desert`.

Note: If your search does not find the text, repeat the exercise. Be careful to type the correct criteria in Step 3. One common error is pressing Enter at the end of the search condition, an action that adds a `[HRt]` code to the search.

Step 5: Press Search Forward (F2) twice: once to repeat the search process and a second time to accept the current search condition `painted desert` which displays at the bottom of the screen.

After the first occurrence of `Painted Desert` is found, the message `* Not found *` appears briefly in the lower-left corner of the screen to indicate that no more instances of the phrase appear in the text.

Searching for Embedded Words and Whole Words

The word *the* presents a search problem. It is a whole word and also part of other words. To search for any occurrence of the three characters *the* throughout the current STATES4.LST document, follow these steps:

Step 1: Move the cursor to the upper left corner of the current document by pressing Home, Home, up arrow.

Step 2: Access the **Search** pull-down menu and select **Forward** (or press F2).

Step 3: At the prompt `->Srch:` on the status line, type **the** and press Forward Search (F2) to begin the search.

Note: You do not have to delete the search condition used in the previous search operation. Just start typing the new condition; the screen display of the previous condition disappears.

Step 4: Press F2 twice to repeat the next occurrence of `the`.

Step 5: Repeat the search several times.

If you continue the search to the bottom of the document, WordPerfect finds *the* both as a frequently used whole word and as a string of three characters embedded in *Then, their, northern, southern*, and *authentic*. To modify the search to find only the whole word the, follow these steps:

Step 1: Move the cursor to the upper left corner of the current document by pressing Home, Home, up arrow.

Step 2: Access the **S**earch pull-down menu and select **F**orward (or press F2).

Step 3: At the prompt `->Srch:` on the status line, type **the** with a space on either side (that is, press the space bar, type **the**, and press the space bar).

Step 4: Press Forward Search (F2) to begin the search.

Step 5: Press F2 twice to repeat the search.

Step 6: Repeat the search several times. Now only the whole word `the` is found.

Using Wild Cards To Find Spelling Variations

Use the ^X option when you are uncertain of the exact spelling of a word. Inserting ^X instead of a character that can vary causes WordPerfect to search for matching words but to accept any character instead of the ^X character.

Suppose that you are aware of an incorrect spelling in a document, and you want to see where it occurs. For example, in SEARCH4.DOC, *from* is misspelled as *form* in some places. To find all words that start with *f*, end with *m*, and have any two characters in the middle, follow these steps:

Step 1: Clear the screen without saving the current document and retrieve SEARCH4.DOC.

Step 2: Notice the incorrect spelling of `form` (instead of `from`) in the last line of the first paragraph.

Step 3: Access the **S**earch pull-down menu and select **F**orward (or press F2).

Step 4: At the prompt, type **f**, press Ctrl-V, and then press Ctrl-X. Press Ctrl-V and then Ctrl-X again; then type **m** (but do **not** press Enter). You should see `f^X^Xm` as the search criteria in the lower-left corner of the screen, as shown in figure 4.6.

```
     Illinois.  You'all want to visit Abraham Lincoln's boyhood
home in Springfield.  Then travel north to Chicago.  Visit the
Shedd Aquarium and the Museum of Science and Industry.  While in
the Loop, get a bird's eye view of the city and Lake Michigan form
the top of the Sears Tower.

     Tennessee.  Of course, you'all want to visit Nashville, the
country music capital. Gatlinburg and the Great Smoky Mountain
National Park should also be on your list.

               New Mexico.  Schedule your trip to visit
          Santa Fe during one of the craft festivals.
          Artists from all over the Southwest have their
          works on exhibit.  Arrive at Carlsbad Caverns
          shortly before sunset to witness the mass
          exodus of bats form the depths of the caverns.

               Arizona.  In the northern part of the
          state you'all want to see the Grand Canyon,
          Monument Valley, the Painted Desert, and the
          Meteor Crater.  Drive through scenic Oak Creek
          Canyon and enjoy the natural red hues around
          Sedona.  You'all also want to see the Sonoran
          desert in the southern part of the state and
-> Srch: f^X^Xm
```

Fig. 4.6. Specifying a search condition containing wild cards.

Step 5: Press Forward Search (F2); then press F2 twice to repeat the search.

Step 6: Repeat the search until no more words are found.

You should find three words. In this example, `form` is not supposed to be used. In other situations, searching for `ro` or `or`, `ie` or `ei` may find different correct words. Be careful when using wild cards, particularly in search-and-replace actions discussed later.

Searching Backward

You can begin searching at any point and move backward to the beginning of the document. When you search for several words, it is often handy to search forward for a word, then search backward for the next word. Ordinarily, though, begin a search at the beginning or end of the document.

To search backward for the typing error **you'all**, follow these steps:

Step 1: Move the cursor to the bottom of the current document by pressing Home, Home, down arrow (↓).

Step 2: Access the **S**earch pull-down menu and select **B**ackward (or press Shift-F2).

Step 3: At the prompt `<-Srch:`, type **you'all** and press Search (F2).

Step 4: Press Search Backward (Shift-F2), then F2 to repeat the search.

Step 5: Continue to repeat the search until you see the following message:

```
* Not found *
```

To change the search direction when you repeat the search (see Step 3), press F2 twice to repeat the search forward; press Shift-F2, F2 to repeat the search backward.

Note: If you select Search Forward (F2), causing the prompt `->Srch:` to appear in the lower left corner of the screen, and you then decide to search backward, press the up arrow; the prompt is changed to `<-Srch:`. If you select Search Backward (Shift-F2), pressing the down arrow (↓) reverses the search direction.

Searching for Hidden Codes

You can use Search to find hidden codes and then change the codes manually. The process of searching for hidden codes parallels that of searching for text. At the prompt for a search condition, simply enter the hidden code and begin the search.

To find the hidden code `[Tab]`, follow these steps:

Step 1: Move the cursor to the upper left corner of the current document by pressing Home, Home, up arrow.

Step 2: Press Forward Search (F2).

Note: By using the F2 key, you are using the faster method of accessing Search. If you like, you can access Search by using the pull-down menu system.

Step 3: At the prompt `->Srch:`, press Tab. The search condition changes to `[Tab]`.

Step 4: Press F2 and then press Reveal Codes (Alt-F3 or F11) to see the hidden code `[TAB]` left of the cursor position on the `I` of `Illinois`.

Step 5: Press F2 twice to repeat the search for the next `[Tab]` code.

Step 6: Press Reveal Codes (Alt-F3 or F11) to restore full document display.

You can edit as you search. Once you complete the search for text or hidden codes, you can use any WordPerfect editing function to make manual changes. When you are ready, you can repeat the last search to find the next repetition of text or hidden code requiring an edit.

Searching and Replacing Text and Hidden Codes

You may want to replace or eliminate text or hidden codes found in a search. Search and Replace (Alt-F2) makes this task simple. The search-and-replace operation may begin anywhere in the document and proceed to the end of the document, or it may be confined to a block of text.

Replacing Hidden Codes

If the object of a search is a hidden code created by pressing a key on the keyboard (such as Tab), you can indicate the search criteria by pressing that key. If the object of a search is a hidden code created through menu selections (such as `[L/R Mar:]`), you must access a limited menu displayed in the lower left corner of the screen.

To remove the [Tab] indentations from SEARCH4.DOC, follow these instructions:

Step 1: Position the cursor at the top of the current SEARCH4.DOC document by pressing Home, Home, Home, up arrow.

Step 2: Access the **S**earch pull-down menu and select **R**eplace (or press Alt-F2). At the prompt `w/Confirm? No (Yes)`, press **N**.

Step 3: At the prompt `->Srch:`, press Tab; then press F2.

Step 4: At the prompt `Replace with:`, press F2 to activate the search-and-replace feature, thereby deleting the tab (replacing it with nothing).

All tabs are now removed; the left margin is smooth except for paragraphs about New Mexico and Arizona, whose spacing is controlled through the left/right margins feature.

To remove the `[L/R Mar:]` codes, follow these steps:

Step 1: Move the cursor to the upper left corner of the current document by pressing Home, Home, Home, up arrow.

Step 2: Press Replace (Alt-F2). At the prompt `w/Confirm? No (Yes)`, press **Y**.

Step 3: At the prompt `->Srch:`, press Format (Shift-F8) to access a limited version of the menu levels that create left and right margins.

Step 4: Choose **L**ine (**1**) and then **M**argins (**6**). `[L/R Mar]` appears at the bottom of the screen as the search condition.

Step 5: Press F2. At the prompt `Replace with:`, press (F2). The cursor moves to the first `[L/R Mar]` hidden code above the New Mexico paragraph.

Step 6: At the prompt `Confirm? No (Yes)`, press **Y** to confirm the removal of the first `[L/R Mar]` code.

Step 7: Repeat Step 6 to confirm the removal of the second and last `[L/R Mar]` code after the Arizona paragraph.

Replacing Selected Text

When you search for and replace a correctly spelled word but one that is wrong for the use intended (such as *form* for *from*), use the Confirm option. To practice searching and replacing with confirmation at each occurrence, follow these steps:

Step 1: Move the cursor to the upper left corner of the current document by pressing Home, Home, up arrow.

Step 2: Press Replace (Alt-F2). At the prompt `w/Confirm? No (Yes)`, press **Y**.

Step 3: At the prompt `->Srch:`, type **form** and press F2.

Step 4: At the prompt `Replace with:`, type **from** and press F2. The cursor appears at the first `form`, found at the end of the first paragraph.

Step 5: At the prompt `Confirm? No (Yes)`, press **Y**. `Form` changes to `from` at the end of the first paragraph, and the cursor moves to the next occurrence of `form` in the New Mexico paragraph.

Step 6: Press **Y** for Yes to correct the New Mexico paragraph and complete the current search-and-replace operation.

Replacing Text Globally

Using Search and Replace to confirm the change of each occurrence of the specified criteria certainly works faster than manually searching and editing an entire document. Replacement speeds up even more if you set Confirm to off.

To change *you'll* to *you will* without using Confirm, follow these steps:

Step 1: Move cursor to the upper left corner of the current document by pressing Home, Home, up arrow.

Step 2: Press Replace (Alt-F2); at the prompt `w/Confirm? No (Yes)`, press **N**.

Step 3: At the prompt `->Srch:`, type **you'll**. Press F2.

Step 4: At the prompt `Replace with:`, type **you will** and press F2.

Step 5: Page through the document and note the global change.

For Further Reference

If you would like to know more about WordPerfect codes, consult *Using WordPerfect 5.1*, Special Edition (Que Corporation, Carmel, IN, 1989), Chapter 3.

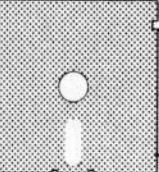

Summary of Concepts

Lesson 4 explains these concepts:

- ❑ Several cursor-movement keys and key combinations move the cursor within a page and between the pages of a document.
- ❑ Additional keys and key combinations delete portions of text.
- ❑ You can delete words, sentences, and paragraphs by selecting menu options.
- ❑ WordPerfect includes the Undelete feature, which permits you to restore the last three deletions.
- ❑ You can enhance text as you type by using boldfacing, underlining, and centering.
- ❑ WordPerfect inserts hidden codes to control document layout (for example, margin codes) and appearance (for example, underlining codes).
- ❑ You can reveal for editing purposes the hidden codes that control a document.
- ❑ WordPerfect supports searching for a specified character string or hidden code.
- ❑ Searching may start at any point in the document and move forward or backward.
- ❑ A search condition typed lowercase finds all uppercase, lowercase, and mixed-case occurrences of the condition. Type a case-specific search condition in mixed case or uppercase.
- ❑ The wild card (entered as Ctrl-V, Ctrl-X) is used to represent any character in a specific position within the search condition. For example, the search condition *b^Xd* finds *bad*, *bed*, and *bid*.
- ❑ WordPerfect supports replacing a specified character string or hidden code, with or without confirmation.

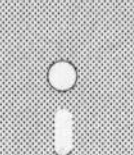

Review Exercises

Practice using the WordPerfect features in this lesson by completing these exercises. If you do not remember how to do something, review the preceding explanations and practice steps.

1. Clear the screen without saving the current document and retrieve CRIMSON4.LTR.
2. Use the Delete-to-end-of-line command to erase the last line of text `Senior Account Representative`.
3. Save the current document to disk under the name PRACTICE.L4, leaving the document on-screen after the save. Hint: Access the **F**ile pull-down menu and select **S**ave, not E**x**it (or press F10).
4. Delete from the current document the statement `corporate reservations department`; then reenter it as bold and underlined.
5. Use Reveal Codes (Alt-F3) to locate the `[BOLD]` and `[UND]` codes that were entered in Step 3 above; then delete the codes.
6. Retrieve STATES4.LST.
7. Do a forward search for any occurrence of the `an` character string.
8. Do a backward search for `and`, limited to the whole word.
9. Search for every two-letter word that begins with `O`.
10. Search for every occurrence of a hard return (`[HRt]`) code.
11. Search for `visit` and replace selected occurrences with `see`.
12. Search for the phrase `you'll want to` and replace all occurrences with the phrase **everyone should**.

Working with Blocks

5

DISK TUTOR

If you haven't yet explored the Disk Tutor, you might want to complete the appropriate tutorial lesson before continuing with this book lesson. If you have already run the tutorial, you might want to run it again and review the pertinent options. The part of the tutorial relevant to this lesson is:

- ❑ Lesson F: Edit a Document

If you complete the options on the Disk Tutor, you will be more familiar with the techniques and commands found in this lesson.

In this lesson, you practice these tasks:

- ❑ Highlighting a block of text
- ❑ Moving or copying a block of text—both within and between documents
- ❑ Deleting a block
- ❑ Saving or appending a block
- ❑ Printing a block
- ❑ Working with windows

You probably often work on a small portion, or *block*, of text. In this lesson, you first learn to mark or highlight a section of a document, and then learn to give commands to manipulate the block. You also learn to view two documents on a single screen.

Understanding How the Block Feature Works

A block of text is highlighted so that it is ready to be used with such commands as Delete, Copy, or Print. Highlighting a block of text requires just three simple steps:

- ❑ Move the cursor to the beginning of the text to be marked.
- ❑ Access the **E**dit pull-down menu and select **B**lock (or press Block, Alt-F4 or F12) to turn on Block.
- ❑ Move the cursor to the end of the block of text to be marked, using any cursor-movement key to complete the highlighting process.

Once you highlight the block, you can issue a command (such as underlining). If you change your mind and decide to cancel highlighting, you can resort to one of three actions:

- ❑ Access the **E**dit pull-down menu and select **B**lock.
- ❑ Press Alt-F4 (or F12 if you have an Enhanced Keyboard), the function-key combination assigned to Block.
- ❑ Press F1, the Cancel function key.

Once you use or cancel the highlighted block, you can highlight a block again. In this section of the workbook, you learn how to block (highlight) text, how to cancel highlighting, and about commands which can be applied to highlighted text.

Highlighting a Block

To highlight a portion of text and then cancel the highlighting, follow these steps:

Step 1: Clear the current screen without saving the previous document and retrieve CRIMSON5.LTR.

Note: The instruction to clear the screen without saving the current document is used many times throughout the workbook. It means to access the **F**ile pull-down menu and select E**x**it (or press F7); when prompted `Save Document? Yes (No)`, press **N**; when prompted `Exit WP? No (Yes)`, press **N**.

Step 2: Move the cursor to the beginning of the first paragraph.

Step 3: Access the **E**dit pull-down menu (see fig. 5.1).

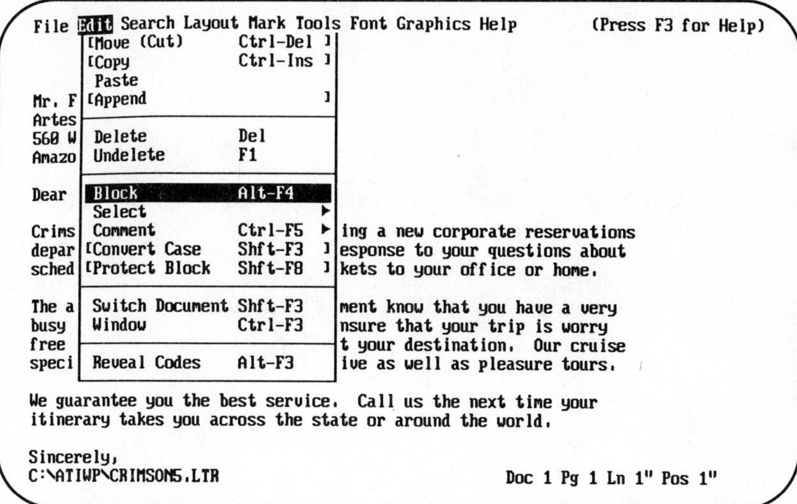
File Edit Search Layout Mark Tools Font Graphics Help (Press F3 for Help)
Move (Cut) Ctrl-Del
Copy Ctrl-Ins
Paste
Append
Delete Del
Undelete F1
Block Alt-F4
Select
Comment Ctrl-F5
Convert Case Shft-F3
Protect Block Shft-F8
Switch Document Shft-F3
Window Ctrl-F3
Reveal Codes Alt-F3
Mr. F
Artes
560 W
Amazo
Dear
Crims ing a new corporate reservations
depar esponse to your questions about
sched kets to your office or home.
The a ment know that you have a very
busy nsure that your trip is worry
free t your destination. Our cruise
speci ive as well as pleasure tours.
We guarantee you the best service. Call us the next time your
itinerary takes you across the state or around the world.
Sincerely,
C:\ATIWP\CRIMSON5.LTR
Doc 1 Pg 1 Ln 1" Pos 1"

Fig. 5.1. The Block option on the Edit pull-down menu.

Step 4: Select **Block**. A flashing message `Block on` appears in the lower left corner of the screen.

Note: Instead of turning on Block as shown in Steps 2 and 3 above, you can simply press Alt-F4 (or F12 if you have an Enhanced Keyboard).

Step 5: Press Enter to highlight the entire first paragraph, as shown in figure 5.2. Pressing Enter causes the cursor to move to the location of the next `[HRt]` code.

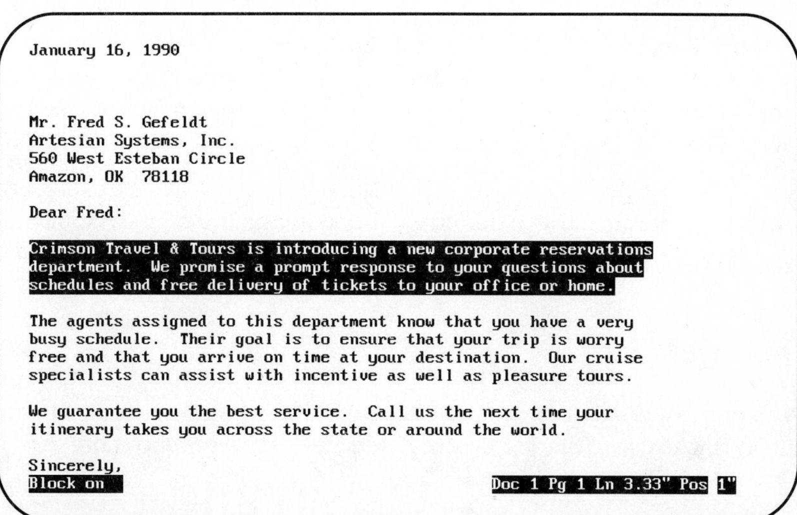
January 16, 1990
Mr. Fred S. Gefeldt
Artesian Systems, Inc.
560 West Esteban Circle
Amazon, OK 78118
Dear Fred:
Crimson Travel & Tours is introducing a new corporate reservations
department. We promise a prompt response to your questions about
schedules and free delivery of tickets to your office or home.
The agents assigned to this department know that you have a very
busy schedule. Their goal is to ensure that your trip is worry
free and that you arrive on time at your destination. Our cruise
specialists can assist with incentive as well as pleasure tours.
We guarantee you the best service. Call us the next time your
itinerary takes you across the state or around the world.
Sincerely,
Block on
Doc 1 Pg 1 Ln 3.33" Pos 1"

Fig. 5.2. A highlighted block of text.

Step 6: To cancel highlighting, access the **E**dit pull-down menu and select **B**lock (or press Alt-F4 or F12).

Applying Commands to Blocked Text

You can apply quite a variety of commands to blocked text. Apply these commands on a block of highlighted text:

- Append
- Block Protect
- Bold
- Center
- Delete
- Flush Right
- Font
  - Appearance (All)
  - Size (All)
- Format
- Macro
- Mark Text
  - Index
  - List
  - Table of Authorities
  - Table of Contents
- Move
  - Block
  - Tabular Column
  - Rectangle
- Print
- Replace
- Save
- Search
- Shell
  - Append
  - Save
- Sort
- Spell
- Style
- Switch
- Tables
- Text In/Out
- Underline

The commands which enhance the appearance of text are presented in Lesson 5. Other commands manipulate blocks of text.

Manipulating Blocks of Text

Using WordPerfect's powerful Block feature, you can move, copy, delete, print, save, or append text blocks of any size. The procedure is as simple as highlighting the text you want to manipulate, selecting the action to be taken, and if necessary telling WordPerfect where to move, copy, or save the block.

Caution: When you edit a document, save your work frequently; if the results are not what you expect, you can retrieve the original document and start over. Saving your work frequently is particularly wise when moving, copying, or deleting text.

Moving a Block

WordPerfect's capability to move blocks can be a powerful editing tool. Knowing that you can always make use of this feature frees you from worrying about preparing a perfect report or letter the first time. Instead, you can get your ideas down quickly and use Block Move later to organize your thoughts.

When you move a block of text, WordPerfect deletes it from one place and inserts it at another place. You can move a block of any size to another place in the document where you are working or you can move a block to another document.

To move a paragraph, follow these steps:

Step 1: Clear the screen without saving the current document and retrieve MOVING5.LTR.

Step 2: Position the cursor at the beginning of the second paragraph.

Step 3: Access the **E**dit pull-down menu and select **B**lock (or press Alt-F4 or F12); move the cursor to the end of the paragraph.

Step 4: Access the **E**dit pull-down menu and select **M**ove (or press Ctrl-F4,1,1). The alternative keystroke sequence in parentheses is interpreted as follows: Press Ctrl-F4, choose **B**lock (**1**) from the menu on the status line, and then choose **M**ove (**1**) from the menu on the status line.

Note: The marked text disappears from the screen, as shown in figure 5.3. If a block of text is not marked, you cannot select Move from the **E**dit pull-down menu or access the Block and Move options when you press Ctrl-F4.

```
Jan 16, 1989


Mr. Fred S. Gefeldt
Artesian Systems, Inc.
560 West Esteban Circle
Amazon, OK  78118

Dear Fred:

The agents assigned to this department know that you have a very
busy schedule.  Their goal is to ensure that your trip is worry
free and that you arrive on time at your destination.  Our cruise
specialists can assist with incentive as well as pleasure tours.


Call us the next time your itinerary takes you across the state or
around the world.  We guarantee you the best service.

Sincerely,


Move cursor; press Enter to retrieve.          Doc 1 Pg 1 Ln 3.67" Pos 1"
```

Fig. 5.3. *The screen display before moved text is received.*

Step 5: At the prompt `Move cursor; press Enter to retrieve.`, located at the bottom of the screen, move the cursor to the blank line before the first paragraph and press Enter.

Step 6: Add blank lines if necessary to correct appearances.

Block Move makes easy work of moving paragraphs. Now, switch two sentences in the third paragraph by completing these steps:

Step 1: Move the cursor to the beginning of the sentence `We guarantee...`, access the **E**dit pull-down menu, and select **B**lock (or press Alt-F4 or F12) to turn on Block.

Step 2: Press the period key to highlight the text up to and including the period.

Step 3: Access the **E**dit pull-down menu and select **M**ove (or press Ctrl-F4,**1**,**1**).

Step 4: Move the cursor to the beginning of the paragraph, position it on the `C` in `Call`, and press Enter.

Step 5: Insert or delete spaces as necessary to correct the paragraph's appearance.

After completing most Move and Copy commands, you may need to add or delete some spaces around the block to ensure that the text fits correctly in its new location. In the previous exercise, you moved a sentence and a paragraph. The paragraphs and sentences in the revised document should appear in the order shown in figure 5.2.

Copying a Block

Block Copy duplicates the highlighted block of text. The original block remains in place, and a copy of the block appears in a new location.

To copy a block of text, follow these steps:

Step 1: Clear the screen without saving the current document and retrieve a new copy of MOVING5.LTR.

Step 2: Position the cursor at the beginning of the second paragraph.

Step 3: Access the **E**dit pull-down menu and select **B**lock (or press Alt-F4 or F12); move the cursor to the end of the paragraph.

Step 4: Access the **E**dit pull-down menu and select **C**opy (or press Ctrl-F4,**1**,**2**).

Note: Although highlighting is removed from the text, the text remains on-screen. If you select Move, highlighted text temporarily disappears from the screen. When you copy text, however, the blocked text remains on-screen and the highlighting disappears. In both situations, the blocked text resides in a temporary storage area until you point with the cursor and press Enter to tell WordPerfect where to move or copy the text.

Step 5: At the prompt `Move cursor; press Enter to retrieve.`, move the cursor to the blank line before the first paragraph and press Enter.

Step 6: Adjust the spacing of blank lines, if necessary.

You copied the block! Note that the paragraph you just copied is in the document twice. Although you can simply move the paragraph, use the extra paragraph to practice deleting a block.

Deleting a Block

You can delete a block of text in three ways: access the **E**dit pull-down menu and select **D**elete; press a function-key combination to access the **M**ove menu, select **B**lock, and then select **D**elete; or press the Del key. Once you practice each method, you can decide which you prefer. If you use the pull-down menu system or press Del, the prompt `Delete Block? No (Yes)` appears, and you can cancel the delete operation. Remember that you can restore text removed with the last three delete commands by using **C**ancel (F1), which is discussed in Lesson 3.

To use the pull-down menu to delete the duplicate paragraph you just created, follow these steps:

Step 1: Position the cursor at the beginning of the first paragraph (the duplicate of the third paragraph).

Step 2: Access the **E**dit pull-down menu and select **B**lock (or press Alt-F4 or F12); move the cursor to the end of the paragraph.

Step 3: Access the **E**dit pull-down menu again and select **D**elete. At the prompt `Delete Block? No (Yes)`, press **Y**. The highlighted block is deleted.

Step 4: In order to practice another method of deleting, restore the deleted text by accessing the **E**dit pull-down menu and selecting **U**ndelete (or press F1); then press **R**estore (**1**).

To delete the restored duplicate paragraph by using the Move (Ctrl-F4) menu, follow these steps:

Step 1: Position the cursor at the beginning of the duplicate paragraph.

Step 2: Access the **E**dit pull-down menu and select **B**lock (or press Alt-F4 or F12); then move the cursor to the end of the paragraph.

Step 3: Press Ctrl-F4.

Step 4: Choose **B**lock (**1**) from the menu on the status line; then choose **D**elete (**3**). The highlighted block is deleted.

Step 5: Restore the deleted text one more time by accessing the **E**dit pull-down menu and selecting **U**ndelete (or press F1); then press **R**estore (**1**).

To delete the restored duplicate paragraph by using Del, follow these steps:

Step 1: Position the cursor at the beginning of the duplicate paragraph.

Step 2: Press Block (Alt-F4 or F12) and move the cursor to the end of the paragraph.

Step 3: Press Del; at the prompt `Delete Block? No (Yes)`, press **Y**.

Saving a Block

As you type a document, you may type a paragraph or some other block of text that you want to use again in another document. A simple way to reuse previously typed text is to save the block to a separate file, independent from the document you are working in.

To save the name and address information from the current document to disk and then verify that the new document exists, follow these steps:

Step 1: Position the cursor at the line before the name-and-address block of MOVING5.LTR.

Step 2: Access the **E**dit pull-down menu and select **B**lock (or press Alt-F4 or F12); move the cursor to the line below the address block.

Step 3: Access the **F**ile pull-down menu and select **S**ave (or press **F10**).

Step 4: At the prompt `Block name:`, type **SAVEIT.V1** and press Enter. After a momentary delay, the file is written.

Step 5: Access the **F**ile pull-down menu and select List **F**iles (or press F5), press Enter to accept the default disk drive path displayed in the lower-left corner, highlight the SAVEIT.V1 file, and press **L**ook (**6**) or Enter.

Step 6: Press Exit (F7) twice: once to restore the List Files screen and again to restore MOVING5.LTR to the screen.

Appending a Block

Append works similarly to Save—except that you add the marked block to an already existing file on disk rather than save the block to a new file. If no file exists on disk, however, the command works exactly like Save and creates a new file.

Caution: A Save command replaces, or writes over, an existing file of the same name.

To append the signature block or closing section of the current document to the text in SAVEIT.V1, follow these steps:

Step 1: Position the cursor at the line preceding the signature block of MOVING5.LTR.

Step 2: Access the **E**dit pull-down menu and select **B**lock (or press Alt-F4 or F12); move the cursor to the line below the signature block.

Step 3: Access the **E**dit pull-down menu, select **A**ppend, and then select To **F**ile (or press Ctrl-F4,1,4).

Step 4: At the prompt `Append to:`, type **SAVEIT.V1** and press Enter.

Step 5: To see the results, access the **F**ile pull-down menu and select List **F**iles (or press F5), accept the current disk drive path, highlight the SAVEIT.V1 file, and press **L**ook (**6**) or Enter.

Step 6: Press Exit (F7) twice: once to restore the List Files screen and again to restore MOVING5.LTR to the screen.

Printing a Block

Printing a block is a quick and easy way to produce hard copy of a portion of text. To print a block, first highlight the text to be printed, select **P**rint from the **F**ile pull-down menu (or press Shift-F7), and press **Y** in response to the screen prompt `Print block? No (Yes)`.

To print the address block from the current document, follow these steps:

Step 1: Move the cursor to the beginning of the address block. Access the **E**dit pull-down menu and select **B**lock (or press **Alt-F4** or **F12**); then highlight the address block.

Step 2: Access the **F**ile pull-down menu and select **P**rint (or press Shift-F7).

Step 3: At the prompt `Print block? No (Yes)`, prepare the printer and press **Y** (press **N** if you do not have a printer on-line).

Working with Two Documents

WordPerfect 5.1 enables you to open two document windows at the same time. So far, you have worked in the first document window (Doc 1 on the status line). Everything that you can do in Doc 1 you can do in Doc 2. In addition, you can move and copy text between the two windows. You can switch between the two windows or split the screen and see both documents at the same time.

Switching between Document Windows

Working with two windows gives you editing flexibility and convenience. To switch between document windows and retrieve files into both windows, follow these steps:

Step 1: Clear the screen without saving the current document.

Step 2: Access the **E**dit pull-down menu and select **S**witch Document (or press Shift-F3) several times; watch the display in the lower-right portion of the screen switch between Doc 1 and Doc 2.

Step 3: Make sure that WordPerfect is switched to Doc 2. Access the **F**ile pull-down menu and select List **F**iles (or press F5); then retrieve CRIMSON5.LTR.

Step 4: Switch to Doc 1.

Step 5: Access the **F**ile pull-down menu and select **R**etrieve (or press Shift-F10). At the prompt Document to be retrieved:, type **CRIMSON5.TOP** and press Enter.

You now have two documents open: CRIMSON5.TOP is Doc 1, currently in view; CRIMSON5.LTR is Doc 2, accessible for full-screen viewing and editing by your pressing Switch (Shift-F3).

Splitting the Screen into Windows

You may find it useful to see parts of two documents at the same time. You may want to use the second document window to keep notes to yourself. Or you may want a copy of the same document in both windows so that you can view different parts simultaneously.

To split the screen to see portions of both Doc 1 and Doc 2 at the same time, follow these steps:

Step 1: Access the **E**dit pull-down menu and select **S**witch Document (or press Shift-F3) to make the current document Doc 2.

Step 2: Access the **E**dit pull-down menu again and select **W**indow (or press Ctrl-F3,1).

Step 3: At the prompt `Number of lines in this window: 24`, type **14** and press Enter.

You see both open documents on-screen, as shown in figure 5.4.

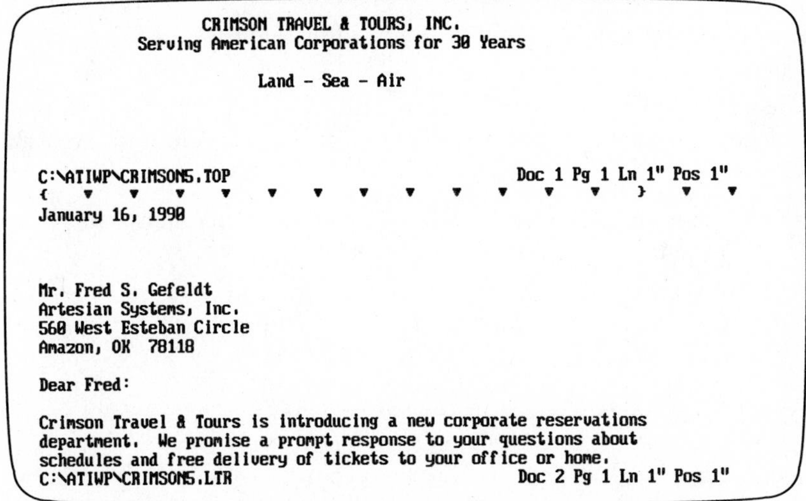

```
                    CRIMSON TRAVEL & TOURS, INC.
            Serving American Corporations for 30 Years

                         Land - Sea - Air



C:\ATIWP\CRIMSON5.TOP                              Doc 1 Pg 1 Ln 1" Pos 1"
{   ▼   ▼   ▼   ▼   ▼   ▼   ▼   ▼   ▼   ▼   ▼   ▼   }   ▼   ▼
January 16, 1990


Mr. Fred S. Gefeldt
Artesian Systems, Inc.
560 West Esteban Circle
Amazon, OK  78118

Dear Fred:

Crimson Travel & Tours is introducing a new corporate reservations
department. We promise a prompt response to your questions about
schedules and free delivery of tickets to your office or home.
C:\ATIWP\CRIMSON5.LTR                              Doc 2 Pg 1 Ln 1" Pos 1"
```

Fig. 5.4. *A split screen displaying two documents.*

A tab ruler splits the screen horizontally just above the date in CRIMSON5.LTR (Doc 2). A maximum of 24 lines of text can appear; you control the size of each window by setting the number of lines in one window. The arrows in the tab ruler point to the current document screen (in this case the arrows point down). When you switch screens by pressing Switch (Shift-F3), the tab-ruler arrows change direction to point to the new current document screen. You have full editing control in either window. Both windows have a status line.

Copying a Block between Windows

To copy CRIMSON5.LTR in Doc 2 to CRIMSON5.TOP in Doc 1, perform these steps:

Step 1: Position the cursor at the top of Doc 2.

Step 2: Access the **E**dit pull-down menu and select **B**lock (or press Alt-F4 or F12); highlight the entire CRIMSON5.LTR document.

Step 3: Access the **E**dit pull-down menu again and select **C**opy (or press Ctrl-F4,1,2).

Step 4: Access the **E**dit pull-down menu a third time and select **S**witch Document (or press Shift-F3) to position the cursor in Doc 1.

Step 5: Move the cursor below the last line of the letterhead and press Enter.

Step 6: Insert or delete blank lines to give the heading and body proper spacing.

You can, incidentally, move and copy between windows whether or not you are using a split screen. To remove the split screen, repeat the same steps for creating the double windows:

Step 1: Access the **E**dit pull-down menu and select **S**witch Document (or press Shift-F3) to position the cursor in Doc 2.

Step 2: Press Ctrl-F3, choose **W**indow (**1**), and at the prompt `Number of lines in this window: 14`, type **24** and press Enter.

Placing a Tab Ruler On-Screen

A tab ruler appears at the bottom of the screen when you alter document tab settings through a Format Line Tab set command sequence (see Lesson 6). Once you establish tab settings, the tab ruler disappears from the screen display.

You may prefer to keep the tab ruler on-screen when you create a document that uses many tab settings. To display a tab ruler, set lines to 23 (one line fewer than the maximum 24).

To display, then remove, the current tab ruler on your screen, perform these steps:

Step 1: Press Ctrl-F3, choose **W**indow (**1**), and at the prompt `Number of lines in this window: 24`, type **23** and press Enter.

Note: The ruler at the bottom of the screen resembles the one in figure 5.5. Left and right margins are marked with curly braces—{}—and tabs are noted with upward-pointing arrows.

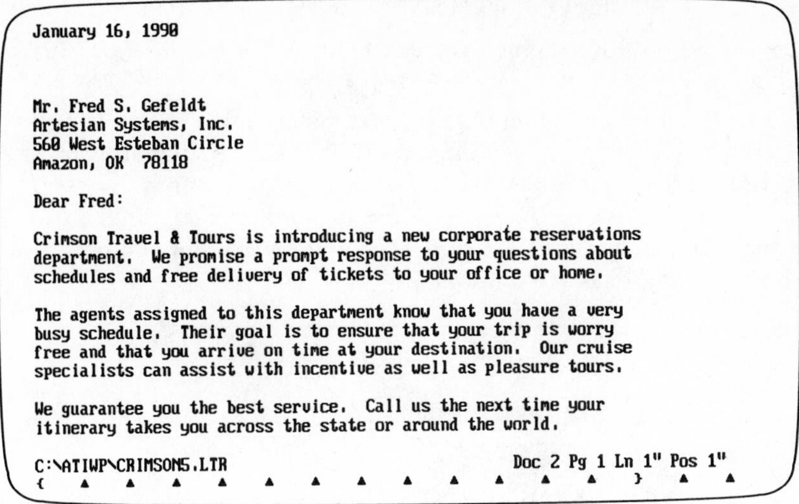

January 16, 1990

Mr. Fred S. Gefeldt
Artesian Systems, Inc.
560 West Esteban Circle
Amazon, OK 78118

Dear Fred:

Crimson Travel & Tours is introducing a new corporate reservations department. We promise a prompt response to your questions about schedules and free delivery of tickets to your office or home.

The agents assigned to this department know that you have a very busy schedule. Their goal is to ensure that your trip is worry free and that you arrive on time at your destination. Our cruise specialists can assist with incentive as well as pleasure tours.

We guarantee you the best service. Call us the next time your itinerary takes you across the state or around the world.

C:\ATIWP\CRIMSON5.LTR Doc 2 Pg 1 Ln 1" Pos 1"

Fig. 5.5. *The tab ruler, displayed at bottom of screen.*

Step 2: Press Ctrl-F3, choose **Window (1)**, and at the prompt `Number of lines in this window: 23`, type **24** and press Enter.

Working with Rectangular Blocks

Being able to work with a continuous block of text, such as a sentence or paragraph, is important in a word processing package. WordPerfect enables you to move, copy, or delete a rectangular block of text within a paragraph or page, leaving text to either side untouched.

To move, copy, delete, or append a rectangle of text that does not include an entire line or paragraph, highlight the desired block, beginning with the upper left corner and ending with the lower right corner. Select the Move Rectangle command sequence and choose the action to perform (for example, Move or Copy). Complete each of the four actions as you do for ordinary block functions.

To copy the rectangular block that contains the middle column of cities from the OFFICES5.LST document to another place in the same document, follow these steps:

Step 1: Clear the screen without saving the current document and retrieve OFFICES5.LST.

Step 2: Move the cursor to the column heading titled `Midwest`.

Step 3: Access the **Edit** pull-down menu; select **Block** (or press Alt-F4 or F12) and highlight the text which ends with `St. Louis`.

Caution: Be sure that the highlighted text matches that shown in figure 5.6, including the three spaces after `St. Louis`. (The highlighting must be as wide at the bottom as the longest name in the column, `Indianapolis` in this case.) In spite of the size of the highlighted area, only the rectangle between the upper-left and lower-right end points of the highlighted area is acted upon.

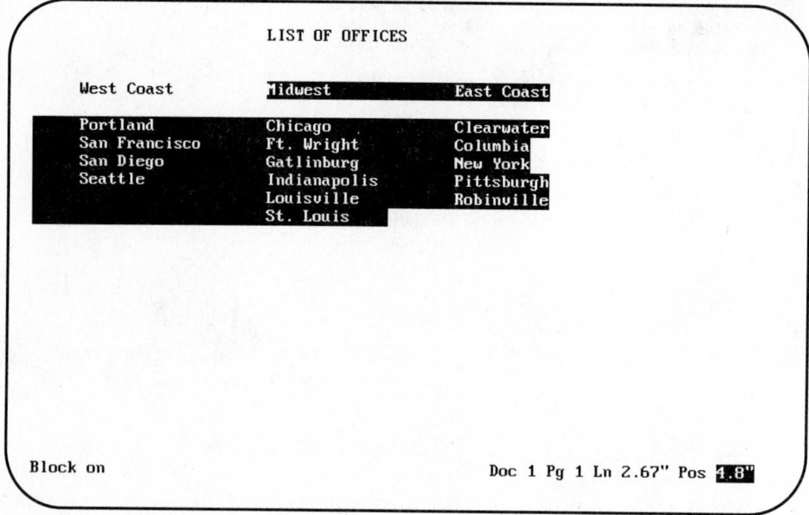

Fig. 5.6. Highlighting a rectangular block.

Step 4: Access the **E**dit pull-down menu, choose S**e**lect, and choose **R**ectangle (or press Ctrl-F4,3).

Note: The highlighted area changes to fit the rectangle marked by the upper-left starting position of the cursor and the lower-right ending position of the cursor.

Step 5: Choose **C**opy (**2**), move the cursor to the line below the last line of city names, and press Enter.

The column of cities marked `Midwest` is duplicated at the bottom of the list, as shown in figure 5.7.

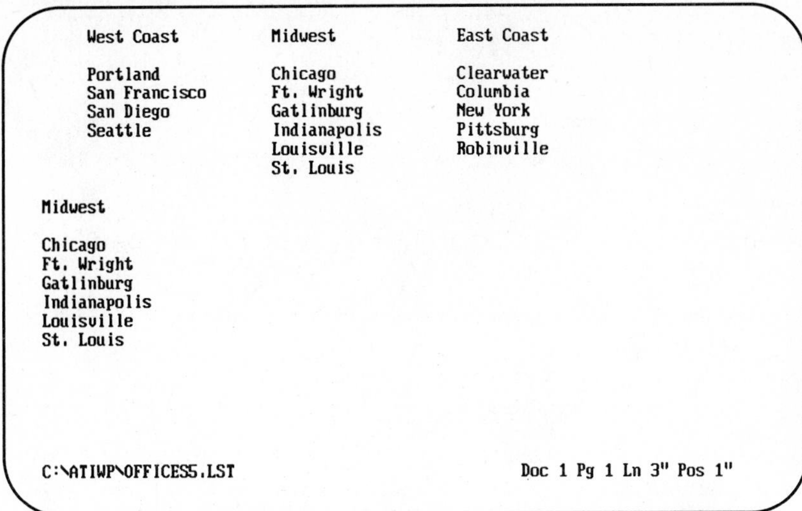

Fig. 5.7. Copying a rectangular block.

To facilitate using the rectangle command, make the bottom entry the longest entry in the list. You may have to pad the right side of that entry with spaces.

You have practiced quite a few block operations in this lesson. Reinforce these concepts by working through the summary exercises that follow.

For Further Reference

If you would like to know more about working with blocks, consult *Using WordPerfect 5.1*, Special Edition (Que Corporation, Carmel IN, 1989), Chapters 2 and 4.

Summary of Concepts

Lesson 5 explains these concepts:

- ❑ Manipulating highlighted blocks of text by using a variety of commands.
- ❑ Activating Block from the **E**dit pull-down menu by selecting **B**lock (or pressing Alt-F4 or F12).
- ❑ Expanding the highlighted text to be acted upon by using the cursor-movement keys.
- ❑ Canceling highlighting from the **E**dit pull-down menu by selecting **B**lock (or pressing Alt-F4 or F1).
- ❑ Invoking Append, Copy, Delete, Move, Print, and Save instructions in order to manipulate portions of highlighted text.
- ❑ Working on two documents at the same time by retrieving one file into Doc 1, selecting the Switch Document (Shift-F3) command, and retrieving a second file into Doc 2.
- ❑ Using the full range of WordPerfect commands in either window or between the two windows.
- ❑ Viewing two documents at the same time using the Screen (Ctrl-F3) command to split the screen.
- ❑ Putting a tab ruler at the bottom of the screen by using WordPerfect's Window command and setting the number of lines to 23.
- ❑ Manipulating a block of text that is not as wide as a line or paragraph by accessing Move Rectangle.

Review Exercises

Practice using the WordPerfect features in this lesson by completing these exercises. If you do not remember how to do something, review the preceding explanations and practice steps.

1. Clear the screen without saving the current document and retrieve COPYEX5. Each paragraph after the Introduction contains a brief description of a WordPerfect feature.
2. Block-copy the paragraph beginning with `Cancel` (paragraph four) to the space between the Introduction paragraph and the Speller paragraph.
3. Block-delete the original paragraph you just copied and adjust the spacing as necessary.
4. Move the paragraph that starts with `Cancel` to the end of the document, immediately after the last paragraph. If necessary, adjust the spacing.
5. Print the document in memory.
6. Block the heading and first paragraph; print only the highlighted text.
7. Save only the Speller paragraph to disk under the name SPELLER.
8. Create two windows, splitting the screen at line 12.
9. Copy the heading and first paragraph from Doc 1 to Doc 2.
10. Remove the split screen, leaving a tab ruler at the bottom of the screen.
11. Remove the tab ruler at the bottom of the screen.
12. Clear the current document screen, retrieve the OFFICES5.LST file, and delete the `Midwest` rectangular block of text.

Formatting and Enhancing Text

6

DISK TUTOR

If you haven't yet explored the Disk Tutor, you might want to complete the appropriate tutorial lesson before continuing with this book lesson. If you have already run the tutorial, you might want to run it again and review the pertinent options. The part of the tutorial relevant to this lesson is:

- ❑ Lesson G: Change Format

If you complete the options on the Disk Tutor, you will be more familiar with the techniques and commands found in this lesson.

In this lesson, you practice these tasks:

- ❑ Set left and right margins
- ❑ Change and delete tabs
- ❑ Use tab alignment
- ❑ Indent text
- ❑ Use flush-right margins
- ❑ Use full justification
- ❑ Hyphenate words
- ❑ Change line spacing
- ❑ Select fonts by name or size
- ❑ Change typeface appearance
- ❑ Enter special characters with Compose

Throughout the *WordPerfect PC Tutor*, you have used WordPerfect's current default margins, tabs, hyphenation, and line spacing when you entered text. For many documents, these automatic settings are adequate. You can, however, change these settings as frequently as necessary within a document.

The Format command (Shift-F8) menu in figure 6.1 shows the four commands and their options that control the appearance of lines, pages, and the overall document: Line, Page, Document, and Other. You also can access these commands by selecting options on the Layout pull-down menu. Most formatting features may be added before you type any text, or they can be added to existing text later.

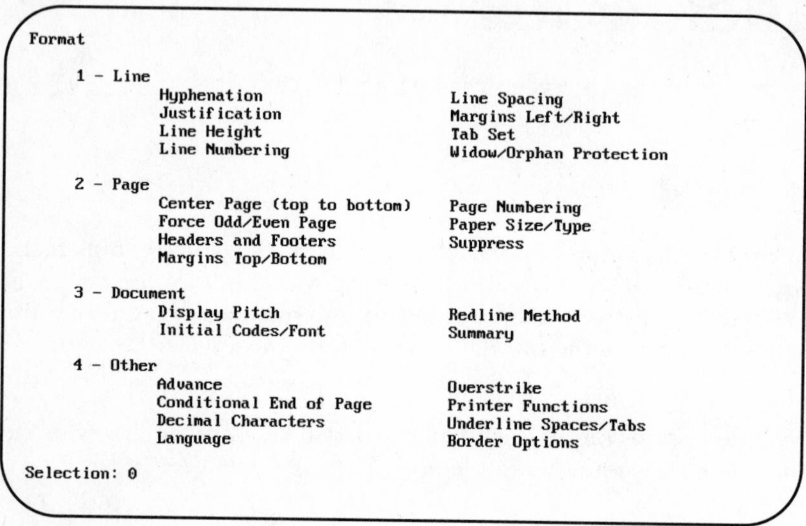

Fig. 6.1. *WordPerfect's formatting options.*

Setting Left and Right Margins and Tab Stops

WordPerfect computes margins as the number of inches from the edge of the paper. You may specify inches, characters, centimeters, or points—depending on how you designate units of measure with Setup. Lesson 1 contains instructions for changing the unit of measure; the figures in the *WordPerfect PC Tutor* reflect the inches setting. WordPerfect also provides four types of tab stops: left, center, right, and decimal. Each type of tab can have a dot leader—a series of periods before the tab.

Setting Left and Right Margins

LESSON FILES

The default left and right margin is 1 inch. To reset the margins in the CRIMSON6.LTR document from 1 inch to .5 inch on the left and from 1 inch to 2.5 inches on the right (to make room for a proofreader to make notes), follow these steps:

Step 1: Clear the screen without saving the current document and retrieve CRIMSON6.LTR.

Note: The instruction to clear the screen without saving the current document is used many times throughout the *WordPerfect PC Tutor*. It means to access the **F**ile pull-down menu and select E**x**it (or press F7); when prompted `Save Document? Yes (No)`, press **N**; when prompted `Exit WP? No (Yes)`, press **N**.

Step 2: Access the **L**ayout pull-down menu and select **L**ines (or press Shift-F8,1). A Format: Line menu similar to the one shown in figure 6.2 appears.

Note: Depending on how WordPerfect is set up on your system, you may see slightly different settings for the Format: Line options.

```
Format: Line

     1 - Hyphenation                        No

     2 - Hyphenation Zone - Left            10%
                            Right           4%

     3 - Justification                      Full

     4 - Line Height                        Auto

     5 - Line Numbering                     No

     6 - Line Spacing                       1

     7 - Margins - Left                     1"
                   Right                    1"

     8 - Tab Set                            Rel: -1", every 0.5"

     9 - Widow/Orphan Protection            No


Selection: 0
```

***Fig 6.2**. A sample Format:Line menu.*

Step 3: Choose **M**argins Left/Right (7). The cursor shifts to the current entry for the left margin.

Step 4: To change the left margin from 1 inch to .5 inch, type **.5** and press Enter.

Step 5: To change the right margin from 1 inch to 2.5 inches, type **2.5** and press Enter.

Step 6: Press Exit (F7) to return to the current document.

Step 7: Press Screen (Ctrl-F3) and choose **R**ewrite (**3**) to reformat the screen to reflect new margin settings.

The text is reformatted on-screen, and the right margin is noticeably wider. Changing the format of a document—such as resetting the margins—does not instantly reformat the text on-screen. The screen display is reformatted the first time the screen is changed. You can change the screen in more than one way: by using the Screen Rewrite option shown in Step 7; by pressing Home, Home, down arrow, and then returning to your position in the document; by pressing PgDn and then PgUp; or by taking other actions that change the screen.

Setting Tab Stops

WordPerfect's default tab stops are set every one-half inch, beginning at the left margin. If you change the left margin, tab settings change also to retain their relationship with the left margin, not with the left edge of the page.

You can set four types of tabs: left, right, center, and decimal. They affect the document in the following ways:

- ❑ *Left tabs*. The first line is indented to the tab stop, and subsequent lines return to the left margin.
- ❑ *Center tabs*. Text centers at the tab stop. Center tabs work very much like the Center command (Shift-F6) except that you can force centering anywhere on the line.
- ❑ *Right tabs*. Text continues left of a right tab stop.
- ❑ *Decimal tabs*. Text or numbers continue to the left until the alignment character (the period or decimal point) is typed; then text or numbers continue to the right. This setup causes alignment around the tab stop. The decimal-tab feature is invoked the same way as Tab Align (Ctrl- F6)—except that Tab Align does not need a preset tab.

You can precede any tab style by a series of dots (periods). Dot leaders are useful for improving the readability of long lists. If, however, you print with proportional fonts, dot leaders can produce unpredictable results.

The tab ruler **[Tab Set:]** is an open code. It therefore stays in effect, beginning where you insert the code, until you insert a new code, reach the end of the document, or delete the code. Properly positioning the cursor in the document before inserting a tab ruler is very important.

To change tab settings for the current document only, follow these steps:

Step 1: Clear the screen without saving the current document.

Step 2: Access the **L**ayout pull-down menu and select **L**ine (or press Shift-F8,1).

Step 3: Choose **T**ab Set (**8**).

Note: The bottom of the screen displays a graphic representation of the current tab stops, called the tab ruler, similar to the one shown in figure 6.3.

```
L....L....L....L....L....L....L....L....L....L....L....L....L....L....L....L...
|    ^    |    ^    |    ^    |    ^    |    ^    |    ^    |    ^    |    ^
0"        +1"       +2"       +3"       +4"       +5"       +6"       +7"
Delete EOL (clear tabs); Enter Number (set tab); Del (clear tab);
Type; Left; Center; Right; Decimal; .= Dot Leader; Press Exit when done.
```

Fig. 6.3. The tab ruler.

Step 4: To delete a single tab stop (for example, the left tab stop denoted by the letter L at +2"—2 inches from the left margin), move the cursor to +2" and press Del.

Step 5: To delete all tab stops right of the cursor, press Ctrl-End.

Step 6: To set a single left tab stop 2 inches from the left margin, move the cursor to +2" on the ruler and press **L**.

Step 7: To set left tab stops at regular intervals—for example, every half-inch beginning one inch from the left margin at any position on the ruler—type **1,.5** and press Enter.

Step 8: Press Exit (F7) enough times to restore the current document.

It is more efficient to set all regularly spaced tab stops first, as you did in Step 7, and then to insert and delete individual tab stops.

Using Left, Right, Center, and Decimal Tabs

WordPerfect's four types of tabs facilitate typing all forms of documents, including those that contain lists, statistics, and other kinds of tables. To practice using the four types of tabs by creating the sales list shown in figure 6.4, follow these steps:

```
                    SALES LIST


               Item Sold                Quantity     Billed

     IBM PS/2 Model 30                      1        850.30
     Paper, Continuous form (20lb)         10        150.00
     Citizen 180D printer                   1        180.00
     Ribbons, Citizen 120/180              25         92.50
     Typing stand                           1         15.75

     TOTAL                                         $1288.55
```

Fig. 6.4. Using tabs in a document.

Step 1: Clear the screen without saving the current document.

Step 2: Access the **Layout** pull-down menu, select **Align**, and select **Center** (or press Shift-F6).

Step 3: Type **SALES LIST** and insert two blank lines.

Step 4: Access the **Layout** pull-down menu and select **Line** (or press Shift-F8,1); then choose **Tab** Set (**8**).

Step 5: If necessary, move the cursor to the left edge of the tab ruler; then press Ctrl-End to remove all tabs.

Step 6: Press **C** for center tab stops at positions `+2"`, `+4.5"`, and `+6"`; then press Exit (F7) enough times to restore the current document screen.

Step 7: Press Tab once and type **Item Sold**; press Tab again and type **Quantity**; press Tab again and type **Billed**. Then insert one blank line.

Note: Page and column headings are now typed. Notice how the column headings center around the tab. You must now set left, right, and decimal tabs to complete the sales list.

Step 8: With the cursor positioned at the beginning of the second blank line below the `Item Sold`, `Quantity`, and `Billed` headings, repeat Steps 4 and 5 to access the Tab menu and clear all tabs.

Step 9: At position `1"`, press **L**.

Step 10: At position `5"`, press **R** and immediately press the period key. The letter `R` should be highlighted on the ruler (the highlight indicates that a dot leader is in effect left of the R tab).

Step 11: At position `6"`, press **D**; then press Exit (F7) enough times to restore the current document screen.

Refer to figure 6.4 to enter the list of items sold, quantity, and amount billed, following these steps:

Step 1: Press Tab; type the first item sold (**IBM PS/2 Model 30**) and press Tab; type the quantity **1** and press Tab; type the amount billed **850.30**, and press Enter.

Step 2: Repeat Step 1 and enter the remaining four items shown in figure 6.4.

Step 3: Space down one blank line from the last item sold, press tab, and type **TOTAL**. To leave quantity blank, press Tab without entering a number; then type **$1288.55** for the total.

WordPerfect has a math-column feature (see Lesson 16) that can automatically calculate the billed total.

Using Margins and Tabs To Style Text

WordPerfect offers several useful indentation features for styling text. The following list notes four of these features:

- ❏ To create a traditionally indented paragraph, simply press Tab and begin typing. The first line is indented, and following lines begin at the left margin.
- ❏ To indent an entire paragraph one tab stop from the left margin, use Indent (F4).
- ❏ To indent both left and right margins (for inserting quotations, for example), use the right-and-left Indent command (Shift-F4).
- ❏ To create a hanging (or outdented) paragraph, use the Indent command (F4); then press Margin Release (Shift-Tab). The first line of the paragraph begins at the left margin, and following lines are indented.

To practice using the right-and-left indent and hanging paragraph features, follow these steps to create the document shown in figure 6.5:

```
                         Announcement

      I am pleased to announce that we have hired several new
people to fill vacancies in the firm.  Please join me in
welcoming them to the company.

John Fox, Director of Marketing, West coast region.  John joins
      us from the Weber Corporation, where he was Assistant
      Marketing Director.

Linda Ann, Office Manager, Indianapolis office.   Linda joins us
      from a local firm where she was in charge of office
      administration and payroll.

Sam Weist, Director of Security, Mid-West region. Sam joins us
      from a local security firm.

               A reception will be held for our
               new people in the conference room,
               Tuesday, January 17, 1990.  All
               employees are invited.


L. C. Tyrant
Director of Personnel
```

Fig. 6.5. *A document with left and right tabs and outdenting.*

Step 1: Clear the screen without saving the current document; type the heading **Announcement**, centering it on the page; and insert one blank line.

Step 2: To create the first paragraph with a traditional indentation, press Tab once, type the paragraph **I am pleased . . .** and insert two blank lines.

Step 3: Type the paragraph about John Fox, using a hanging indent. Access the **L**ayout pull-down menu, select **A**lign, and then select **I**ndent.

Next access the **Layout** pull-down menu, select **Align**, and select **Margin Rel ←**. Type the paragraph and insert one blank line.

Step 4: Type the paragraph about Linda Ann, using a shorter method of creating a hanging outdent. Press F4 (Indent); then press Shift-Tab (Margin Release). Type the paragraph and insert one blank line.

Step 5: Type the remaining paragraph, about Sam Weist, using your preferred method (see Step 3 or Step 4) of specifying a hanging outdent; insert two blank lines.

Step 6: Type the information about the reception. Access the **Layout** pull-down menu, select **Align**, and then select **Indent →←** (or press Shift-F4). Repeat this instruction twice to indent a total of three tab stops. Type the paragraph **A reception will be....**

Step 7: Space two blank lines and type the two signature lines at the bottom of the announcement.

Setting Text Alignment and Spacing

Several commands help to align text. Tab stops, indentation, and margins used in the preceding section facilitate normal typing requirements. The commands that follow help you create interesting styles in your text. For example, dates sometimes are typed flush with the right margin, words may be hyphenated to fill the line better, or line spacing may be varied.

Text is ordinarily left-justified or blocked on the left margin, except for tabs and indentations. Because WordPerfect 5.1 provides left, right, center, and full justification, you can now justify text on the right margin only, center text between margins, or set full justification between the left and right margins (default).

Using Flush Right

Flush Right (Alt-F6) aligns a short line of text at the right margin. When the Flush Right command is typed, the cursor moves to the right margin. As you type, text is entered left of the current cursor position, similar to the way the right tab stop was entered earlier. Right-flush lines must end with a hard return ([HRt]) to work properly.

Practice using Flush Right by following these steps:

Step 1: Clear the screen without saving the current document and retrieve ANNOUNC6.DOC.

Step 2: Insert two blank lines at the top of the document and move the cursor to the first line in the document.

Step 3: Access the **L**ayout pull-down menu, select **A**lign, and then select **F**lush Right (or press Alt-F6). Type **January 2, 1990**.

You can see the effect of using Flush Right in the initial date line of figure 6.6. The effects of using the next three topics (full justification, hyphenation, and line spacing) also are illustrated in figure 6.6.

```
                                                January 2, 1990


                          Announcement

     I am pleased to announce that we have hired several new people
to fill vacancies in the firm.  Please join me in welcoming them to
the company.


John Fox, Director of Marketing, West coast region.  John joins us
     from the Weber Corporation, where he was Assistant Marketing
     Director.

Linda Ann, Office Manager, Indianapolis office.   Linda  joins  us
     from a local firm where she was in charge of office adminis-
     tration and payroll.

Sam Weist, Director of Security, Mid-West region. Sam joins us from
     a local security firm.


               A reception will be held for our new

               people in the conference room, Tues-

               day, January 17, 1990.  All employ-

               ees are invited.


L. C. Tyrant
Director of Personnel
```

Fig. 6.6. *An example of flush-right text, full justification, hyphenation, and double-spacing.*

Using Full Justification

Full justification causes all lines to start at the left margin and end at the right margin, except the last line of a paragraph, single lines, and lines with tabs and indentations. To execute this feature, WordPerfect inserts extra spaces between each word on a line until the line ends exactly on the right margin.

You can change justification anywhere in the document. You can change the default—full justification—permanently by using the Setup menu (Shift-F1), selecting **I**nitial **S**ettings (**5**), choosing **I**nitial **C**odes (**4**), and entering the code you prefer. For example, you may want left justification, which leaves a smooth left margin and a jagged right margin.

As has been noted, WordPerfect offers four types of justification: full, left, center, and right justification. Full justification gives printed documents a professional, formal look. Hyphenation also can help full justification look better by reducing the number of blank spaces at the ends of lines. Otherwise, the jagged right margin produced by left justification (specified by the setting **F**ull justification **O**ff) looks best.

You cannot see the effect of full justification (or right justification only) on the current document screen. Access the Print menu and view or print the document to see the smooth right margin.

Full-justify the announcement on the current document screen by following these steps:

Step 1: Move the cursor to the upper left corner of the document by pressing Home, Home, Home, up arrow.

Step 2: Access the **L**ayout pull-down menu and select **L**ine (or press Shift-F8,1). Choose **J**ustification (**3**), press **F**ull (**4**) to turn on full justification, and press Exit (F7) to return to the current document.

Note: Text on the document screen still appears jagged along the right margin.

Step 3: Access the **F**ile pull-down menu and select **P**rint (or press Shift-F7). Select **V**iew Document (**6**) and Full Page (**3**) to see the final document on-screen.

Step 4: Press Exit (F7) to restore the current document.

Using Hyphenation

When a line of text becomes too long to fit within the margins, the last word in the line wraps to the next line. With short words, wrapping is not a problem. With long words, however, two potential problems exist. If the line is not justified to the right margin (right or full justification), large gaps occur at the right margin, making the margin appear too jagged. If justification is on, large spaces between words become visually distracting.

Hyphenating a long word at the end of a line solves the problem and creates a visually attractive printed document. Using hyphenation is a two-step process. First, access the Setup Environment menu and set the prompt for hyphenation. Your choices are **Never** (**1**), **When** Required (**2**), and **Always** (**3**). When you select **Never**, WordPerfect 5.1 hyphenates words automatically. If **When** Required or **Always** is selected, you may be asked to reposition the hyphen or to accept the hyphen inserted by WordPerfect 5.1. Words are hyphenated according to information in two external files—the dictionary WP{WP}US.LEX and a special hyphenation file WP{WP}US.HYC—or according to internal rules.

Once you set the hyphenation mode, you can access the Format: Line menu, select the hyphenation option, and select **Yes** or **No** to turn hyphenation on and off. If you are prompted to hyphenate words when you enter or edit text, a suggested hyphenation appears with the prompt `Position hyphen; Press ESC`. At this prompt, you can accept the suggested hyphenation by pressing Esc or change the position of the hyphen and then press Esc. To change the position of the hyphen, press the right-arrow and left-arrow keys until the hyphen is in place.'

If you do not want to be interrupted by hyphenation, turn the feature off until you finish entering or editing text. If you set manual hyphenation on after text is entered, words to be hyphenated are presented one at a time. If automatic hyphenation is turned on, the text is hyphenated without prompting. Hyphenation involves a complicated set of rules, which you can change.

To practice manual hyphenation, follow these steps:

Step 1: Position the cursor in the upper-left corner of the announcement concerning new employees by pressing Home, Home, Home, up arrow.

Step 2: Access the **F**ile pull-down menu and select Set**u**p (or press Shift-F1); then select **E**nvironment (**3**).

Step 3: Select **P**rompt for Hyphenation (7), select **A**lways (3), and press Exit (F7) to restore the current document.

Step 4: Access the **L**ayout pull-down menu and select **L**ine (or press Shift-F8 and then choose **L**ine (**1**)); select H**y**phenation (**3**) and press **Y**es to turn on hyphenation.

Step 5: Press Exit (F7) to return to the current document and press PgDn. The prompt `Position hyphen; press ESC adminis-tration` appears at the bottom of the screen.

Caution: Words presented for manual hyphenation on-screen may vary from those shown in figure 6.6, depending on your margin and font settings.

Step 6: Practice using the right arrow and left arrow to move the suggested hyphen to a position of your choice; then return the hyphen to the suggested position and press Esc.

Step 7: Press Esc to accept each remaining suggested hyphenation.

To restore the current document to its prehyphenated appearance in order to repeat the hyphenation process in automatic mode, follow these steps:

Step 1: Press Home, Home, Home, up arrow to move the cursor to the top left corner of the document.

Step 2: Press Reveal Codes (Alt-F3 or F11). The code `[Hyph On]` appears.

Step 3: Position the highlight bar on `[Hyph On]` and press Del to remove the hyphenation code. Press Reveal Codes (Alt-F3 or F11) to restore full-screen display of the document.

Step 4: Delete the hyphens that appear in the document and press Home, Home, Home, up arrow to move the cursor to the top left corner of the document.

Note: To remove hyphens in large documents, use Search and Replace (refer to Lesson 3). Search for the Ctrl-Hyphen code and replace with no code.

Step 5: Access the **F**ile pull-down menu and select Set**u**p (or press Shift-F1), and select **E**nvironment (**3**).

Step 6: Select **P**rompt for Hyphenation (**7**), select **N**ever (**1**), and press Exit (F7) to restore the document.

Step 7: Access the **L**ayout pull-down menu and select **L**ine (or press Shift-F8,1). Select H**y**phenation (**3**) and press **Y**es to turn on hyphenation.

Step 8: Press Exit (F7) to return to the current document and press PgDn.

When you return to the current document, you find it automatically hyphenated, as shown in figure 6.6. If you use automatic mode, you may find it easier to do all the hyphenating at one time after the document is complete.

Setting Line Spacing

WordPerfect's default is single-spacing. You can, however, set line spacing at any number with up to two decimal places. You may choose double-spacing or triple-spacing to allow room for handwritten comments on draft documents. Consider specifying 1.25 or 1.5 to set spacing between single and double line to improve readability.

Determine line spacing by positioning the cursor where spacing is to change and inserting the code to change spacing. You can change spacing as you type the document or after the document is complete; you can also use several different spacing settings in a single document.

Use double-spacing in the current document by following these steps:

Step 1: Move the cursor to the line preceding the sentence `A reception will be....`

Step 2: Access the **L**ayout pull-down menu and select **L**ine (or press Shift-F8,1). Choose Line **S**pacing (**6**).

Step 3: Type **2**, press Enter, and press Exit (F7) to restore the current document. Move the cursor to the end of the announcement. The rest of the document is now double-spaced.

Step 4: To mark the place to restore single-spacing, move the cursor to the line below the sentence `All employees are invited.`

Step 5: Access the **L**ayout pull-down menu and select **L**ine (or press Shift-F8,1). Choose Line **S**pacing (**6**), type **1**, and press Enter. Press Exit (F7) to restore the current document.

Step 6: Access the **F**ile pull-down menu and select **P**rint (or press Shift-F7). Then select either **F**ull Document (**1**) to print the announcement or **V**iew Document (**6**) to see the announcement on-screen.

Your printout or screen display containing flush-right text, full justification, hyphenation, and line spacing should appear as you see it in figure 6.6.

Using Font Menu Options To Enhance Text

One exceptional feature of WordPerfect 5.1 is its capability of getting the most out of any printer. Although only some text enhancements are visible on-screen depending on the monitor used, you can see the effect off all settings on the printed page.

To select a font (print style) by its name or by its size and to alter its appearance, position the cursor where you want the change, and then invoke the appropriate codes. Fonts are open codes, affecting the document until the end of the document or until you insert another code into the document.

The range of available attributes varies according to the capability of your printer. If you have just a text printer, your choices may be more limited than the choices provided by a printer with both text and graphics capabilities. Laser printers offer the largest selection of features.

It is impractical to devise an extensive font-change exercise that everyone can do, considering the wide range of printers available. Therefore, the following instructions lead you only through accessing various font menus; it's more useful to experiment with printed output on your own.

Choosing a Font by Name

When you install a printer in WordPerfect, you select an initial font, also called the default base font. The base font is the font in which text is normally printed. Also, when you install a printer, print fonts specific to that printer are placed on your disk. These print fonts are listed in the Base Font menu.

To invoke a specific font by its name, position the cursor where you want the font change to begin, access the Base Font menu, highlight the appropriate font, and press Enter. Using Reveal Codes (Alt-F3 or F11), you can see the font code in your document. For example, the 10-pitch Courier font appears as `[Font:Courier 10cpi]`. To access the Font menu, which contains the Base Font option, follow these steps:

Step 1: Access the F**o**nt pull-down menu (or press Ctrl-F8).

Note: Although the font menu's appearance depends on whether you use the pull-down menu or press Ctrl-F8 (see fig. 6.7), both versions of the menu provide the same powerful features.

Access the Font pull-down menu.

Press Ctrl-F8 to access the font-menu display at the bottom of the screen.

Step 2: Press Enter to accept the highlighted Base Font option on the F**o**nt pull-down menu (or choose Base **F**ont (**4**) if you accessed a font menu by pressing Ctrl-F8 in Step 1). A list similar to the one shown in figure 6.8 appears, showing available fonts.

Step 3: View the available options for your system (an asterisk marks the current base font); then press Exit (F7) or Cancel (F1) to restore the WordPerfect editing screen.

The Base Font submenu option displays a list of fonts for the printer you installed. The list in figure 6.8 supports the Hewlett-Packard LaserJet Series II printer. You will

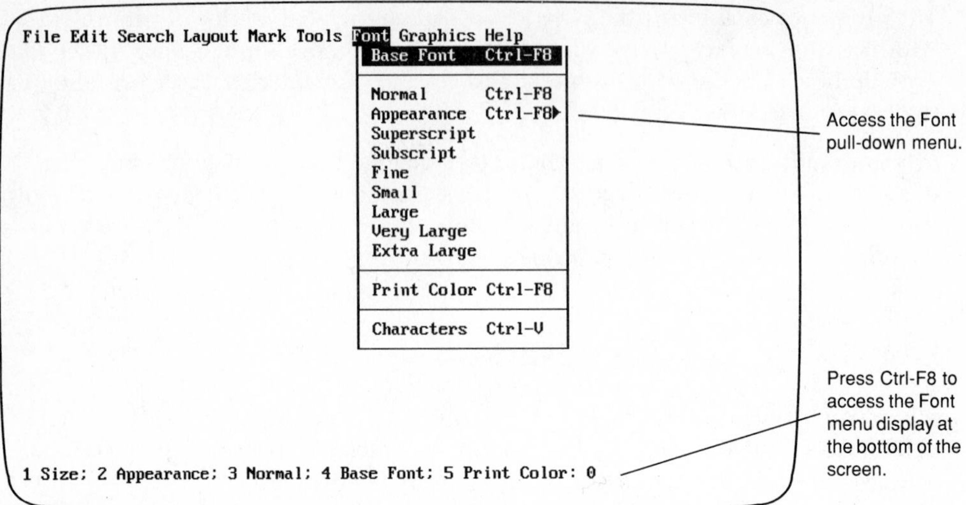

Fig. 6.7. Two versions of the Font main menu.

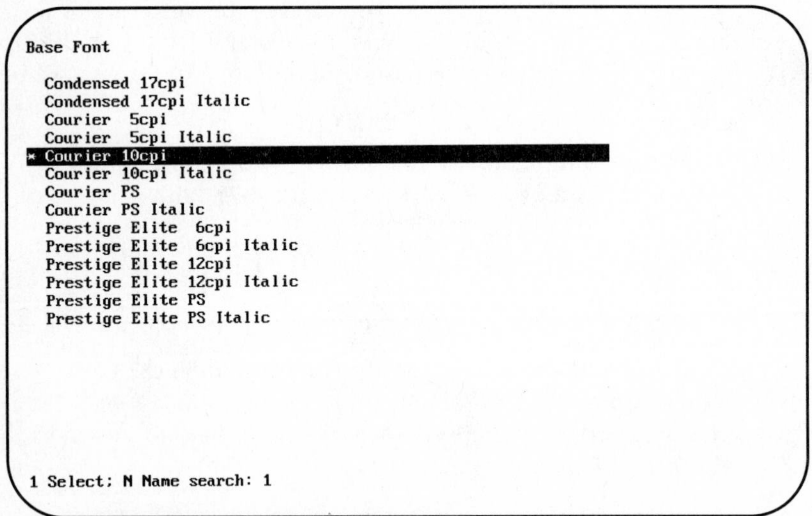

Fig. 6.8. A sample display of available base fonts.

most likely see a different menu on your screen. To change the base font anywhere in the current document, use the up arrow and down arrow to highlight a new base-font choice; then choose **Select (1)**.

Selecting a Font by Size

Access Size menu options in one of two ways: Access the **Font** pull-down menu or press Ctrl-F8 and select **Size (1)**. The Size menu presents seven choices of print size, as shown in figure 6.9 (figure 6.7 shows the corresponding choices on the **Font** pull-down menu).

```
1 Suprscpt; 2 Subscpt; 3 Fine; 4 Small; 5 Large; 6 Vry Large; 7 Ext Large: 0
```

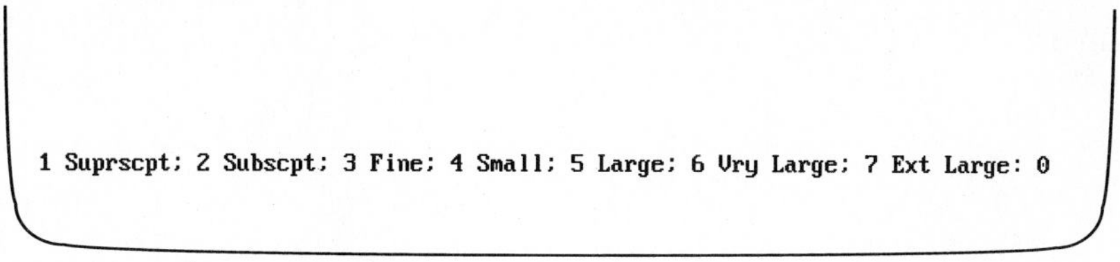

***Fig. 6.9.** The Font Size options.*

Font sizes range from very small superscript (Su**p**rscpt) to extra large (**E**xt Large). The actual size depends on your printer. Sizes 1 through 4 are incrementally smaller than the current base font. Sizes 5 through 7 are incrementally larger than the current base font. When you select one of these font sizes, WordPerfect 5.1 selects the incremental size you choose, based on which font size is currently in use. The results, therefore, depend on the font size in use and the font sizes installed on your printer. To view the options for selecting a font by size, follow these steps:

Step 1: Access the F**o**nt pull-down menu (or press Ctrl-F8,1).

Note: The choices Su**p**erscript, Su**b**script, **F**ine, **S**mall, **L**arge, **V**ery Large, and **E**xtra Large appear on the F**o**nt pull-down menu. If you press Ctrl-F8 and choose **S**ize (**1**), an abbreviated list of these choices appears at the bottom of the screen, as shown in figure 6.9.

Step 2: Look at the available options; then press Exit (F7) or Cancel (F1) to restore the WordPerfect editing screen.

To change the font size temporarily in relation to the current base font, highlight your choice on the F**o**nt pull-down menu or select a number from the options at the bottom of the screen.

Changing Typeface Appearance

The Appearance menu presents nine options for changing the appearance of the selected font. Choices such as outline, shadow, small capital letters, bold, italic, and underline are appropriate for headings, titles, letterheads, book and magazine titles, foreign words, and captions. Appearance changes such as strikeout and redline emphasize document changes and revisions. To view the options for changing the appearance of the typeface, do the following:

Step 1: Access the F**o**nt pull-down menu and select **A**ppearance (or press Ctrl-F8,2). The Font Appearance menu appears, as shown in figure 6.10.

```
1 Bold 2 Undln 3 Dbl Und 4 Italc 5 Outln 6 Shadw 7 Sm Cap 8 Redln 9 Stkout: 0
```

Fig. 6.10. *The Font Appearance options.*

Note: The choices **B**old, **U**nderline, **D**ouble Underline, **I**talics, **O**utline, Sh**a**dow, Small **C**ap, **R**edline, and **S**trikeout appear on the Font Appearance pop-up menu. If you pressed Ctrl-F8 and chose **A**ppearance (**2**), an abbreviated list of the choices appears at the bottom of the screen (see fig. 6.10).

Step 2: Press Cancel (F1) or Exit (F7) to return to the current document screen.

Experiment with using these options on your own documents and equipment. Consult your printer manual for features supported by your printer. If you incorporate font choices into style sheets, you can develop "jazzed up" printed output much more easily. You can read about style sheets in Lesson 10.

Enhancing Text with the Block Command

After you mark off text with the Block command, you can change the appearance of the highlighted text. You can emphasize an important paragraph by making it bold, for example, or you can call attention to a single word by underlining it. You can center a title, redline edited text, or strike out text to be deleted. The Block command allows you to enhance a section of text as small as a single letter or as large as the entire document.

Boldfacing and Underlining a Block

In Lesson 3, you produced boldfaced and underlined text as you typed. You may, however, find it easier to type text without incorporating special characteristics and then enhance the text later by using Block.

Try enhancing a letterhead that does not include special display features. To bold a block of text, follow these steps:

Step 1: Clear the screen without saving the current document and retrieve CRIMSON6.TOP.

Step 2: Access the **E**dit pull-down menu and select **B**lock (or press Alt-F4 or F12). Press End to highlight the entire line.

Step 3: Access the F**o**nt pull-down menu, select **A**ppearance, and select **B**old (or press F6).

To underline a block of text, follow these steps:

Step 1: Position the cursor at the beginning of the second line of the heading, access the **E**dit pull-down menu, and select **B**lock (or press F4 or F12); highlight the line.

Step 2: Access the F**o**nt pull-down menu, select **A**ppearance, and select **U**nderline (or press F8).

To apply underline and bold features to the same text, follow these steps:

Step 1: Position the cursor at the beginning of the third line of the heading, access the **E**dit pull-down menu, and select **B**lock (or press Alt-F4 or F12), and highlight the line.

Step 2: Press Bold (F6).

Step 3: Block the third line of the heading again.

Step 4: Press Underline (F8).

Step 5: Access the **F**ile pull-down menu and select **P**rint (or press Shift-F7). Select either **F**ull Document (**1**) to print the announcement or **V**iew Document (**6**) to see the announcement on-screen.

Step 6: Press Exit (F7) enough times to restore the CRIMSON6.TOP document to the screen.

The final document resembles what you see in figure 6.11—if your printer supports boldface and underlining.

```
CRIMSON TRAVEL & TOURS, INC.
Serving American Corporations for 30 Years

Land - Sea - Air
```

Fig. 6.11. *Using Block to boldface and underline text.*

Changing Case

To change a block of text to all lowercase or all uppercase, you do not have to retype the block. A simple command, the Switch command, does the typing for you, changing the text from uppercase to lowercase. WordPerfect leaves certain letters capitalized, including the first letter of sentences and the letter I when it occurs by itself.

To switch all characters in the CRIMSON6.TOP document to uppercase, follow these steps:

Step 1: Clear the screen without saving the current document and retrieve CRIMSON6.TOP.

Step 2: Access the **E**dit pull-down menu and select **B**lock (or press Alt-F4 or F12); then highlight the three lines of heading.

Step 3: Access the **E**dit pull-down menu, select Con**v**ert Case, and then select To **U**pper (or press Shift-F3,1).

The letterhead appears in all uppercase letters.

Entering Special Characters with Compose

You can print more characters than are available on your keyboard if your printer has graphics capabilities. These additional characters, stored in WordPerfect character sets (see fig. 6.12), can be reproduced through the use of Compose code Ctrl-2 or Ctrl-V. In Lesson 8 you learn to print the Compose characters supported by your printer.

Sample Printout of CHARACTR.DOC

Multinational 2
Charset: 2
Contains: Rarely-used non-capitalizable multinational characters and diacriticals.

2,0 . Dot Below
2,1 .. Double Dot Below
2,2 • Centered Ring
2,3 ˳ Ring Below
2,4 ' Apostrophe Accent Above Off Center
2,5 ‸ Circumflex Below
2,6 ‗ Double Underline
2,7 _ Macron Below (Underline)
2,8 ĸ Lowercase Greenlandic k
2,9 ̮ Half Circle Below
2,10 ' Vertical Tilde
2,11 ' Inverted Apostrophe Accent Above
2,12 ' Inverted Mirrored Apostrophe Accent Above
2,13 , Mirrored Apostrophe Accent Below
2,14 ¸ Right Cedilla
2,15 ˛ Non-connecting Cedilla (Mirrored Ogonek)
2,16 ˩ Hook (Tail) to the Left
2,17 ˪ Hook (Tail) to the Right
2,18 ' Vertical Mark
2,19 ' Horn
2,20 , Low Rising Tone Mark
2,21 ˛ Rude
2,22 ' Ayn
2,23 ' Alif/Hamzah
2,24 ˇ Upadhmaniya
2,25 ˇ Candrabindu
2,26 ˊ Mjagkij Znak
2,27 ˝ Tverdyj Znak

Fig. 6.12. A printout of a portion of the CHARACTR.DOC file.

Ctrl-2, the primary Compose key sequence, works everywhere in the program, including submenus and the macro editor. The alternative Compose key sequence—Ctrl-V—works in the main editing screen but does not work in all submenus. Some users prefer Ctrl-V because it displays the prompt `(Key =)` on-screen to remind you that WordPerfect is waiting for you to enter a character reference number or mnemonic combination.

WordPerfect's Compose feature provides two ways to enter special characters: a numeric method and a mnemonic method. To use the numeric method, press Compose (Ctrl-2 or Ctrl-V) and type a two-part character number (see the left-hand column in fig. 6.12 for examples). To use the mnemonic method, press Compose and type the component characters (such as **c** and /) that together form a new character (¢). WordPerfect software includes two files to determine which nonkeyboard characters your printer supports.

Testing Your Printer Capability

The WordPerfect Conversion disk contains two files—CHARMAP.TST and CHARACTR.DOC—that provide additional information about the WordPerfect character sets. You can print CHARMAP.TST in each of your base fonts to see which characters your printer can print and to determine which characters must be drawn graphically. You can print CHARACTR.DOC on any printer with graphics capability to obtain a complete list of each character, its character number, as well as its descriptive name. To see CHARACTR.DOC, follow these steps:

Step 1: Find CHARACTR.DOC on your hard disk or on your WordPerfect 5.1 Conversion disk.

Note: CHARACTR.DOC is *not* on your practice disk.

Step 2: Clear the screen without saving the current document and retrieve CHARACTR.DOC.

Step 3: Scroll through the document on-screen by using the cursor-movement keys.

Step 4: Access the **F**ile pull-down menu and select **P**rint (or press Shift-F7). Select **F**ull Document (**1**) to print the file.

Using the Numeric Method To Compose Characters

The numeric method composes nonkeyboard characters stored in the WordPerfect 5.1 character set by referencing applicable code numbers. For example, **2,6** is the code that produces a double underline (see fig. 6.12). To create the symbol for one-half (1/2), follow these steps:

Step 1: Clear the screen without saving the current document.

Step 2: Press Ctrl-2, type **4,17**, and press Enter.

Note: The symbol 1/2 appears on-screen if your monitor is capable of displaying the character. If your screen cannot display the one-half symbol, you see a small box (■) in its place. Keep available the CHARACTR.DOC you just printed so that you can look up other characters.

Using the Mnemonic Method to Compose Characters

The mnemonic method refers to specifying two keyboard symbols which compose a special character. For example, the cent symbol (¢) is composed of the letter c and the slash (/). To compose the cent symbol, follow these steps:

Step 1: Clear the screen without saving the current document.

Step 2: Press Ctrl-2, type the lowercase letter **c** followed by the slash (/).

Note: You can type either the **c**/ or the /**c** sequence.

In this lesson you practiced a variety of techniques for formatting and enhancing text. Reinforce these concepts by working through the summary exercises that follow.

For Further Reference

If you would like to learn more about enhancing your documents, consult *Using WordPerfect 5.1*, Special Edition (Que Corporation, Carmel, IN, 1989), chapters 5, 8, 15, and 21.

Summary of Concepts

Lesson 6 explains these concepts:

- ❑ Set margins by specifying the number of characters, inches, or centimeters from the left and right edges of the paper.
- ❑ Format lists creatively by employing WordPerfect's four types of tabs (left, right, center, and decimal).
- ❑ Vary the document display by indenting and outdenting text. For example, indent both left and right margins when you include a quotation.
- ❑ Change the line spacing by specifying a number, including up to two decimal places.
- ❑ Use Flush Right to align a single line of text with the right margin.
- ❑ Align text against left and right margins using WordPerfect's four justification settings: left, center, right, and full (the default).
- ❑ Use manual or automatic hyphenation to reduce blank spaces that may appear when you print right-justified, word-wrapped text.
- ❑ Determine a document's "look" by using a variety of base fonts.
- ❑ Specify a variety of font sizes in relation to the current base font.
- ❑ Enhance the display of selected words or phrases within a document (boldface, underline, and so on), by using Block to mark text and to select the appropriate appearance option.
- ❑ Load WordPerfect's CHARMAP.TST and CHARACTR.DOC files to test the capabilities of your printer.
- ❑ Compose a variety of special characters not found on the keyboard by using WordPerfect 5.1's numeric and mnemonic methods.

Review Exercises

Practice using the WordPerfect features in this lesson by completing these exercises. If you do not remember how to do something, review the preceding explanations and practice steps.

1. Clear the screen without saving the current document and retrieve CRIMSON6.LTR. Change the left margin to .5 inch and the right margin to 2.5 inches. Either view the document or print it to see the results.
2. Using left tabs, create a phone list in which names begin in position 1.5", area codes begin in position 5.5" (use a dot leader), and phone numbers begin in position 6.5".
3. Create a list of bills you owe, using the following format:

   Owed to   Date due   Amount   Balance

   Set a left tab at position 1.5", a left tab at position 4.5", a decimal tab at position 5.5", and another decimal tab at position 6.5". Enter at least five items.
4. Using the Flush Right command to specify the margin, add the current date to the top of the list of bills you created in exercise 3.
5. Retrieve CRIMSON6.LTR and hyphenate the text manually. Repeat this exercise, using automatic hyphenation.
6. Create a memo to your employees or friends, announcing an open house at your home. Include the invitation in paragraph one, include directions in paragraph two, and suggest dress or provide other instructions in paragraph three. Indent paragraph one an extra tab stop from both the left and right margins.
7. Practice enhancing the memo you created in exercise 6, using a variety of font changes supported by your printer. Access the Print menu, and view or print enhancements.
8. Clear the screen without saving the current document, retrieve ANNOUNC6.DOC, and place the paragraph symbol (¶) at the beginning of each paragraph.

Formatting Pages and Designing Documents

7

In this lesson, you practice these tasks:

- ❑ Set top and bottom page margins and center text between margins
- ❑ Position a page number and start a new page number
- ❑ Specify page headers and page footers
- ❑ Number pages in a header or footer
- ❑ Suppress page headers, footers, and numbers
- ❑ Keep text together by using the Conditional End Of Page feature, the Block Protect feature, and the Widow/Orphan Protection feature
- ❑ Specify paper size
- ❑ Change initial codes in a document

In this lesson, you use WordPerfect formatting features to design clear, interesting, and readable documents. Designing a document requires you to make format choices that affect the entire document or to choose among formatting options that control pages or groups of pages. This lesson focuses on formatting the page.

Most formatting features are established through the Format menu, shown in figure 7.1.

```
Format

     1 - Line
              Hyphenation                          Line Spacing
              Justification                        Margins Left/Right
              Line Height                          Tab Set
              Line Numbering                       Widow/Orphan Protection

     2 - Page
              Center Page (top to bottom)          Page Numbering
              Force Odd/Even Page                  Paper Size/Type
              Headers and Footers                  Suppress
              Margins Top/Bottom

     3 - Document
              Display Pitch                        Redline Method
              Initial Codes/Font                   Summary

     4 - Other
              Advance                              Overstrike
              Conditional End of Page              Printer Functions
              Decimal Characters                   Underline Spaces/Tabs
              Language                             Border Options

Selection: 0
```

***Fig.* 7.1.** *The Format menu.*

You see four kinds of format commands: Line, Page, Document, and Other. In Lesson 6, you practiced using several Format: Line commands, including those that control hyphenation, justification, left and right margins, and tab settings. Now you will practice using additional options in all four groups.

Determining Page Layout

Text on a page ordinarily forms a rectangle, with margins on all four sides. With WordPerfect, you can even center the text within the margins. In the preceding lessons you set left and right margins. To complete the page layout, you may now need to adjust top and bottom margins.

You also have centered text between right and left margins—as you typed and with a block command. You can, in addition, center less than a page of text between top and bottom margins. This feature is quite useful when you make cover pages.

Setting Top and Bottom Margins

The top margin sets the distance from the top edge of the paper to the first line of print. Similarly, the bottom margin sets the distance from the last line of print to the bottom edge of the paper.

You can place margin settings anywhere in the text; these settings affect all pages after they are set. You can change margin settings as often as you need to. If you want a certain margin setting to apply to the entire document, set it at the beginning of the first page. WordPerfect 5.1's default margins are, for example, 1 inch on all four sides of the paper. You can, however, change the default settings by changing initial codes, as illustrated in the last section of the lesson.

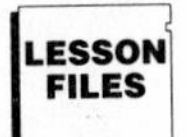

To change the top margin in CRIMSON7.LTR, follow these steps:

Step 1: Clear the screen without saving the current document and retrieve CRIMSON7.LTR.

Note: The instruction to clear the screen without saving the current document is used many times throughout the workbook. It means to access the **F**ile pull-down menu and select E**x**it (or press F7); when you are prompted `Save Document? Yes (No)`, press **N**; when you are prompted `Exit WP? No (Yes)`, press **N**.

Step 2: Access the **F**ile pull-down menu and select **P**rint (or press Shift-F7). Select **V**iew Document (**6**) and then choose to view the document at either 100% (**1**) or Full Page (**3**). Notice the current size of the top margin and press Exit (F7) to restore document display.

Step 3: Access the **L**ayout pull-down menu and select **P**age (or press Shift-F8,2); then choose **M**argins (**5**).

Step 4: Type **2.5** as the top margin and press Exit (F7) enough times to return to the current document.

Step 5: Access the **F**ile pull-down menu and select **P**rint (or press Shift-F7). Select **V**iew Document (**6**) and then choose to view the document at either 100% (**1**) or Full Page (**3**). Notice the increase in the top margin. Press Exit (F7) to restore document display.

Follow a similar procedure to set a bottom margin.

Centering Text Top to Bottom

Sometimes you may want to override the top and bottom margins and center text an equal distance from the top and bottom of the page. You may, for example, want to center text on the cover page of a report, as illustrated in figure 7.2.

```
WordPerfect 5

A Report on Office Productivity

Prepared by:

Lee A. Metzelaar

April 1, 1990
```

Fig. 7.2. Text centered top to bottom.

To practice centering the text of the cover page shown in figure 7.2, follow these steps:

Step 1: Clear the screen without saving the current document and retrieve COVER7.DOC.

Step 2: Access the **File** pull-down menu and select **Print** (or press Shift-F7). Select **View** Document (**6**) and then choose the Full Page (**3**) option. The text begins at the top of the page. Press Exit (F7) to restore the document display.

Step 3: Move the cursor to the top of the page by pressing Home, Home, Home, up arrow.

Step 4: Access the **Layout** pull-down menu and select **Page** (or press Shift-F8,2).

Step 5: Choose **Center** Page (top to bottom) (**1**) and choose **Yes**. Press Exit (F7) until the document is restored to the screen.

Step 6: Access the **File** pull-down menu and select **Print** (or press Shift-F7). Then select **View** Document (**6**) and choose the Full Page (**3**) option. The text is now centered on the page. Press Exit (F7) to restore document display.

If you view the current document by using Reveal Codes (Alt-F3), the page-centering code appears as `[Center Pg]`. To center text perfectly, remove any excess hard returns ([HRt]) below the last printed line on the page. Otherwise, WordPerfect 5.1 includes them as part of the text to be centered.

Numbering Pages

Numbering pages automatically is as simple as telling WordPerfect where you want the number to appear on the page. The default setting is no page numbering. The page-numbering menu (see fig. 7.3) controls page numbering. To activate automatic page numbering, do these three steps:

- ❑ Turn on automatic page numbering by telling WordPerfect where to position the page number (the default is off).
- ❑ Tell WordPerfect what page number to start with (the default is 1).
- ❑ Tell WordPerfect whether page numbering should be suppressed on any page, such as page 1.

```
Format: Page Numbering

     1 - New Page Number       1

     2 - Page Number Style     ^B

     3 - Insert Page Number

     4 - Page Number Position No page numbering
```

Fig. 7.3. The Format: Page Numbering menu.

Positioning the Page Number

The page number can appear in any of six positions on the page or in either of two positions on alternating pages. Choose the position from the visual page-number menu shown in figure 7.4.

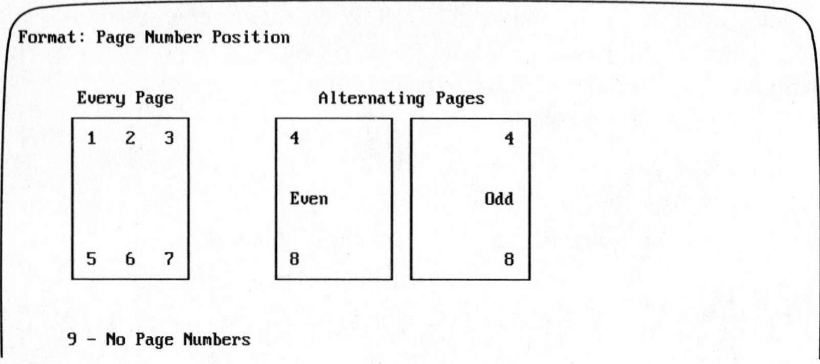

Fig. *7.4. The Format: Page Number Position menu.*

To turn on page numbering and to position page numbers at the bottom center of the page, follow these steps:

Step 1: Clear the screen without saving the current document and retrieve PAGES7.LST.

Step 2: Access the **L**ayout pull-down menu and select **P**age (or press Shift-F8,2); then choose Page **N**umbering (**6**).

Step 3: Select Page Number **P**osition (**4**).

Step 4: Choose (**6**) to position page numbers at the bottom center of every page (see fig. 7.4); then press Exit (F7) to restore the document.

Page numbers do not appear on-screen. You see them only when you print or view the document. To view the page numbering on several pages of the current document, follow these steps:

Step 1: Access the **F**ile pull-down menu and select **P**rint (or press Shift-F7). Select **V**iew Document (**6**); then choose 100% (**1**).

Step 2: Press Home, down arrow to display the bottom half of page 1 and to see page number 1.

Step 3: Press PgDn and then Home, down arrow to see page number 2 at the bottom of the second page.

Step 4: Press Exit (F7) to restore the current document.

Starting a New Page Number

Sometimes you want to start a document with a page number other than 1. You may, for example, store chapters in a book as separate documents, and Chapter 2 must start with page 37. Access the Format: Page screen to select the option that sets a new page number.

To change the page numbering of PAGES7.LST so that page numbers begin at 37, follow these steps:

Step 1: Move the cursor to the upper left corner of the current document by pressing Home, Home, Home, up arrow.

Step 2: Access the **L**ayout pull-down menu and select **P**age (or press Shift-F8,2). Choose Page **N**umbering (**6**), and then choose **N**ew Page Number (**1**).

Step 3: Type **37** and press Enter; then press Exit (F7) to restore the current document.

Note: WordPerfect inserts the code `[Pg Num:37]`, which you can see if you access Reveal Codes (Alt-F3 or F11).

Step 4: To view the document, access the **F**ile pull-down menu and select **P**rint (or press Shift-F7). Select **V**iew Document (**6**); then choose 100% (**1**).

Step 5: Press Home, down arrow to display the bottom half of page 1 and see page number 37.

Step 6: Press PgDn and then Home, down arrow to see the page number 38 at the bottom of the second page. Press Exit (F7) to restore the current document.

Step 7: To delete the page-number code and restore the default starting page number 1, access the **E**dit menu and select **R**eveal Codes (or press Alt-F3 or F11). Position the cursor on the code `[Pg Num:37]`; press Del and press Alt-F3 or F11 to turn off Reveal Codes.

You also can set page numbers to Roman numerals by entering the starting Roman numeral in lowercase.

Suppressing Page Numbers

The page-number display is often suppressed on the first page of a document. Page numbering still, however, includes the first page. The Format: Suppress menu (see fig. 7.5) controls the suppression of page numbers, headers, and footers.

```
Format: Suppress (this page only)

     1 - Suppress All Page Numbering, Headers and Footers

     2 - Suppress Headers and Footers

     3 - Print Page Number at Bottom Center  No

     4 - Suppress Page Numbering             No

     5 - Suppress Header A                   No

     6 - Suppress Header B                   No

     7 - Suppress Footer A                   No

     8 - Suppress Footer B                   No
```

Fig. 7.5. *The Format: Suppress menu.*

To suppress the page number from the first page of the current document, follow these steps:

Step 1: Move the cursor to the upper left corner of the current document by pressing Home, Home, Home, up arrow.

Step 2: Access the **L**ayout pull-down menu and select **P**age (or press Shift-F8,2). Choose S**u**ppress (this page only) (**8**).

Step 3: Choose Suppress **P**age Numbering (**4**), press **Y**, and press Exit (F7) to restore the current document.

Note: WordPerfect inserts the code `[Suppress:PgNum]`, which you see if you access Reveal Codes (Alt-F3 or F11). The first page number, 1, is suppressed; page numbering begins on the next page with number 2.

Step 4: To see the document, access the **F**ile pull-down menu and select **P**rint (or press Shift-F7). Select **V**iew Document (**6**) and then choose 100% (**1**).

Step 5: Press Home, down arrow to display the bottom half of page 1. A page number does not appear.

Step 6: Press PgDn and then Home, down arrow to view page number 2 at the bottom of the second page. Press Exit (F7) to restore the current document.

Step 7: To delete the suppress code and restore the page number display on page 1, access the **E**dit menu and select **R**eveal Codes (or press Alt-F3 or F11). Next, position the cursor on the code `[Suppress:PgNum]`, press Del, and press Alt-F3 or F11 to turn off Reveal Codes.

Using Page Headers and Footers

A *page header* is a block of text that repeats at the top of each page in a multiple-page document. A *page footer* is a block of text that repeats at the bottom of each page. Headers and footers can appear on all pages, on only even pages, or on only odd pages You can have two headers and footers per page. Using the even/odd page option, you can also create alternating headers and footers.

Headers and footers occupy space between margins and text. WordPerfect inserts approximately one line space between the header or footer and the text. If you want more space, include blank lines at the bottom of the header or at the top of the footer. You can edit and delete both headers and footers.

You cannot see headers and footers on-screen. Select the View Document option from the Print menu to see the repeating text.

Creating a Header and a Footer

You can create headers at any place in the document. If, however, you create one in a place other than the beginning of the document, the header or footer may move if you add or delete text.

To create both a header and a footer in the current PAGES7.LST document, follow these steps:

Step 1: Clear the screen without saving the current document and retrieve PAGES7.LST.

Step 2: Access the **L**ayout pull-down menu and select **P**age (or press Shift-F8,2). Choose **H**eaders (**3**).

Step 3: Choose Header **A** (**1**) from these options at the bottom of the screen:

`1 Header A; 2 Header B: 0.`

Step 4: Choose Every **Page** (**2**) from the following options at the bottom of the screen:

`1 Discontinue;2 Every Page;3 Odd Pages;4 Even Pages; 5 Edit:0`

Note: You now see a blank screen, except for the status-line prompt `Header A: Press EXIT when done` at the bottom. Use this screen to enter the header that will appear at the top of each page. You may type any text and enter font codes, lines, and other graphics. The header may not exceed the length of the page.

Step 5: At the left margin, type **CRIMSON TOURS TRAVEL TIP** and press Enter twice.

Step 6: Press Exit (F7) once to return to the Format: Page screen.

Step 7: Choose **F**ooters (**4**), select Footer **A** (**1**), and then choose Every **P**age (**2**).

Note: You now see another blank screen with the status line prompt `Footer A: Press EXIT when done`. Use this screen to enter the footer for the bottom of each page.

Step 8: Press Enter twice to space two blank lines, press Flush Right (Alt-F6), and type **Have a nice day!**

Step 9: Press Exit (F7) enough times to restore the current document.

Step 10: To see the document, access the **F**ile pull-down menu and select **P**rint (or press Shift-F7); then select **V**iew Document (**6**). Choose 100% (**1**) to see the header.

Step 11: Press Home, down arrow to display the bottom half of page 1 and to see the footer.

Step 12: Press PgDn and then Home, down arrow to see the header and footer on page 2. Press Exit (F7) to restore the current document.

Notice how much better a document looks when you style it with headers and footers. In Steps 5 and 8 you pressed Enter twice to add spacing between the header and text and between the footer and text. Consider putting the page number in the header or footer too—the result may look more professional.

Numbering Pages within a Header or Footer

You can add automatic page numbers to a header or footer by inserting a Ctrl-B (hold Ctrl down and press B). The symbol ^B appears in the header or footer to indicate automatic page numbering. When the document is printed, or viewed, page numbers replace the ^B symbol. You also can dress up the page number by including the word **Page** (Page ^B) or setting the number off with hyphens (- ^B -).

To place the page number in the upper right corner of a document within the header, follow these steps:

Step 1: Clear the screen without saving the current document and retrieve PAGESNR7.LST.

Step 2: Access the **L**ayout pull-down menu and select **P**age (or press Shift-F8,2). Choose **H**eaders (**3**).

Step 3: Choose Header **A** (**1**), then **E**dit (**5**).

Step 4: Position the cursor at the end of the first line after TIP. Press Flush Right (Alt-F6).

Step 5: Type **Page** (include one space after the word) and then press Ctrl-B.

Step 6: Press Exit (F7) enough times to restore the current document.

Step 7: To see the document, press Print (Shift-F7), select **V**iew Document (**6**), and then choose 100% (**1**). Use PgUp and PgDn to inspect all pages. Press Exit (F7) to restore the current document.

The default starting page number in a header is 1. You can set the default to a number other than 1 by following the procedures discussed earlier in "Starting a New Page Number."

Suppressing Headers, Footers, and Page Numbers

On some documents, the first page should not include headers, footers, and page numbers. The procedure for suppressing all three is similar to the process used to suppress only page numbers. Take just a moment to review the procedure without performing the steps:

- ❑ Move the cursor to the top of the page where you want to suppress the header, footer, or page number.
- ❑ Access the **L**ayout pull-down menu and select **P**age (or press Shift-F8,2). Select S**u**ppress (this page only) (**8**).
- ❑ Select the header, footer, or page numbers to be suppressed and press Exit (F7) to restore the document.

Alternating Headers or Footers

Some document designs (books, for example) require that different headers appear on odd and even pages or that the page numbers alternate to the outside edge of the page. In a bound document, even-numbered pages are usually on the left; odd pages, on the right.

In the following steps you practice putting the page number on the outside edge of the page and putting alternating headers along the inside edge, next to the spine or binding. To create a header on the right (odd-numbered) pages, follow these steps:

Step 1: Clear the screen without saving the current document and retrieve PAGES7.LST.

Step 2: Access the **L**ayout pull-down menu and select **P**age (or press Shift-F8,2). Choose **H**eaders (**3**) and then select Header **A** (**1**).

Step 3: Choose **O**dd Pages (**3**) to access the blank header screen. Type **Have a nice trip!** (but do not press Enter).

Step 4: Press Flush Right (Alt-F6); type **Page**. Press the space bar, press Ctrl-B, and then press Enter twice to include blank lines in the header.

Step 5: Press Exit (F7) once to return to the Format: Page menu.

To create a different header on the left (even-numbered) pages, follow these steps:

Step 1: Select **H**eaders (**3**), Header **B** (**2**), and **E**ven Pages (**4**).

Step 2: Type **Page**, press the space bar, and press Ctrl-B.

Step 3: Press Flush Right (Alt-F6), type **CRIMSON TRAVEL TIPS**, and press Enter twice to include blank lines in the header.

Step 4: Press Exit (F7) enough times to return to the current document.

Step 5: To see the document, press Print (Shift-F7), select **V**iew Document (**6**), and then choose 100% (**1**). Use PgUp and PgDn to inspect all pages; press Exit (F7) to restore the current document.

Page numbers are on the outside edges of the pages, and the comments `Have a nice trip!` and `CRIMSON TRAVEL TIPS` are on the inside edges at the binding.

Consider using within headers and footers the font codes supported by your printer. In Lesson 18 you learn an easy way to create lines that you can incorporate within headers and footers.

Determining Available Text Lines

Take a moment to reflect on page design. Because you can see only 24 lines of a document on-screen at one time, you have to rely on the status line to tell you the cursor's position by page and line. The sample page layout in figure 7.6 shows specifications for top and bottom margins, left and right margins, header and footer areas, and the remaining text area.

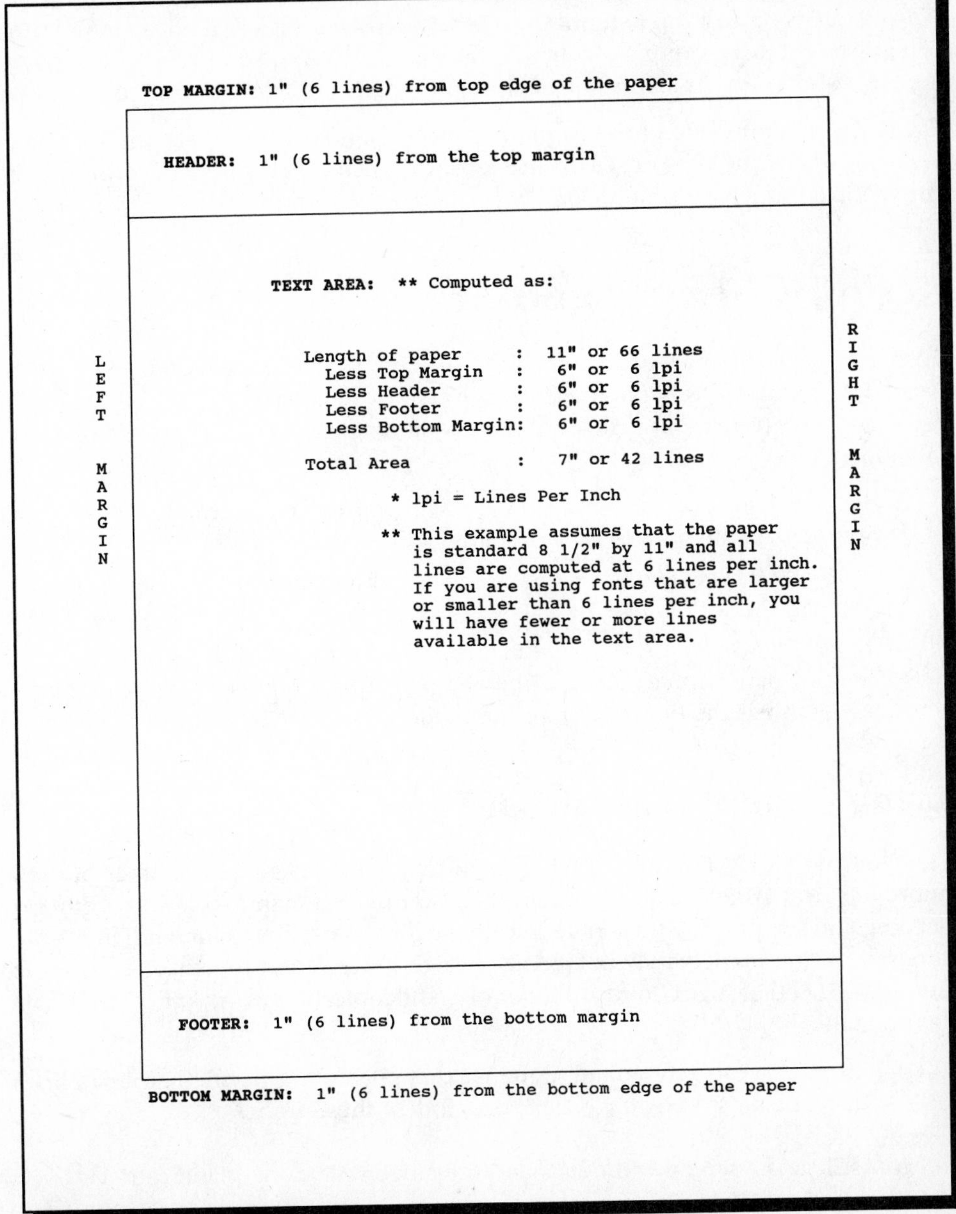

Fig. 7.6. Designing a page layout.

The sample layout calls for a page that is 11 inches long (or 66 lines, based on 6 lines per inch). You can, however, instruct WordPerfect to use any size of page—as you see later in this lesson. Of course, you do not use the whole page for any document; you reserve room for margins at the top and the bottom of the page. If you accept WordPerfect's default top and bottom margins, you have just 9 inches, or 54 lines, of text area (11 inches minus 2 inches for the margins). As you enter text on the page, the line counter on the status line begins counting from 1" to 10" (or 7 to 54 lines).

Figure 7.6 demonstrates how to plan a page layout and compute the text area available on a page. If you set up the layout depicted in figure 7.6, WordPerfect automatically begins another page after you type 42 lines of text.

Keeping Text Together

Even though you may prefer the default automatic page-break feature in WordPerfect, you may sometimes want to override established page breaks. You can use three ways to prevent text from being split by a page break. Use one of these methods:

- ❑ The *Conditional End of Page* feature, which prevents a certain number of lines from being split by a page break
- ❑ The *Block Protect* feature, which prevents a block of text from being split by a page break
- ❑ The *Widow/Orphan Protection* feature, which prevents leaving the first line of a paragraph as the last line of a page (orphan) or the last line of a paragraph as the first line of a page (widow)

Using Conditional End of Page

Use the Conditional End of Page command to keep a designated number of lines unbroken by a page break. For example, use this command to hold together a heading and the first few lines of text following it. To use the command, move the cursor to a line immediately before the text to be grouped together, specify the Conditional End of Page command sequence, and indicate the number of lines to be kept together.

To practice the command sequence that prevents a specified group of lines from being split with a page break, follow these steps:

Step 1: Clear the screen without saving the current document and retrieve CONDEOP7.LST.

Step 2: Press PgDn to display the second page; then press the up arrow several times.

Step 3: Compare the current screen display with the portion of CONDEOP7.LST shown in figure 7.7. Note the soft page break (a single dotted line) that splits the second paragraph under `Graphics`.

```
Graphics

WordPerfect offers you five different types of boxes: figure, table
box, text box, user-defined box and equation. You follow the same
steps to create each box, and you can include text, graphics, or
equations in any type of box. The distinction exists primarily for
design convenience--you define each type of box as having specific
elements.

As you plan your document, decide in advance the use of each of the
--------------------------------------------------------------------------
different types of boxes and how each is to look. For example, in
a newsletter, you may decide to use figure boxes to hold graphics
created in another program. In this case, define the figure box
with single borders. You may decide to use table boxes to call out
important text in your document. In this case, define the table
box with thick top and bottom borders and no side borders. You may
want to put the nameplate in a text box defined with thick top and
bottom borders and 10% gray shading. You may decide to use user-
defined boxes for major headlines, defined with no borders or
shading.

C:\ATIWP\CONDEOP7.LST                      Doc 1 Pg 1 Ln 8.17" Pos 1"
```

Fig. *7.7. A page break before the use of Conditional End of Page.*

Step 4: Position the cursor just above the line `As you plan your document...`, which appears at the bottom of the first page.

Step 5: Access the **L**ayout pull-down menu and select **O**ther (or press Shift-F8,4). Choose **C**onditional End of Page (**2**).

Step 6: In response to the prompt `Number of Lines to Keep Together:`, type **3** and press Enter.

Step 7: Press Exit (F7) to restore the current document.

Step 8: Press the down arrow enough times to see the new page break that appears above the second paragraph under `Graphics` (see fig. 7.8).

```
Graphics

WordPerfect offers you five different types of boxes: figure, table
box, text box, user-defined box and equation.  You follow the same
steps to create each box, and you can include text, graphics, or
equations in any type of box.  The distinction exists primarily for
design convenience--you define each type of box as having specific
elements.
================================================================================
As you plan your document, decide in advance the use of each of the
different types of boxes and how each is to look.  For example, in
a newsletter, you may decide to use figure boxes to hold graphics
created in another program.  In this case, define the figure box
with single borders.  You may decide to use table boxes to call out
important text in your document.  In this case, define the table
box with thick top and bottom borders and no side borders.  You may
want to put the nameplate in a text box defined with thick top and
bottom borders and 10% gray shading.  You may decide to use user-
defined boxes for major headlines, defined with no borders or
shading.

C:\ATIWP\CONDEOP7.LST                                 Doc 1 Pg 2 Ln 1.33" Pos 1"
```

Fig. 7.8. The page break after the use of Conditional End of Page.

Conditional End of Page is an excellent feature to build into style sheets or macros (see Lesson 10).

Using Block Protect

Block Protect serves essentially the same purpose as Conditional End of Page: both prevent a designated group of lines from being split by a page break. The difference between the commands involves the manner in which text is specified. Using Block Protect, you highlight a block of text and then select the Protect command. After you execute the command sequence, the highlighted block is pulled together on one side of the page break.

Now repeat the preceding exercise, using Block Protect instead of Conditional End of Page. Just follow these steps:

Step 1: Clear the screen without saving the current document and retrieve CONDEOP7.LST.

Step 2: Move the cursor to the line that precedes the second paragraph under `Graphics` (that is, move the cursor to the line that precedes `As you plan your document...`).

Step 3: Access the **E**dit pull-down menu and select **B**lock (or press Alt-F4 or F12). Highlight to the end of the paragraph.

Step 4: Access the **Edit** pull-down menu and select Protect Block (or press Shift-F8 and press **Y** to protect the block).

Step 5: Confirm that the page break shifts to the position shown in figure 7.8.

Preventing Widows and Orphans

To prevent widows and orphans, move the cursor to the top of the document, access the Format: Line menu, and turn on the feature. As you type a document with the automatic page-break feature on, any widows and orphans adjust position to join related text. The default setting is off.

To practice the command, follow these steps:

Step 1: Clear the screen without saving the current document and retrieve CONDEOP7.LST.

Step 2: View the current document by pressing Print (Shift-F7), View Document (**6**), and then Full Page (**3**). The last line of page 1 is an orphan (the first line of a paragraph that is the last line of a page).

Step 3: Exit (F7) to the current document and move the cursor to the top of page 1 by pressing Home, Home, Home, up arrow.

Step 4: Access the **L**ayout pull-down menu and select **L**ine (or press Shift-F8,1).

Step 5: Choose **W**idow/Orphan Protection (**9**) and press **Y** to turn on the feature.

Step 6: Press Exit (F7) and move to the top of the second page to see that the first line of the paragraph is no longer an orphan, as shown in figure 7.9.

Remember, the Widows/Orphans Protection feature ensures only that the first and last lines of a paragraph are not on a page by themselves. Use Block Protect or Conditional End of Page to keep an entire block of text together.

Creating and Selecting Paper and Form Sizes

With WordPerfect you can specify the size, type, orientation, and location of the paper (form) on which to print a document. Generally, the default settings are for 8 1/2-by-11-inch paper. With WordPerfect you can select from among a number of

```
Graphics

WordPerfect offers you five different types of boxes: figure, table
box, text box, user-defined box and equation. You follow the same
steps to create each box, and you can include text, graphics, or
equations in any type of box. The distinction exists primarily for
design convenience--you define each type of box as having specific
elements.

---------------------------------------------------------------------------
As you plan your document, decide in advance the use of each of the
different types of boxes and how each is to look. For example, in
a newsletter, you may decide to use figure boxes to hold graphics
created in another program. In this case, define the figure box
with single borders. You may decide to use table boxes to call out
important text in your document. In this case, define the table
box with thick top and bottom borders and no side borders. You may
want to put the nameplate in a text box defined with thick top and
bottom borders and 10% gray shading. You may decide to use user-
defined boxes for major headlines, defined with no borders or
shading.

C:\ATIWP\CONDEOP7.LST                          Doc 1 Pg 2 Ln 1.33" Pos 1"
```

Fig. *7.9. Removing an orphan.*

other commonly used forms such as legal (8 1/2-by-14-inch) or envelope (9 1/2-by-4-inch). You can also create additional forms to suit your printing needs.

Creating a Paper Size and Form

If the form you want to use in your printer is not defined by WordPerfect, you must create a new form and then select it for use in the current document. The process is simple: access the Format: Page menu, choose Paper **S**ize/Type (**7**), choose **A**dd (**2**), and follow the on-screen instructions.

Suppose that you want to use an 8 1/2-by-3-inch envelope in your laser printer. To create the new paper definition, follow these steps:

Step 1: Clear the screen without saving the current document; then access the **L**ayout pull-down menu and select **P**age (or press Shift-F8,2). Choose Paper **S**ize/Type (**7**) (see fig. 7.10).

Note: The paper types that display vary according to the current printer selected. Figure 7.10 reflects LaserJet Series II paper-type definitions.

Step 2: Choose **A**dd (**2**) from the menu at the bottom of the screen to access the Format: Paper Type menu (see fig. 7.11).

Format: Paper Size/Type

Paper type and Orientation	Paper Size	Prompt	Loc	Font Type	Double Sided	Labels
Envelope - Wide	9.5" x 4"	No	Manual	Land	No	
Legal	8.5" x 14"	No	Contin	Port	No	
Legal - Wide	14" x 8.5"	No	Contin	Land	No	
Standard	8.5" x 11"	No	Contin	Port	No	
Standard - Wide	11" x 8.5"	No	Contin	Land	No	
[ALL OTHERS]	Width ≤ 8.5"	Yes	Manual		No	

Fig. 7.10. *The Format: Paper Size/Type menu.*

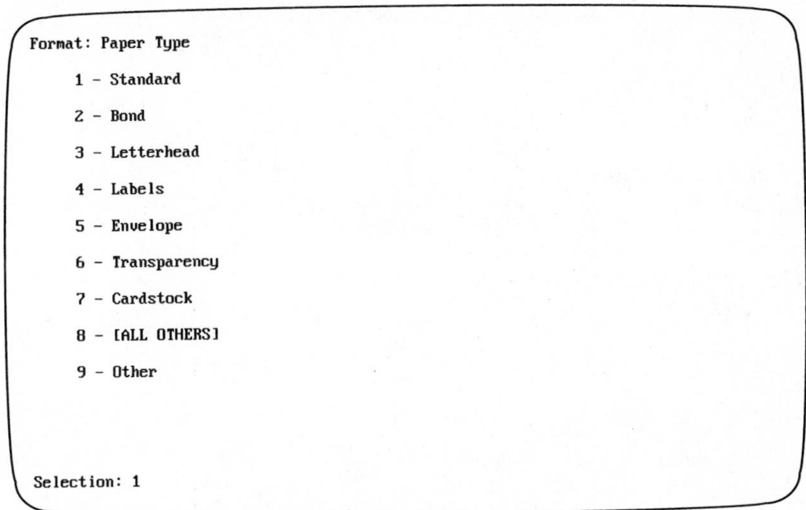

Format: Paper Type
1 - Standard
2 - Bond
3 - Letterhead
4 - Labels
5 - Envelope
6 - Transparency
7 - Cardstock
8 - [ALL OTHERS]
9 - Other
Selection: 1

Fig. 7.11. *The Format: Paper Type menu.*

Step 3: Choose **E**nvelope (**5**) as the paper type. Make sure that the Format: Edit Paper Definition screen (see fig. 7.12) appears.

Note: At this point, you can accept the paper definition by pressing Exit (F7). Or you can edit the paper definition by selecting from the menu shown in figure 7.12. In this workbook illustration, you change the size and orientation of the new envelope form and set up a prompt for manual feed.

Step 4: Choose Paper **S**ize (**1**). Predefined sizes display on-screen, as shown in figure 7.13.

```
Format: Edit Paper Definition

        Filename                    HPLASEII.PRS

    1 - Paper Size                  8.5" x 11"

    2 - Paper Type                  Envelope

    3 - Font Type                   Portrait

    4 - Prompt to Load              No

    5 - Location                    Continuous

    6 - Double Sided Printing       No

    7 - Binding Edge                Left

    8 - Labels                      No

    9 - Text Adjustment - Top       0"
                          Side      0"

Selection: 0
```

Fig. 7.12. The Format: Edit Paper Definition menu.

```
Format: Paper Size                Width  Height

    1 - Standard                  (8.5" x 11")

    2 - Standard Landscape        (11" x 8.5")

    3 - Legal                     (8.5" x 14")

    4 - Legal Landscape           (14" x 8.5")

    5 - Envelope                  (9.5" x 4")

    6 - Half Sheet                (5.5" x 8.5")

    7 - US Government             (8" x 11")

    8 - A4                        (210mm x 297mm)

    9 - A4 Landscape              (297mm x 210mm)

    o - Other
```

Fig. 7.13. The Format: Paper Size menu.

Step 5: Select **O**ther (**O**). At the prompt `Width: 0"`, type **8.5** and press Enter. At the prompt `Height: 0"`, type **3** and press Enter.

Note: After you enter the height, the Format: Edit Paper Definition menu reappears on-screen.

Step 6: Choose **F**ont type (**3**); then choose **L**andscape (**2**) from the Orientation menu at the bottom of the screen.

Step 7: Choose P**r**ompt to Load (**4**); then choose **Y**es.

Step 8: Choose **L**ocation (**5**); then choose **M**anual (**3**) from the menu options at the bottom of the screen.

Note: Your screen display should reflect the settings in figure 7.14.

```
Format: Edit Paper Definition

        Filename                     HPLASEII.PRS

     1 - Paper Size                  8.5" x 3"

     2 - Paper Type                  Envelope - Wide

     3 - Font Type                   Landscape

     4 - Prompt to Load              Yes

     5 - Location                    Manual

     6 - Double Sided Printing       No

     7 - Binding Edge                Left

     8 - Labels                      No

     9 - Text Adjustment - Top       0"
                           Side      0"
```

***Fig. 7.14.** The Edit Paper Definition screen, which reflects new settings.*

Step 9: Press Exit (F7) to return to the Format: Paper Size/Type screen; verify that your new envelope form appears on the list (see fig. 7.15).

Step 10: Press Exit (F7) enough times to restore the blank document screen.

Now that the new paper size and form are specified, you can select the combination for use at any time. Because you added the size-and-form combination to your library of paper definitions, you do not have to repeat this process each time you want to use the new form.

Format: Paper Size/Type

Paper type and Orientation	Paper Size	Prompt	Loc	Font Type	Double Sided	Labels
Envelope - Wide	8.5" x 3"	Yes	Manual	Land	No	
Envelope - Wide	9.5" x 4"	No	Manual	Land	No	
Legal	8.5" x 14"	No	Contin	Port	No	
Legal - Wide	14" x 8.5"	No	Contin	Land	No	
Standard	8.5" x 11"	No	Contin	Port	No	
Standard - Wide	11" x 8.5"	No	Contin	Land	No	
[ALL OTHERS]	Width ≤ 8.5"	Yes	Manual		No	

1 Select; 2 Add; 3 Copy; 4 Delete; 5 Edit; N Name Search: 1

Fig. 7.15. *The Format: Paper Size/Type menu, which lists the new envelope form.*

Selecting a Paper Size and Form

Paper sizes supported by WordPerfect 5.1 are described in files referred to as *forms* or *paper definitions*. To change a paper definition for the current document (for example, to specify the option Envelope—Wide 8.5" x 3" instead of the option Standard 8.5" x 11"), simply select the Paper **S**ize/Type (7) option from the Format: Page menu, highlight the Envelope—Wide 8.5" x 3" paper definition, and press **S**elect (**1**). WordPerfect embeds the appropriate paper-size code at the current cursor position. The code alters the paper size of the current document. The line counter (Ln) and cursor position (Pos) reflect the new page size as you create and move through the new document. If you are unsure which paper size is in use, access the Format: Page screen (Shift-F8) and visually check the paper definition displayed next to Paper **S**ize/Type (7).

To select the new envelope-size definition created in the previous illustration, follow these steps:

Step 1: Access the **L**ayout pull-down menu and select **P**age (or press Shift-F8,2).

Step 2: Select Paper **S**ize/Type (7), highlight the option Envelope Wide 8.5 x 3, and press **S**elect (**1**).

Note: The Format: Page screen (see fig. 7.16) now indicates that the new form is selected.

```
Format: Page

     1 - Center Page (top to bottom)     No

     2 - Force Odd/Even Page

     3 - Headers

     4 - Footers

     5 - Margins - Top                   0.5"
                   Bottom                0.5"

     6 - Page Numbering

     7 - Paper Size                      8.5" x 3"
               Type                      Envelope

     8 - Suppress (this page only)
```

Fig. *7.16. The Format: Page menu, which reflects a change in the paper size and type.*

Step 3: Press Exit (F7) to restore the document screen.

Step 4: To view the embedded paper definition code, access the **E**dit pull-down menu and select **R**eveal Codes (or press Alt-F3 or F11).

Note: The code `[Paper Sz/Typ:8.5" x 3",Envelope]` appears in Reveal Codes mode. Now you can begin to type the contents of an envelope.

Step 5: To view the size of the currently defined envelope, press Enter until a single dashed line (indicating a soft page break) appears on-screen.

Step 6: Note the small number of text lines available between the top and bottom margins of the currently defined envelope.

Step 7: Clear the screen without saving the current document.

Each time you access a blank document screen, the default paper size/type is in effect. Repeat these steps to switch to a different paper size.

Deleting a Paper Size and Form

If you no longer use a defined paper size and form, you can remove the definition. Access the Format: Page menu, select the Paper Size/Type screen, highlight the size and form type to be deleted, and press **D**elete (**4**). To delete the definition for the 8 1/2-by-3-inch envelope, follow these steps:

Step 1: Access the **L**ayout pull-down menu and select **P**age (or press Shift-F8,2).

Step 2: Select Paper **S**ize/Type (**7**), highlight the option Envelope Wide 8.5" x 3", and press **D**elete (**4**).

Step 3: In response to the prompt `Delete paper definition?`, press **Y**.

Step 4: Press Exit (F7) enough times to restore the document screen.

You should now be comfortable creating, selecting, and deleting paper size forms. To edit an existing form, follow the same steps for adding a paper size and form, except select **E**dit (**4**) instead of **A**dd (**2**).

If you make selections from the Page: Format menu when you create a document, WordPerfect embeds one or more codes that affect only the current document. You can, however, establish *initial codes*, which affect all documents.

Setting Initial Codes

WordPerfect establishes defaults for a variety of settings. For example, the default for justification is full justification, and margins are set to 1 inch on all sides. If you want other settings, you can set them each time you create a document. You can, however, establish new codes to control all new documents by entering the settings you prefer into the Initial Codes screen.

When you create a new document, WordPerfect 5.1 uses the codes in the Initial Codes screen instead of its original default settings. To practice setting initial codes, specify left justification and set the top and bottom margins to one-half inch by following these steps:

Step 1: Access the **F**ile pull-down menu, select Se**t**up, and select **I**nitial Settings (or press Shift-F1,4). Then select Initial **C**odes (**5**).

Note: A split screen, similar to the one that appears in Reveal Codes mode, appears. If initial codes are already established on your system, the codes appear in the bottom half of the screen. Otherwise, the screen appears empty.

Caution: If initial codes are already established on your system, and you share your system with other users, note the codes in use and restore them once you complete the next exercise. Skip Step 2 if the `[Just:Left]` code already appears on the initial codes screen; skip Step 3 if a `[T/B Mar:0.5",0.5"]` code already appears on the Initial Codes screen.

Step 2: Access the **L**ayout pull-down menu and select **L**ine (or press Shift-F8,1). Choose **J**ustification (**3**) and then choose **L**eft (**1**).

Step 3: Press Esc or Cancel (F1) once to return to the main Format menu. Choose **P**age (**2**); then choose **M**argins (**5**).

Step 4: Type **.5** and press Enter to set the top margin; type **.5** and press Enter to set the bottom margin; then press Exit (F7) to restore the Initial Codes screen (see fig. 7.17).

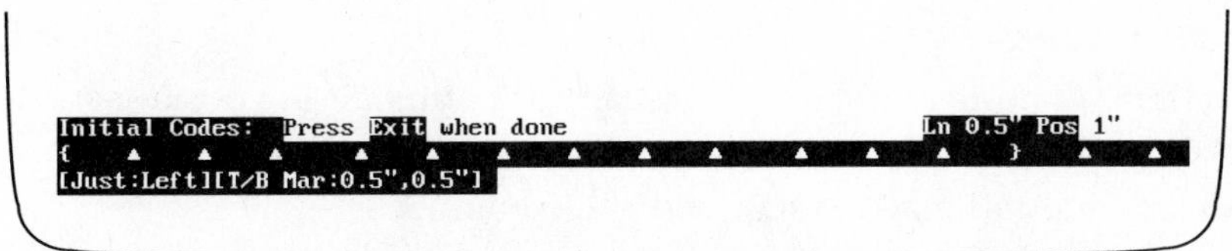

***Fig.** 7.17. The Initial Codes screen, reflecting two settings.*

Step 5: Press Exit (F7) enough times to restore the document screen.

The codes displayed in the Initial Codes screen in figure 7.17 affect all new documents, although you do not see the codes in the new documents. These revised initial codes do not affect the current document or previously created documents stored on disk.

To restore the initial codes in effect before the last exercise, follow these steps:

Step 1: Access the **F**ile pull-down menu, select Set**u**p, and select **I**nitial Settings (or press Shift-F1,4). Choose Initial **C**odes (**5**).

Step 2: If you established a `[Just:Left]` initial code in the preceding exercise, position the cursor on the left-justification code and press Del.

Step 3: If you established a `[T/B Mar:0.5",0.5"]` code in the preceding exercise, position the cursor on the top/bottom margin code and press Del.

Step 4: Press Exit (F7) enough times to restore the document screen.

For Further Reference

If you would like to know more about designing documents, consult *Using WordPerfect*, Special Edition (Que Corporation, Carmel, IN, 1989), Chapter 6.

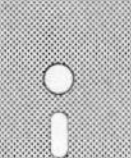

Summary of Concepts

Lesson 7 explains these concepts:

- ❑ Page layout includes setting margins and centering text.
- ❑ You can set top and bottom margins as well as left and right margins.
- ❑ You can center text between top and bottom margins as well as between left and right margins.
- ❑ WordPerfect supports a variety of automatic page-numbering positions and lets you number pages within a header or footer.
- ❑ A document does not have to start with page number 1.
- ❑ You may use up to two headers and two footers in a single document.
- ❑ You can suppress headers, footers, and page numbering on individual pages.
- ❑ You can keep a section of text from being broken by an automatic page break by grouping a number of lines through the Conditional End of Page command, the Block Protect command, or the Widow/Orphan Protection feature.
- ❑ Soft page breaks are created automatically as the total of the text lines, header/footer lines, and margin lines exceed the size of the paper specified to WordPerfect.
- ❑ Use hard page breaks to force text to remain on the current page—regardless of subsequent additions or deletions of text.
- ❑ WordPerfect defines commonly used paper types and sizes supported by the current printer.
- ❑ You can define additional paper types and sizes by accessing the Format: Page, Paper Size/Type menu options.
- ❑ WordPerfect establishes defaults for a variety of settings. Examples of such defaults include full justification and 1-inch margins.
- ❑ You can establish your own codes to control all new documents by entering the preferred settings into the Initial Codes screen.

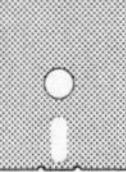

Review Exercises

Practice using the WordPerfect features in this lesson by completing the following exercises. If you do not remember how to do something, review the explanation.

1. Clear the screen without saving the current document, retrieve OFFICES7.LST, and change the top margin to 15.
2. Clear the screen without saving the current document, retrieve OFFICES7.LST, and center the text between top and bottom margins.
3. Access the Print menu to view the centered text in the previous exercise.
4. Specify page numbering in the upper right corner of the current document.
5. Clear the screen without saving the current document and create a new document named FRIENDS.LST. Enter data about four friends, one friend to a page. Use a hard break to separate the four pages. On each page, put in the following pieces of information, with blank lines between items:

   Name:

   Address:

   City, State, ZIP:

   Home phone:

   Work phone:

   Birthday:
6. Establish a header that includes the centered text **List of My Friends**.
7. Set up a footer with the label **yourname—1990** left-aligned and the page number right-aligned.
8. Review the "Determining Available Text Lines" section and compute the number of print lines (including text, header, and footer lines) available on a legal-size form with default margin settings.
9. Define a half-sheet (5.5-by-8.5-inch) paper or form size, suitable for printing memos.
10. Establish an initial code to set left and right margins at 2 inches. Test the results of the 2-inch-margin initial code by typing text into a new document; then restore the original initial code settings.

Using the Speller and Thesaurus

8

In this lesson, you practice these tasks:

- ❏ Install and set up the Speller and Thesaurus
- ❏ Select correct spellings and skip correctly spelled words
- ❏ Edit words and add words to the dictionary
- ❏ Eliminate double words
- ❏ Look up words in the Speller
- ❏ Spell-check blocks
- ❏ Correct irregular case
- ❏ Add words to the dictionary
- ❏ Use the Thesaurus menu
- ❏ Look up words in the Thesaurus
- ❏ Extend a Thesaurus word search
- ❏ View a word in context
- ❏ Replace words with the Thesaurus

Veteran writers and editors consult the dictionary and thesaurus as tools of their trade. WordPerfect's Speller and Thesaurus provide two valuable tools for increasing your writing efficiency and accuracy. The Speller, which contains more than 100,000 words, helps you proofread by searching for spelling mistakes and common typing errors such as transposed, missing, extra, or wrong letters, and double words—like `the the`. You can even look up words when you know what they sound like but do not know how they are spelled.

You can also look up words before you add them to the document, add words to the dictionary, create custom dictionaries, and purchase dictionaries for other languages.

The Speller contains only the correct spelling of words; it does not contain definitions. If you need to look up a word's meaning, use a conventional dictionary. The Speller dictionary also contains correct hyphenation locations for every word WordPerfect includes in the dictionary, making automatic hyphenation with 5.1 work more efficiently (Lesson 6 discusses hyphenation).

Although you can use the mouse to invoke the Speller or Thesaurus from the **T**ools pull-down menu and to select menu options, you cannot select replacement words with the mouse.

Setting Up the Speller and Thesaurus

You can find the Speller and Thesaurus on one 3 1/2-inch disk or two separate 5 1/4-inch disks. To install the Speller and Thesaurus, see the WordPerfect reference manual. Select the Basic choice from the installation options and follow the screen instructions. Make copies of the original disks, store the original disks in a safe place, and use the copies.

The main dictionary file, WP{WP}US.LEX, contains the main and common word lists. A new file, WP{WP}US.SPW, must be located in the same directory as the dictionary files. The first time you add a word to the dictionary, a supplemental dictionary file, WP{WP}US.SUP, is created. WP{WP}US.THS, the main Thesaurus file, contains the Thesaurus's word lists.

Hard disk users have several options for storing Speller and Thesaurus files. The two features can be stored in separate directories on the disk, in one large directory, with other WordPerfect programs, or on a virtual disk. Direct WordPerfect to the location of the Speller and Thesaurus through the Setup (Shift-F1) command.

Changing your WordPerfect Setup is outside the scope of this book. Figure 8.1, however, reproduces a typical Setup: Location of Files screen (accessed through the key combination Shift-F1, **6**), which shows the location of **T**hesaurus/Spell/ Hyphenation main and supplementary files (**3**).

If you do not specify where WordPerfect files are stored, Wordperfect looks for them in the current directory. Once you tell WordPerfect the location of your Speller and Thesaurus files, you need only issue the command to start the Speller or Thesaurus—WordPerfect uses the files specified in Setup.

```
Setup: Location of Files

     1 - Backup Files                      C:\WP51\BACKUP

     2 - Keyboard/Macro Files              C:\WP51\KBMAC

     3 - Thesaurus/Spell/Hyphenation
                       Main                C:\WP51\DIC51
                       Supplementary       C:\WP51\DIC51

     4 - Printer Files                     C:\WP51

     5 - Style Files                       C:\WP51\STYLES
              Library Filename             LIBRARY.STY

     6 - Graphic Files                     C:\WP51\GRAPH51

     7 - Documents                         C:\WP51\QUE51
```

Fig. 8.1. *The Setup: Location of Files screen.*

Using the Speller

WordPerfect's Spell command (Ctrl-F2) compares each word in your document against the words in the dictionary file. The dictionary contains a list of common words most frequently used and a list of main words generally found in dictionaries. WordPerfect checks the common word list first, then the main word list, then, if necessary, any supplementary dictionary. The supplementary dictionary contains words that you add to the Speller.

The spell checker is not a grammar editor. It cannot find typographical errors like `them` instead of `then`. Both of these words are spelled correctly. To catch similar errors, you must still proofread carefully. The Speller does, however, contain some variant words such as `doughnut` and `donut`.

Selecting Correct Words and Adding Words to the Dictionary

After you invoke the Speller, it checks every word of your document with the dictionary. If the word does not appear in the dictionary, the Speller highlights the word and presents a list of possible correct spellings, along with a menu. You can choose an action from the menu or select the correct spelling from the list. If you select a correct spelling, the word you choose replaces the incorrect word in the document.

If the Speller cannot find a correct spelling, the word isn't necessarily misspelled; the word may, for example, be the name of a person or place not ordinarily found in any dictionary. In that case, skip the word or add the word to the supplemental dictionary.

Remember, WordPerfect 5.1 uses the dictionary to determine where to hyphenate words. If you add a word to the dictionary, first insert soft hyphens (press Ctrl and the hyphen key at the same time) at places in the word that can be hyphenated. Soft hyphens appear in printer and screen displays only if the word ends a sentence and is split between two lines.

The document in figure 8.2 offers several opportunities for correcting spelling. To spell-check SPELL8.CHK, follow these steps:

```
I am sory that I will not be abel to attend the comittee bord
meating next week.  I will be in Alamagordo viziting a rellative
sick with newmonya.
```

Fig. 8.2. Spelling errors in the SPELL8.CHK document.

Step 1: Clear the screen without saving the current document and retrieve SPELL8.CHK.

Note: The instruction to clear the screen without saving the current document is used many times throughout the workbook. It means to access the **F**ile pull-down menu and select E**x**it (or press F7); when prompted `Save Document? Yes (No)`, press **N**; when prompted `Exit WP? Yes (No)`, press **N**.

Step 2: Access the **T**ools pull-down menu and select Sp**e**ll (or press Ctrl-F2).

Step 3: The first highlighted word (to indicate a word not in the dictionary) is `sory`. Your screen display should resemble the list of possible correct spellings and the Not Found: menu shown in figure 8.3.

Note: Your options now include selecting an action from the Not Found: menu, pressing Enter to see more words, or pressing a letter that corresponds to the correct spelling shown in the list. If you select a correct spelling, that word replaces `sory`. Spell then looks for more misspelled words.

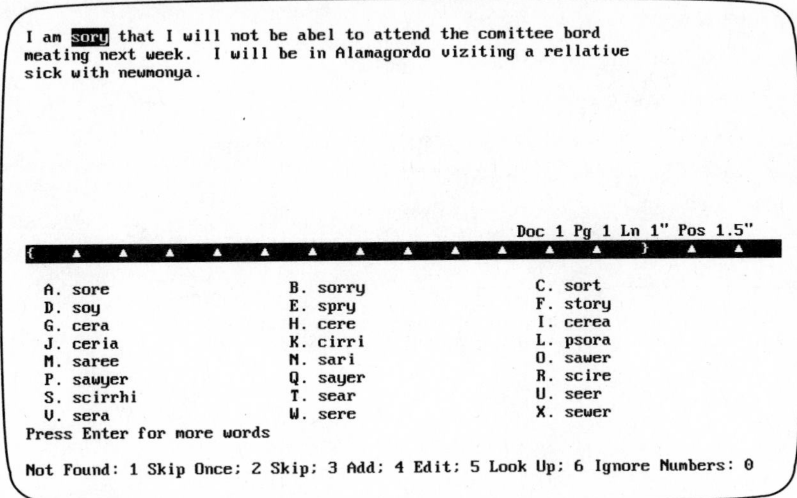

I am sory that I will not be abel to attend the comittee bord
meating next week. I will be in Alamagordo viziting a rellative
sick with newmonya.
Doc 1 Pg 1 Ln 1" Pos 1.5"
A. sore
B. sorry
C. sort
D. soy
E. spry
F. story
G. cera
H. cere
I. cerea
J. ceria
K. cirri
L. psora
M. saree
N. sari
O. sawer
P. sawyer
Q. sayer
R. scire
S. scirrhi
T. sear
U. seer
V. sera
W. sere
X. sewer
Press Enter for more words
Not Found: 1 Skip Once; 2 Skip; 3 Add; 4 Edit; 5 Look Up; 6 Ignore Numbers: 0

Fig. 8.3. *The display of possible spellings and the Not Found: menu.*

Caution: Make a selection from the Not Found: menu by selecting the number of your choice. You do not have the option of selecting by number or letter from this menu.

Step 4: Press Enter to see more words; then press Enter again to see the original list of words.

Step 5: Press **B** to select the correct spelling `sorry`, and notice the automatic correction of the word as well as the shift of highlighting to the next misspelled word.

Step 6: Press **D** to select `able` for `abel`.

Step 7: Press **A** to select `committee` for `comittee`.

Step 8: Press **C** to select `board` for `bord`.

Step 9: Press **C** to select `meeting` for `meating`.

Note: No word list appears for `Alamagordo`, which is spelled correctly but is not in the dictionary. You can add the word to the supplemental dictionary by selecting Add (**3**). If you do not use it again, you may prefer not to add it. Other choices applicable at this point include Skip

Once (1) or Skip (2). Skip (2) ignores `Alamagordo` for the rest of the document. Skip Once (1) ignores the word just one time.

Step 10: Press Skip (2) to skip `Alamagordo` as a misspelling anywhere else in the document.

Step 11: Press **A** to select `visiting` for `viziting`.

Step 12: Press **A** to select `relative` for `rellative`.

Step 13: Press **E** to select `pneumonia` for `newmonya`.

Step 14: Note the word count; follow the screen instructions—`Press any key to continue`—to exit from the Speller.

The document is now correct, as shown in figure 8.4.

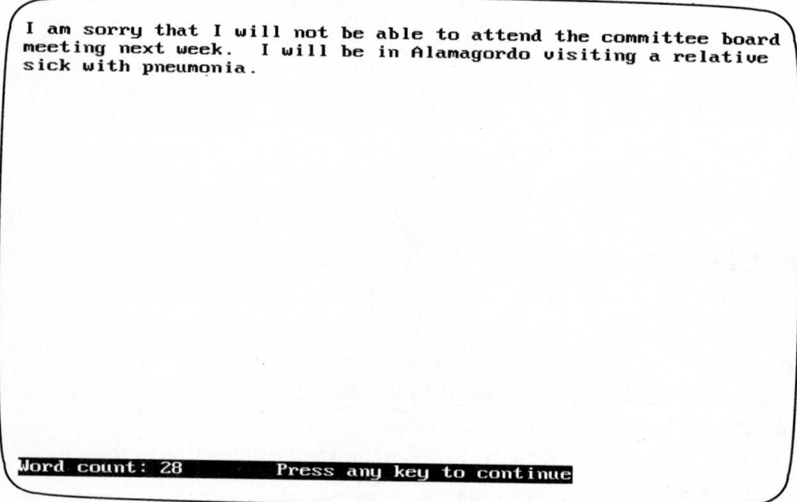

I am sorry that I will not be able to attend the committee board
meeting next week. I will be in Alamagordo visiting a relative
sick with pneumonia.
Word count: 28
Press any key to continue

***Fig. 8.4.** The SPELL8.CHK document, corrected with the Speller.*

Notice how the speller attempts to find the word phonetically, as it does with `newmonya`. In most cases, the correct spelling is among the first five words on the list.

To stop the Speller before the page or document is completely checked, press Cancel (F1). When the Speller completes the spell check or is interrupted, a word count appears at the bottom of the screen (see fig. 8.4). Press any key to return to the current document screen.

Editing Words and Eliminating Double Words

The previous exercise includes a correct word (`Alamagordo`) that is not in the dictionary. When you come to that word, you have several choices. You can skip the word or add it to the dictionary. Other options are available on the Not Found: menu, including editing a misspelled word or deleting duplicate words. Using the SPELL8.LTR document shown in figure 8.5, practice the options Skip, Edit, and Delete 2nd, described next.

If a highlighted word is wrong but is not in the dictionary, you can edit the word. If you select Edit (4), the cursor moves to the misspelled word, and you have full editing control until you press Exit (F7). If two words are run together, move the cursor between the two words and press the space bar. If you just pressed wrong keys, type the word again. You also can type a different word. To return to the Speller, press Exit (F7). The edited word is spell-checked again.

```
Jan 16, 1990


Mr. Fred S. Gefeldt
Artesian Systems, Inc.
560 West Esteban Circle
Amazon, OK  78118

Dear Fred:

Crimson Travel & Tours is introducing a newcorporate reservations
department.  We promise a prompt response to your questions about
schedules and free delivery of tickets to your office or home.

The agents assigned to this department knowthat you have a very
busy schedule.  Their goal is to ensure that your trip is worry
free and that you arrive on on time at your destination.  Our
cruise specialists can assist with incentive as well as pleasure
tours.

We guarantee you the the best service.  Call us the next time your
itinerary takes you across the state or around the world.

Sincerely,


Aimee Lockyer
Senior Account Representative
```

Fig. 8.5. The SPELL8.LTR document.

If the Speller finds a double word, such as `on on`, the Double Word: menu appears at the bottom of the screen (see fig. 8.6). You can skip (**1** or **2**) or edit the double word. An additional choice, Delete 2nd (**3**), removes the second, or duplicate, word. You can also choose the option Disable Double Word Checking (**5**). Type the number of your choice to select from the double-word menu.

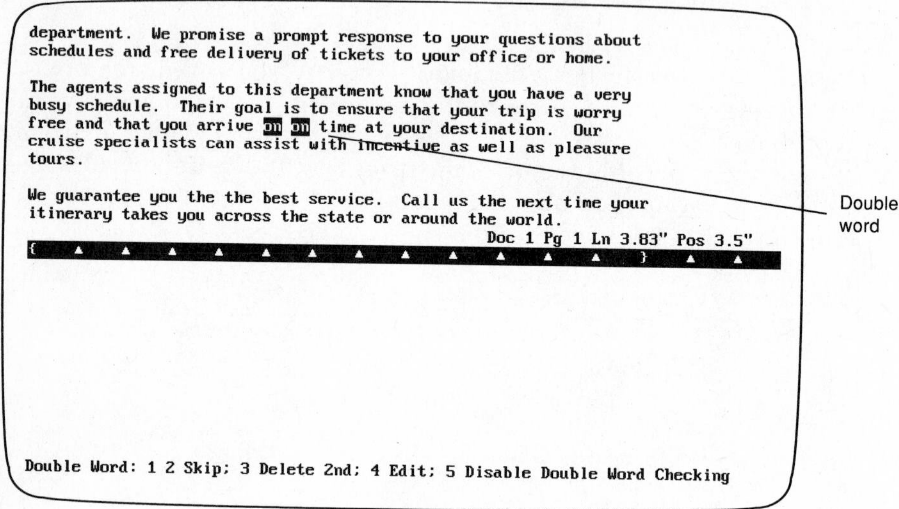
department. We promise a prompt response to your questions about
schedules and free delivery of tickets to your office or home.
The agents assigned to this department know that you have a very
busy schedule. Their goal is to ensure that your trip is worry
free and that you arrive on on time at your destination. Our
cruise specialists can assist with incentive as well as pleasure
tours.
We guarantee you the the best service. Call us the next time your
itinerary takes you across the state or around the world.
Doc 1 Pg 1 Ln 3.83" Pos 3.5"
Double Word: 1 2 Skip; 3 Delete 2nd; 4 Edit; 5 Disable Double Word Checking
Double word

Fig. 8.6. The Double Word: menu.

To spell-check the SPELL8.LTR document, follow these steps:

LESSON
FILES

Step 1: Clear the screen without saving the current document and retrieve SPELL8.LTR.

Step 2: Access the **T**ools pull-down menu and select Spell (or press Ctrl-F2); then select **D**ocument (**3**).

Step 3: Skip the first three spelling errors (`Gefeldt`, `Artesian`, and `Esteban`); they are correct.

Step 4: At the error `newcorporate`, press Edit (**4**).

Step 5: Make sure that WordPerfect is not in typeover mode, move the cursor to the letter `c`, and press the space bar.

Step 6: To return to the Speller, follow the instructions at the bottom of the screen to press Exit (F7).

Step 7: At the error `knowthat`, insert a space between `know` and `that`; press Exit (F7) to return to the Speller.

Step 8: At the error `on on`, note the appearance of the Double Word: menu shown in figure 8.6; press Delete 2nd (**3**).

Step 9: At the error `the the`, press Delete 2nd (**3**).

Step 10: Accept the last two highlighted words by pressing Skip (**2**); to exit from the Speller, follow the screen instructions `Press any key to continue.`

Looking Up a Nondocument Word in the Speller

The Check: menu offers two methods for looking up a word without spell-checking a page or document. You can check a single word in the current document or look up a word independent of the current document.

To spell-check a word in the current document, move the cursor to any character position within the word to be checked. Select the spell-check option **W**ord (**1**). If the word is spelled correctly, the cursor shifts to the next word. Press Exit (F7) to leave the Check: menu. If the word is not spelled correctly, a list of suggested spellings appears on-screen along with the Not Found: menu options.

To check a word that is not part of the document, select the spell-check **L**ook Up (**5**) option. When you see the prompt `Word or word pattern:` in the lower left corner, type the word you want to spell-check. The Speller shows you all possibilities. When you use Look Up, you cannot select a word and automatically insert it in your document. Write down your choice, exit from the Look Up operation, and type the word.

To check the spelling of `recieve` and `good`, follow these steps:

Step 1: Clear the screen without saving the current document.

Step 2: Access the **T**ools pull-down menu and select Spell (or press Ctrl-F2); then select **L**ook Up (**5**).

Step 3: At the prompt `Word or word pattern:`, type **recieve**, press Enter, and notice that the correct spelling `receive` appears as the only suggested spelling.

Step 4: At the prompt `Word or word pattern:`, type **good**, press Enter, and notice the list of quite a few suggested spellings.

Step 5: Press Exit (F7) enough times to restore the current document screen.

Using Wild Card Characters To Look Up a Word

Instead of trying to spell precisely the word you want, use an asterisk (*) to replace an unknown number of characters or a question mark (?) to replace a single unknown character. The Speller displays all words that match that pattern.

To look up `na?al` and `na*al`, follow these steps:

Step 1: Access the **T**ools pull-down menu and select Sp**e**ll (or press Ctrl-F2); then select **L**ook Up (**5**).

Step 2: At the prompt `Word or word pattern:`, type **na?al** and press Enter. A list of three words appears.

Step 3: At the prompt `Word or word pattern:`, type **na*al** and press Enter. A longer list of words appears.

Step 4: Press Exit (F7) enough times to restore the current document screen.

Spell-Checking a Block

To spell-check part of the whole document, use Block. Remember that you can spell-check a word, a page, or a whole document by using the Check: menu. You can spell-check blocks of text by highlighting the block, then selecting Spell. The Check: menu is bypassed, and checking begins immediately. If a word is not found, the Not Found: menu and word list appear.

To spell-check paragraph two of the SPELL8.LTR document, follow these steps:

Step 1: Clear the screen without saving the current document and retrieve SPELL8.LTR.

Step 2: Position the cursor at the start of the second paragraph (starting at `The agents...`), press Block (Alt-F4 or F12), and highlight the entire paragraph.

Step 3: Access the **T**ool pull-down menu and select Sp**e**ll (or press Ctrl-F2); make necessary corrections.

Step 4: Exit from the Speller and restore the current document.

Correcting Irregular Case

The WordPerfect 5.1 speller checks for irregular case. For example, if you type `BOston`, the speller stops and presents the Irregular Case: menu, shown in figure 8.7.

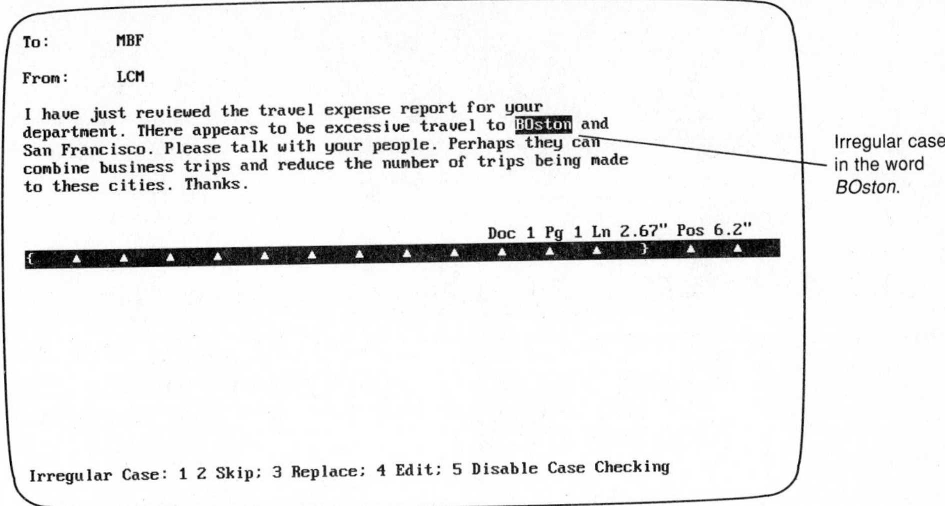
To: MBF

From: LCM

I have just reviewed the travel expense report for your department. THere appears to be excessive travel to BOston and San Francisco. Please talk with your people. Perhaps they can combine business trips and reduce the number of trips being made to these cities. Thanks.

Doc 1 Pg 1 Ln 2.67" Pos 6.2"

Irregular Case: 1 2 Skip; 3 Replace; 4 Edit; 5 Disable Case Checking

Irregular case in the word *BOston*.

Fig. 8.7. *The Irregular Case: menu.*

Using the Irregular Case: menu, you can choose Skip—option (**1**) or (**2**)—to skip the word, thus accepting it; Replace (**3**) to accept the word; Edit (**4**) to edit the word manually; or Disable Case Checking (**5**). If a document contains several valid words, acronyms, or formulas with irregular case, disable case-checking.

To spell-check a document with irregular-case errors, follow these steps:

LESSON FILES

Step 1: Clear the screen without saving the current document and retrieve TRAVEL8.MEM.

Step 2: Access the **T**ools pull-down menu and select Sp**e**ll (or press Ctrl-F2); then select **D**ocument (**3**).

Step 3: Press Skip (**2**) when you are prompted to correct the initials `MBF` and `LCM`.

Step 4: Press Replace (**3**) when you are prompted by the Irregular Case: menu to correct `THere` and `BOston`.

Using the Thesaurus

The Thesaurus can add freshness and variety to your writing by suggesting alternative words. The Thesaurus also helps you search for just the right word.

Suppose, for example, that you want to describe someone as *nice* but want a more forceful or professional word. Select the Thesaurus and choose the option for looking up a word. When you are prompted, type **nice**. A list of synonyms and antonyms appears. You can direct the Thesaurus to explore any of the words on-screen.

To use the Thesaurus, though, you must know how to spell the word. If you are unsure of the spelling, use the Speller to look up the word, incorporating the wild-card characters * and ?.

Starting the Thesaurus

You can start the Thesaurus in several ways. You can generate a list of words associated with another, specific word by placing the cursor on any character within the word and starting the Thesaurus (Alt-F1). As an alternative, you can place the cursor on a blank line and press Thesaurus (Alt-F1). At the prompt `Word:` in the lower left corner of the screen, enter the word you want to look up in the Thesaurus. The MEMO8.THE document shown in figure 8.8 provides several opportunities for using the Thesaurus.

To access MEMO8.THE and look up `permit`, follow these steps:

LESSON FILES

Step 1: Clear the screen without saving the current document and retrieve MEMO8.THE.

```
May 21, 1990

Memorandum

To:       MBF

From:     LCM

I have just interviewed Linda Ann and feel she would fit your
operation nicely.  Linda's educational background is just what
you need.  Her personality is super and would permit her to work
effectively with others.  Based on Linda's work experience she is
bright, resourceful and certainly not lazy.  Please include her
in your schedule of interviews.  Thanks.




C:\ATIWP\MEMO8.THE                          Doc 1 Pg 1 Ln 1" Pos 1"
```

Fig. 8.8. *The MEMO8.THE document.*

Step 2: Move the cursor to any letter in the word `permit`.

Step 3: Access the **T**ools pull-down menu and select **T**hesaurus (or press Alt-F1).

You invoked the Thesaurus and looked up the word where the cursor was positioned. Now look at the Thesaurus menu in figure 8.9.

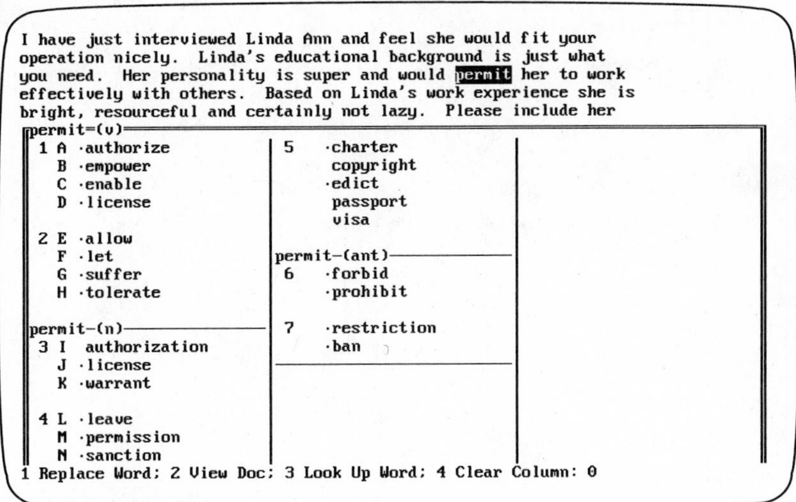

***Fig. 8.9.** The Thesaurus word list for* `permit`.

Understanding the Thesaurus Menu

The Thesaurus display shown in figure 8.9 has three basic parts: the text, the word list, and the menu. The text at the top of the page shows the word being looked up (highlighted) and the text surrounding the word.

The typical word list contains several pieces of information:

- The *headword* (`permit` in fig. 8.9) precedes each grouping of similar words.
- The *part of speech* refers to the types of words that follow. In WordPerfect, parts of speech include adjectives (`a`), nouns (`n`), verbs (`v`), and antonyms (`ant`). In figure 8.9, (`v`), (`n`), and (`ant`) apply.
- *Subgroups* of words organize synonyms and antonyms by meaning or part of speech. For example, figure 8.9 shows seven numbered

subgroups. Subgroup 1 lists four action verbs. Subgroup 2 suggests four verbs suitable in a passive context. Subgroup 6 lists antonyms that are verbs, whereas subgroup 7 lists antonyms that are nouns.

- The *reference menu* indicates the letters (A through N in fig. 8.9) left of each word. Press the letter that corresponds to the replacement word you want or to a word that may offer more Thesaurus word choices.
- *Bullets* (the small dots at the left of the words), denote words that are themselves headwords.

The Thesaurus menu appears on the status line. Type the number of your choice to select from the Thesaurus menu. Your options include these:

- Replace Word (**1**)

  Select a word from the word list to replace the word that you looked up.
- View Doc (**2**)

  Scroll the text at the top of the page for a better sense of the context around the original word.
- Look Up Word (**3**)

  Type a new word or point to a reference number from the word list for a new word. Words with bullets that appear on the word list are also headwords that contain related words to consider.
- Clear Column (**4**)

  Clear all words from the current column.

Using a Thesaurus Suggestion To Replace a Word

To complete the search for a synonym to replace `permit`, select `enable` from the word list by following these steps:

Step 1: Choose Replace Word (**1**).

Step 2: Note the status line prompt `Press letter for word` and press **C** to select `enable`.

WordPerfect returns to the current document screen. Inspect the MEMO8.THE document. `Permit` changes to `enable` .

Extending a Thesaurus Word Search

Sometimes you must be more creative about searching for your word. When the first list of words does not offer a suitable synonym or antonym, extend the search with words on the first list. To illustrate an extended search for a replacement of the word `super`, follow these steps:

Step 1: Position the cursor within the word `super`.

Step 2: Access the **T**ools pull-down menu and select **T**hesaurus (or press Alt-F1).

Note: A blank word list and the message `Word not found:` appear. The message appears for only a moment in the lower left corner of the screen. At the next prompt—`Word:`—type any word that generally describes what you want to say.

Step 3: Type **nice** and press Enter.

Note: The newly generated word list offers you several possibilities (see fig. 8.10). Assume that `congenial` seems the best replacement choice, but extend the search on `congenial` to look for an even better word. If the word for the extended search appears on the screen with a bullet in front of it, simply press the letter to the left of the bullet. If the word does not appear on the screen or appears without a bullet, you must select Look Up Word (3) and type the word.

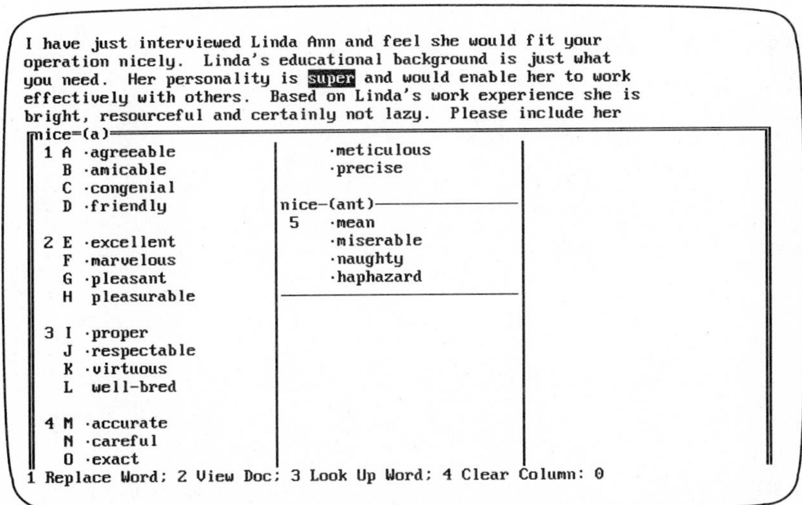

Fig. 8.10. *The Thesaurus word list for nice.*

Step 4: Press **C** to view extended search results in the second column.

Note: The second word list, shown in figure 8.11, appears. The reference letters (`A`, `B`, `C`) move to the new list. Choosing a word from the old list now requires clearing the current column.

```
I have just interviewed Linda Ann and feel she would fit your
operation nicely.  Linda's educational background is just what
you need.  Her personality is super and would enable her to work
effectively with others.  Based on Linda's work experience she is
bright, resourceful and certainly not lazy.  Please include her
nice=(a)                  congenial=(a)
 1    ·agreeable           1 A ·affable
      ·amicable              B ·agreeable
      ·congenial             C ·cordial
      ·friendly              D ·pleasant
                             E ·sociable
 2    ·excellent
      ·marvelous           2 F ·compatible
      ·pleasant              G ·harmonious
       pleasurable           H ·sympathetic

 3    ·proper             congenial-(ant)
      ·respectable         3 I ·unpleasant
      ·virtuous
      well-bred

 4    ·accurate
      ·careful
      ·exact
1 Replace Word; 2 View Doc; 3 Look Up Word; 4 Clear Column: 0
```

Fig. 8.11. *The extended Thesaurus word list for* `nice`.

Step 5: Choose Clear Column (**4**).

Step 6: Press the up arrow and down arrow to scroll the contents of the column so that the screen appears the same as the one in figure 8.10 when you finish.

Step 7: Press the left arrow and right arrow to switch the reference letters between the first and second column. Be sure that the reference letters are in the first column when you finish.

Step 8: Press Replace Word (**1**) and press **C** to select `congenial`.

Looking Up a Nondocument Word in the Thesaurus

To look up a word not included in the current document, place the cursor on a blank line and press Thesaurus (Alt-F1). Because you have not specified a word for the Thesaurus to look up, blank columns and the prompt `Word:` appear. Type the word that is to be the object of the search.

To look up *fabulous*, which is not in the current document, follow these steps:

Step 1: Move the cursor to a blank line.

Step 2: Access the **T**ools pull-down menu and select **T**hesaurus (or press Alt-F1).

Step 3: At the prompt `Word:`, type **fabulous** and press Enter.

Step 4: After viewing the list of synonyms and antonyms for *fabulous*, press Exit (F7) to return to the current document screen without selecting a new word.

The Thesaurus is a simple but powerful WordPerfect feature that can improve your written work. Use it to find just the right words to say what you mean or to vary your usual choice of words.

For Further Reference

If you would like to learn more about using the Thesaurus and Speller, consult *Using WordPerfect 5.1*, Special Edition (Que Corporation, Carmel, IN, 1989), Chapter 7 and Appendix A.

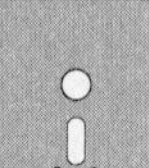

Summary of Concepts

Lesson 8 explains these concepts:

- ❑ WordPerfect 5.1 includes Speller and Thesaurus features.
- ❑ Use the Setup: Location of Files menu to direct WordPerfect to the Speller and Thesaurus utility files.
- ❑ You can spell-check any word in the current document or look up a word not in the current document.
- ❑ You can spell-check a word, a page, an entire document, or you can limit the check to a specified block.
- ❑ When you use the Speller, WordPerfect highlights any word that does not appear in its dictionaries. You can skip, replace, edit, or add the word to the WordPerfect dictionary system.
- ❑ Spell-checking includes searching for double words and finding irregularities in case.
- ❑ Use Cancel (F1) to end a spell-check operation before it is complete or to cancel a word search in the Thesaurus.
- ❑ You can find synonyms and antonyms for any word in the current document or specify a Thesaurus search on a word not in the current document.
- ❑ You can increase the number of words from the original word list produced in a Thesaurus operation.
- ❑ To replace a word in the current document, choose a reference letter from the list of words.

Review Exercises

Practice using the WordPerfect features in this lesson by completing the following exercises. If you do not remember how to do something, review the explanation and practice the tasks again.

1. Clear the screen without saving the current document.
2. Create a short paragraph summarizing your reaction to the Speller and Thesaurus capabilities of WordPerfect 5.1. Include a few misspelled words, at least one double word, and some descriptive adjectives such as *wonderful*. Type your name at the end.
3. Save the document created in the preceding exercise as SPELL.TST.
4. Spell-check the entire SPELL.TST document, correct any misspellings, delete the second of any double words, and add your name to the dictionary.
5. Spell-check a word not in your new document.
6. Clear the screen without saving the corrected document and retrieve SPELL.TST, which contains the original errors.
7. Block the first half of the paragraph and spell-check only the marked block.
8. Clear the screen without saving the current document, access a blank document screen, and look up various spellings of `b?ke` and `b*ke`.
9. Type the sentence **Now is the time for all good men to come to the aid of their country**.
10. With the Thesaurus, find a substitute for `aid`, and replace the original word.
11. Look up *simple* in the Thesaurus.
12. Find an antonym for *end* in the Thesaurus.

Printing a WordPerfect Document

9

DISK TUTOR

If you haven't yet explored the Disk Tutor, you might want to complete the appropriate tutorial lesson before continuing with this book lesson. If you have already run the tutorial, you might want to run it again and review the pertinent options. The part of the tutorial relevant to this lesson is

- ❑ Lesson H: Print a Document

If you complete the options on the Disk Tutor, you will be more familiar with the techniques and commands found in this lesson.

In this lesson, you practice these tasks:

- ❑ Select a printer from a list of installed printers
- ❑ Print multiple copies
- ❑ Select print quality
- ❑ Print from disk, using the main Print menu
- ❑ Print by using List Files
- ❑ View and control printer status
- ❑ Determine printer capabilities

With all of WordPerfect 5.1's sophisticated tools to aid you in composing and formatting a document, you can lose sight of the program's primary function: committing your words to paper. Many WordPerfect print features have been redesigned in version 5.1 to take advantage of the latest advances in printer technology.

In this lesson, you examine several important aspects of printing. First, select the printer you are using. Next, select the print quality and number of copies to be printed. You can queue several documents to print, change the order of the queue, temporarily halt the printing of a document, restart a print job, and cancel one or more print commands.

WordPerfect 5.1 offers three test documents that help you determine the capabilities of your current printer. Remember, for example, from Lesson 6 that you can compose characters and symbols not on your keyboard. One of the test documents tells you which composed characters your printer can print.

Using Options on the Main Print Menu

The main Print menu (see fig. 9.1) controls printing and printer-related activities. Seven Print menu choices control printing the current document or a document on disk, printing selected (multiple) pages, viewing the document on-screen, and initializing the printer.

```
Print

     1 - Full Document
     2 - Page
     3 - Document on Disk
     4 - Control Printer
     5 - Multiple Pages
     6 - View Document
     7 - Initialize Printer

Options

     S - Select Printer                  HP LaserJet Series II
     B - Binding Offset                  0"
     N - Number of Copies                1
     U - Multiple Copies Generated by    WordPerfect
     G - Graphics Quality                Medium
     T - Text Quality                    High



Selection: 0
```

Fig. 9.1. *The main Print menu.*

Six additional *options* control printer-related activities. You can select which printer you are using or install a new printer. You can specify a binding offset, which adds extra room to inside margins that are to be bound or hole-punched. Use this menu to specify the number of copies to be printed and to indicate whether WordPerfect 5.1 or the printer controls making copies. You can also select printing draft-quality, medium-quality, or high-quality text and graphics.

You have learned several features shown on the Print menu. In Lesson 3 you used **Full Document (1)** to print the entire current document and **Page (2)** to print the page in the document marked by the current cursor position. In Lessons 6 and 7 you used the **View Document (6)** option to see the effects of settings not visible on the document screen (such as right justification).

Initializing the Printer

You should initialize the printer at the start of each WordPerfect 5.1 editing session only if you have a printer that uses soft fonts. *Soft fonts* are stored on disk and downloaded as needed to a laser printer's internal memory. Complete the following steps only if you use soft fonts and have not yet initialized your printer during the current editing session:

Step 1: Access the **File** pull-down menu and select **Print** (or press Shift-F7). Select **Initialize Printer (7)**.

Step 2: In response to the prompt `Proceed with Printer Initialization? No (Yes)`, press **Y**.

Do not print until indicators quit flashing on the laser printer. It may take several minutes to download all the soft fonts.

Selecting the Printer

Printers are like people from around the world; they do not speak the same language. Printer manufacturers, in an effort to differentiate themselves and provide unique features, have developed proprietary printer command languages. Even different models of the same manufacturer may use incompatible commands.

WordPerfect has researched hundreds of available printers and developed printer files for most printers. Printer files translate the formatting codes in your document to the command language of the printer attached to your computer. These files are stored on the Printer disks shipped with WordPerfect 5.1. When WordPerfect 5.1 was installed on your system, one or more printers should have been specified for use.

Once printers are installed, but before you print, you must access the Print: Select Printer menu and select the printer you want to use. Once you select a printer, it remains the default printer until you make another selection. To view the process of using the Print menu to select a printer without changing the current printer, follow these steps:

Step 1: Access the **File** pull-down menu and select **Print** (or press Shift-F7).

Step 2: Choose **Select Printer (S)**.

Note: You should see a Print: Select Printer menu similar to the one illustrated in figure 9.2. The list of installed printers on your menu may vary. To select a printer, highlight the printer and choose **S**elect (**1**). Do not choose a printer different from the default printer in this exercise.

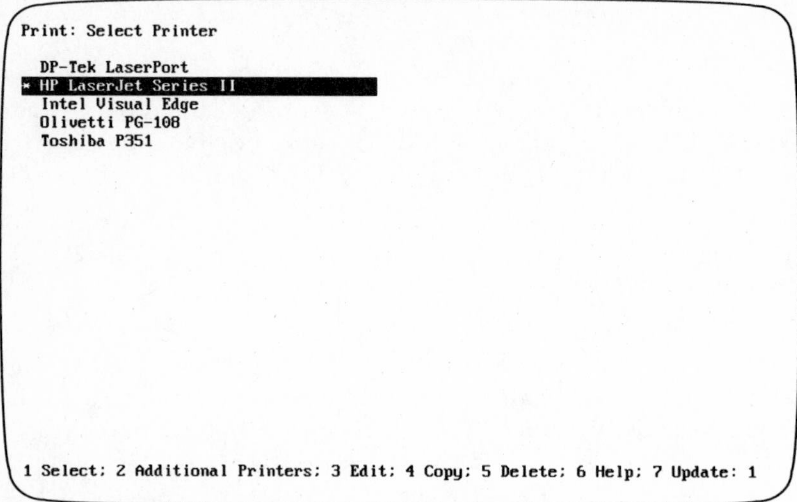

Fig. 9.2. *The Print: Select Printer menu.*

Step 3: Press Cancel (F1) or Exit (F7) until the document screen appears on your monitor.

Selecting Print Quantity

If you need more than one copy of the print job, select from the print options **N**umber of Copies (**N**). Some printers can reprint a job a number of times after receiving the printer information only once. If your printer has this capability, specify M**u**ltiple Copies Generated (**U**), then **P**rinter (**2**) to increase print speed.

To print multiple copies of the ANNOUNC9.DOC document, follow these steps:

Step 1: Clear the screen without saving the current document and retrieve the ANNOUNC9.DOC document.

Note: The instruction to clear the screen without saving the current document is used many times throughout the *WordPerfect PC Tutor*. It means to access the **F**ile pull-down menu and select Exit (or press

F7); when prompted Save Document? **Y**es (**N**o), press **N**; when prompted Exit WP? **N**o (**Y**es), press **N**.

Step 2: Access the **F**ile pull-down menu and select **P**rint (or press Shift-F7).

Step 3: Choose **N**umber of Copies (**N**), type **2**, and press Enter.

Step 4: Choose M**u**ltiple Copies Generated by (**U**).

Step 5: Choose **P**rinter (**2**) from the menu at the bottom of the screen to speed printing.

Note: If your printer cannot print multiple copies without the help of WordPerfect 5.1, the Multiple Copies Generated setting changes back to **W**ordPerfect (**1**).

Step 6: Choose **F**ull Document (**1**).

Two copies of the ANNOUNC9.DOC document are printed. The **P**rinter (**2**) option is useful to laser printer users because the document does not have to be formatted twice, once for each time it is printed.

Selecting Print Quality

Use the **G**raphics Quality (**G**) option on the Print menu to control the degree of resolution (sharpness) that the printer uses to print graphics images. Use the **T**ext Quality (**T**) option to control the sharpness of text in a document. There are four options on both menus. Use Do **N**ot Print (**1**) if your printer experiences problems printing text and graphics together. Print graphics or text first; then feed the paper through again and print the other.

You may choose **D**raft (**2**), **M**edium (**3**), or **H**igh (**4**) resolution output. As you increase resolution, you also increase printing time and wear on the printer ribbon or cartridge. Medium resolution usually produces a very good document.

To set both graphics and text to medium resolution and to restore the current document screen without executing a print command, follow these steps:

Step 1: Access the **F**ile pull-down menu and select **P**rint (or press Shift-F7).

Step 2: Choose **G**raphics Quality (**G**); then choose **M**edium (**3**).

Step 3: Choose **T**ext Quality (**T**); then choose **M**edium (**3**).

Step 4: Press Exit (F7) until you return to the current document screen.

Text and graphics quality settings are document-specific. They remain in effect for that document until you change them.

Changing a Print Menu Default

If you change Print menu defaults frequently, you can change them "permanently" by using the Setup: Print Options menu. For example, if you print many variations of a document before you produce a final copy, you can change the print quality defaults from Medium for graphics and High for text to Draft for both settings. Then, on the less frequent occasions when you need medium-quality or high-quality text, make the change on the Print menu. To alter permanent settings, just access the Setup menu, access the initial settings submenu, choose the print options, and make the required changes. Figure 9.3 illustrates the Setup: Print Options menu.

```
Setup: Print Options

     1 - Binding Offset                    0"

     2 - Number of Copies                  1
         Multiple Copies Generated by      WordPerfect

     3 - Graphics Quality                  Medium

     4 - Text Quality                      High

     5 - Redline Method                    Printer Dependent

     6 - Size Attribute Ratios - Fine      60%
         (% of Normal)          Small      80%
                                Large      120%
                           Very Large      150%
                          Extra Large      200%
                      Super/Subscript      60%



Selection: 0
```

Fig. 9.3. *The Setup: Print Options menu.*

Options 1 through 4 are explained in a previous section that introduces the Print menu options. Select **R**edline Method (**5**) to mark printed text by placing a small character under each letter to be marked or a symbol in the margin next to each line that is to be marked. One use for redline is to highlight changes to a document.

Select **S**ize Attribute Ratios (**6**) to alter the default percentage differences of selected fonts in relation to the current base font. To understand this option, assume that the current base font is Dutch Roman 14pt, which you specified after accessing the Font (Ctrl-F8), Base **F**ont (**4**) menu. Further assume that you now select a font by size such as Very Large after accessing the Font (Ctrl-F8), **S**ize (**1**) menu (refer to

Lesson 6). Text affected by the new font setting is 150 percent larger than the previous text, according to the default percentage for Very Large shown in figure 9.3. Use the Setup: Print Options menu to change default percentages.

To practice changing, then restoring your Print menu defaults, follow these steps:

Step 1: Access the **File** pull-down menu, select Set**u**p, and select **I**nitial Settings (or press Shift-F1,4); then choose **P**rint Options (**8**).

Step 2: Choose **S**ize Attribute Ratios (**6**).

Step 3: Press Enter three times to position the cursor on 150%, defining Very Large.

Step 4: Type **175** and press Enter.

Step 5: Press Exit (F7) enough times to restore the current document.

Note: Until you repeat the process to change the Very Large size attribute ratio, selecting the Very Large font by size (refer to Lesson 6) produces text 175 percent larger than the base font instead of 150 percent larger than the base font.

Step 6: To restore the original specification for the Very Large ratio, access the **F**ile pull-down menu, select Set**u**p, and select **I**nitial Settings (or press Shift-F1,4). Choose **P**rint Options (**8**).

Step 7: Choose **S**ize Attribute Ratios (**6**) and press Enter three times to position the cursor on 150%, defining Very Large.

Step 8: Type 150, press Enter, and press Exit (F7) enough times to restore the current document.

You have just practiced selecting several important options from the Print menu and changing a Print menu default by using the Setup: Print Options menu. You will use these options frequently.

Printing from Disk

Using WordPerfect, you can print a document directly from disk without displaying the document on-screen. You can perform this operation from the main Print menu or from the List Files screen. The time it takes to print from disk varies according to the Fast Save setting (on or off) in effect at the time the document was saved.

When you print from disk, you can specify all pages (the default) or only selected pages. Specify individual pages separated by commas and continuous pages separated by hyphens. For example, to limit a document printout to pages 1, 3, and 5 through 15, type **1,3,5-15** and press Enter in response to the prompt `Pages: (All)`.

Understanding the Fast Save Feature

To reduce the time to save a document, WordPerfect does not store formatting specifications if the Fast Save feature is active (the default in WordPerfect 5.1). On the other hand, WordPerfect 5.1 must then take additional time to format when you print the document. If you turn Fast Save off, you increase the time needed to save a document but decrease the time needed to print a document.

To turn Fast Save on or off, follow these steps:

Step 1: Access the **F**ile pull-down menu, select Se**t**up, and select **E**nvironment (or press Shift-F1,3).

Step 2: Select **F**ast Save (unformatted) (**5**) and then select **Y**es or **N**o.

Step 3: Press Exit (F7) to return to the current document screen.

Printing from Disk, Using the Main Print Menu

When you know the name of the file you want to print, use the following method to type the name of the file and to specify the pages you want printed.

You must know the complete file name before you start this operation. No provision is made for looking at the List Files screen once you press Print.

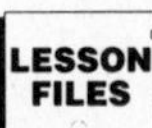

To print from disk by using the Print menu, follow these steps:

Step 1: Access the **F**ile pull-down menu and select **P**rint (or press Shift-F7).

Step 2: Choose **D**ocument on Disk (**3**).

Step 3: Type the file name CRIMSON9.LTR and press Enter. The message `Page(s): (All)` appears at the bottom of the screen.

Step 4: Press Enter to print the entire document.

Note: If you have a printer different from the one in use at the time the lesson-disk files were stored, you see the prompt `Document not formatted for current printer. Continue? No (Yes)`. If you do not see the message, skip to Step 6.

Step 5: Choose **Y**es to continue printing. The message `Formatting for current printer` appears briefly in the lower left corner of the screen.

Step 6: Press Exit (F7) to restore the current document screen.

Printing from Disk, Using List Files (F5)

If you are unsure about the name of the file you want to print, use List Files (F5) to display the files. You can highlight the file and instruct WordPerfect to print it.

To print with List Files, follow these steps:

Step 1: Access the **File** pull-down menu and select **List Files** (or press F5); then press Enter to display the list of *WordPerfect PC Tutor* Lesson files on the current directory.

Step 2: Move the highlight bar to CRIMSON9.LTR.

Step 3: Choose **Print** (**4**).

Step 4: When you are prompted `Pages: (All)`, press Enter to print the entire document.

Step 5: If you see the prompt `Document not formatted for current printer. Continue? No (Yes)`, press **Y** to format the document for the current printer and to complete the print operation.

Step 6: Press Exit (F7) until the current document appears on-screen.

Controlling the Printer

WordPerfect 5.1's Control Printer feature is a powerful tool for managing printing activities. You can cancel individual print jobs, cancel all jobs, or display a list of all jobs waiting to be printed. You can move any print job to the top of the list. You can even suspend printing temporarily and then resume printing if the printer jams or needs a new ribbon.

Viewing Current Print Jobs

The Print: Control Printer screen shown in figure 9.4 illustrates the organization of current print-job information. The most important print job is the one currently printing. WordPerfect maintains constant watch over the status of the print job and continually updates the Control Printer screen.

```
Print: Control Printer

Current Job

Job Number: None                              Page Number:  None
Status:     No print jobs                     Current Copy: None
Message:    None
Paper:      None
Location:   None
Action:     None


Job List

Job  Document             Destination         Print Options



Additional Jobs Not Shown: 0



1 Cancel Job(s); 2 Rush Job; 3 Display Jobs; 4 Go (start printer); 5 Stop: 0
```

Fig. 9.4. *The Print: Control Printer screen, showing no print jobs.*

Current print-job information includes the following items:

- *Job Number*: Numbers each print job sequentially during the current editing session.
- *Status*: Indicates what action WordPerfect 5.1 is taking with the current print job.
- *Message*: Provides a brief description of problems or displays `None`.
- *Paper*: Reflects the paper size defined for the current print job (refer to Lesson 7).
- *Location*: Reflects the location of paper for the current print job.
- *Action*: Prompts for user activity required before printing continues, or displays `None`.
- *Page Number*: Indicates which page number is printing, according to WordPerfect 5.1. The number on-screen may, however, not be the page number you see on the printer. If your printer has a buffer—extra memory—the page indicated may still be in the printer's buffer, waiting to be printed.
- *Current Copy*: Indicates how many copies are to be printed and which copy is currently printing.

Information about other jobs waiting to print also appears on this screen under Job List, including the name, source (screen or disk file), and destination (such as LPT1, indicating a standard parallel printer). Special Print Options, such as Rush, are also indicated.

Using the Control Printer Menu

The bottom line of the Print: Control Printer screen (see fig. 9.4) presents five printer control options: Cancel Job(s), **R**ush Job, **D**isplay Jobs, **G**o (start printer), and **S**top. Use **C**ancel Job(s) to terminate one or more print jobs. Type the number of the job to be canceled or an asterisk (*) to cancel all jobs. You are asked to confirm this request.

Use **R**ush Job (**2**) to print any job immediately, no matter how far down it is in the list of waiting jobs. If you interrupt a job currently printing, WordPerfect 5.1 automatically resumes printing when the rush job finishes. WordPerfect 5.1 prompts you to change forms if necessary. **D**isplay Jobs (**3**) displays waiting jobs not shown on the current screen. **G**o (start printer) (**4**) resumes printing after a form change or if the job is halted through the use of **S**top (**5**). Use **S**top (**5**) to stop or suspend printing without canceling the print job.

To view print-job status and practice using Control Printer menu options, set up two print jobs and stop printing. Ordinarily you interrupt jobs waiting to print by using **S**top (**5**) on the Control Print menu. The lesson files are so short, however, that both jobs will print before you can abort printing through the use of menus. To force a halt in printing for this exercise, take your printer off-line. Follow these steps to set up printing two files and access the Print: Control Printer screen:

Step 1: Take your printer out of Ready mode, or turn it off temporarily.

Step 2: Access the **F**ile pull-down menu and select List **F**iles (or press F5) and press Enter to access the current directory.

Step 3: Highlight ANNOUNC9.DOC and choose **P**rint (**4**).

Step 4: When you are prompted `Page(s): (All)`, press Enter.

Step 5: If you are prompted `Document not formatted for current printer. Continue? No (Yes)`, press **Y**.

Step 6: Highlight CRIMSON9.LTR and choose **P**rint (**4**).

Step 7: When you are prompted `Page(s): (All)`, press Enter.

Step 8: If you are prompted `Document not formatted for current printer. Continue? No (Yes)`, press **Y**.

Step 9: Press Exit (F7) until the current document returns to the screen.

Step 10: Access the **F**ile pull-down menu and select **P**rint (or press Shift-F7). Choose **C**ontrol Printer (**4**).

The Print: Control Printer menu (see fig. 9.5) should appear on-screen. Notice that two jobs appear on the job list. The status of job 1—your jobs may be numbered differently if you have previously printed a document—is `Printing`. The message `Printer not accepting characters` and the action `Check cable, make sure printer is turned ON` appear on-screen because the printer is not in ready mode. Do not ready your printer yet.

```
Print: Control Printer

Current Job

Job Number: 1                                   Page Number:  1
Status:     Printing                            Current Copy: 1 of 1
Message:    Printer not accepting characters
Paper:      None
Location:   None
Action:     Check cable, make sure printer is turned ON


Job List

Job  Document             Destination          Print Options
 1   (Disk File)          LPT 1                Text=Draft
 2   (Disk File)          LPT 1                Text=Draft


Additional Jobs Not Shown: 0



1 Cancel Job(s); 2 Rush Job; 3 Display Jobs; 4 Go (start printer); 5 Stop: 0
```

Fig. 9.5. The Print: Control Print screen—print jobs pending.

Rushing a Print Job

Use the **R**ush Job (**2**) option to advance a particular job to immediate printing. To move job 2 into position for printing, follow these steps:

Step 1: Choose **R**ush Job (**2**).

Step 2: When you are prompted `Rush which job? 2`, press Enter.

Job 1 and job 2 change places on the job list. In addition, the print option for job 2 now reads `RUSH, Text=Draft`. To move job 1 back into position for printing, repeat Steps 1 and 2, specifying that job 1 should be rushed.

Canceling a Print Job

To cancel a print job waiting on the print list, use the **C**ancel (**1**) option. If you cancel the job currently printing, press Enter. If the printer does not respond immediately, you may see the message `Press Enter if printer doesn't respond.` To cancel the current print job, follow these steps:

Step 1: Choose **C**ancel Job(s) (**1**).

Step 2: When you are prompted `Cancel which job? (*=All Jobs)`, press Enter to indicate the current job.

The current job is removed from the screen, and the next job on the list becomes the current job.

Restarting a Print Job

To restart a job, use the **G**o (start printer) (**4**) option located at the bottom of the Print: Control Printer screen. If the job consists of one page or if printing is suspended on page 1, then printing restarts on page 1. If, however, printing is halted on a page number other than 1, you are prompted to indicate a restart page.

The current print job is stopped according to the `Status:` line. The indicated `Action:` is `Fix printer (check cable, make sure printer is turned ON) press "G" to restart, "C" to cancel.` Be sure to read all messages on-screen and take appropriate action before you restart.

To restart printing, follow these steps:

Step 1: Put the printer on-line to clear the action message.

Step 2: Choose **G**o (start printer) (**4**) to restart the print job.

Note: The Current Job status report now indicates that no jobs are waiting to print.

Step 3: Press Exit (F7) to restore the current document screen.

Determining Your Printer's Capabilities

WordPerfect 5.1 provides three documents to help you determine your printer's capabilities. One document, PRINTER.TST, tests how well the currently selected printer definition can produce a variety of text *sizes* and *appearances*. The one-page output varies with the base fonts available. Figure 9.6 illustrates a printout of the PRINTER.TST document on a LaserJet Series II printer. The base fonts available at the time include Swiss and Dutch Times Roman fonts up to point size 36.

WordPerfect 5.1 Printer Test

WordPerfect 5.1 has many new features such as labels, spreadsheet imports, tab sets relative to margins, pull-down menus, mouse support, and more advanced macro and merge functions. WordPerfect 5.1 also supplements your printer's available characters by graphically printing over 1,500 international, legal, math, scientific, and typographical characters.

Japanese ど Copyright © Hand ☞ Greek Δ

Equations can be created using WordPerfect's Equation feature.

$$\int_0^\infty x^{n-1}e^{-x}dx = \int_0^1\left(\log\frac{1}{x}\right)dx = \frac{1}{n}\prod_{m=1}^{\infty}\frac{\left(1+\frac{1}{m}\right)}{1+\frac{n}{m}} = \Gamma(n)\ ,\ n\neq 0,-1,-2,-3,\ldots$$

The Tables feature in WordPerfect 5.1 creates, formats, and edits tables easily. The Tables Options[1] can be used to improve the appearance of the table.

Print Attributes	567,845.56	Centered	Right Aligned
	67,887.47	Shadow	SMALL CAPS
	635,733.03	Redline	~~Strikeout~~

Fine, Small, Normal, Large, Very Large, Extra Large, Super-script, and Subscript are some of the printing features that have made **WordPerfect the world's number one word processor.**

You can create ruled and numbered paper by using User Boxes with numbers and graphic lines as borders. Text size and *appearance* may be changed without affecting the numbers or lines.

Integrating Text and Graphics

Graphic images can be scaled, rotated, and moved. You can indicate the style of the border and include a caption.

MOUSE

The graphic image can be placed anywhere on the page, inserted in a line, tied to a paragraph, or included in a header or footer.

[1]Although only double and single lines are used in this table, many other border styles are available including dashed lines, dotted lines, thick lines, extra thick lines, and no lines at all.

This document printed in WordPerfect 5.1 - May 29, 1990 11:49 am.

Fig. 9.6. The PRINTER.TST document, printed on a laser printer.

After you specify a particular base font, print CHARMAP.TST to find out which characters will or will not print, given the font selected. Using WordPerfect 5.1 and the currently selected printer, print CHARACTR.DOC to show all the graphic characters available.

To perform the following exercises, you must access the documents PRINTER.TST, CHARMAP.TST, and CHARACTR.DOC that you copied from the original WordPerfect disks at the time of installation. Find them in the directory where printer files are stored. If you do not know the name of that directory, access the Setup: Location of Files screen by pressing Shift-F1, then choosing **L**ocation of Files (**6**). Note the subdirectory displayed next to **P**rinter Files (**4**). Use List Files to view the directory contents to verify the location of the three files. If you cannot find these files, contact another WordPerfect 5.1 user in your office or computer lab.

Printing the Test Document

Examine figure 9.6 carefully. The figure illustrates the results of a printer test in which a LaserJet Series II printer and a variety of downloadable or soft fonts were used. Notice that many features are used, such as graphics symbols, the equation editor, underlining and bold print, varying type fonts, user boxes, footnotes, page footings, and graphics integration.

To print the PRINTER.TST document and view the printer capabilities of your system, using the current base font setting as a basis, follow these steps:

Step 1: Access the **F**ile pull-down menu and select List **F**iles (or press F5).

Step 2: Select the subdirectory where the PRINTER.TST document is located and highlight PRINTER.TST.

Step 3: Choose **P**rint (**4**).

Step 4: When you are prompted `Page(s): (All)`, press Enter.

Step 5: If you are prompted `Document not formatted for current printer. Continue? No (Yes)`, press **Y**.

Note: Depending on the current printer definition, you may experience a delay before the one-page document prints.

Step 6: Press Exit (F7) to restore the current document screen.

Compare your printer's capabilities with those in figure 9.6. If your printer does not have graphics capability, you will notice several features missing from your PRINTER.TST document when you compare the output to figure 9.6.

Printing the WordPerfect Character Sets

Two other files provided by WordPerfect provide additional information about the WordPerfect 5.1 character sets. You can print CHARMAP.TST in each of your base fonts to see *only those characters that your printer can print* (as opposed to characters that can be drawn graphically through the use of compose techniques, discussed in Lesson 6).

Print CHARACTR.DOC on any printer to obtain a *complete list of all characters* in the 12 WordPerfect character sets along with the associated compose codes and character names. If your printer does not have graphics capability, some characters do not print.

Warning: If you print the document on a graphics printer, be prepared for a long print job. Printing CHARACTR.DOC on a LaserJet Series II takes nearly two hours!

To print the CHARMAP.TST document, using the currently selected base font, follow these steps:

Step 1: Access the **F**ile pull-down menu and select List **F**iles (or press F5).

Step 2: Select the subdirectory where the CHARMAP.TST document is located and highlight CHARMAP.TST.

Step 3: Choose **P**rint (**4**) to print the WordPerfect test document that lists only the characters supported by the current base font and printer definition.

Step 4: When you are prompted `Page(s): (All)`, press Enter.

Step 5: If you are prompted `Document not formatted for current printer. Continue? No (Yes)`, press **Y**.

Step 6: After the CHARMAP.TST document prints, press Exit (F7) to restore the current document screen.

To perform the same test, using a different base font, select the font and repeat Steps 1 through 6. To take the time to print a complete list of characters, repeat the steps in the preceding exercise, substituting CHARACTR.DOC in place of CHARMAP.TST in Step 2. Recall, however, that it could take several hours to print CHARACTR.DOC.

For Further Reference

If you would like to know more about printing with laser printers, consult *Using WordPerfect 5.1*, Special Edition (Que Corporation, Carmel, IN, 1989), Chapters 8, 9, and 10.

Summary of Concepts

Lesson 9 explains these concepts:

- ❑ Access the main Print menu to control printing and printer-related options.
- ❑ To print a WordPerfect document, you must select a printer definition file from a list of installed printers.
- ❑ Select text and graphics print quality from the main Print menu.
- ❑ Use the main Print menu also to determine the number of copies to be printed and whether WordPerfect 5.1 or the printer controls making copies.
- ❑ Change Print menu defaults through the Setup, Initial Settings, and Printer Options menu.
- ❑ Print some or all pages from disk by using the main Print menu or List Files.
- ❑ Use the Control Printer screen to determine the status of the printer, cancel print jobs, rush one print job ahead of another, and suspend or start a print job.
- ❑ Print the one-page PRINTER.TST document to see whether the currently defined printer alters character size and appearance specific to the base font in use.
- ❑ Print CHARMAP.TST to determine which characters can be printed (as opposed to composed graphically) by the currently defined printer.
- ❑ Print CHARACTR.DOC to produce a lengthy listing of all characters supported by WordPerfect, along with character descriptions and compose codes.

Review Exercises

Practice using the WordPerfect features in this lesson by completing the following exercises. If you do not remember how to do something, review the explanation and practice the tasks again.

1. Clear the screen without saving the current document.
2. Access the list of printer definitions and review your choices.
3. Select, if you have more than one choice, a different printer. Then return the printer selection to its original setting.
4. Set the printer text quality to High.
5. Set the printer graphics quality to Medium.
6. Set the Print menu defaults for text and graphics to Medium.
7. Print ANNOUNC9.DOC from disk, using List Files.
8. Print CRIMSON9.LTR from disk, using the Print menu.
9. Take your printer off-line to force a subsequent display of a printer problem message; then use List Files to select any three Lesson files for printing.
10. Access the Printer Control menu, study the messages, and cancel all print jobs on the jobs list.
11. Access the Base Font menu (Ctrl-F8,4) and select an alternative base font if one is available.
12. Reprint CHARMAP.TST, using the new base font, and restore the original base font.

Learning WordPerfect's Advanced Features

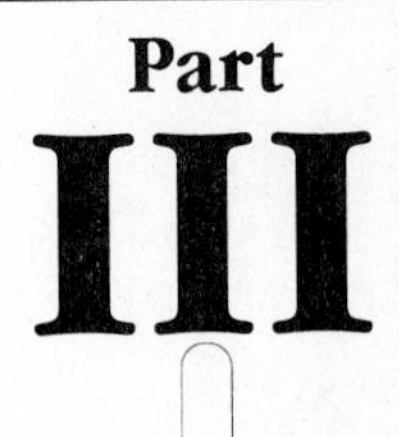

In Part II you learned the basic skills needed to create, edit, and print out documents with WordPerfect. Now you are ready to learn more advanced features of WordPerfect. The Lessons in Part III will help you save time and gain more control over your documents.

- ❑ Use List Files in Lesson 10
- ❑ Save time with macros and styles in Lesson 11
- ❑ Merge files in Lesson 12
- ❑ Sort and select data in Lesson 13
- ❑ Organize document references in Lesson 14
- ❑ Use footnotes, endnotes, outlines, and line numbers in Lesson 15
- ❑ Work with text columns in Lesson 16
- ❑ Calculate with math columns in Lesson 17
- ❑ Work with tables in Lesson 18
- ❑ Integrate text and graphics in Lesson 19

Using List Files

10

In this lesson, you practice these tasks:

- ❑ Understand the List Files screen
- ❑ Change the current directory
- ❑ Rename a file
- ❑ Use Look to preview a file
- ❑ Copy, move, print, and delete a file
- ❑ Use the Short/Long display
- ❑ Use Name Search to locate a file name
- ❑ Mark text for multiple file action
- ❑ Use Word Search to locate files

Before you begin this lesson, be sure to have a formatted 5 1/4- or 3 1/2-inch disk handy. You should also have WordPerfect installed on a hard disk system with one floppy disk drive, and the current directory should hold your WordPerfect document files. You may have to modify instructions that refer to specific disk drives if you have a dual-floppy-disk system without a hard disk.

WordPerfect's List Files feature can help you use DOS to manage disk files. This powerful feature is actually more "friendly" than DOS. Without leaving the WordPerfect program, you can use List Files to change disk directories and drives, to preview documents, and to move, copy, rename, and mark files so that you can move, copy, search, or delete more than one file at a time. List Files can even search documents and mark those containing specified words and phrases.

Note: The figures in this lesson use List Files displays that probably do not match those on your screen; the results you get with List Files will match the files stored on your disk.

Understanding the List Files Screen

You were introduced to the List Files (F5) command and screen displays (see fig. 10.1) when you retrieved a file in Lesson 3. You accessed the List Files screen again in Lesson 9 to print a document stored on disk. Now learn more about the screen information and menus before you use other List Files commands.

```
06-05-90  09:26a              Directory C:\WP51\QUEDISK\*.*
Document size:          0  Free: 12,320,768 Used:     167,806      Files:       76

 .    Current     <Dir>                          ..     Parent     <Dir>
ANNOUNC5.DOC     1,847  03-13-90 08:04a  |  ANNOUNC8.DOC    1,432  03-31-90 06:57p
BIRTH12 .LST     1,863  04-21-90 05:45a  |  BLKSRT12.DOC    1,648  04-13-90 10:40p
CLIP18A .DOC     1,822  05-15-90 09:34a  |  CLIP18B .DOC    6,719  05-05-90 02:04a
COL3-15 .DOC     2,234  04-29-90 04:12p  |  CONDEOP6.LST    3,357  05-15-90 09:35a
COPYEX4 .        2,383  03-11-90 09:44a  |  COVER13 .MRK    3,601  04-22-90 07:49a
COVER6  .DOC     2,653  03-16-90 10:02a  |  CRIM11A .PRI    1,475  05-15-90 09:37a
CRIM11A .SEC     1,130  04-15-90 09:33a  |  CRIMSO10.LTR    1,346  04-14-90 10:25p
CRIMSO11.LTR     1,484  04-14-90 10:24p  |  CRIMSON2.LTR    1,327  05-15-90 08:10a
CRIMSON2.TOP       609  05-15-90 09:39a  |  CRIMSON3.LTR    1,335  05-15-90 08:11a
CRIMSON4.LTR     1,327  03-11-90 06:05a  |  CRIMSON4.TOP      609  05-15-90 09:40a
CRIMSON5.LTR     1,085  03-13-90 05:20a  |  CRIMSON5.TOP      609  03-14-90 11:50a
CRIMSON6.LTR     1,327  03-16-90 09:14a  |  CRIMSON8.LTR    1,265  04-01-90 11:34a
CRIMSON9.LTR     1,879  05-15-90 09:42a  |  DELNO14 .DOC    4,529  04-23-90 02:57p
DOCREF13.EX      3,400  04-22-90 09:37a  |  EDFOOT14.DOC    4,529  04-23-90 03:02p
EDIT18  .TBL     2,412  05-15-90 09:43a  |  ENDNO14 .DOC    4,485  04-28-90 05:30p
EXERCIS9.DOC     3,129  05-15-90 09:44a  |  EXERCISE.14     4,043  04-25-90 10:48p
FOOTEN14.DOC     4,582  04-25-90 07:37a  |  FOOTNO14.DOC    3,943  04-23-90 09:17a
GETTY15 .ADD     3,477  05-15-90 09:45a  ▼  INDEX13 .DOC    1,401  04-22-90 08:01a

1 Retrieve; 2 Delete; 3 Move/Rename; 4 Print; 5 Short/Long Display;
6 Look; 7 Other Directory; 8 Copy; 9 Find; N Name Search: 6
```

Heading information

File information

List Files menu

Fig. 10.1. The List Files screen.

Understanding Heading Information

The first two lines of the List Files screen shown in figure 10.1 form the heading. If you have more files than can be shown on one screen, the heading remains on-screen as the list of files scrolls up and off the screen. This heading contains useful information.

The first heading line displays, from left to right, the system date and time (shown as 24-hour time) and the disk drive, path, and directory listed. You may find the drive and path on your list different from the one in figure 10.1 (`C:\WP51\QUEDISK\*.*`) if your disk is organized differently.

The second heading line displays the size of the document being edited, the amount of free space on the disk drive, the amount of space used in the current directory, and the number of files in the current directory.

Understanding File Information

The largest section of the List Files screen is a two-column list of files (in alphabetical order) in the current directory. Across the line you see the file name, followed by the file size, and then the date and time the file was created or last changed.

Entries displaying `<DIR>` refer to another subdirectory. Figure 10.2 shows a sample WordPerfect directory that has 10 subdirectories listed before individual file names.

```
06-05-90  09:35a               Directory C:\WP51\*.*
Document size:          0   Free:  8,579,072 Used:  3,633,409       Files:        92

 .    Current     <Dir>                         |  ..    Parent      <Dir>
BACKUP  .         <Dir>  05-29-90 12:14p        |  DIC51    .        <Dir>  05-29-90 12:15p
GRAPH51 .         <Dir>  05-29-90 12:16p        |  KBMAC    .        <Dir>  05-29-90 12:15p
QUE51   .         <Dir>  05-29-90 12:16p        |  QUEDISK  .        <Dir>  05-29-90 04:23p
SPELL51 .         <Dir>  06-05-90 09:33a        |  STYLES   .        <Dir>  05-29-90 12:15p
WPDATA  .         <Dir>  06-05-90 09:33a        |  8514A    .VRS     4,862  01-19-90 12:00p
AD       .WPM       178  02-23-90 12:57p        |  ALTI     .WPM       123  02-23-90 03:01p
ALTRNAT  .WPK       919  01-19-90 12:00p        |  ATI      .VRS     6,036  01-19-90 12:00p
BOX      .WPM       168  01-21-90 12:26p        |  CHARACTR.DOC     43,029  01-19-90 12:00p
CHARMAP  .TST    42,530  01-19-90 12:00p        |  CODES    .WPM     7,403  01-19-90 12:00p
CONVERT  .EXE   109,049  01-19-90 12:00p        |  CURSOR   .COM     1,452  01-19-90 12:00p
DBLIST   .SF     14,405  01-18-90 10:17a        |  DIAB620  .PRS     1,743  02-28-90 03:38p
DPTEKLAS.PRS     11,073  02-28-90 02:02p        |  EGA512   .FRS     3,584  01-19-90 12:00p
EGAITAL  .FRS     3,584  01-19-90 12:00p        |  EGASMC   .FRS     3,584  01-19-90 12:00p
EGAUND   .FRS     3,584  01-19-90 12:00p        |  EMPLOYEE.TXT      8,254  01-18-90 08:35a
ENDFOOT  .WPM     3,871  01-19-90 12:00p        |  ENHANCED.WPK      3,571  01-19-90 12:00p
EQUATION.WPK      2,974  01-19-90 12:00p        |  FIXBIOS  .COM        50  01-19-90 12:00p
FOOTEND  .WPM     3,833  01-19-90 12:00p        |  GENIUS   .VRS    12,353  01-19-90 12:00p
GRAB     .COM    16,450  01-19-90 12:00p        ▼  GRAPHCNV.EXE    111,104  01-19-90 12:00p

1 Retrieve; 2 Delete; 3 Move/Rename; 4 Print; 5 Short/Long Display;
6 Look; 7 Other Directory; 8 Copy; 9 Find; N Name Search: 6
```

Fig. 10.2. The List Files screen with subdirectories.

If you have more files than can be shown on-screen, the excess files scroll up or down off the screen. The heading at the top of the screen and the menu at the bottom of the screen, however, remain in view. The vertical line separating the two columns of file names displays an arrowhead, pointing up and/or down, indicating that more files are out of view in the specified direction.

Understanding the List Files Menu

The bottom part of the List Files screen contains two menu lines that provide access to WordPerfect's 10 powerful List Files features shown in figure 10.2. To select a feature, press the corresponding number, 1 through 9, or press the highlighted letter that appears on-screen. For example, you can press **2** or **D** to select Delete; or you can press only **N** to select Name Search.

Adding Practice Files

Before you begin the List Files exercises that follow (such as exercises to delete files), safeguard your existing lesson disk files by creating some practice files. To create these files, follow these steps:

Step 1: Clear the screen without saving the current document.

Note: The instruction to clear the screen without saving the current document is used many times throughout the workbook. It means to access the **File** pull-down menu and select **Exit** (or press F7); when you are prompted `Save Document? Yes (No)`, press **N**; when you see the prompt `Exit WP? No (Yes)`, press **N**.

Step 2: Type **This is a practice file** as the first and only line of the new document.

Step 3: Press Save (F10), type **DELETEME.001** when you see the prompt `Document to be saved:`, and press Enter.

Step 4: Repeat Step 3, editing the file name portion of the disk drive\path\file name display to read **DELETEME.002** instead of `DELETEME.001`.

Step 5: Repeat Step 4 three times to create DELETEME.003, DELETEME.004, and DELETEME.005.

Step 6: Repeat Step 4 twice to create RENAMEME.001 and MOVEDOC.001.

Step 7: Select **Exit** (or press F7); when you see the prompt `Save Document? Yes (No)`, press **N**; when you are prompted `Exit WP? No (Yes)` press **N**.

Using Retrieve

List File's **Retrieve (1)** option and the Retrieve (Shift-F10) command used from within WordPerfect work the same way (see Lesson 2). Both retrieve files from disk into the computer's memory. If a file is already in memory, the new file is loaded into memory at the position of the cursor. Before you retrieve a second file, you are prompted `Retrieve into current document? (Y/N)` for permission to combine the two documents.

New with WordPerfect 5.1 is the capability to retrieve DOS text files with the **Retrieve (1)** option. The **Text In (5)** option in previous versions is replaced by **Short/Long Display (5)**.

Using Delete

The more you use WordPerfect, the more you accumulate files that you no longer need and that should be removed from the disk. Using the Delete feature is as easy as highlighting the unwanted file, selecting **Delete (2)** from the menu, and answering a prompt by pressing **Y** for Yes. You can delete several files at one time by first highlighting, then marking, each file with an asterisk.

To practice deleting one file named DELETEME.001, follow these steps:

Step 1: Access the **File** pull-down menu and select List **Files** (or press F5).

Step 2: Press Enter to access the current directory containing the lesson-disk files and the newly created practice files.

Step 3: Using cursor arrow keys, highlight the file DELETEME.001.

Step 4: Press **Delete (2)**, and at the prompt `Delete filename? No (Yes)`, press **Y**.

The List Files screen is rewritten, and the deleted file no longer appears. Be careful not to remove the wrong files. Once you delete a file, WordPerfect has no way to undelete the file or files. Some software products, however, such as PC Tools or Norton Utilities, can undelete the files. Regular backup copies of data files spare you the interruption and embarrassment of losing important data.

To delete several files at one time, perform these steps:

Step 1: Move the cursor to the DELETEME.002 file and press the * (asterisk) key.

Step 2: Repeat Step 1, marking the files DELETEME.003, DELETEME.004, and DELETEME.005.

Step 3: Select **Delete (2)**; when you see `Delete marked files? No (Yes)`, press **Y**.

Step 4: When you are prompted `Marked files will be deleted. Continue? No (Yes)`, press **Y**.

Step 5: Press Exit (F7) to return to the current document.

Hint: You can copy seldom-used files from a hard disk to a floppy disk and then delete the files on the hard disk to free hard disk space.

Using Move/Rename

When you organize your disk directories, you may need to rename files or move them to a different directory. For example, you may want to change a file name to a more meaningful one. Or you may decide to create a new subdirectory and then move files from another directory to the new directory.

Use Move/Rename to change the name of a file in the current directory or to copy a file to a new location when you remove it from the original location. You also can change the file name during a copy process illustrated later.

When you highlight a file name and select Move/Rename, the prompt `New Name: old filename` appears. The prompt `New Name: C:\WP51\QUEDISK\RENAMEME.001` appears after you highlight the file RENAMEME.001 and select Move/Rename—if C: is the current disk drive and \WP51\QUEDISK is the current path and current directory. To rename a file, change the file name. The new name appears instead of the old name. To move a file, change either or both the disk drive name and path.

Renaming a File

To rename the RENAMEME.001 file as NEWNAME.V01, follow these steps:

Step 1: Access the **F**ile pull-down menu and select List **F**iles (or press F5).

Step 2: Press Enter to access the current directory containing the lesson files.

LESSON FILES

Step 3: Highlight the RENAMEME.001 file name.

Step 4: Press **M**ove/Rename (**3**).

Step 5: At the prompt `New Name: your disk drive\path\RENAMEME.001`, edit the RENAMEME.001 part of the display to read **NEWNAME.001**; press Enter.

The name is changed and repositioned on-screen immediately.

Moving a File

When you move a file, WordPerfect deletes the file from the current directory and copies the file to its new location. Before you delete a file from the hard disk, you may want to copy the file onto a floppy disk. Move/Rename does all this work in one command.

To move NEWNAME.001 from the hard disk to the disk in drive A, follow these steps:

Step 1: Insert the formatted disk into the A: disk drive.

Step 2: Highlight the MOVEDOC.001 file name on the current List Files display.

Step 3: Press **Move/Rename (3)**.

Step 4: At the prompt `New Name: your disk drive\path\MOVEDOC.001`, edit the disk drive and path part of the current display to read **A:**; press Enter.

Step 5: Press Exit (F7) to restore the current document screen.

The file MOVEDOC.001 is removed from the current directory and transferred to the disk in drive A.

To move more than one file at a time, mark each file with an asterisk before you select the Move/Rename command and proceed as if you were moving one file. At the prompt `Move marked files? No (Yes)`, press **Y**. At the prompt `Move marked files to:`, enter the destination disk drive, path, and subdirectory. When you move several files at one time, you cannot rename the files.

Using Print

The **Print (4)** option prints the highlighted file or files on disk to the currently selected printer. You can read more about printing in Lessons 3 and 9.

To execute a print command from the List Files display, simply highlight the file to print and choose **Print (4)**. If you print only the highlighted file, you are prompted `Page(s): (All)`, and you can specify the pages to be printed. To set up multiple files for printing, mark the files with the asterisk (*) before selecting the print option from the menu. You are prompted `Print marked files? No (Yes)`.

Using Short/Long Display

Each time you accessed List Files (F5) in earlier lessons of the workbook, you viewed a short display of file names. Files were arranged in two columns of 18 files each. If, however, you specify a long display, files are listed one per line. Figure 10.3 illustrates both the short display and long display.

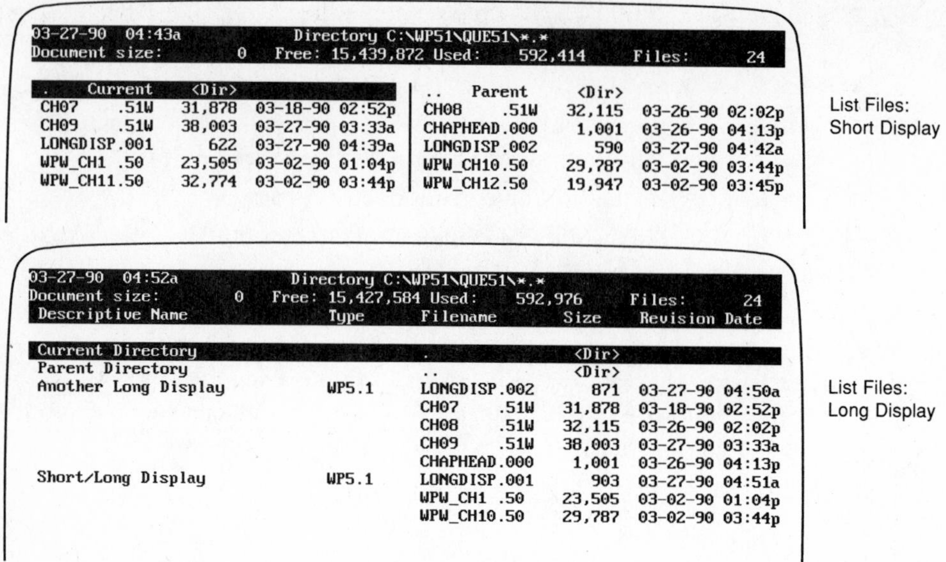

```
03-27-90  04:43a              Directory C:\WP51\QUE51\*.*
Document size:          0   Free: 15,439,872 Used:     592,414      Files:        24

 .    Current     <Dir>                          ..     Parent      <Dir>
CH07      .51W   31,878  03-18-90 02:52p   CH08      .51W   32,115  03-26-90 02:02p
CH09      .51W   38,003  03-27-90 03:33a   CHAPHEAD.000      1,001  03-26-90 04:13p
LONGDISP.001        622  03-27-90 04:39a   LONGDISP.002        590  03-27-90 04:42a
WPW_CH1  .50     23,505  03-02-90 01:04p   WPW_CH10.50      29,787  03-02-90 03:44p
WPW_CH11.50      32,774  03-02-90 03:44p   WPW_CH12.50      19,947  03-02-90 03:45p
```

List Files:
Short Display

```
03-27-90  04:52a              Directory C:\WP51\QUE51\*.*
Document size:          0   Free: 15,427,584 Used:     592,976      Files:        24
 Descriptive Name                 Type       Filename        Size    Revision Date

 Current Directory                           .               <Dir>
 Parent Directory                            ..              <Dir>
 Another Long Display             WP5.1      LONGDISP.002      871  03-27-90 04:50a
                                             CH07      .51W 31,878  03-18-90 02:52p
                                             CH08      .51W 32,115  03-26-90 02:02p
                                             CH09      .51W 38,003  03-27-90 03:33a
                                             CHAPHEAD.000    1,001  03-26-90 04:13p
 Short/Long Display               WP5.1      LONGDISP.001      903  03-27-90 04:51a
                                             WPW_CH1  .50   23,505  03-02-90 01:04p
                                             WPW_CH10.50    29,787  03-02-90 03:44p
```

List Files:
Long Display

Fig. 10.3. *The Short/Long List Files display.*

In the long display, information on the right side of the line is the same as that in the short display. On the left side of the line you see the descriptive name of the file and the type of file—information drawn from document summary information stored in the document. The long display, unlike the short display, shows only WordPerfect 5 and 5.1 files.

Using the long display effectively requires three steps. First, access the Setup: Document Management/Summary screen and turn on the document summary feature. Second, create a new document (or edit an existing document) and complete information on a document summary screen when you save the file. Third, access List Files, choose Short/Long Display, and select Long Display.

To access the Document Management/Summary screen (see fig. 9.4) and turn on the document summary feature, follow these steps:

Step 1: Access the **F**ile pull-down menu and select Set**u**p (or press Shift-F1); then choose **E**nvironment (**3**).

Step 2: Choose **D**ocument Management/Summary (**4**) to access the screen shown in figure 10.4.

```
Setup: Document Management/Summary

     1 - Create Summary on Save/Exit    No

     2 - Subject Search Text            RE:

     3 - Long Document Names            No

     4 - Default Document Type
```

Fig. 10.4. The Setup:Document Management/Summary Screen.

Step 3: Choose **C**reate Summary on Save/Exit (**1**). When you are prompted `No (Yes)`, press **Y**.

Step 4: Press Exit (F7) until the current document screen appears.

To create a document SAMPLONG.W51 and fill in a document summary screen after initiating a save command, follow these steps:

Step 1: Access a blank document screen, type **Sample Long Name File**, and press Enter.

Step 2: Access the **F**ile pull-down menu and select **S**ave (or press F10).

Note: Because the document summary feature is active, a blank document summary screen (see fig. 10.5) appears.

```
Document Summary

        Revision Date

     1 - Creation Date  06-05-90 09:38a

     2 - Document Name
         Document Type

     3 - Author
         Typist

     4 - Subject

     5 - Account

     6 - Keywords

     7 - Abstract



Selection: 0                    (Retrieve to capture; Del to remove summary)
```

Fig. 10.5. A blank document summary screen.

Step 3: Choose Document **N**ame (**2**), type **Sample Long File Name**, and press Enter.

Step 4: For Document Type, type **W51** and press Enter.

Step 5: Press Exit (F7).

Step 6: At the prompt `Document to be saved: SAMPLONG.W51`, press Enter.

To list files by using the long display, follow these steps:

Step 1: Access the **F**ile pull-down menu and select List **F**iles (or press F5).

Step 2: Press Enter to access the current directory.

Step 3: Choose **S**hort/Long Display (**5**).

Step 4: When you are prompted `1 Short Display; 2 Long Display: 2`, press **2** or **L**.

Step 5: Press Enter to accept the current directory.

Step 6: Scroll through the directory until you see the SAMPLONG.W51 file (see fig. 10.6).

```
10-01-90  06:12p              Directory C:\ATIWP\*.*
Document size:      740   Free:    563,200 Used:     319,529     Files:       82
 Descriptive Name                Type      Filename          Size    Revision Date

                                           NUMBER19.DOC      1,351  05-06-90 11:44a
                                           OFFICES5.LST      1,364  05-04-90 07:26a
                                           OFFICES7.LST      1,342  05-15-90 09:51a
                                           OUTL15A .DOC      2,330  04-20-90 07:12p
                                           OUTL15B .DOC      1,729  04-24-90 05:39a
                                           OUTL15C .DOC      1,826  04-24-90 12:06p
                                           PAGES4  .LST      1,284  03-10-90 09:33a
                                           PAGES7  .LST      1,108  03-08-90 08:53p
                                           PAGESNR7.LST      1,894  03-10-90 07:38a
                                           PRES13  .MRG      3,658  04-13-90 08:44a
                                           RATIFY13.LST        655  04-21-90 09:33a
 Sample Long File Name           W51       SAMPLONG.W51        740  10-01-90 06:07p
                                           SEARCH4 .DOC      2,216  03-10-90 10:08a
                                           SPELL8  .CHK        470  03-10-90 02:02p
                                           SPELL8  .LTR      1,352  03-31-90 07:15a
                                           STATES13.LST      2,125  03-10-90 10:05a
                                           STATES19.LST      2,125  05-15-90 09:55a
                                           STATES4 .LST      2,125  03-10-90 10:05a

1 Retrieve; 2 Delete; 3 Move/Rename; 4 Print; 5 Short/Long Display;
6 Look; 7 Other Directory; 8 Copy; 9 Find; N Name Search: 6
```

***Fig. 10.6.** A long display of Document Summary results.*

Step 7: Press Exit (F7) to restore the current document screen.

To restore the short display in List Files, follow these steps:

Step 1: Access the **F**ile pull-down menu and select List **F**iles (or press F5). Press Enter to access the current directory.

Step 2: Choose **S**hort/Long Display (**5**).

Step 3: When you are prompted `1 Short Display; 2 Long Display: 1`, press **1** or **S**.

Step 4: Press Exit (F7) to view the short display of file names.

Step 5: Press Exit (F7) to restore the current document.

To access the Document Management/Summary screen and turn off the document summary feature, follow these steps:

Step 1: Access the **F**ile pull-down menu and select Se**t**up (or press Shift-F1); then choose **E**nvironment (**3**).

Step 2: Choose **D**ocument Management/Summary (**4**).

Step 3: Choose **C**reate Summary on Save/Exit (**1**). When you are prompted `Yes (No)`, press **N**.

Step 4: Press Exit (F7) to restore the current document.

Note: Features such as those in Step 3 that you turn on and off by pressing Y or N appear dynamically on-screen. If the feature is turned off, you see the prompt `No (Yes)`. But if the feature is turned on, you see `Yes (No)`.

Using Look

Look (**6**) displays the highlighted file on-screen without retrieving it into WordPerfect. Because **L**ook (**6**) is the default option on the List Files menu, you can access it by pressing Enter. When you use the Look option, you cannot edit the file that appears. Look is, however, a powerful tool for searching through directories for the right file for retrieving, copying, moving/renaming, or deleting.

In Look mode, you can move through the document by using most cursor-movement keys. Pressing **S** starts and stops continuous downward scrolling. The speed of your computer, however, may make continuous scrolling too fast for useful browsing. When you access Look mode, you see a new prompt, `LOOK: 1 NextDoc; 2 Prev Doc: 0`, at the bottom of the screen. When you are in Look mode, press **1** or **N** or PgDn to see the next document in the directory; press **2** or **P** or PgUp to look at the previous document.

You also can use Forward Search (F2) and Backward Search (Shift-F2) to locate text in a document. You cannot, however, use the extended search to see into headers, footers, or footnotes.

With Look, you can check other directories by highlighting the directory name, pressing **L**ook (**6**), and pressing Enter. The directory changes so that you can look into any file. If you exit from List Files, the current directory is restored to the directory in use when you entered List Files.

Looking at a File

Looking into any file listed is as simple as highlighting that file name and pressing Enter. **L**ook (6) is the default List Files menu selection.

To look into a file in the current directory, follow these steps:

Step 1: Access the **F**ile pull-down menu and select List **F**iles (or press F5). Press Enter to access the current directory.

LESSON FILES

Step 2: Highlight the CRIMSO10.LTR file name and press Enter (or **L** or **6**).

Step 3: Press and hold down the down arrow to scroll to the bottom of the document.

Step 4: Press Home, Home, up arrow to return to the top of the document.

Step 5: Press **S** to scroll down.

Searching a File

When you are looking in a file, use Forward and Backward Search to find key words and text.

Caution: The Look option places the cursor at the bottom of the first screen. Because Forward Search does not check text above the cursor, be sure to move the cursor to the top of the document before you begin the search.

The CRIMSO10.LTR file should be on-screen from the previous steps. To search forward through CRIMSO10.LTR for Honolulu, follow these steps:

Step 1: Press Home, Home, up arrow to return to the top of the document.

Step 2: Press Forward Search (F2). When you are prompted `Srch:`, type **honolulu**; then press (F2).

Step 3: Press Exit (F7) twice to restore the current document.

Practice looking through any file on your current directory. Also feel free to look into any other directories listed. You learn to access other directories in the next section.

Using Other Directory

In Lesson 3, you learned to change the current directory permanently by typing an equal sign (=) and an alternative directory path immediately after you press List

Files (F5). You learned also to change the current directory temporarily by typing an alternative directory path without an equal sign after you press List Files (F5).

Use **O**ther Directory (7) to change the current directory permanently after the List Files display appears on-screen. At least two directories appear at the top of the List Files screen: Current<DIR> and Parent<DIR>; other directories may be set up on your system. If a directory other than Current <Dir> or Parent<Dir> is highlighted, and you choose **O**ther Directory, the prompt New directory =, followed by the name of the highlighted directory, appears at the bottom of the screen. If a file name or Current<Dir> is highlighted, then the prompt redisplays the current directory. If Parent<Dir> is highlighted, the parent directory of the current subdirectory appears.

Pressing Enter after you see the New directory = prompt causes another prompt—Dir—to appear, followed by the new directory name and file specification for all files (*.*). You can edit both specifications. You can, for example, create a new directory by entering a nonexistent name and pressing **Y** in response to the prompt Create directory name? No (Yes).

Switching to an Existing Directory

To change the current directory to the parent directory permanently and then restore the directory containing the lesson files as the current directory, follow these steps:

Step 1: Access the **F**ile pull-down menu and select List **F**iles (or press F5).

Step 2: Write down (or remember) the directory path displayed at the bottom of the screen so that you can restore the path in Step 8; then press Enter.

Step 3: Highlight the parent directory, select **O**ther Directory (7), and press Enter twice.

Step 4: Highlight a file name and press **L**ook (6).

Note: If WordPerfect cannot read your highlighted file, you may see strange symbols or characters on the screen.

Step 5: Press Exit (F7) twice to restore the current document screen.

Step 6: Access the **F**ile pull-down menu and select List **F**iles (or press F5). Note the default display of the directory path you selected in Step 3.

Step 7: Press Enter to access the List Files display of files in the parent directory.

Step 8: Highlight the name of the directory containing the lesson-disk files (see Step 2).

Step 9: Select **O**ther Directory (7). Press Enter twice to set permanently the current directory as the directory containing the lesson-disk files.

Step 10: Press Exit (F7) to restore the current document screen.

Creating a Directory

Suppose that you decide to create a new subdirectory in which to store documents. In such a case, it is too awkward to exit from WordPerfect, create the subdirectory, return, and use it. Use the Other Directory command to accomplish the task.

To explore creating the new subdirectory A:\NEWDIR from within WordPerfect, perform these steps:

Step 1: Place a formatted disk in drive A.

Step 2: Access the **F**ile pull-down menu and select List **F**iles (or press F5), press Enter to access the current directory, and select **O**ther Directory (7).

Step 3: When you are prompted `New directory your disk drive\path`, type **A:\NEWDIR** and press Enter.

Step 4: See the prompt `Create A:\NEWDIR? No (Yes)` on the status line and press **Y** to create the new directory.

Step 5: Press Exit (F7) twice to restore the current document screen.

Deleting a Directory

Use Other Directory to delete as well as to create subdirectories. When you delete a subdirectory, make sure that it is empty of other files and directories. To delete the subdirectory created on the A: disk drive in the preceding exercise (the directory is empty of files), follow these steps:

Step 1: Be sure that the disk containing the new directory NEWDIR is in drive A.

Step 2: Access the **F**ile pull-down menu and select List **F**iles (or press F5).

Step 3: See the prompt at the bottom of the screen displaying the current directory, type **A:**, and press Enter.

Step 4: Highlight the entry `NEWDIR . <Dir>` and choose **D**elete (**2**).

Step 5: When you are prompted `Delete A:\NEWDIR? No (Yes)`, press **Y**.

Note: The List Files screen is reorganized, and `NEWDIR. <Dir>` is deleted.

Step 6: Press Exit (F7) to restore the current document screen.

Become comfortable with Other Directory as soon as possible. Spend some time moving around your disk drives and directories.

Using Copy

With the Copy (**8**) option, you can copy one or more files from the current directory to the same subdirectory, other subdirectories, and other disk drives. Use this option to make backup copies of your files. Copy is similar to Move. Both commands copy files, but Move deletes the original file after a copy is made.

You should make a backup copy of files when you finish working and before you turn the power off. Many systems that fail do so when the power is first turned on and the initial surge of current hits the computer and disk-drive chips. If the file to be copied already exists on the destination disk drive, you see the message `Replace your disk drive\path\filename? No (Yes).`

Copying a File to the Same Directory

Every file name in a disk directory must be unique. Suppose that you want to make a temporary copy of a file as you make changes. You must give the copy a different name from the original. One way to do so is to use the same file name but change the extension. For example, copy the CRIMSO10.LTR file and name the copy CRIMSON.BAK.

To make a backup copy of the CRIMSO10.LTR file in the same directory, follow these steps:

Step 1: Access the **F**ile pull-down menu and select List **F**iles (or press F5). Press Enter to access the current directory.

Step 2: Highlight the CRIMSO10.LTR file name.

Step 3: Select Copy (**8**).

Step 4: When you are prompted `Copy this file to:`, type **CRIMSON.BAK** and press Enter.

Step 5: Press Home, Home, up arrow to highlight `<Current><Dir>`. Press Enter twice to reorganize the List Files screen. Both CRIMSO10.LTR and CRIMSON.BAK appear.

Note: You must reorganize the screen to see the file name you just created.

Step 6: Press Exit (F7) until the current document appears on-screen.

Copying a File to a Different Directory

Copying a file to a different directory involves nearly the same process as copying a file to the same directory. The main difference is that when you copy a file to a different directory, you must include the location of the destination directory. A file name is not required. The file being copied can retain its original name because it is going to a new directory.

To copy a file to a different directory (in this exercise, disk drive A), follow these steps:

Step 1: Place a formatted disk in drive A.

Step 2: Access the **File** pull-down menu and select List **Files** (or press F5). Press Enter to access the current directory.

Step 3: Highlight the CRIMSO10.LTR file name and select **Copy** (**8**).

Step 4: When you are prompted `Copy this file to:`, type **A:** and press Enter.

Step 5: Press Exit (F7) to restore the current document screen.

Copying Multiple Files to a Different Directory

Copying multiple files to another directory involves a process similar to that of copying one file. The difference is that all files to be copied must be marked with an asterisk (*).

To copy several files to a different directory (in this exercise, disk drive A:), follow these steps:

Step 1: Access the **File** pull-down menu and select List **Files** (or press F5). Press Enter to access the current directory.

LESSON FILES

Step 2: Mark the files CRIMSO10.LTR, CRIMSON.BAK, and SAMPLONG.W51 with an asterisk (*).

Step 3: Select **Copy** (**8**).

Step 4: When you are prompted `Copy marked files? No (Yes)`, press **Y**.

Step 5: When you are prompted `Copy all marked files to:`, type **A:** and press Enter.

Step 6: When you are prompted `Replace A:\CRIMSO10.LTR? No (Yes)`, press **Y**.

Step 7: Press Exit (F7) until the current document screen appears.

Copying files to different directories on the hard disk entails a similar process. Instead of specifying disk drive A, however, you must specify the entire path pointing to the directory where you want to put the copied files.

Marking All Files for List Files Operations

In earlier exercises, you marked files by highlighting them one at a time and pressing the asterisk (*) key. With WordPerfect, you can also mark all files at once. Marking all files in the directory at once is an easy way to prepare the directory for backup to another directory or disk or to delete all files and start fresh. To mark all files at one time, follow these steps:

Step 1: Access the **F**ile pull-down menu and select List **F**iles (or press F5). Press Enter to access the current directory.

Step 2: Press Home and then type * (asterisk) to mark all files.

Note: At this point, apply one of several List Files commands to all marked files (such as delete or copy).

Step 3: Press Home and then type * to unmark all files that are marked.

Step 4: Press Exit (F7) until the current document screen appears.

Remember that the Home and asterisk (*) keys mark all files if none are marked. If any files are marked, pressing Home, * clears all marks instead of marking all files.

Limiting the Display of File Names

Limiting the number of files on the List Files screen reduces the amount of unrelated information on-screen. If you plan to search files (a process illustrated in the next section), the fewer files you have to search, the faster the search. To limit the files that are seen, change the DOS all-files option (*.*) to identify the specific files you want displayed.

To limit the number of files on the List Files screen to only those files that begin with S, follow these steps:

Step 1: Access the **F**ile pull-down menu and select List **F**iles (or press F5).

Step 2: View the prompt `Dir your disk drive:\your path\*.*` at the bottom of the screen, edit the *.* portion to read **S*.***, and then press Enter.

Note: On-screen you see only the file names that begin with `S`. Your screen should look like the one in figure 10.7.

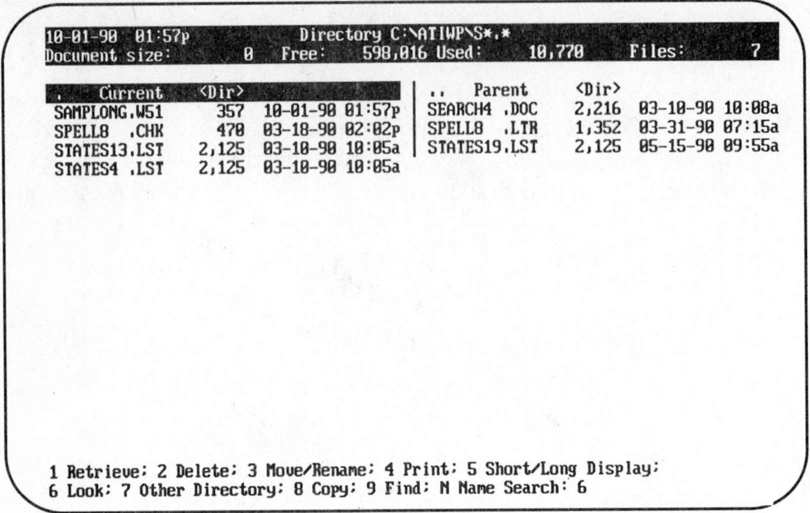

***Fig. 10.7.** Limiting the List Files screen display.*

Step 3: Press Exit (F7) to restore the current document screen.

To limit the display further and include only files beginning with ST, follow these steps:

Step 1: Access the **F**ile pull-down menu and select List **F**iles (or press F5).

Step 2: See the prompt `Dir your disk drive:\your path\*.*` at the bottom of the screen, edit the *.* portion to read **ST*.***, and press Enter.

Note: Only files with names beginning with `ST` appear on-screen. You can further limit the number of files on this screen by marking specific files with an asterisk (*).

Step 3: Press Exit (F7) to restore the current document screen.

If you are unfamiliar with DOS file-naming conventions and the use of wild-card characters to retrieve files, consult your DOS reference manual.

Using Find

Use **F**ind (9) to locate a group of file names by using a character pattern; to search document summary screens, the first page, or entire documents for a character pattern, word, or phrase; and to search for conditions in the document summary screens. Files that meet the search criteria are marked with an asterisk (*).

You may limit the search with any marking technique to point to specific files. You can even use Find to limit the files to one criterion and then use Find again to further limit the files.

Find options include searching for groups of file names—**N**ame (**1**)—by using DOS wild-card techniques; searching document summaries—**D**oc Summary (**2**)—for word patterns; searching the first page—First **P**g (**3**) or **E**ntire Doc (**4**)—for a word pattern; searching the document summary conditions such as revision date, author, typist, and account—**C**onditions (**5**); and reversing the results of a find operation—**U**ndo (**6**). At the conclusion of a Find search, the screen is reorganized to display only the file names that meet search conditions.

Searching the First Page of All Documents

To search the first page of all documents in the current directory, follow these steps:

Step 1: Access the **F**ile pull-down menu and select List **F**iles (or press F5); then press Enter to access the current directory.

Step 2: Choose **F**ind (**9**) and view the Find menu options at the bottom of the screen (see fig. 10.8).

```
CRIMSON6.LTR    1,327  03-16-90 09:14a │ CRIMSON8.LTR    1,265  04-01-90 11:34a
CRIMSON9.LTR    1,879  05-15-90 09:42a │ DELNO14 .DOC    4,529  04-23-90 02:57p
DOCREF13.EX     3,400  04-22-90 09:37a │ EDFOOT14.DOC    4,529  04-23-90 03:02p
EDIT18  .TBL    2,412  05-15-90 09:43a │ ENDNO14 .DOC    4,485  04-28-90 05:30p
EXERCIS9.DOC    3,129  05-15-90 09:44a │ EXERCISE.14     4,043  04-25-90 10:48p
FOOTEN14.DOC    4,582  04-25-90 07:37a │ FOOTNO14.DOC    3,943  04-23-90 09:17a
GETTY15 .ADD    3,477  05-15-90 09:45a ▼ INDEX13 .DOC    1,401  04-22-90 08:01a

Find: 1 Name; 2 Doc Summary; 3 First Pg; 4 Entire Doc; 5 Conditions; 6 Undo: 0
```

***Fig. 10.8.** The Find menu options accessed with List Files.*

Step 3: Choose First **P**g (**3**).

Step 4: At the prompt `Word pattern:`, type **WordPerfect** and press Enter.

Note: Figure 10.9 shows the results of the Find search (your list of files may vary).

```
10-01-90  01:57p              Directory C:\ATIWP\*.*
Document size:          0  Free:    598,016 Used:       76,656     Files:        21

 .   Current    <Dir>                     |  ..   Parent    <Dir>
 CLIP19A .DOC   1,822  05-15-90 09:34a    |  CLIP19B .DOC   6,719  05-05-90 02:04a
 CONDEOP7.LST   3,357  05-15-90 09:35a    |  COPYEXS .      2,383  03-11-90 09:44a
 COVER7  .DOC   2,653  03-16-90 10:02a    |  DELNO15 .DOC   4,529  04-23-90 02:57p
 DOCREF14.EX    3,400  04-22-90 09:37a    |  EDFOOT15.DOC   4,529  04-23-90 03:02p
 EDNO15  .DOC   4,485  04-20-90 05:30p    |  EXERCISE.15    4,043  04-25-90 10:48p
```

Fig. 10.9. The results of a Find search on all files.

Step 5: Press Exit (F7) to restore the current document screen.

Using the Conditions Menu

Use the Find: Conditions menu (see fig. 10.10) for the greatest flexibility in specifying search criteria.

```
Find: Conditions                                          Files Selected:    59

     1 - Perform Search
     2 - Reset Conditions

     3 - Revision Date - From
                         To

     4 - Text - Document Summary
                First Page
                Entire Document

     5 - Document Summary
         Creation Date - From
                         To
         Document Name
         Document Type
         Author
         Typist
         Subject
         Account
         Keywords
         Abstract

Selection: 1
```

Fig. 10.10. The Find: Conditions menu options.

Perform Search (1) starts the search. When the search is finished, WordPerfect 5.1 displays a file list containing only those files matching the search criteria. A note at the top of the screen indicates the number of files selected to be searched.

Reset Conditions (**2**) reverses the results of the last search. Use the Revision **D**ate (**3**) to select documents according to the date the documents were last revised. Use **T**ext (**4**) to search a document summary, a document's first page, or an entire document for a specified word pattern. Or use Document **S**ummary (**5**) to select documents by data in any document summary field.

Selecting **D**oc Summary (**2**), First **P**g (**3**), or **E**ntire Doc (**4**) from the basic Find menu accesses one of the three options that appear also after you select **T**ext (**4**) from the Find: Conditions menu. Document Summary is, however, more flexible than its List Files: Find counterpart. You can search the whole summary or any individual field: date, name, subject, author, typist, or comments.

To perform a search on the author field in the document summary, follow these steps:

Step 1: Access the **F**ile pull-down menu and select List **F**iles (or press F5). Press Enter to accept the current directory containing the lesson-disk files.

Step 2: Choose **F**ind (**9**) and then choose **C**onditions (**5**).

Step 3: Choose Document **S**ummary (**5**).

Step 4: Press Enter four times to position the cursor on the Author field.

Step 5: Type **Fox** and press Enter.

Step 6: Press Exit (F7) to position the cursor on the selection prompt at the bottom of the screen.

Step 7: Choose **P**erform Search (**1**).

Note: Files EXRCIS10.DOC and PAGES10.DOC are displayed as the result of a search for files in which the document summary indicates Fox as the author.

Step 8: Press Exit (F7) to restore the current document screen.

WordPerfect actually searches for a pattern of characters, not a word. Thus if you tell WordPerfect to search for `bank`, it finds several words with `bank` in them, such as banker, bankroll, and bankruptcy.

Using Name Search

Name Search (**N**) moves the highlight bar to the file name as you type the name. To highlight the file name TESTPLAN.DOC, press Name Search (**N**) and press **T**. The highlight moves to the first file beginning with `T`. Press **E**, and the highlight moves to the first file that begins with `TE`. This feature is particularly useful when your directory contains more files than can be displayed on-screen.

To name-search the file STATES4.LST, follow these steps:

Step 1: Access the **F**ile pull-down menu and select List **F**iles (or press F5). Press Enter.

Step 2: Choose **N**ame Search (**N**).

Step 3: Press **S**. The cursor moves to the first file on-screen that starts with S.

Step 4: Press **T**.

Step 5: Press **A**.

Step 6: Press Enter or an arrow key to exit from the name search.

Step 7: Press Exit (F7) to restore the current document screen.

As you become a veteran WordPerfect user, your document directories grow to perhaps several hundred files. The Name Search command is an especially handy tool then.

For Further Reference

If you would like to know more about using List Files, consult *Using WordPerfect 5.1*, Special Edition (Que Corporation, Carmel, IN, 1989), Chapters 3, 8, and 10.

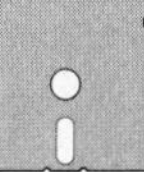

Summary of Concepts

Lesson 10 explains these concepts:

- ❏ You can access a list of all files on the current disk drive and directory. The list includes the file name, size, date, and time each file was created.
- ❏ You can access 10 powerful disk management commands when you are in List Files mode.
- ❏ Use the List Files Retrieve option to load files into memory.
- ❏ Use the List Files Delete option to remove one or more files or directories from disk.
- ❏ Use the List Files Move/Rename option to rename a file or to move a file from one directory to another.
- ❏ Use the List Files Print option to print a file on disk.
- ❏ Use the List Files Short/Long Display option to view files one per line, including selected data items from document summaries.
- ❏ Use the List Files Look option to view files without loading them into memory.
- ❏ Use the List Files Other Directory option to change the current directory or to add a directory.
- ❏ Use the List Files Copy option to make a second (backup) copy of one or more files.
- ❏ Use the List Files Find command to search for specific document content.
- ❏ Use the List Files Name Search command to move the highlighter to a specific file name with just a few keystrokes.

Review Exercises

Practice using the WordPerfect features in this lesson by completing the following exercises. If you do not remember how to do something, review the explanation and practice the steps.

1. Access a blank document screen.
2. Create and save four practice files: ERASEME.1, ERASEME.2, COPYME.1, and CHANGEME.1.
3. Use the List Files Name Search option to verify the existence of new files on your current directory.
4. Mark both ERASEME files and then delete the marked files.
5. Look at the first page of the PGES10.DOC file.
6. Rename the CHANGEME.1 file, using CHANGED.1 as the file name.
7. Copy the PAGES10.DOC file to PAGES.BAK.
8. Use Name Search to locate CRIMSO10.LTR.
9. Mark all files in the directory at once; then unmark all marked files.
10. Use Find to search for all files that contain the word Illinois in the first page.

Using Macros and Styles

11

In this lesson, you practice these tasks:

- ❑ Distinguish among types of macros
- ❑ Create, test, and run a macro
- ❑ Create a macro pause to accept data
- ❑ Use the macro-editor feature
- ❑ Manage macro files
- ❑ Create a style
- ❑ Save and edit a style
- ❑ Create and use a style library

WordPerfect 5.1's macro capability is one of the program's most useful and exciting features. Although a macro is nothing more than a series of keystrokes saved to a file, a macro can save you much time and effort. Once you create a macro, you can call on it to type keystrokes you stored earlier.

A style is a powerful tool you can use to control the format of a single document or a group of documents. You can include text, most formatting codes, and graphics in a style and store the style for repeated use.

Using Macros

You have probably noticed that the more you use WordPerfect, the more you repeat many tasks. These tasks can include typing the same headings, signature blocks, and stock phrases; deleting sentences and paragraphs; indenting lists; invoking WordPerfect commands to set margins, underline, or bold text; and setting formats for columns.

You can create a macro to do nearly any task that you can accomplish with a series of keystrokes. You can even have one macro call another macro when the first one finishes executing. A macro can repeat itself or pause and wait for you to enter information before it continues.

Macros are powerful, yet they are simple to create because WordPerfect can "learn" keystrokes as you type them. To create and use a macro that types the name WordPerfect, for example, follow these steps:

- ❑ Turn on the Macro Definition feature.
- ❑ Name and briefly describe the macro.
- ❑ Type the keystrokes to be stored (such as WordPerfect).
- ❑ Turn off Macro Definition.
- ❑ Activate the macro when you need it by pressing the Macro key and typing the name of the macro.

Understanding Types of Macros

You can create and run four kinds of macros: Alt-letter macros, descriptive macros, unnamed macros, and keyboard macros. WordPerfect assigns a .WPM (WordPerfect macro) extension to each macro.

An Alt-letter macro is named with the Alt key plus a letter from A to Z—for example, Alt-K or Alt-X. A descriptive macro has a name of one to eight characters, such as TABS or MARGINS5. An unnamed macro is, from a user's point of view, named with the Enter key; WordPerfect assigns the macro name WP{WP}.WPM. You create a keyboard macro by redefining any key in WordPerfect. For instance, you can redefine the F8 function key (Underline) to turn on italics instead of underline.

Caution: Before you create a macro, save any current document to disk and access a blank document screen. Typing on a blank document screen prevents you from adding unwanted keystrokes to your current document. As an added reason for caution, many macros (including ones in this workbook) include initial instructions to clear the screen without saving the current document.

Caution: When you name a macro, you see the following prompt if the macro name is already in use:

```
macroname.WPM Already Exists: 1 Replace; 2 Edit; 3 Description: 0
```

If you select **R**eplace (**1**), the new keystrokes you enter overwrite the previous definition. If you doubt the purpose or content of the existing macro, select

Description (3) to view the user-provided description or **Edit (2)** to view the description and macro code before you overwrite a previous definition.

Creating and Testing an Alt-letter Macro

You can store frequently used words or phrases as Alt-letter macros, ready for use in two keystrokes. To create a simple Alt-letter macro that types the term WordPerfect 5.1 at the current cursor location, follow these steps:

Step 1: Clear the screen without saving the current document.

Note: The instruction to clear the screen without saving the current document is used many times throughout the workbook. It means to access the **File** pull-down menu and select **Exit** (or press F7). When you are prompted `Save Document? Yes (No)`, press **N**; when you see the prompt `Exit WP? No (Yes)`, press **N**.

Step 2: Access the **Tools** pull-down menu, select **Macro**, and choose **Define** (or press Ctrl-F10).

Step 3: At the prompt `Define macro:`, press Alt-W to name the macro.

Caution: If you encounter a message that ALTW.WPM already exists after you press Alt-W, choose **Description (3)**. If the description reads `Insert WordPerfect 5.1`, the macro was created during this exercise by another book user. Press Cancel (F1), repeat Steps 2 and 3, select **Replace (1)**, and continue with Step 4. If the description reads differently, the macro probably represents a real macro stored on your system, one that you should not overwrite. Press Cancel (F1) and repeat Steps 2 and 3, substituting another letter for the practice macro name such as Alt-Z.

Step 4: At the prompt `Description:`, type **Insert WordPerfect 5.1**.

Note: The blinking prompt `Macro Def` appears in the lower left corner of the screen. WordPerfect is now in "learning" mode. Any keystrokes you type are stored as part of the macro, including corrections.

Step 5: Type **WordPerfect 5.1** and press Enter.

Step 6: Press Macro Define (Ctrl-F10) to turn off the macro learn feature.

Note: The flashing `Macro Def` message disappears, and the Alt-letter macro Alt-W is now stored to disk as ALTW.WPM.

To use the new macro in several situations, follow these steps:

Step 1: Clear the screen without saving the current document.

Step 2: Press Alt-W to insert WordPerfect 5.1 on the screen at the current cursor position.

Step 3: Press Enter, press Center (Shift-F6), and press Alt-W.

Step 4: Press Enter, press Flush Right (Alt-F6), and press Alt-W.

The macro works as if you were typing individual keystrokes. In Steps 2, 3, and 4, the Alt-W macro places "WordPerfect 5.1" at the left margin, in the center of the page, and flush to the right margin, respectively. You can include other formatting such as margin settings as part of the macro.

Creating and Testing a Descriptive Macro

Creating a descriptive macro follows nearly the same procedure as in creating an Alt-letter macro. Simply provide a one- to eight-character name instead of pressing Alt in combination with a letter of the alphabet after you begin a macro definition.

To create a macro that initially clears the screen without saving the current document and produces a standard memo heading, follow these steps:

Step 1: Clear the screen without saving the current document.

Step 2: Access the **T**ools pull-down menu, select **M**acro, and choose **D**efine (or press Ctrl-F10).

Step 3: At the prompt `Define macro:`, type **MEMODEMO** and press Enter to name the macro.

Step 4: At the prompt `Description:`, type **PRACTICE MEMO HEADING** and press Enter. The flashing message `Macro Def` appears in the lower left corner of the screen.

Step 5: Press Exit (F7) and press **N** to clear the screen without saving the current document. Press **N** to remain in WordPerfect.

Step 6: Press Center (Shift-F6), type **MEMORANDUM** and press Enter twice.

Step 7: Press Center (Shift-F6) and enter the current system date by pressing Date (Shift-F5) and selecting Date **C**ode (**2**). Press Enter three times.

Step 8: Type **To:** and press Enter twice.

Step 9: Type **From:** and press Enter twice.

Step 10: Type **Subj:** and press the up arrow four times (or until the cursor is located at the end of the `To:` line); then press Indent (F4) twice.

Step 11: Press Macro Define (Ctrl-F10) to end macro definition; then store the MEMODEMO macro on disk as MEMODEMO.WPM.

Step 12: Clear the screen without saving the current document.

The macro is complete and stored on disk. To test the new macro, follow these steps:

Step 1: Access the **T**ools pull-down menu, select **M**acro, and choose E**x**ecute (or press Alt-F10).

Step 2: At the prompt `Macro:`, type **MEMODEMO** and press Enter.

Figure 11.1 illustrates the results of executing the memo heading macro (the date will vary, displaying your current system date). Remember to be careful if you execute a macro that contains an early instruction to exit from the current document without saving it. If the current screen contains text you want to retain, invoke a save command before you execute the macro.

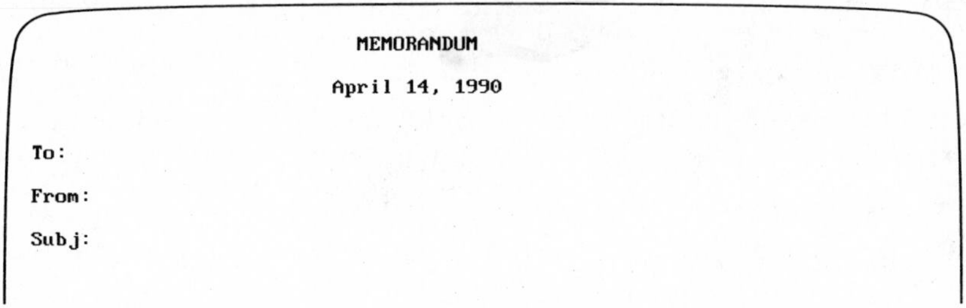

***Fig. 11.1.** The results of executing the MEMODEMO descriptive macro.*

Making a Macro Pause

In a macro, you can include a pause that allows you to enter text during macro execution. When you finish entering text, simply press Enter to continue the macro. To insert a pause in a macro, press Macro Commands (Ctrl-PgUp) when you are in Macro Def mode and at a point in the commands where you want the macro to pause. The following menu appears:

```
1 Pause; 2 Display; 3 Assign; 4 Comment; 0
```

Selecting **P**ause (**1**) inserts the WordPerfect {PAUSE} command in the macro, but you do not see any change on-screen. When the executing macro encounters {PAUSE}, the macro stops. At this point, you can type any text you want. When you press Enter, the macro continues.

To create another version of the memo heading macro, adding pauses so that you can type the To:, From:, and Subj: lines as the heading is being created, follow these steps:

Step 1: Clear the screen without saving the current document.

Step 2: Access the **T**ools pull-down menu, select **M**acro, and choose **D**efine (or press Ctrl-F10).

Step 3: At the prompt `Define macro:`, type **NEWMEMO** and press Enter to name the macro.

Step 4: At the prompt `Description:`, type **MEMO HEADING—pause for user input** and press Enter.

Note: The message `Macro Def` appears flashing in the lower left corner of the screen, indicating that you are in learn mode. As you enter the macro code in Steps 5 through 13, you may make a typing error or two. Correct errors as you go along. All keystrokes are learned (stored) when Macro Def mode is active.

Step 5: Press Exit (F7) and press **N** to clear the screen without saving the current document. Press **N** to remain in WordPerfect.

Step 6: Type **MEMORANDUM**; then press Enter two times.

Note: Do not center the title at this point in the illustration. You center the text during an edit example to follow.

Step 7: Press Date (Shift-F5), choose Date **C**ode (**2**), and press Enter three times.

Step 8: Type **To:** and press Indent (F4) twice.

Step 9: Press Ctrl-PgUp, choose **P**ause (**1**), and press Enter three times.

Step 10: Type **From:** and press Indent (F4) once.

Step 11: Press Ctrl-PgUp, choose **P**ause (**1**), and press Enter three times.

Step 12: Type **From:** and press Indent (F4) once.

Step 13: Press Ctrl-PgUp, choose **P**ause (**1**), and press Enter four times.

Step 14: Press Macro Define (Ctrl-F10) to end macro definition; then store the NEWMEMO macro on disk as NEWMEMO.WPM.

The macro is complete and stored on disk. Remember, NEWMEMO.WPM clears the screen without saving the current document and creates a memo heading. If you have a document on-screen that you want to keep, save it to disk before you execute this macro. If this situation creates a problem, you learn later how to edit the macro and to change the problem instructions.

When you execute the NEWMEMO macro, the cursor stops at the To: line first. Type the text you want to enter on this line and press Enter. The macro continues to the `From:` and `Subj:` lines. Enter the text on each of these lines and press Enter to continue. To test the new macro, follow these steps:

Step 1: Access the **T**ools pull-down menu, select **M**acro, and choose E**x**ecute (or press Alt-F10).

Step 2: At the prompt `Macro:`, type **NEWMEMO** and press Enter.

Step 3: At the `To:` line, type **WordPerfect 5.1 Users** and press Enter.

Step 4: At the From: line, type **Que Corporation** and press Enter.

Step 5: At the `Subj:` line, type **Using the WordPerfect PC Tutor** and press Enter.

Note: The heading you created appears at the top of the screen, as you see in figure 11.2. You supply the variable portions of the memo heading from the keyboard; WordPerfect supplies the fixed portions of the heading stored in the macro.

```
MEMORANDUM

October 11, 1990

To:        WordPerfect 5.1 Users

From:      Que Corporation

Subj:      Using the WordPerfect PC Tutor
```

Fig. 11.2. The results of executing a macro that pauses for user input.

Step 6: Press Reveal Codes (Alt-F3 or F11) to view the codes that control the memo heading created by a macro that paused for user input (see fig. 11.3).

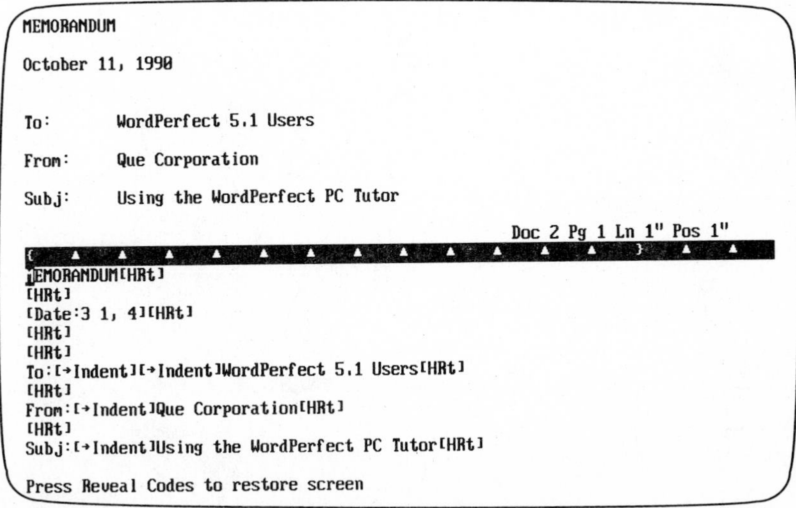

MEMORANDUM
October 11, 1990
To: WordPerfect 5.1 Users
From: Que Corporation
Subj: Using the WordPerfect PC Tutor
Doc 2 Pg 1 Ln 1" Pos 1"
MEMORANDUM[HRt]
[HRt]
[Date:3 1, 4][HRt]
[HRt]
[HRt]
To:[→Indent][→Indent]WordPerfect 5.1 Users[HRt]
[HRt]
From:[→Indent]Que Corporation[HRt]
[HRt]
Subj:[→Indent]Using the WordPerfect PC Tutor[HRt]
Press Reveal Codes to restore screen

Fig. 11.3. Viewing codes after executing a macro that pauses for user input.

Step 7: Press Reveal Codes (Alt-F3 or F11) to restore full document display.

Using the Macro Editor

To revise a macro, you can replace the macro and enter all new code, or you can edit the existing code. The number of changes may dictate which method to use. As a general rule, replace a short macro and edit a long macro.

When you invoke Macro Define (Ctrl-F10) and specify a macro file name that already exists, you see this prompt:

```
macroname.WPM is Already Exists: 1 Replace; 2 Edit; 3 Description: 0
```

To replace the existing macro, choose **R**eplace (**1**), enter the new description, and enter the codes when you see the flashing `Macro Def` message in the lower left corner of the screen.

To edit the macro, choose **E**dit (**2**) at the prompt. A macro editing screen appears. Figure 11.4 illustrates the codes controlling NEWMEMO.WPM, which pauses for user input. Once you understand how to interpret the codes, you can, with practice, become adept at revising macros with the macro editor as opposed to creating all new code in Macro Def mode.

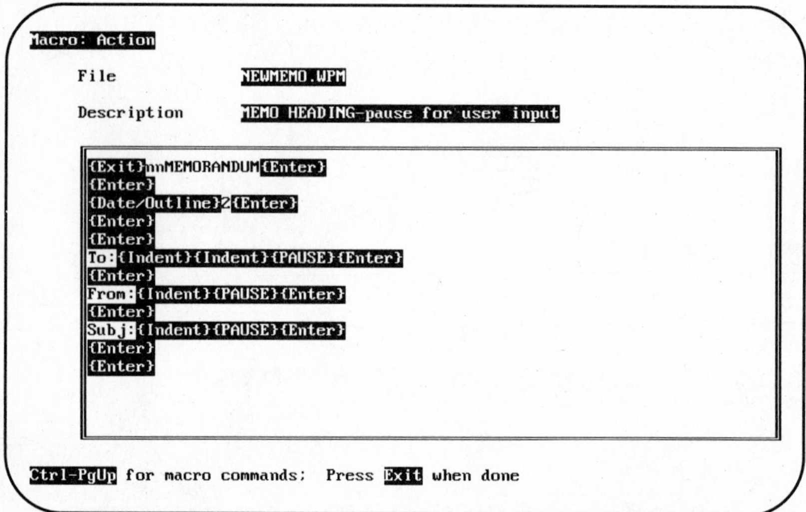

Macro: Action
File NEWMEMO.WPM
Description MEMO HEADING-pause for user input
{Exit}nnMEMORANDUM{Enter}
{Enter}
{Date/Outline}2{Enter}
{Enter}
{Enter}
To:{Indent}{Indent}{PAUSE}{Enter}
{Enter}
From:{Indent}{PAUSE}{Enter}
{Enter}
Subj:{Indent}{PAUSE}{Enter}
{Enter}
{Enter}
Ctrl-PgUp for macro commands; Press Exit when done

***Fig. 11.4.** The Macro: Action screen before editing.*

Reading and understanding the macro code is not difficult if you remember the meaning of the keystrokes. Read the macro code in figure 11.4 as follows:

- `{Exit}nnMEMORANDUM{Enter}{Enter}`: Presses Exit (F7), responds **no** to both saving the current document and exiting from WordPerfect, types **MEMORANDUM**, and presses Enter twice.
- `{Date/Outline}2{Enter}{Enter}{Enter}`: Selects Date/Outline (Shift-F5), chooses Date Code (**2**), and presses Enter three times.
- `To:{Indent}{Indent}{PAUSE}{Enter}{Enter}`: Types **To:**, presses Indent (F4) twice, pauses to accept user input, and presses Enter twice.
- `From:{Indent}{PAUSE}{Enter}{Enter}`: Types **From:**, presses Indent (F4) once, pauses to accept user input, and presses Enter twice.
- `Subj:{Indent}{PAUSE}{Enter}{Enter}{Enter}`: Types **Subj:**, presses Indent (F4) once, pauses to accept user input, and presses Enter three times.

At the end of the last line, the macro stops operating and returns the control of WordPerfect 5.1 to you in the current document screen. The cursor is positioned two lines below the `Subj:` line where you can begin typing the body of the memo.

To change the NEWMEMO macro to center both the title MEMORANDUM and the current date, you may find it easier to edit the macro than to re-create all the macro code. To edit the NEWMEMO macro, follow these steps:

Step 1: Clear the screen without saving the current document.

Step 2: Access the **T**ools pull-down menu, select **M**acro, and choose **D**efine (or press Ctrl-F10).

Step 3: When you are prompted `Macro Define:`, type **NEWMEMO** and press Enter.

Step 4: When you are prompted `NEWMEMO.WPM Already Exists`, select **E**dit (**2**).

Step 5: Position the cursor on the letter `M` in `MEMORANDUM` in the first line of the macro code.

Step 6: Press Center (Shift-F6).

Step 7: Move the cursor to the beginning of line three, positioning the cursor on the first curly bracket `{` at the front of `{Date/Outline}`.

Step 8: Press Center (Shift-F6). Be sure that your macro code revisions reflect those shown in figure 11.5.

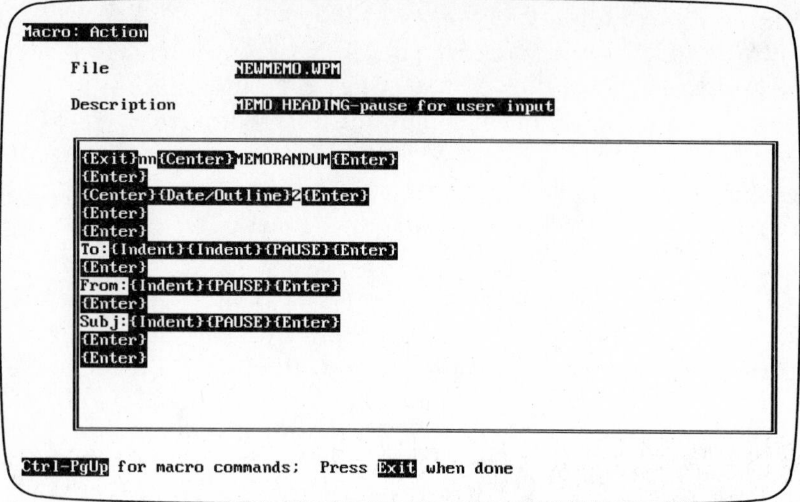

Macro: Action
File NEWMEMO.WPM
Description MEMO HEADING-pause for user input
{Exit}mn{Center}MEMORANDUM{Enter}
{Enter}
{Center}{Date/Outline}2{Enter}
{Enter}
{Enter}
To:{Indent}{Indent}{PAUSE}{Enter}
{Enter}
From:{Indent}{PAUSE}{Enter}
{Enter}
Subj:{Indent}{PAUSE}{Enter}
{Enter}
{Enter}
Ctrl-PgUp for macro commands; Press Exit when done

Fig. 11.5. *The Macro: Action screen after editing to insert center codes.*

Step 9: Press Exit (F7) to restore the current document screen.

Editing is over, and the revised NEWMEMO macro is stored on disk as NEWMEMO.WPM. To execute the macro and see the changes you made, follow these steps:

Step 1: Access the **T**ools pull-down menu, select **M**acro, and choose **E**xecute (or press Alt-F10).

Step 2: At the prompt `Macro:`, type **NEWMEMO** and press Enter.

Step 3: View the centered title and current system date.

Step 4: Complete the entry for the `To:`, `From:`, and `Subj:` lines, as shown in figure 11.6.

```
                    MEMORANDUM

                  October 11, 1990

To:       WordPerfect 5.1 Users

From:     Que Corporation

Subj:     Using the WordPerfect PC Tutor
```

Fig. 11.6. *The results of executing a revised macro.*

Managing Your Macro Files

You may want to keep your macros in a separate library or even to organize several libraries for them. For example, you can develop macros that serve personal needs and others that serve business needs. If two people share the same system, each may have a unique set of macros and therefore need different libraries.

If you have a hard disk, you can organize macros in one or more subdirectories on the hard disk or even maintain and execute macros from a floppy disk. If you use a dual-floppy-disk system, you can organize personal macros on one disk and business macros on another disk.

WordPerfect offers you flexibility for accessing your macros. You can establish a default location for a macro library with the Setup menu, or you can specify a disk drive, path, and directory when you execute a macro. To set a default macro library location, access the **F**ile pull-down menu and select Se**t**up (or press Shift-F1). Choose **L**ocation of Files (**6**); choose Keyboard/Macro Files (**2**); and enter the disk drive, path, and directory name. Figure 11.7 illustrates a default macro library location at C:\WP51\KBMAC.

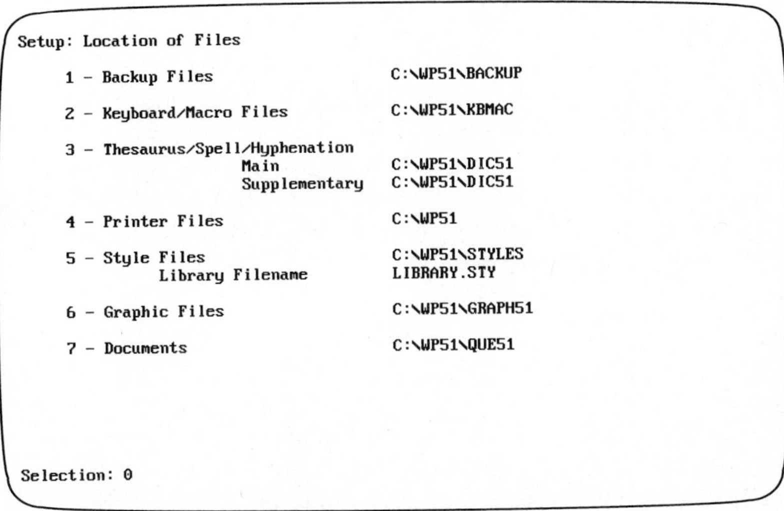

Fig. 11.7. *A sample location of Keyboard/Macro Files.*

You may also specify the disk drive, path, and directory as part of the file name. Suppose, for example, that your default macro library is established on a hard disk but that you want to run a macro from a floppy disk. Insert into the disk drive

(drive A) the floppy disk containing the macro. Access the **T**ools pull-down menu, select **M**acro, and choose **E**xecute (or press Alt-F10). At the prompt `Macro:`, type **A:** followed immediately by the name of the macro.

Consider another example. Suppose that the macro you want to invoke is located on the hard disk in a library other than the library you defined as the default through the Setup menu. Simply indicate the full path followed by the macro name after you begin executing the macro. For example, if the macro is located on drive D in the BIGMAC subdirectory, type **D:\WP51\BIGMAC\macroname** when you see the prompt `Macro:`.

If you do not remember what a macro does, you can highlight the file name after you press List Files (F5) and select **L**ook (**6**). The description entered at the time the macro was created appears at the top of the screen.

Properly accessing WordPerfect macros improves the usefulness of the macro feature. Plan and organize your macro libraries to serve your specific needs, which may be as simple as putting everything in one directory or as sophisticated as organizing several directories. These chapters provide a wide variety of macro applications. For now, you have the skills to use macros in many routine situations.

Using Styles

Whether you manually insert style characteristics (such as margins, fonts, and appearance settings) into documents or use macros, you may find subsequent editing of styles tedious. To specify an alternative style, you must find every place the original style appears in the document and change each occurrence. For example, if you underline text and later decide that you prefer boldfaced text, you must find every place where underlining is used in the document and change every code from underline to bold.

As an alternative, WordPerfect provides a feature with which you can store one or more characteristics, such as underlining, as a style (named, for example, ENHANCE). After you store underlining, you simply establish underlined text in a document by using the Style feature instead of the Underline (F8) command—and store the document with its attached style. If you later decide that you prefer boldface to underlining, just change the appropriate code in the style named ENHANCE.

Once you create a style, you can save it as part of the current document. You can also save it to a style library for use with other documents.

Defining Open, Paired, and Outline Styles

You will find three types of WordPerfect styles: open, paired, and outline.

Open styles remain in effect until you override the style codes, either by using another style or by inserting other formatting codes manually. You do not turn off open styles. Margins are an example of open styles. A margin code affects the document from the place where it is inserted until another margin code is inserted.

Paired styles are turned on and off throughout the document. For example, Underline is a paired style code, turned on at the beginning of the text to be underlined and turned off again at the end of the underlined text. Underline, bold, and italics are stored as paired style codes.

Outline styles organize and format hierarchical material. An outline style is a family of up to eight open or paired styles assigned to a specific outline or paragraph-numbering level. Outline styles, a hybrid of the Outline and Styles features, are discussed in Lesson 15.

Using an Open Style

Figure 11.8 illustrates Styles menu options across the bottom of the screen and provides a sample list of currently defined styles. WordPerfect provides some styles, such as Bibliogrphy (Bibliography) and Pleading (Header for numbered pleading paper). Other styles are user-defined, such as the DOT open style described as `Dingbat 14pt dot bullet` in figure 11.8.

```
Styles

  Name          Type      Description

  A&M LTR HEAD  Open      A & M Corporate Letterhead
  AAITALIC      Paired    ITALICS
  ATYPE         Paired    Type face for type strings
  Bibliogrphy   Paired    Bibliography
  Doc Init      Paired    Initialize Document Style
  Document      Outline   Document Style
  DOT           Open      Dingbat 14pt dot bullet
  FIGURE        Open      Hands-on figure specs.
  FOXMETZ       Open      Fox-Metzelaar ltr head
  H-LINE        Open      Horizontal line left to right
  HANDS-ON TAB  Open      Tab setting for hands-on steps
  INDENT        Outline   Indents each level one tab stop
  LOGO-DUTCH    Open      A&M Heading (no line)
  LOGO-TRM      Open      A&M Heading (w/line and large heading)
  MARGINS       Open      T/B .5 L/R 1.0
  PageNum       Open      Page numbering supp head/foot
  Pleading      Open      Header for numbered pleading paper
  Right Par     Outline   Right-Aligned Paragraph Numbers
  SQUARE        Open      Dingbat 14pt square bullet

1 On; 2 Off; 3 Create; 4 Edit; 5 Delete; 6 Save; 7 Retrieve; 8 Update: 1
```

Fig. 11.8. A sample Styles screen display, including menu options.

Select **C**reate (3) to access a screen on which to enter text and codes. Select **S**ave (6) to store the newly created style for use with more than one document. Access the previously stored style by selecting **R**etrieve (7).

Creating a Style

To access the Styles screen, follow these steps:

Step 1: Clear the screen without saving the current document.

Step 2: Access the **L**ayout pull-down menu and select **S**tyles (or press Alt-F8).

You should see the menu options across the bottom of the screen. The defined styles on your screen display may vary from those shown in figure 11.8.

In Lesson 3, you combined two documents to form a letterhead over a letter (CRIMSON3.LTR). As an alternative, you can create a style sheet containing a letterhead that you can use repeatedly to position a letterhead on a new or existing document. Assume that you would like to include open codes to set justification to Left, turn Widow/Orphan Protection on, and center page numbering at the bottom of each page in the document.

To create a letterhead style containing these open codes, follow these steps:

Step 1: Select **C**reate (3) to access the Styles: Edit menu (see fig. 11.9).

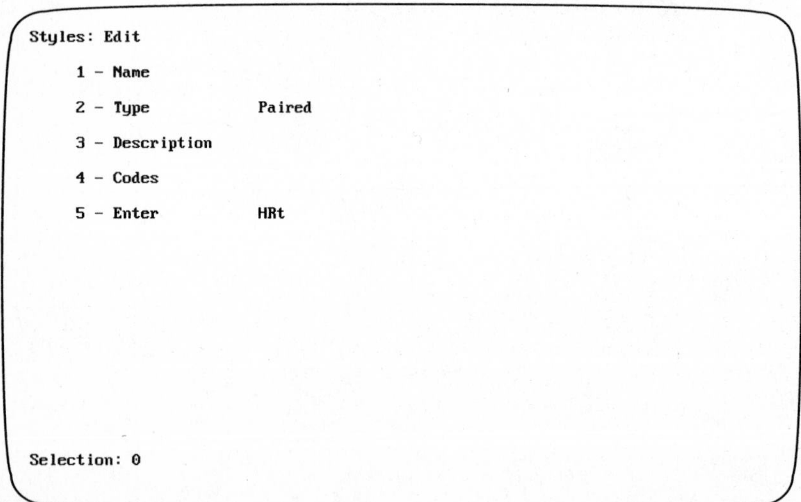

Fig. 11.9. *The Styles: Edit menu.*

Step 2: Select **N**ame (**1**), type LETTERHEAD, and press Enter.

Step 3: Select **T**ype (**2**) and then choose **O**pen (**2**) from the menu options that appear at the bottom of the screen.

Note: The Styles: Edit menu now displays only four choices that are appropriate to open style sheets, as compared to the five options shown in figure 11.9.

Step 4: Select **D**escription (**3**), type **Crimson letterhead**, and press Enter.

Step 5: Choose **C**odes (**4**).

Note: The screen that appears is similar to the Reveal Codes screen (see fig. 11.10). Use the upper half of the screen to enter open codes and the first half of paired codes. Enter the second half of paired codes in the lower half of the screen.

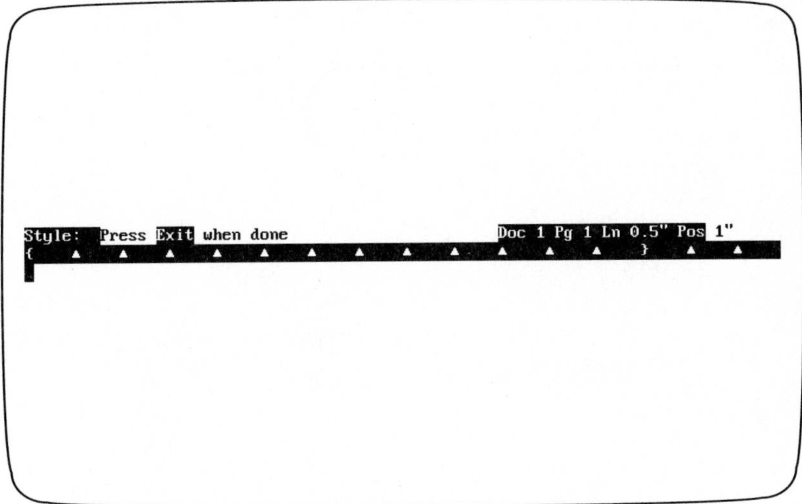

Fig. 11.10. *The style codes screen before codes and text are entered.*

Step 6: Access the **L**ayout pull-down menu and select **L**ine (or press Shift-F8,1).

Step 7: Choose **J**ustification (**3**) and choose **L**eft (**1**).

Step 8: Choose **W**idow/Orphan Protection (**9**), select **Y**es, and press Exit (F7) to return to the Styles split screen.

Note: The codes `[Just:Left][W/O On]` appear in the first line of the bottom half of the Styles split screen.

Step 9: Access the **L**ayout pull-down menu and select **P**age (or press Shift-F8,2).

Step 10: Choose Page **N**umbering (**6**), choose Page Number **P**osition (**4**), and type **6** to center page numbering at the bottom of every page in the document.

Step 11: Press Exit (F7) to restore the Styles split screen.

You entered the open codes that control the document as a whole. The codes `[Just:Left][W/O On][Pg Numbering:Bottom Center]` appear in the first line of the bottom half of the Styles split screen. To complete the letterhead by adding three lines of text, one of which is enhanced with boldface, follow these steps:

Step 1: Press Center (Shift-F6), press Bold (F6), type **CRIMSON TOURS & TRAVEL, INC.**, press Bold (F6), and press Enter twice.

Step 2: Press Center (Shift-F6), type **Serving Corporate America for 30 Years**, and press Enter three times.

Step 3: Press Center (Shift-F6), type **Land - Sea - Air**, and then press Enter three times.

Step 4: Press Home, Home, Home, up arrow to position the cursor on the first code. Be sure that your screen resembles the one shown in figure 11.11.

Step 5: Press Exit (F7) twice to restore the Styles menu options across the bottom of the screen (see fig. 11.8).

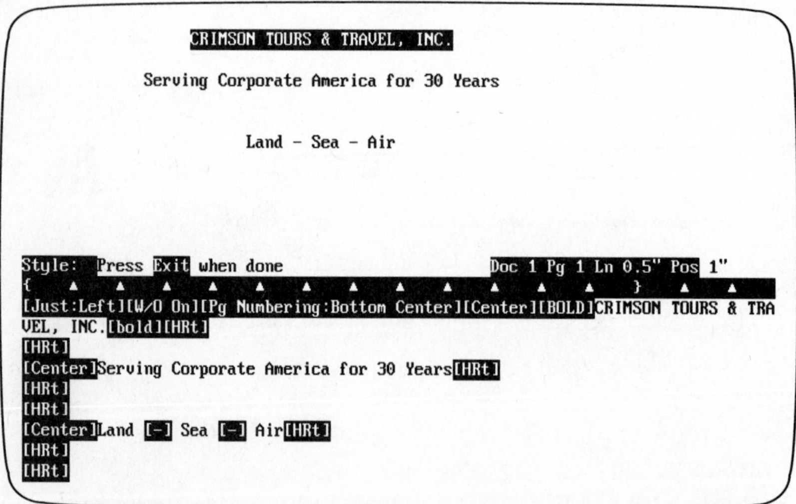

***Fig. 11.11.** The style codes screen after codes and text are entered.*

Saving a Style in a Style Library

Once you create a style sheet, you can file it on disk and use it again. To save a style sheet unique to the current document, simply save the document to disk. If you plan to use the style sheet in other documents, save the style sheet to a styles library.

To save the newly created LETTERHEAD style sheet to a style library, follow these steps:

Step 1: Be sure that the Styles menu options appear across the bottom of the screen, as shown in figure 11.8; choose **S**ave (**6**).

Step 2: In response to the prompt `Filename:`, type **CRIMSON.LIB** and press Enter.

Note: Even though the style itself is named LETTERHEAD, it is stored under a selected library named CRIMSON.LIB, which can hold many other styles established for the CRIMSON firm.

Note: If you see the message `Replace CRIMSON.LIB? No (Yes)`, press **Y**.

Step 3: Press Exit (F7) to restore the current document screen.

Saving a Style as Part of a Document

To use a style, first note whether the name of the style appears after you select Style (Alt-F8); if the name doesn't appear, retrieve the style library containing the style you want. Then highlight the name of the style and choose **O**n (**1**). Be sure to save the document if you want to retain the new style settings.

To insert the style LETTERHEAD above the body of a letter stored as CRIMSO11.LTR, follow these steps:

Step 1: Access the **F**ile pull-down menu and select E**x**it (or press F7). When prompted `Save document? Yes (No)`, press **N**. When prompted `Exit WP? No (Yes)`, press **N**.

LESSON FILES

Step 2: Access the **F**ile pull-down menu and select **R**etrieve (or press Shift-F10). When prompted `Document to be retrieved:`, type **CRIMSO11.LTR** and press Enter.

Step 3: Access the **L**ayout pull-down menu and select **S**tyles (or press Alt-F8).

Note: The display area above the Styles main menu does not list the LETTERHEAD style sheet. You must tell WordPerfect to attach the CRIMSON.LIB style library to the current document.

Step 4: Choose **R**etrieve (**7**). When you are prompted `Filename:`, type **CRIMSON.LIB** and press Enter.

Step 5: In response to the message `Style(s) already exist. Replace? No (Yes)`, press **Y** to attach the styles in CRIMSON.LIB to the current document.

Step 6: Highlight the file name LETTERHEAD and choose **On** (**1**).

Note: The contents of the LETTERHEAD style are inserted at the top of the document.

Step 7: Access the **File** pull-down menu and select **Print** (or press Shift-F7). Select **View** Document (**6**) to see the bold enhancement to the firm name in the first line of the letterhead.

Step 8: Press Exit (F7) enough times to restore the current document screen.

Step 9: Press Save (F10) and specify the file name CRIMCODE.LTR.

Using Reveal Codes To View a Style Code

You should now have a complete letter on the current document screen, including the letterhead inserted at the top of the document after you attached the CRIMSON library of styles and selected LETTERHEAD. Use Reveal Codes to view a style code.

To view the open style code generating the letterhead in the current document, follow these steps:

Step 1: Access the **Edit** pull-down menu and choose **Reveal** Codes (or press Alt-F3 or F11).

Step 2: Notice the `[Open Style:LETTERHEAD]` code in the first line of the Reveal Codes display on the bottom half of the screen, as illustrated in figure 11.12.

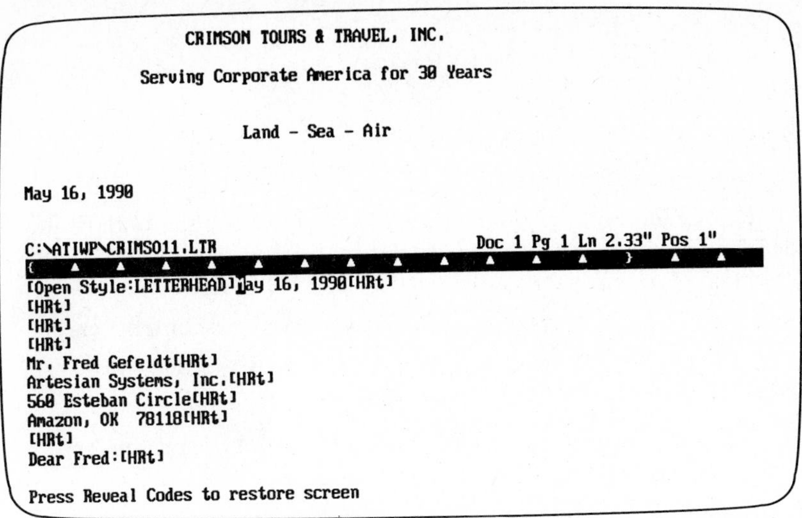
CRIMSON TOURS & TRAVEL, INC.

Serving Corporate America for 30 Years

Land - Sea - Air

May 16, 1990

C:\ATIWP\CRIMSO11.LTR Doc 1 Pg 1 Ln 2.33" Pos 1"

[Open Style:LETTERHEAD]May 16, 1990[HRt]
[HRt]
[HRt]
[HRt]
Mr. Fred Gefeldt[HRt]
Artesian Systems, Inc.[HRt]
560 Esteban Circle[HRt]
Amazon, OK 70118[HRt]
[HRt]
Dear Fred:[HRt]

Press Reveal Codes to restore screen

Fig. 11.12. *Using Reveal Codes to view an Open Style code.*

Note: You can view the style codes when you are in Reveal Codes mode, but you cannot edit style codes from Reveal Codes mode.

Step 3: Position the cursor on the `[Open Style:LETTERHEAD]` code to view the multiple-line display of the style's contents.

Step 4: Access the Edit pull-down menu and choose **R**eveal Codes (or press Alt-F3 or F11) to turn off Reveal Codes.

Editing a Style

As your needs change, so will your style sheets. For example, suppose that you decide that underlining is more appropriate than bolding for the company name in the letterhead. To make the change and incorporate the change into every document containing the letterhead style code, simply highlight the LETTERHEAD style on your style sheets menu, choose **E**dit (**4**), and change the codes.

To change LETTERHEAD so that you underline the company name rather than boldface it, follow these steps:

Step 1: Access the **L**ayout pull-down menu and select **S**tyles (or press Alt-F8) to access the Styles menu options at the bottom of the screen.

Step 2: If the name LETTERHEAD does not appear in the list of style names, choose **R**etrieve (**7**), type CRIMSON.LIB, press Enter, and select **Y**es to replace.

Step 3: Highlight the LETTERHEAD style sheet.

Step 4: Select **E**dit (4) to access the Styles: Edit menu.

Step 5: Choose **C**odes (4).

Step 6: Highlight the initial **[BOLD]** code and press Delete.

Step 7: Press Underline (F8), press End, and press Underline (F8).

Note: If your screen displays underlining, you can see the underlining under the firm name. Otherwise, turn on Reveal Codes and highlight the style code to verify that underline codes are in effect.

Step 8: Press Exit (F7) enough times to restore the current document screen.

To see that the change is automatically incorporated into stored documents containing the LETTERHEAD open style code, follow these steps:

Step 1: Clear the screen without saving the current document and retrieve the CRIMCODE.LTR you saved in a previous exercise.

Step 2: Be sure that the firm name appears underlined instead of in boldface (use **V**iew Document (6) from the Print menu if your screen does not display underlining).

Creating a Paired Style

Any paired WordPerfect 5.1 code can be easily incorporated in a paired style. Two commonly used paired codes are Bold (F6) and Underline (F8). Creating a paired style sheet is similar to creating an open style sheet except that you must include the ending code in a paired style sheet.

To access the screen to include paired codes that boldface text in a style called ENHANCE, follow these steps:

Step 1: Clear the screen without saving the current document and retrieve CRIMSO11.LTR.

Step 2: Access the **L**ayout pull-down menu and select **S**tyles (or press Alt-F8).

Step 3: Select **C**reate (3) to access the Styles: Edit menu.

Step 4: Select **N**ame (**1**), type **ENHANCE**, and press Enter.

Step 5: Select **D**escription (3), type Bold selected text, and press Enter.

Step 6: Choose **C**odes (**4**).

The initial style codes screen for paired codes (see fig. 11.13) is similar to that for open codes (see fig. 11.10). However, a box appears in the upper half of the paired codes screen, which displays the notation `Place Style On Codes above, and Style Off Codes below`. The cursor is initially located above the box. Enter open codes and the beginning code of a paired code above the box; enter the ending code of a paired code below the box. Use cursor-movement keys to move between boxes.

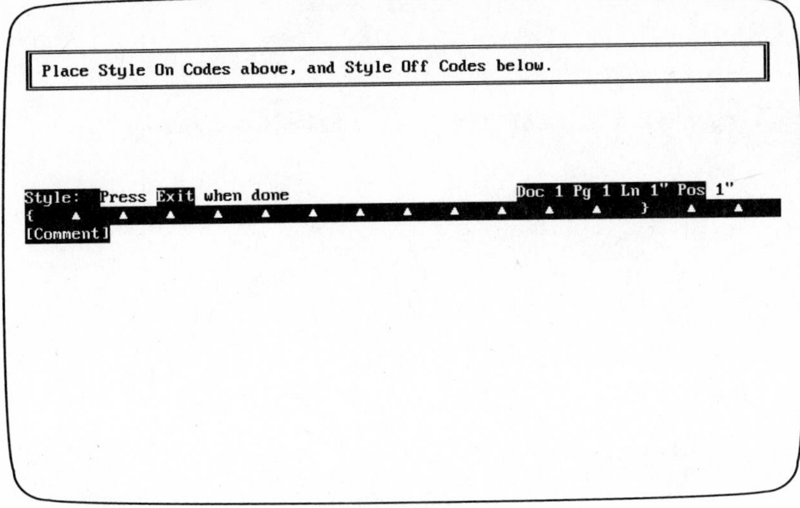

Fig. 11.13. A style paired codes screen before codes are entered.

The [Comment] marks the spot for text that will be surrounded by the paired codes. You are not limited to the number of codes you can enter into the box. If, however, you keep style sheets simple, you will find them easier to troubleshoot and edit.

To enter the codes to bold text, follow these steps:

Step 1: If the current cursor position is not above the box, press Home, Home, Home, up arrow.

Step 2: Press Bold (F6).

Step 3: Press Home, Home, Home, down arrow to position the cursor below the box.

Step 4: Press Bold (F6).

Figure 11.14 illustrates the display of paired codes in the bottom portion of the screen—similar to a Reveal Codes mode display.

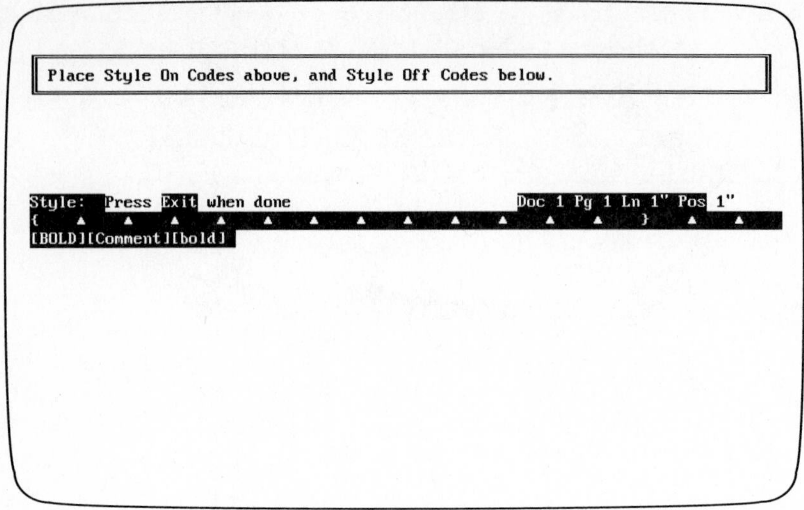

Fig. 11.14. *The paired codes screen after codes have been entered.*

Now that you entered the codes to boldface text, exit from the style screen and put the ENHANCE style to work. To boldface existing text, follow these general instructions: highlight the text, access style sheets, highlight the ENHANCE style sheet, and select **On** (**1**). If you have a lot of text to enhance, create a macro that turns on Block, pauses so that you can highlight the block to be enhanced, and inserts the style sheet when you press Enter.

You must also save the current document if you want to save the style sheet as part of the document. If you want to share the style sheet with other documents, also save the current style library, including the new style sheet, back to disk.

To boldface a phrase in the CRIMSO11.LTR, follow these steps:

Step 1: Press Exit (F7) enough times to restore the display of the CRIMSO11.LTR document.

Step 2: Position the cursor in the second paragraph, on the `w` in `worry free`.

Step 3: Access the **E**dit pull-down menu and select **B**lock (or press Alt-F4 or F12).

Step 4: Highlight the phrase `worry free` located in paragraph two.

Step 5: Access the **L**ayout pull-down menu and select **S**tyles (or press Alt-F8).

Step 6: Highlight the style sheet ENHANCE and choose **On** (**1**).

The `Block On` message disappears, and the phrase worry free appears highlighted to indicate that it is marked for bold printing.

You may think that it is more efficient to boldface the marked text by pressing Bold (F6) instead of performing Steps 5 and 6. In this short example of boldfacing text in one document, you are correct. Remember, however, that you can store many codes in a single style and that you can save a style for use with other documents.

Now that you know how to use a style to enhance existing text, apply the same technique to enhancing text as you type. Follow these steps:

Step 1: Press Home, Home, Home, down arrow and position the cursor three lines below the last line typed.

Step 2: Access the **L**ayout pull-down menu and select **S**tyles (or press Alt-F8).

Step 3: Highlight the style name ENHANCE and choose **O**n (**1**).

Step 4: Type **P.S. You would not believe how beautiful Tahiti is this time of year—the ideal place for your next sales conference.**

Step 5: Press End to end the style sheet.

You can also stop using the style by pressing right arrow or by accessing the Style menu (Alt-F8) and choosing Off (**2**).

In this lesson you practiced relatively simple applications for both macros and styles. Experiment with both features to develop your knowledge of the power of WordPerfect.

For Further Reference

For an extended discussion on creating, using, and storing macros, including unnamed and keyboard macros as well as Alt-letter and descriptive macros, consult *Using WordPerfect 5.1*, Special Edition, (Que Corporation, Carmel, IN, 1989), Chapters 11 and 12.

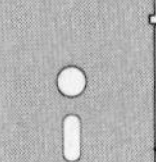

Summary of Concepts

Lesson 11 explains these concepts:

- ❑ You can capture any WordPerfect keystrokes, store them within a macro, and automatically repeat the keystrokes by running the macro.
- ❑ You can create and run four kinds of macros: Alt-letter macros, descriptive macros, unnamed macros, and keyboard macros.
- ❑ WordPerfect assigns a .WPM (WordPerfect macro) extension to each macro.
- ❑ Creating a macro is quite simple: press Macro Define (Ctrl-F10), provide the name and a brief description of the macro, type the keystrokes to be stored, and press Ctrl-F10 to toggle off Macro Define.
- ❑ To edit a macro, press Macro Define (Ctrl-F10), specify an existing macro name, and replace or edit the code.
- ❑ To make a macro pause for user entry from the keyboard, access Macro Commands (Ctrl-PgUp) and choose Pause (**1**). Wordperfect inserts a {PAUSE} code in the macro.
- ❑ Hard disk users generally establish library files of macros in a subdirectory other than the WordPerfect document subdirectory.
- ❑ Styles contain user-defined editing codes and text.
- ❑ You can attach styles to a specific document or store them in style libraries to be used in other documents.
- ❑ There are three types of styles; Open, Paired, and Outline.
- ❑ Open styles remain in effect until you override the style codes, either by using another style or by inserting other formatting codes manually.
- ❑ Paired styles, such as bold and underline, are turned on and off throughout the document.
- ❑ Outline style sheets are used to control the indentation and format of up to eight levels of outline.
- ❑ You can view style codes in Reveal Codes mode, but you must access the Styles (Alt-F8) menu to edit style codes.

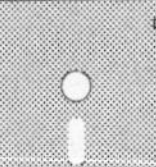

Review Exercises

Practice using the WordPerfect features in this lesson by completing these exercises. If you do not remember how to do something, review the explanation and practice the tasks again.

1. Clear the screen without saving the current document.
2. Create and run a macro that types the name of the city in which you live.
3. Replace the macro created in exercise 2 with a macro that first clears the screen, then types your complete address, including a five-digit ZIP code.
4. Edit the macro created in exercise 3 by changing the five-digit ZIP code to a nine-digit ZIP code.
5. Create a macro that prompts for user entry of name and birthday information.
6. Display the macro code for NEWMEMO and be sure that you understand each part of the code.
7. Edit the macro code displayed in exercise 6 to eliminate clearing the screen before you prompt the user.
8. Create an open style sheet that sets top and bottom margins at .5 inch, left and right margins at 1.25 inches, page numbering at the bottom center of the page, and your name and address centered at the top of the page as a letterhead.
9. Access CRIMSO11.LTR, create a paired style sheet that italicizes text, and italicize the first sentence of paragraph one.

Using Merge

12

In this lesson, you practice these tasks:

- ❑ Differentiate between fixed and variable data
- ❑ Create a primary merge document
- ❑ Create a secondary merge file
- ❑ Execute a merge
- ❑ Alter merge codes
- ❑ Eliminate blank lines in merge results
- ❑ Include dates in merged documents
- ❑ Merge data from the keyboard
- ❑ Create labels by using Merge

Most word processors provide a merge capability so that you can combine data that does not change with data that does change. WordPerfect 5.1 has a powerful merge feature that automates a number of routine chores and allows you to assemble a rather complex document with ease. You can use Merge to create custom letters, contracts, mailing and filing labels, invitations, and any other document that combines a standard format with some varying information.

This lesson helps you understand primary (fixed data) and secondary (variable data) files, learn the available codes, merge text files, and print labels.

Understanding a Merge

Merge operations blend fixed data with variable data. Figure 12.1 illustrates the top portion of the CRIMSON letter used throughout the workbook. In figure 12.1, XXXXs represent variable data: four address lines (full name, company name, street address, city-state-ZIP code) and the portion of the salutation line after Dear.

```
                 CRIMSON TRAVEL & TOURS, INC.
         Serving American Corporations for 30 Years

                      Land - Sea - Air

May 16, 1990


XX. XXXX XXXXXXX
XXXXXXXX XXXXXXX, XXX.
XXX XXXXXXX XXXXXXX
XXXXXX, XX  XXXXX

Dear XXXXX:

Crimson Travel & Tours is introducing a new corporate reservations
department.  We promise a prompt response to your questions about
schedules and free delivery of tickets to your office or home.
```

Fig. 12.1. *A document displaying XXXXs for variable data; other content is fixed data.*

All remaining information—text, numbers, symbols, and formatting codes controlling the layout of the document—in figure 12.1 is fixed. You can type the fixed or standard parts of a document once and store them as a "boilerplate" or model for merging with a file of variable data.

Figure 12.2 illustrates a custom letter produced by blending specific variable data about one client with general fixed data.

```
                    CRIMSON TRAVEL & TOURS, INC.
              Serving American Corporations for 30 Years

                         Land - Sea - Air

     May 16, 1990


     Mr. Fred Gefeldt
     Artesian Systems, Inc.
     560 Esteban Circle
     Amazon, OK  78118

     Dear Fred:

     Crimson Travel & Tours is introducing a new corporate reservations
     department.  We promise a prompt response to your questions about
     schedules and free delivery of tickets to your office or home.
```

Fig. 12.2. *A merge that combines fixed data with variable data to produce a finished document.*

To use the merge capability, store fixed information in a primary merge file, or primary file, and merge the primary file with the variable data. WordPerfect 5.1 provides several methods for inserting variable information into a merge. The most common method involves placing the variable information in a secondary merge file, or secondary file, which you can develop on any database or file management program supported by WordPerfect 5.1. You can also merge variable data into the primary document from the keyboard or from a WordPerfect secondary file—the methods illustrated in the workbook.

The primary file controls the merge operation. To create the primary file, type the document the way you ordinarily do, including format codes. In addition, enter merge codes that show where each item of variable information is to be placed. When you execute a merge, the program reads the primary file and pulls in variable information from the file sources designated by the merge codes. Variable information appears in the locations marked by the associated merge codes.

You can create the primary and secondary merge files in either order. Often your variable data already exists in secondary files created through other database software. Using Merge is then a matter of creating the primary file in WordPerfect 5.1 and using the variable data.

Building a Simple Merge

Suppose that you want to merge your customer information into the Crimson letter that you worked with in previous lessons. Planning your merge is important. You can adapt the CRIMSO12.LTR document illustrated in figure 12.2 as the primary merge file.

Examine the CRIMSO12.LTR document to determine the information that changes with each letter (variable data). The information that changes includes the customer's full name, company name, street address, city, state, ZIP code, and first name. You may also include telephone number. Although phone number is not merged into this primary document, it adds to our information about customers and can be used in other merged documents listing customers and phone numbers. It is easier to include data initially than to add it later.

Each piece of information—such as full name or city—is a field. Related fields (all data about one customer) form a record. To use WordPerfect's merge capability, you must set up fields and enter data in a secondary merge file and create a reference to the secondary file field names in the primary merge document.

Creating the Secondary File

To create the secondary file, begin with a blank document. On the first page, set up the names of the fields. On the second and subsequent pages, enter data into fields in the order in which the fields were set up on the first page.

Each page constitutes a record. Consider the first page the Field Names record and remaining pages as individual customer records.

Creating the Field Names Record

To create the Field Names record in the secondary file, follow these steps:

Step 1: Clear the current document screen without saving the current document.

Note: The instruction to clear the screen without saving the current document is used many times throughout the workbook. It means to access the **F**ile pull-down menu and select E**x**it (or press F7); when you are prompted `Save Document? Yes (No)`, press **N**; when you see the prompt `Exit WP? No (Yes)`, press **N**.

Step 2: Access the **T**ools pull-down menu and select Me**r**ge Codes (or press Shift-F9).

Note: Figure 12.3 illustrates using the pull-down menu system for Step 2. If instead you press Shift- F9, you see the menu options **F**ield, **E**nd Record, **I**nput, **P**age Off, **N**ext Record, and **M**ore across the bottom of the screen.

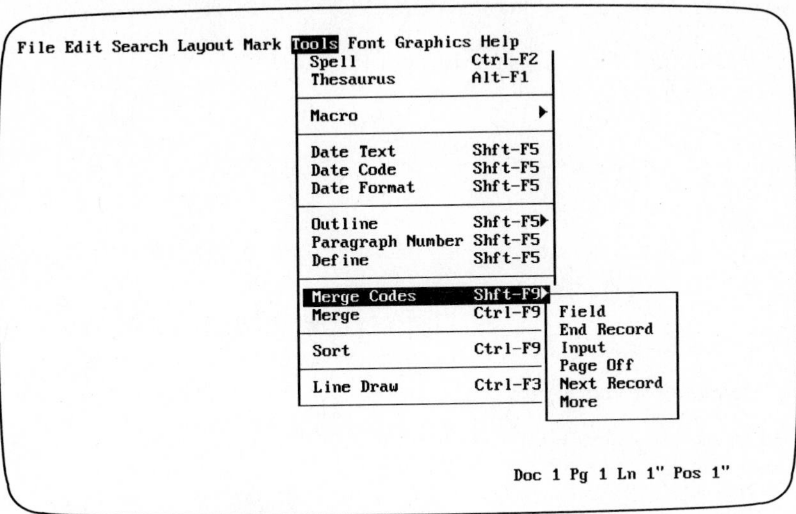

Fig. 12.3. Merge Codes options.

Step 3: Choose **M**ore (**6**) to access a pop-up menu of merge codes in the upper right corner of the screen (see fig. 12.4).

Step 4: Type **F** to position the highlight bar on the first merge code starting with `F`, press the down arrow to highlight the `{FIELD NAMES}` option, and press Enter.

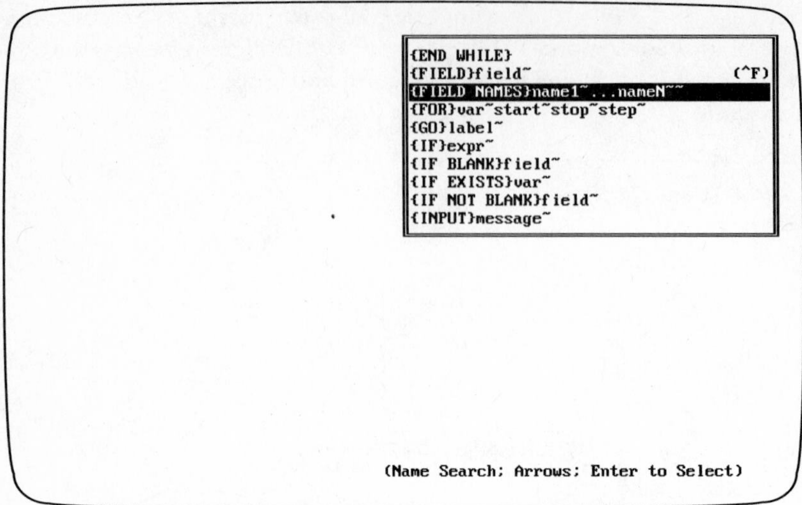

Fig. 12.4. *The Merge Codes selection box.*

Step 5: When you are prompted in the lower left corner of the screen `Enter Field 1:`, type **FullName** and press Enter.

Step 6: When you are prompted `Enter Field 2:`, type **Company** and press Enter.

Step 7: When you see the prompt `Enter Field 3:`, type **Street** and press Enter.

Step 8: At the prompt `Enter Field 4:`, type **CityStateZip** and press Enter.

Note: Three pieces of data are contained in field 4. It is acceptable to combine data into one field. The data must, however, be used as one field and cannot be split up.

Step 9: When you are prompted `Enter Field 5:`, type **Phone** and press Enter.

Step 10: When you see the prompt `Enter Field 6:`, type **FirstName** and press Enter.

Step 11: Press Enter to finish setting up the Field Names record.

The Field Names record is now complete, as illustrated in figure 12.5. Pressing Enter in Step 11 terminates the record with the {END RECORD} code. The cursor is positioned at the top of the second page (note the `Pg 2` in the cursor position status displayed in the lower right corner of the screen), marking the spot for entering the variable data.

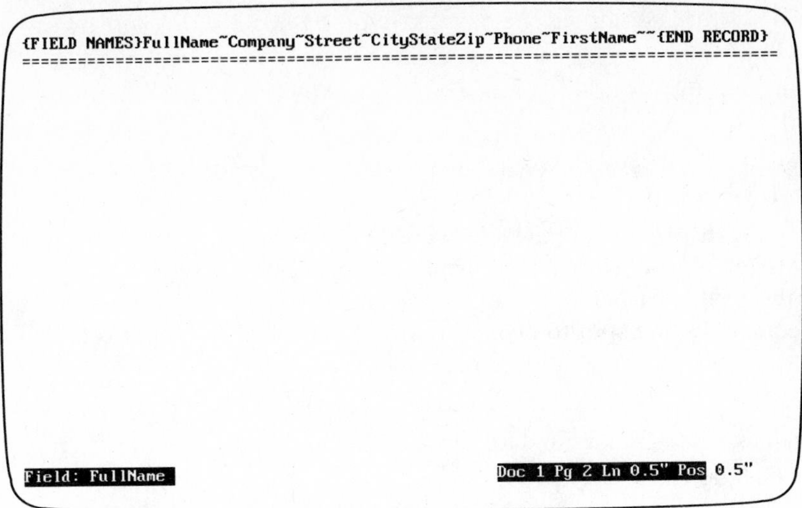

Fig. 12.5. A secondary file displaying the Field Names record.

Entering Variable Data

The message `Field: FullName` appears in the lower left corner of the screen, prompting you to enter the full name of the first customer. You are prompted to enter data for each field in the record in sequence. Conclude entry in a field by pressing End Field (F9). Once you complete data entry for all fields within one record, terminate entry in the record with an End Record code (Shift-F9,2).

You can edit a secondary file the same way you edit any document. Be careful not to remove an `{END FIELD}` or `{End Record}` code, or the wrong data appears in the merge.

To complete the first record, follow these steps:

Step 1: When you are prompted `Field: FullName`, type **Ms. Anna Marie Enloe** and press End Field (F9).

Step 2: When you see the prompt `Field: Company`, type **The OSU** and press End Field (F9).

Step 3: When you see `Field: Street`, type **100 Learning Rd.** and press End Field (F9).

Step 4: At the prompt `Field: CityStateZip`, type **Columbus, OH 43221** and press End Field (F9).

Step 5: When you are prompted `Field: Phone`, type **614/333-0988** and press End Field (F9).

Step 6: At the prompt `Field: FirstName`, type **Anna Marie** and press End Field (F9).

Step 7: Access the Tools pull-down menu and select Merge Codes (or press Shift F-9); then choose **E**nd Record (**2**).

Your screen should display the initial Field Names record and the completed record for Ms. Anna Marie Enloe, as shown in figure 12.6. WordPerfect inserts a page break (indicated by the double dashed line beneath each record). The cursor is positioned on page three, marking the spot to begin entering the second customer record.

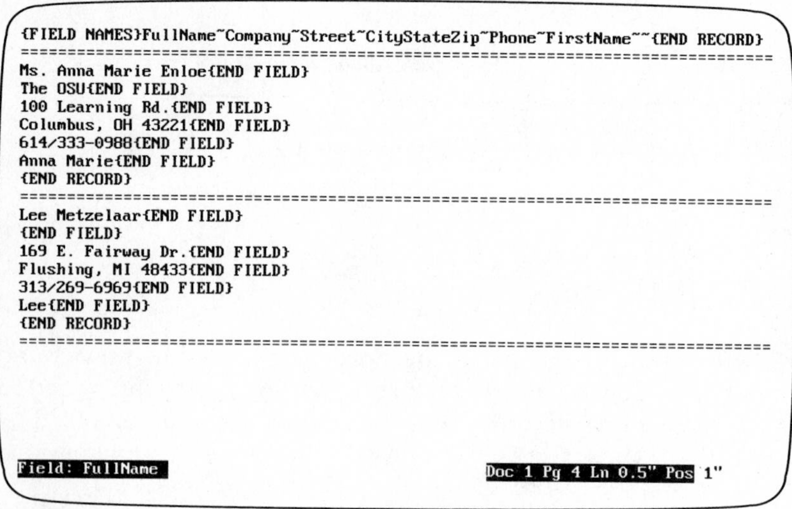

{FIELD NAMES}FullName~Company~Street~CityStateZip~Phone~FirstName~~{END RECORD}
Ms. Anna Marie Enloe{END FIELD}
The OSU{END FIELD}
100 Learning Rd.{END FIELD}
Columbus, OH 43221{END FIELD}
614/333-0988{END FIELD}
Anna Marie{END FIELD}
{END RECORD}
Lee Metzelaar{END FIELD}
{END FIELD}
169 E. Fairway Dr.{END FIELD}
Flushing, MI 48433{END FIELD}
313/269-6969{END FIELD}
Lee{END FIELD}
{END RECORD}
Field: FullName
Doc 1 Pg 4 Ln 0.5" Pos 1"

Fig. 12.6. *A secondary merge file with two customer records.*

To complete the second record, follow these steps:

Step 1: When you are prompted `Field: FullName`, type **Lee Metzelaar** and press End Field (F9).

Step 2: At the prompt `Field: Company`, press End Field (F9).

Note: Some fields may not have an entry. For example, a customer may not be affiliated with a company; therefore, a company entry is not applicable. Press End Field (F9) without typing field contents if you want the contents of a field to be blank.

Step 3: When you are prompted `Field: Street`, type **169 E. Fairway Dr.** and press End Field (F9).

Step 4: When you are prompted `Field: CityStateZip`, type **Flushing, MI 48433** and press End Field (F9).

Step 5: At the prompt `Field: Phone`, type **313/269-6969** and press End Field (F9).

Step 6: When you are prompted `Field: FirstName`, type **Lee** and press End Field (F9).

Step 7: Access the Tools pull-down menu and select Merge Codes (or press Shift-F9). Choose End Record (**2**).

Step 8: Press Exit (F7), press Y in response to the prompt `Save document? Yes (No)`, type MERGESEC as the file name, and press Enter.

The secondary merge file (see fig. 12.6) is completed and stored on disk. You can use the data stored in this file with any primary file.

Creating the Primary File

To execute a merge operation, you need a primary file containing fixed text and codes as well as a secondary file containing variable data. To edit the CRIMSO12.LTR document with merge codes and save the revision as the primary file, follow these steps:

Step 1: Clear the current document screen and retrieve the CRIMSO12.LTR document (see fig. 12.2).

Step 2: Position the cursor at the beginning of the first line of the address block (`Mr. Fred Gefeldt`).

Step 3: Press Ctrl-End to delete the line.

Step 4: Access the **T**ools pull-down menu and select Me**r**ge Codes (or press Shift-F9); choose **F**ield (**1**).

Step 5: When you are prompted `Enter Field:` at the bottom of the screen, type **FullName** and press Enter.

Note: You are entering the field names you created in the secondary merge file. As you type, the field name appears at the bottom of the screen until you press Enter. Then the merge code is transferred to the document.

Step 6: Position the cursor at the beginning of the second line of the address block (`Artesian Systems`) and press Ctrl-End to delete the line.

Step 7: Access the **T**ools pull-down menu and select Me**r**ge Codes (or press Shift-F9); choose **F**ield (**1**).

Step 8: When you are prompted `Enter Field:`, type **Company** and press Enter.

Step 9: Position the cursor at the beginning of the third line of the address block and press Ctrl-End to delete the line.

Step 10: Access the **T**ools pull-down menu and select Me**r**ge Codes (or press Shift-F9); choose **F**ield (**1**).

Step 11: At the prompt `Enter Field:`, type **Street** and press Enter.

Step 12: Position the cursor at the beginning of the fourth line of the address block and press Ctrl-End to delete the line.

Step 13: Access the **T**ools pull-down menu and select Me**r**ge Codes (or press Shift-F9); choose **F**ield (**1**).

Step 14: When you are prompted `Enter Field:`, type **CityStateZip** and press Enter.

Step 15: Position the cursor on the `F` in `Fred` in the greeting line and delete `Fred`.

Step 16: Access the **T**ools pull-down menu and select Me**r**ge Codes (or press Shift-F9); choose **F**ield (**1**).

Step 17: When you are prompted `Enter Field:`, type **FirstName** and press Enter.

Note: Figure 12.7 illustrates the revised CRIMSO12.LTR document, now a primary document ("boilerplate" or model) for a merge operation.

```
                CRIMSON TRAVEL & TOURS, INC.
          Serving American Corporations for 30 Years

                      Land - Sea - Air


May 16, 1990


{FIELD}Fullname~
{FIELD}Company~
{FIELD}Street~
{FIELD}CityStateZip~

Dear {FIELD}FirstName~:

Crimson Travel & Tours is introducing a new corporate reservations
department. We promise a prompt response to your questions about
schedules and free delivery of tickets to your office or home.

The agents assigned to this department know that you have a very
busy schedule. Their goal is to ensure that your trip is worry
free and that you arrive on time at your destination. Our cruise
specialists can assist with incentive as well as pleasure tours.
C:\ATIWP\CRIMSO12.LTR                    Doc 1 Pg 1 Ln 3.33" Pos 2.5"
```

Fig. 12.7. A primary merge file with field name specifications.

Step 18: Press Exit (F7), press **Y** in response to the prompt `Save document? Yes (No)`, type **MERGEPRI**, and press Enter.

Both files needed for a merge—primary file and secondary file—are now stored on disk.

Executing the Merge

Merge the variable data for each customer record in the secondary file with the fixed data in the primary file to produce a series of custom letters as finished documents.

To execute the merge, follow these steps:

Step 1: Clear the current document screen without saving the current document.

Step 2: Access the **T**ools pull-down menu and select **M**erge (or press Ctrl-F9,1).

Step 3: When you are prompted `Primary file:`, type **MERGEPRI** and press Enter.

Note: Figure 12.8 illustrates the screen prompts that appear during execution of a merge. You can type the requested file name, or you can select List Files (F5) and select the file from the list of files on the current directory.

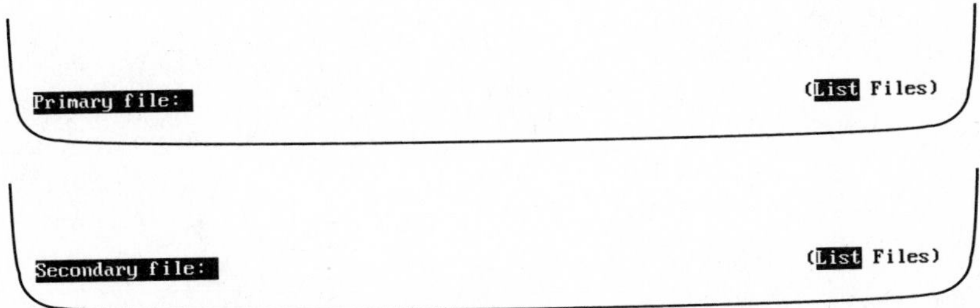

Fig. 12.8. Screen prompts during a merge operation.

Step 4: When you are prompted `Secondary file:`, type **MERGESEC** and press Enter.

Note: Check the bottom line of your screen for messages. If the merge works properly, you see the message `* Merging *`. At the end of the merge, WordPerfect creates a single document; each page within the document is a custom letter. You can print the merged letters immediately or save the document to disk for later printing.

Step 5: Press Home, Home, up arrow to view the first custom letter to Anna Marie Enloe.

Step 6: Press PgDn to view the second custom letter, shown in figure 12.9.

```
                CRIMSON TRAVEL & TOURS, INC.
          Serving American Corporations for 30 Years

                      Land - Sea - Air

May 16, 1990


Lee Metzelaar

169 E. Fairway Dr.
Flushing, MI 48433

Dear Lee:

Crimson Travel & Tours is introducing a new corporate reservations
department.  We promise a prompt response to your questions about
schedules and free delivery of tickets to your office or home.

The agents assigned to this department know that you have a very
busy schedule.  Their goal is to ensure that your trip is worry
free and that you arrive on time at your destination.  Our cruise
specialists can assist with incentive as well as pleasure tours.
                                         Doc 1 Pg 2 Ln 1" Pos 1"
```

Fig. 12.9. A second custom letter in the merged document.

If your merge does not work properly, check the files you created for errors (primary file MERGEPRI shown in figure 12.7 and secondary file MERGESEC shown in figure 12.6). Make sure, for example, that the field names in the Field Names record in the secondary file are spelled the same way as in the primary file. Make corrections as necessary and repeat Steps 1 through 4.

If you cannot find the source of an error, you can continue the workbook exercises by using backup primary (CRIM12A.PRI) and secondary (CRIM12A.SEC) files provided with the lesson disk.

Making Changes to Merge Files

You created and merged a primary and secondary file. But even the best-planned merge eventually needs changing, because your needs change. You may need to add or delete records to the secondary file, update existing data, and add and delete record fields. You can even enter a code to eliminate any field in the primary document for which the associated field in a secondary file record is blank.

Eliminating Blank Fields in Merged Documents

Missing data is a common problem when you merge data. In figure 12.9, the line between Lee Metzelaar and 169 E. Fairway Dr. is blank because the secondary file does not contain a company name for this person.

You can remove blanks from merged documents by using WordPerfect 5.1's merge codes {IF NOT BLANK Company~} and {END IF} in the primary document. Place the codes around the **[HRt]** code that creates the blank line. The command tests the field between the codes, and if the field's contents in the secondary file are blank, the text and hidden codes between {IF NOT BLANK} and {END IF} are suppressed.

To eliminate blank lines in merged documents because no company name exists, follow these steps:

Step 1: Clear the screen without saving the current document and retrieve the MERGEPRI primary document you created earlier.

Note: If the primary document MERGEPRI you created doesn't work, retrieve the backup lesson-disk file CRIM12A.PRI instead.

Step 2: Position the cursor at the beginning of the second line of the address block `{FIELD}Company~`.

Step 3: Access the **T**ools pull-down menu, select Me**r**ge Codes, and choose **M**ore (or press Shift-F9,6).

Step 4: Type **I** to position the highlight bar on the first merge code starting with `I`, highlight `{IF NOT BLANK}field~` in the selection box, and press Enter.

Step 5: When you are prompted `Enter Field:`, type **Company** and press Enter.

Step 6: Position the cursor at the beginning of the third line of the address block (`{FIELD}Street~`).

Step 7: Access the **T**ools pull-down menu, select Me**r**ge Codes, and choose **M**ore (or press Shift-F9,6).

Step 8: Highlight `{END IF}` in the selection box and press Enter.

Note: Your revised merge codes should appear as shown in the top half of figure 12.10. The bottom half of figure 12.10 shows those same codes in Reveal Codes mode.

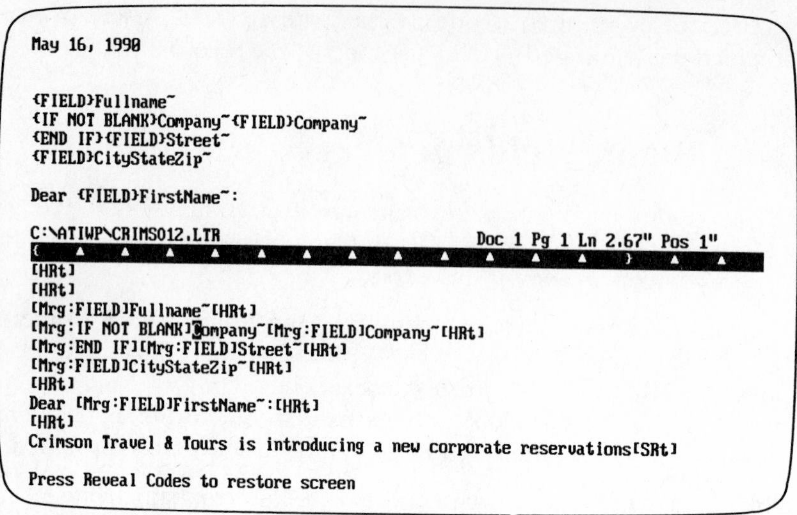
```
May 16, 1990

{FIELD}Fullname~
{IF NOT BLANK}Company~{FIELD}Company~
{END IF}{FIELD}Street~
{FIELD}CityStateZip~

Dear {FIELD}FirstName~:

C:\ATIWP\CRIMS012.LTR                          Doc 1 Pg 1 Ln 2.67" Pos 1"
[HRt]
[HRt]
[Mrg:FIELD]Fullname~[HRt]
[Mrg:IF NOT BLANK]Company~[Mrg:FIELD]Company~[HRt]
[Mrg:END IF][Mrg:FIELD]Street~[HRt]
[Mrg:FIELD]CityStateZip~[HRt]
[HRt]
Dear [Mrg:FIELD]FirstName~:[HRt]
[HRt]
Crimson Travel & Tours is introducing a new corporate reservations[SRt]

Press Reveal Codes to restore screen
```

***Fig. 12.10.** A primary document containing an* {IF NOT BLANK} *code.*

Step 9: Press Exit (F7), press **Y** in response to the prompt Save document? Yes (No), type **MERGEPRI.V2**, and press Enter.

Note: In real merge situations, save the revised primary document under the same name as the original. For workbook illustrations, use a slightly different name each time (in this case, add the extension V2 for version 2) so that you can restart an exercise without reworking all illustrations in the lesson.

To execute the merge again, follow these steps:

Step 1: Clear the screen without saving the current document.

Step 2: Access the **T**ools pull-down menu and select **M**erge (or press Ctrl-F9,1).

Step 3: When you are prompted Primary file:, type **MERGEPRI.V2** and press Enter.

Step 4: When you see the prompt Secondary file:, type **MERGESEC** and press Enter.

Note: If you cannot get the secondary file MERGESEC to work, type the name of the backup lesson-disk file CRIM12A.SEC instead of MERGESEC.

Step 5: After the merge operation is complete, press PgUp and then PgDn to position the cursor at the top of the second custom letter.

Note: Your screen display should resemble the one in figure 12.11. Notice that a blank line no longer appears between the name Lee Metzelaar and the associated address.

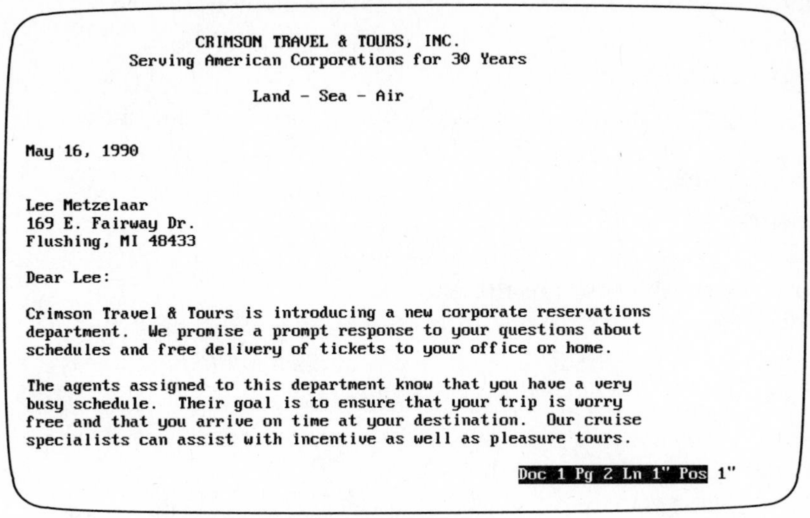

```
            CRIMSON TRAVEL & TOURS, INC.
     Serving American Corporations for 30 Years

                  Land - Sea - Air


May 16, 1990


Lee Metzelaar
169 E. Fairway Dr.
Flushing, MI 48433

Dear Lee:

Crimson Travel & Tours is introducing a new corporate reservations
department.  We promise a prompt response to your questions about
schedules and free delivery of tickets to your office or home.

The agents assigned to this department know that you have a very
busy schedule.  Their goal is to ensure that your trip is worry
free and that you arrive on time at your destination.  Our cruise
specialists can assist with incentive as well as pleasure tours.
                                          Doc 1 Pg 2 Ln 1" Pos 1"
```

***Fig. 12.11.** A second custom letter—blank company name line deleted.*

Altering Fields in Primary and Secondary Files

Sometimes, no matter how carefully you plan a merge, you discover after you begin to create a secondary file that you need to add a field or two. To delete a field, do nothing to the secondary file. Instead, remove references to unwanted fields in the primary file. Adding a field, however, requires a little more consideration.

First you must change the {FIELD NAMES} record in the secondary file, adding the new field name to the list of existing names. If records are already entered into the secondary file, you must update those records with the new data.

Alter the primary file too, inserting a code to reference the new field of data in the secondary file. Add a new field at the end of the Field Names record in the secondary file. Because you can use secondary-file fields in any order within the primary file, the fields don't need to be set up in any particular order in the secondary file. However, the file must be in a consistent order from record to record.

To add a field called Position to the secondary file, which contains each customer's title (for example, President or Director of Sales), follow these steps:

Step 1: Clear the screen without saving the current document and retrieve your MERGESEC file (or CRIM12A.SEC if your file does not work).

Note: Your screen should display the Field Names record and two customer records shown in figure 12.6.

Step 2: Move the cursor to the `{FIELD NAMES}` line on page 1 and position it on the second tilde (~) symbol of the two symbols immediately preceding the `{END RECORD}` code.

Step 3: Type **Position~**.

Note: You must save and retrieve the modified secondary file before WordPerfect 5.1 recognizes the added field.

Step 4: Save the secondary file to disk, using the name MERGESEC.V2.

Step 5: Clear the screen without saving the current document and retrieve the newly revised MERGESEC.V2 document.

Step 6: Press the down arrow until you see the prompt `Field: Position` in the bottom left corner of the screen.

Step 7: Type **General Manager** and press End Field (F9) to update the first customer record on page 2.

Step 8: Press the down arrow until you see the prompt `Field: Position` in the bottom left corner of the screen.

Step 9: Type **Independent Contractor** and press End Field (F9).

The File Names record and customer records in your secondary file should reflect the position-related changes shown in figure 12.12.

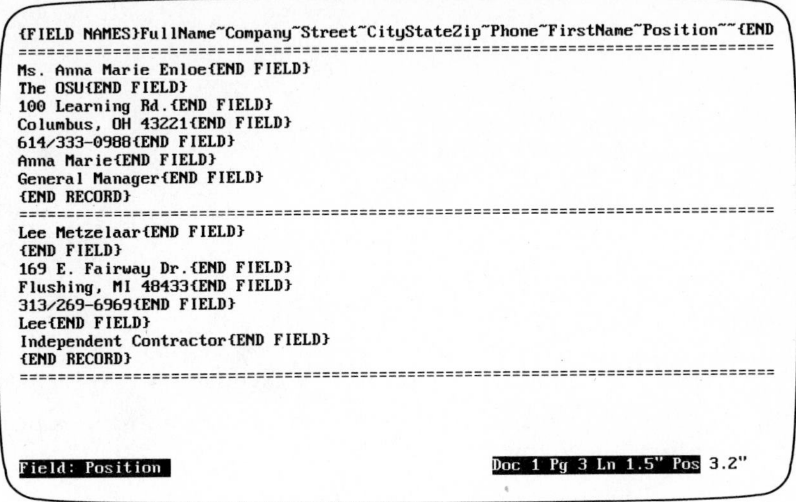

```
{FIELD NAMES}FullName~Company~Street~CityStateZip~Phone~FirstName~Position~~{END
================================================================================
Ms. Anna Marie Enloe{END FIELD}
The OSU{END FIELD}
100 Learning Rd.{END FIELD}
Columbus, OH 43221{END FIELD}
614/333-0988{END FIELD}
Anna Marie{END FIELD}
General Manager{END FIELD}
{END RECORD}
================================================================================
Lee Metzelaar{END FIELD}
{END FIELD}
169 E. Fairway Dr.{END FIELD}
Flushing, MI 48433{END FIELD}
313/269-6969{END FIELD}
Lee{END FIELD}
Independent Contractor{END FIELD}
{END RECORD}
================================================================================

Field: Position                                        Doc 1 Pg 3 Ln 1.5" Pos 3.2"
```

Fig. 12.12. *A secondary file revised to include position data.*

Step 10: Save the updated secondary file to disk as MERGESEC.V3.

To insert a code for the new field in the address block of the primary document, follow these steps:

Step 1: Clear the screen without saving the current document and retrieve the MERGEPRI.V2 document.

Step 2: Move the cursor to the beginning of the second line of the address block—Company~Company~.

Step 3: Access the **T**ools pull-down menu, select Me**r**ge Codes, and choose **F**ield (or press Shift-F9,1).

Step 4: When you are prompted `Enter Field:`, type **Position** and press Enter twice.

Note: Your codes in the primary document should include the position code shown in figure 12.13.

```
May 16, 1990

{FIELD}FullName~
{FIELD}Position~
{IF NOT BLANK}Company~{FIELD}Company~
{END IF}{FIELD}Street~
{FIELD}CityStateZip~

Dear {FIELD}FirstName~:
```

Fig. 12.13. A primary file revised to include a position code.

Step 5: Save the primary file to disk, using the name MERGEPRI.V3.

To execute the merge and view the merged document containing position information in the custom letters, follow these steps:

Step 1: Clear the screen without saving the current document.

Step 2: Access the **T**ools pull-down menu and select **M**erge (or press Ctrl-F9,1).

Step 3: When you are prompted `Primary file:`, type **MERGEPRI.V3** and press Enter.

Step 4: When you are prompted `Secondary file:`, type **MERGESEC.V3** and press Enter.

Step 5: After the merge operation is complete, press PgUp to view the first custom letter that displays `General Manager` as the position description.

Step 6: Press PgDn to view the second custom letter that displays `Independent Contractor` as the position description.

Remember that in workbook illustrations you receive step-by-step instructions to view the merge results. But you can also print output immediately after a merge output or save the merged document to disk for later printing.

Including Dates in Merged Documents

You may want to insert the current date into the merge document each time you perform a particular merge. You can do this by placing a {DATE} code in the primary file.

The {DATE} merge code causes WordPerfect 5.1 to insert the date on which the document is merged. If you want the date on which the document is printed to appear on the finished document, insert the date by using the Date Code feature of Date/Outline (Shift-F5).

To insert the date in the final document at merge time and execute the merge, follow these steps:

Step 1: Clear the screen without saving the current document and retrieve the MERGEPRI.V3 document.

Step 2: Move the cursor to the beginning of the date line and press Ctrl-End.

Step 3: Access the **T**ools pull-down menu and select Me**r**ge Codes (or press Shift-F9).

Step 4: Choose **M**ore (**6**), highlight `{DATE}`, and press Enter.

Step 5: Save the primary file to disk by using the name MERGEPRI.V4 and access a blank document screen.

Step 6: Access the **T**ools pull-down menu and select **M**erge (or press Ctrl-F9,1).

Step 7: When you are prompted `Primary file:`, type **MERGEPRI.V4** and press Enter.

Step 8: When you are prompted `Secondary file:`, type **MERGESEC.V3** and press Enter.

Step 9: After the merge is complete, press PgUp to view the current date in the first custom letter.

Step 10: Press PgDn to view the current date in the second custom letter.

The merged results should display the current date. If you save the results and print them another day, the custom letters reflect the printing date.

Merging Variable Data from the Keyboard

When you perform a merge, you may want to enter from the keyboard all or part of the information that is usually in the secondary file. When you choose this technique, WordPerfect 5.1 stops as it processes each record in the secondary file and waits for you to enter the data. This arrangement is useful when some secondary file information changes each time you do the merge.

To set up, in the primary document, a code that causes a pause in the CRIMSON letter merge, thus allowing you to enter the name of the account representative, follow these steps:

Step 1: Clear the screen without saving the current document and retrieve the MERGEPRI.V4 document.

Step 2: Move the cursor to the beginning of the line containing the name of the Senior Account Representative, Linda Wiest, and press Ctrl-End.

Step 3: Access the **T**ools pull-down menu and select Me**r**ge Codes (or press Shift-F9).

Step 4: Choose **More** (**6**), highlight `{INPUT}message~`, and press Enter.

Step 5: When you are prompted `Enter message:` at the bottom of the screen, type **Senior Account Rep's name** and press End Field (F9).

Note: Figure 12.14 illustrates the addition of the {INPUT} code in the primary document; the {INPUT} code pauses a merge to allow entry from the keyboard.

```
We promise to provide you the best service.  Call us the next time
your itinerary takes you across the state or around the world.

Sincerely,


{INPUT}Type Senior Account Rep's name~
Senior Account Representative
```

Fig. 12.14. *Adding an {INPUT} code to the primary document.*

Step 6: Save the primary file to disk, using the name MERGEPRI.V5.

To execute the merge and enter the account representative's name on each custom letter from the keyboard, follow these steps:

Step 1: Access the **T**ools pull-down menu and select **M**erge (or press Ctrl-F9,1).

Step 2: When you are prompted `Primary file:`, type **MERGEPRI.V5** and press Enter.

Step 3: When you are prompted `Secondary file:`, type **MERGESEC.V3** and press Enter.

Note: After the merge is complete, you should see the prompt `Type Senior Account Rep s name` in the lower left corner of the screen, as shown in figure 12.15.

```
We promise to provide you the best service.  Call us the next time
your itinerary takes you across the state or around the world.

Sincerely,



Type Senior Account Rep's name                      Doc 1 Pg 1 Ln 6.33" Pos 1"
```

Fig. 12.15. *A screen prompt requesting data entered from the keyboard.*

Step 4: Type **Linda Robling** and press End Field (F9) to enter an account representative's name in the first custom letter.

Step 5: Type **Linda Wiest** and press End Field (F9) to enter another account representative's name in the second custom letter.

Step 6: Use cursor-movement keys to scroll through the merged document and view the account representatives' names entered from the keyboard during a merge operation.

Workbook merge illustrations are confined to creating merged documents, but WordPerfect also supports producing labels through the use of its merge capability.

Generating Mailing Labels

Mailing labels are a classic application of merge capabilities. WordPerfect has always had the capability to create mailing labels. But in WordPerfect 5.1, a new approach is taken to positioning information correctly on label stock.

Labels come in many sizes and can be printed in up to five columns across the screen. Labels are also used for many purposes besides mailing. For example, you may want to create labels for file folders, storage bins, and Rolodex files.

Creating a Label Definition

The first step in generating labels involves creating a label definition. To create a label definition, define a paper size and type showing the number of labels, the dimensions of each label, the arrangement of labels on the paper, and the margins for each label.

To create a label definition for the Crimson Travel & Tours, Inc. customer file, follow these steps:

Step 1: Access the **L**ayout pull-down menu and select **P**age (or press Shift-F8,2).

Step 2: Choose Paper **S**ize (7).

Step 3: Choose **A**dd (**2**).

Step 4: Choose **L**abels (**4**).

Step 5: Choose La**b**els (**8**), and when you are prompted `No (Yes)`, press **Y**.

You are now ready to complete the Format: Labels menu. In this exercise you use most of the specifications shown. Change your Format: Labels screen (see fig. 12.13) to indicate that you are printing one column of labels, each label with four lines or rows of print:

Step 1: Choose **N**umber of Labels (**2**), type **1**, and press Enter; then type **4** and press Enter.

Step 2: Press Exit (F7) twice to display the new label definition on the Format: Paper Size/Type screen (see fig. 12.16).

```
Format: Paper Size/Type

                                                               Font  Double
Paper type and Orientation   Paper Size      Prompt  Loc      Type  Sided   Labels

Envelope - Wide              8.5" x 3"        Yes    Manual   Land  No
Envelope - Wide              9.5" x 4"        No     Manual   Land  No
Labels                       8.5" x 11"       No     Contin   Port  No      1 x 4
Legal                        8.5" x 14"       No     Contin   Port  No
Legal - Wide                 14" x 8.5"       No     Contin   Land  No
Standard                     8.5" x 11"       No     Contin   Port  No
Standard - Wide              11" x 8.5"       No     Contin   Land  No
[ALL OTHERS]                 Width ≤ 8.5"     Yes    Manual         No
```

***Fig. 12.16.** The new label definition: 1 x 4.*

Using the Label Definition

Once you create and save the label definition, you can access a blank document screen, select the label definition, and perform the merge. To select the labels definition you just created, follow these steps:

Step 1: Clear the screen without saving the current document.

Step 2: Access the **L**ayout pull-down menu and select **P**age (or press Shift-F8,2).

Step 3: Choose Paper **S**ize (7) and highlight the new definition.

Step 4: Choose **S**elect (**1**).

Step 5: Press Exit (F7) enough times to restore the current document screen.

To create the primary labels file, follow these steps:

Step 1: Press Home, Home, up arrow to position the cursor at the top of the document.

Step 2: Access the **T**ools pull-down menu and select **M**erge Codes (or press Shift-F9); select **F**ield (**1**).

Step 3: When you are prompted `Enter Field:`, type **FullName**. Press End Field (F9) and Enter.

Step 4: Press Shift-F9, choose **F**ield (**1**), type **Company**, press End Field (F9), and press Enter.

Step 5: Press Shift-F9, choose **F**ield (**1**), type **Street**, press End Field (F9), and press Enter.

Step 6: Press Shift-F9, choose **F**ield (**1**), type **CityStateZip**, press End Field (F9), and press Enter.

Step 7: Position the cursor at the beginning of the second line of the address block `{FIELD}Company~`.

Step 8: Access the **T**ools pull-down menu, select Me**r**ge Codes, and choose **M**ore (or press Shift-F9,6).

Step 9: Use arrow keys to highlight `{IF NOT BLANK}field~` in the selection box and press Enter.

Step 10: When you are prompted `Enter Field:`, type **Company** and press Enter.

Step 11: Position the cursor at the beginning of the third line of the address block (`{FIELD}Street~`).

Step 12: Access the **T**ools pull-down menu, select Me**r**ge Codes, and choose **M**ore (or press Shift-F9,6).

Step 13: Highlight `{END IF}` in the selection box and press Enter.

Step 14: Save the primary file to disk, using the name LABELPRI.

To execute the merge, follow these steps:

Step 1: Access the **T**ools pull-down menu and select **M**erge (or press Ctrl-F9,1).

Step 2: When you are prompted `Primary file:`, type **LABELPRI** and press Enter.

Step 3: When you are prompted `Secondary file:`, type **MERGESEC.V3** and press Enter.

After the merge is complete, you should see the merge results on-screen, as shown in figure 12.17. Remember that you can print merged results immediately or save the merged document to disk for later printing.

```
Ms. Anna Marie Enloe
The OSU
100 Learning Rd.
Columbus, OH 43221

==============================================================================
Lee Metzelaar
169 E. Fairway Dr.
Flushing, MI 48433
```

***Fig. 12.17.** The label merge results.*

For Further Reference

If you would like to learn more about specifying various sizes and arrangements of labels, see *Using WordPerfect 5.1*, Special Edition, (Que Corporation, Carmel, IN, 1989), Chapter 13.

Summary of Concepts

Lesson 12 explains these concepts:

- ❑ A merge blends information from the keyboard with a primary document or blends information from each record in a secondary file with a primary document or label.
- ❑ Merge codes embedded in primary and secondary files coordinate the merge operations.
- ❑ A primary file contains fixed text and codes that call for certain items to be entered from the keyboard or to be pulled from a secondary merge file.
- ❑ A secondary file consists of records that have a number of related pieces of information (fields) in a specific order.
- ❑ A field in a secondary file must end with the code {END FIELD}.
- ❑ A record in a secondary file must end with the code {END RECORD} followed by a hard page break (Ctrl-Enter).
- ❑ The {FIELD}field~ code in a primary file calls information from a specific field in the secondary file.
- ❑ Use the {IF NOT BLANK} and {END IF} merge codes to eliminate the hard return if the contents of a field are blank.
- ❑ Use the {INPUT}Message code to pause a merge and display a message prompting for the entry of specific variable data from the keyboard.
- ❑ To create labels by using the merge capability, set up a primary document containing a label definition and merge the document with a secondary file containing name and address data.

Review Exercises

1. Clear the screen without saving the current document, create the following primary file, and save the file as MEMOHEAD.PF:

   Memo

   To:

   From:

   Date:

   Subject:

2. Modify the MEMOHEAD.PF file to include status line prompts for the type of keyboard entry required. Save the modified primary file as MEMOHEAD.PF.

3. Execute the merge with keyboard entry to the MEMOHEAD.PF primary file. Because you are not using a secondary file, press Enter when you are prompted for the name of the secondary file. When you are prompted for data, make up appropriate information for at least two memos. (You do not need to type the body of the memo.)

4. Create the secondary file OFFICERS.SF. Include two fields: addressee and position. Enter data for the following three records and save the file:

   Scott Robling
   Comptroller

   Dave Keller
   Director of Training

   Sam Wiest
   Operations Manager

5. Modify the MEMOHEAD.PF document to insert, on the To: line, the name of the addressee, a comma, and a space, followed by the person's title. The remaining three lines require input from the keyboard. Save the file as BOARDMTG.PF.

6. Merge the secondary file OFFICERS.SF with the primary file BOARDMTG.PF. If the merge works properly, the first To: line in the first custom memo appears as this message:

```
To: Scott Robling, Comptroller
```

13

Sorting and Selecting Data

In this lesson, you practice these activities:

- ❑ Learn WordPerfect's database terms
- ❑ Sort numbers, lines, and paragraphs
- ❑ Sort a block
- ❑ Sort merge files
- ❑ Select records by using a global key
- ❑ Select records by using simple and complex formulas
- ❑ Select records from a block

WordPerfect's database capabilities are limited; it can sort document contents in a designated order or select document contents to meet specified criteria. Its database features are not as powerful as those in stand-alone database software, but WordPerfect can help you manage numbers, lines, paragraphs, and merge files in documents.

In this lesson, you first review fundamental database terms and then explore the basic operation of Sort and Select. WordPerfect 5.1 includes a powerful new table feature for managing data. Lesson 18 includes a discussion of sorting and selecting techniques used with tables.

Understanding WordPerfect's Database Terms

A database is a collection of records; a record consists of one or more related pieces of information; each item within a record is a field. For example, all the information about a product held in inventory (fields such as inventory number, description, location, stock on hand) composes the record for that product. All the records as a group compose the inventory database.

WordPerfect can manipulate three types of records: a line, a paragraph, and a secondary merge file record. A line record ends with a hard or soft return. A paragraph record ends with two hard returns. In a secondary merge file, a field ends with an {END FIELD} merge code, and a record ends with an {END RECORD} merge code (see Lesson 12).

Using WordPerfect's Sort feature, you can arrange records in numeric or alphabetic order. Using the Select feature, you can "filter" a file for information that meets certain criteria. You can select up to nine different criteria, or keys, during a Sort and Select operation. You may, for example, apply Sort and Select commands to a secondary data file to generate an alphabetical listing of clients in the Indianapolis area who own a personal computer, earn over $50,000 a year, and own homes.

Using the Sort Feature

When you use Sort, WordPerfect prompts for both an input and an output file. The input file is the original database to be sorted (stored on disk). The output file is the sorted (or selected) file viewed on-screen or stored on disk. You can sort a block as well as lines, paragraphs, or secondary merge files.

Note: If database contents are blocked (highlighted) before you initiate a Sort operation, you do not see prompts to direct input from the screen and output to the screen.

Sorting Lines

A common application of Line Sort is the sorting of a list of names in a document. To sort a list of the 13 states that ratified the Constitution of the United States, follow these steps:

Step 1: Clear the screen without saving the current document and retrieve the RATIFY13.LST document, which contains a list of 13 states (the list is not in alphabetical order).

Note: The instruction to clear the screen without saving the current document is used many times throughout the workbook. It means to access the **F**ile pull-down menu and select E**x**it (or press F7); when you are prompted `Save Document? Yes (No)`, press **N**; and when you are prompted `Exit WP? No (Yes)`, press **N**.

Step 2: Access the **T**ools pull-down menu or press Merge/Sort (Ctrl-F9).

Note: Figure 13.1 illustrates accessing the Sort option through the Tools pull-down menu. If you press Ctrl-F9, you see the menu options **M**erge (**1**), **S**ort (**2**), and **C**onvert Old Merge Codes (**3**) across the bottom of the screen.

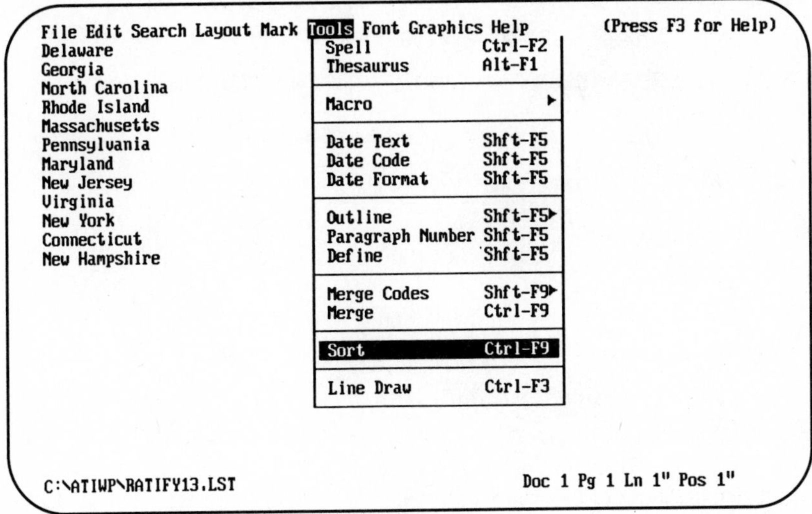

Fig. 13.1. An unsorted list of states and the Sort menu option.

Step 3: Select **S**ort (**2**).

Step 4: In response to the prompt `Input file to sort: (Screen)`, press Enter to sort the document currently in memory.

Step 5: In response to the prompt `Output file for sort: (Screen)`, press Enter to send the sorted output to the screen.

Note: The screen divides into halves, as shown in figure 13.2. The top half displays as much as possible of the file to be sorted. The bottom half displays the Sort definition screen and Sort menu.

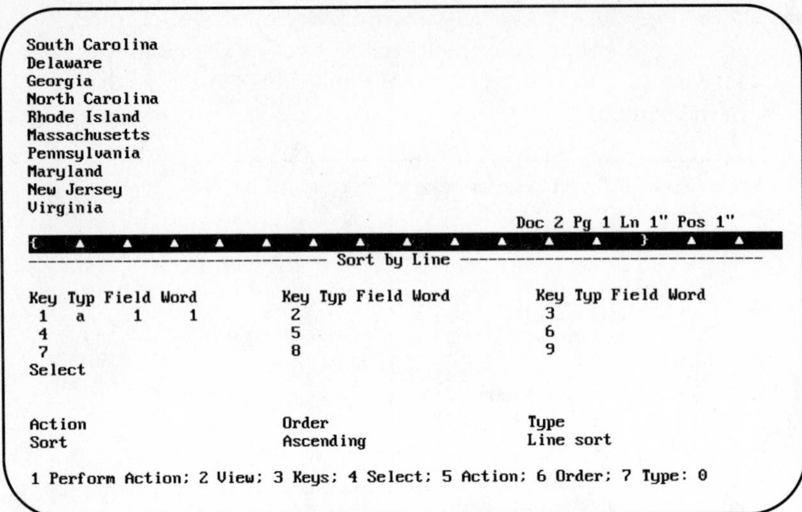

South Carolina
Delaware
Georgia
North Carolina
Rhode Island
Massachusetts
Pennsylvania
Maryland
New Jersey
Virginia
Doc 2 Pg 1 Ln 1" Pos 1"
Sort by Line
Key Typ Field Word
1 a 1 1
4
7
Key Typ Field Word
2
5
8
Key Typ Field Word
3
6
9
Select
Action
Sort
Order
Ascending
Type
Line sort
1 Perform Action; 2 View; 3 Keys; 4 Select; 5 Action; 6 Order; 7 Type: 0

Fig. 13.2. *The Sort definition screen with default settings.*

Step 6: Press **P**erform Action (**1**) to sort.

After a slight delay—during which you see messages at the bottom of the screen indicating that records are being examined, selected, sorted, and transferred—the sorted results appear on- screen. You should see an error in your sort results, as illustrated in figure 13.3.

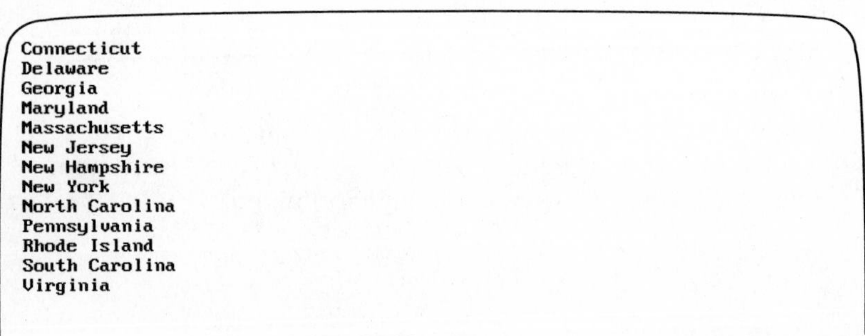

Fig. 13.3. *The initial line sort results; New Hampshire out of order.*

New Hampshire appears after New Jersey in the alphabetized listing. (Your screen display may show another arrangement of the three states that begin with New because records are sorted according to the first word in each line.) To correct the order, follow these steps:

Step 1: Access the **T**ools pull-down menu and select **S**ort (or press Ctrl-F9,2).

Step 2: Press Enter twice to indicate input from the screen and output to the screen.

Step 3: Select **K**eys (**3**). The cursor shifts to the Key 1 area in the bottom half of the screen.

Step 4: Press Enter or the right arrow to accept the default Key 1 Typ definition, which indicates an alphanumeric sort (a).

Note: The message Type: a = Alphanumeric; n = Numeric; Use arrows; Press Exit when done appears across the bottom of the screen.

Step 5: Press Enter or the right arrow to accept the default Key 1 Field definition, which indicates the first field in the file (1).

Step 6: Press Enter or the right arrow to accept the default Key 1 Word definition, which indicates the first word within the first field (1). The cursor shifts to Key 2.

Step 7: Press Enter to select the default alphanumeric (a) as the Key 2 Typ and press Enter to accept (1) as the Key 2 Field.

Step 8: Type **2** to specify a secondary sort on the second word within the first field (see fig 13.4).

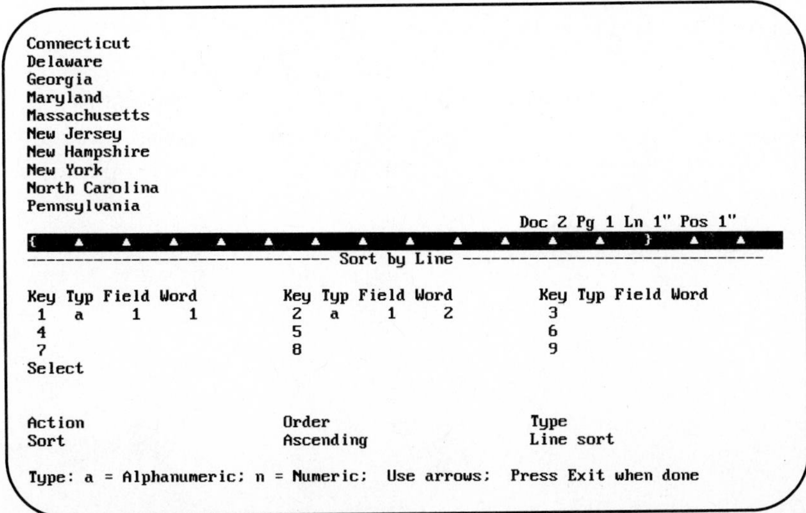

Fig. 13.4. Setting specifications for a two-key sort.

Step 9: Press Exit (F7) to return to the Sort menu.

Step 10: Press **P**erform Action (**1**) to sort.

All states should now appear in alphabetical order. Be careful when you set up the keys for a sort; always check that the results are sorted correctly.

Sorting Paragraphs

A WordPerfect database can contain paragraphs, each separated by two hard returns. If a database is arranged in paragraphs, you cannot sort a line, a field, or a word within a field. You can, however, provide some structure in the paragraph database on which to search. In the example to follow, use the STATES13.LST file containing summary paragraphs about places to visit in various states. Each paragraph is structured with the name of the state as the first word. To practice sorting paragraphs, perform these steps:

Step 1: Clear the screen without saving the current document, retrieve the STATES13.LST document, and note the initial order of states (Illinois, Tennessee, New Mexico, Arizona, Colorado, Kansas).

Step 2: Access the **T**ools pull-down menu and select **S**ort (or press Ctrl-F9,2).

Step 3: Press Enter twice to indicate input from the screen and output to the screen.

Step 4: Choose **T**ype (7) and select **P**aragraph (**3**).

Step 5: Select **K**eys (**3**).

Step 6: Press Ctrl-End to delete former specifications except for the default settings for Key 1 (see fig. 13.5).

Note: Each time you access the Sort specifications screen, the codes most recently used in the current editing session appear instead of the defaults. This feature is helpful when you are performing a sort that involves criteria similar to those used in the most recent Sort operation.

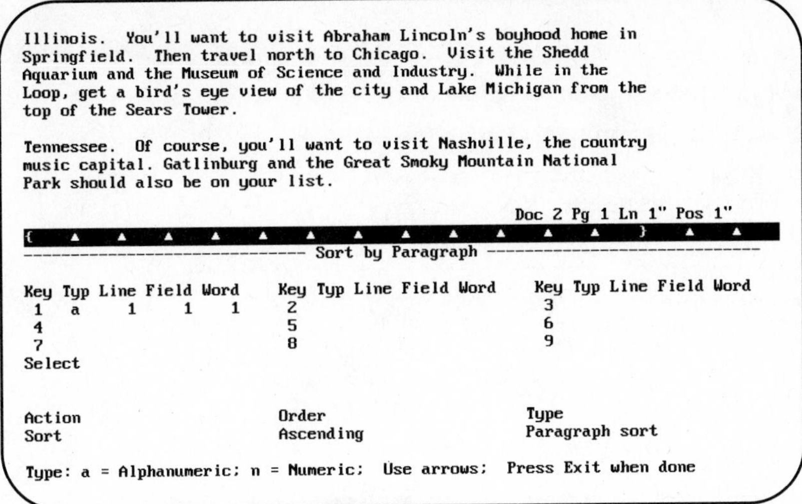
```
Illinois.  You'll want to visit Abraham Lincoln's boyhood home in
Springfield.  Then travel north to Chicago.  Visit the Shedd
Aquarium and the Museum of Science and Industry.  While in the
Loop, get a bird's eye view of the city and Lake Michigan from the
top of the Sears Tower.

Tennessee.  Of course, you'll want to visit Nashville, the country
music capital. Gatlinburg and the Great Smoky Mountain National
Park should also be on your list.
                                                Doc 2 Pg 1 Ln 1" Pos 1"

------------------------------ Sort by Paragraph ------------------------------

Key Typ Line Field Word     Key Typ Line Field Word     Key Typ Line Field Word
 1   a    1     1    1       2                           3
 4                           5                           6
 7                           8                           9
Select


Action                      Order                       Type
Sort                        Ascending                   Paragraph sort

Type: a = Alphanumeric; n = Numeric;  Use arrows;  Press Exit when done
```

Fig. 13.5. *Setting paragraph sort specifications.*

Step 7: Press Exit (F7) once to restore the Sort menu options at the bottom of the screen.

Step 8: Press **P**erform Action (**1**) to sort.

Note: After a slight delay, the states—including the associated descriptive paragraphs—should appear in alphabetical order (Arizona, Colorado, Illinois, Kansas, New Mexico, Tennessee).

You just applied line and paragraph sorts to an entire document. You can also sort only a part of the file.

Sorting a Block

To sort less than an entire file, use WordPerfect's Block feature to mark the block of data to be sorted; then complete the usual sorting routine. To practice sorting blocks within a document, rearranging some names and descriptions of new employees according to their surnames, follow these steps:

Step 1: Clear the screen without saving the current document and retrieve BLKSRT13.DOC.

Step 2: Position the cursor on the blank line just above the John Fox information.

Step 3: Press Block (Alt-F4 or F12).

Step 4: Move the cursor to the line just below the description of Sam Weist.

Step 5: Access the **T**ools pull-down menu and select **S**ort (or press Ctrl-F9).

Step 6: Choose **T**ype (**7**) and select **P**aragraph (**3**).

Step 7: Select **K**eys (**3**), press the right arrow three times until the cursor is on Word specification for Key 1, and type 2 (see fig. 13.6).

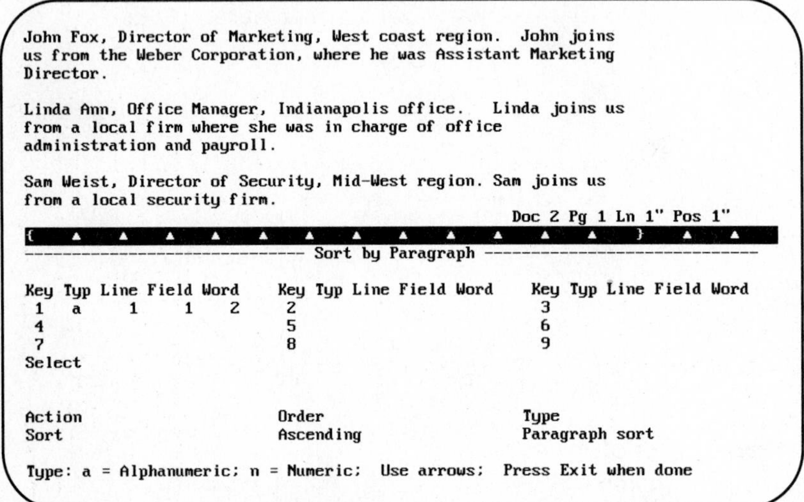

```
John Fox, Director of Marketing, West coast region.  John joins
us from the Weber Corporation, where he was Assistant Marketing
Director.

Linda Ann, Office Manager, Indianapolis office.   Linda joins us
from a local firm where she was in charge of office
administration and payroll.

Sam Weist, Director of Security, Mid-West region. Sam joins us
from a local security firm.
                                                   Doc 2 Pg 1 Ln 1" Pos 1"
---------------------------- Sort by Paragraph ----------------------------

Key Typ Line Field Word    Key Typ Line Field Word    Key Typ Line Field Word
 1   a    1     1    2      2                          3
 4                          5                          6
 7                          8                          9
Select


Action                     Order                      Type
Sort                       Ascending                  Paragraph sort

Type: a = Alphanumeric; n = Numeric;  Use arrows;  Press Exit when done
```

13.6. Setting block sort specifications.

Step 8: Press Exit (F7) to restore the Sort menu at the bottom of the screen.

Step 9: Select **P**erform Action (**1**).

Note: After a short delay, the blocked section of the document sorts by paragraphs and displays employee information in last-name order: `Ann, Fox, and Weist.`

Sorting a Secondary Merge File

A secondary merge file—discussed in Lesson 11—is a form of database. Each field, ending with the merge code {END FIELD}, can be used as a sort or selection key. Each record, ending with the merge code {END RECORD}, can be selected, sorted, or both.

The file PRES13.MRG contains the names and fictitious addresses of presidents of the United States. To sort the list of presidents by last name, follow these steps:

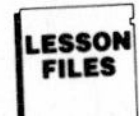

Step 1: Clear the screen without saving the current document and retrieve PRES13.MRG.

Step 2: Access the **T**ools pull-down menu and select **S**ort (or press Ctrl-F9,2).

Step 3: Press Enter twice to indicate input from the screen and output to the screen.

Step 4: Choose **T**ype (**7**) and select **M**erge (**1**).

Step 5: Press **K**eys (**3**), position the cursor at the Key 1 definition, and type the codes **a 1 1 1** (see fig. 13.7).

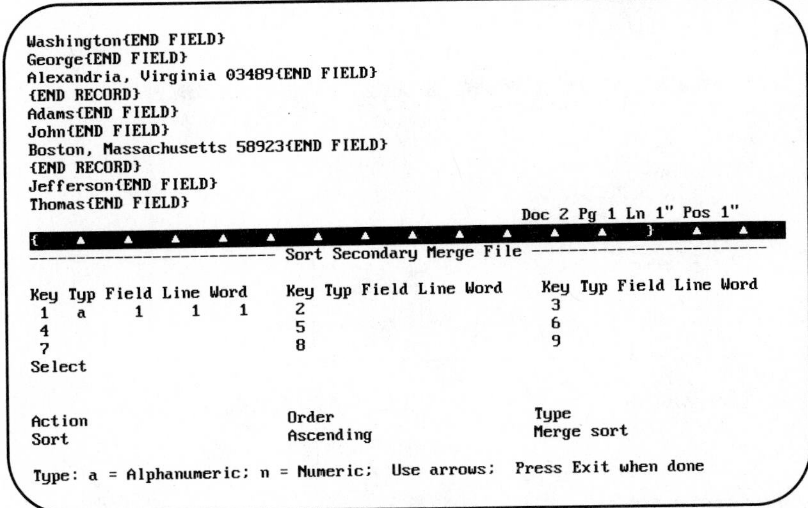

Fig. 13.7. *Setting a sort condition on the first word of the first field in merge records.*

Step 6: Press Exit (F7) to restore the Sort menu at the bottom of the screen.

Step 7: Press **P**erform Action (**1**).

Note: After a short delay, 39 merge records appear in alphabetical order, according to last name of the president.

To reorder the merge records according to ZIP code, follow these steps:

Step 1: Access the **T**ools pull-down menu and select **S**ort (or press Ctrl-F9,2).

Step 2: Press Enter twice to indicate input from the screen and output to the screen.

Step 3: Choose **Type** (**7**) and select **Merge** (**1**).

Step 4: Press **Keys** (**3**), position the cursor at the Key 1 definition, type the codes **3 1 -1** (see fig. 13.8), and press Exit (F7) to restore the Sort menu at the bottom of the screen.

Note: The code 3 indicates that sorting is to be done on the third field (ZIP code). The code -1 indicates that ZIP code is the first entry from the end of the field.

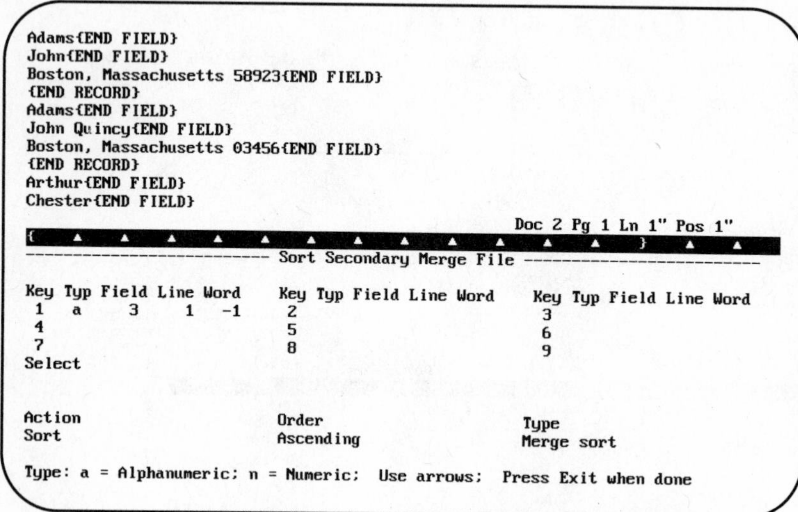

***Fig. 13.8.** Setting a sort condition on the last word of the third field in merge records.*

Step 5: Press **Perform Action** (**1**).

Note: After a short delay, merge records appear in numeric order according to ZIP code.

You just used three sort capabilities of WordPerfect: sorting lines, sorting paragraphs, and sorting merge files. In addition, you applied a paragraph sort to a block of data within the file.

You can also select—or select and sort—only those records meeting conditions you designate.

Using the Select Feature

Using Select, you can extract records meeting specified criteria, such as all records from a birthday list database that have a birthday month of August or the record for one person's birthday. Select criteria can be complex, such as all records in which last name equals Beckman, birth month equals March, and day within birthday month equals 6.

You can use WordPerfect to perform a global search of the entire file, or you can use a formula to limit selection to a specified field or fields. You can simply select records, or you can select and sort the results.

The document BIRTH13.LST (see the following section) contains records for illustrating various Select capabilities. Each line of information about one individual is a record. Each record contains four fields of data: last name (LNAME), first name (FNAME), birthday month (BMONTH), and day of birth within the month (BDAY). When you create a line (or paragraph) database, fields are separated by tab codes.

Using Select with a Global Key

Initiate a Select operation the same way you start a Sort operation—access the **T**ools pull-down menu or press Merge/Sort (F9) and select **S**ort. Next choose Select (**4**) from the Sort menu and enter your criteria for selection as a formula, using the available math operators displayed across the bottom of the screen.

When you perform a global search, enter the formula **keyg=** followed by your select condition or conditions. The g in keyg indicates a global search that overrides any specifications concerning individual keys. To select records containing the word `April` in any field in a list of birthdays, follow these steps:

Step 1: Clear the screen without saving the current document and retrieve BIRTH13.LST (see fig. 13.9).

Birthday List

LNAME	FNAME	BMONTH	BDAY
Keller	Theresa	September	5
McClelland	Ryan	October	1
Beckman	Len	March	21
Fox	April	July	23
Clements	Donna	February	18
Robling	Linda	August	21
Beckman	Mary	June	30
Fox	Tim	January	2
Beckman	Richard	March	29
Fox	Bonnie	January	11
Clements	Kasey	July	9
Strauss	Judy	April	15
Jackson	Ann	December	10
Weist	Linda	June	17
Love	Linda	May	14
Enloe	James	November	11
Enloe	Ree	September	21
Fox	Amy	October	1
Beckman	Marie	March	10
Beckman	Steve	November	21

C:\ATIWP\BIRTH13.LST Doc 1 Pg 1 Ln 0.5" Pos 0.5"

Fig. 13.9. *The BIRTH13.LST database.*

Step 2: Access the **T**ools pull-down menu and select **S**ort (or press Ctrl-F9,2).

Step 3: Press Enter twice to indicate input from the screen and output to the screen.

Step 4: Choose **T**ype (7) and select **L**ine (**2**).

Step 5: Choose **S**elect (4) and type **keyg=april** (see fig. 13.10).

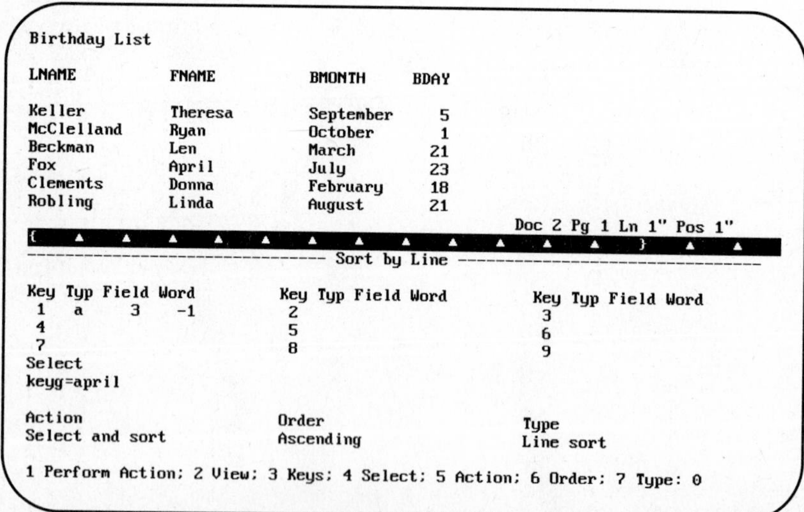

Birthday List

LNAME	FNAME	BMONTH	BDAY
Keller	Theresa	September	5
McClelland	Ryan	October	1
Beckman	Len	March	21
Fox	April	July	23
Clements	Donna	February	18
Robling	Linda	August	21

Doc 2 Pg 1 Ln 1" Pos 1"

Sort by Line

Key	Typ	Field	Word	Key	Typ	Field	Word	Key	Typ	Field	Word
1	a	3	-1	2				3			
4				5				6			
7				8				9			

Select
keyg=april

Action: Select and sort — Order: Ascending — Type: Line sort

1 Perform Action; 2 View; 3 Keys; 4 Select; 5 Action; 6 Order; 7 Type: 0

Fig. 13.10. *Setting a global select condition.*

Step 6: Press Exit (F7) to restore the Sort menu at the bottom of the screen and choose **P**erform Action (**1**).

Note: Verify that two records are extracted from the database: one containing the FNAME (first name) `April` and the other containing the BMONTH (birth month) `April`.

Using Select with a Simple Formula and One Key

The global selection in the preceding exercise searched the entire database. To focus the search on one data field, the select criteria must refer to one of the nine key fields displayed above the select area. To extract all records from the birthday list in which the first name (FNAME) is `April`, follow these steps:

Step 1: Clear the screen without saving the current document and retrieve BIRTH13.LST.

Step 2: Access the **T**ools pull-down menu and select **S**ort (or press Ctrl-F9,2).

Step 3: Press Enter twice to indicate input from the screen and output to the screen.

Step 4: Choose **K**eys (**3**) and enter **2 1** in the Key 1 area.

Note: The **2 1** specification for the first key indicates a search of alphanumeric first word contents in field 2 (FNAME).

Step 5: Press Exit (F7) to restore the Sort menu at the bottom of the screen.

Step 6: Choose **S**elect (**4**) and type **key1=april** to limit record selection to only those records meeting the condition of April as a first name (see fig. 13.11).

```
Birthday List

LNAME          FNAME          BMONTH     BDAY

Keller         Theresa        September    5
McClelland     Ryan           October      1
Beckman        Len            March       21
Fox            April          July        23
Clements       Donna          February    18
Robling        Linda          August      21
                                                    Doc 2 Pg 1 Ln 1" Pos 1"
------------------------------- Sort by Line -------------------------------

Key Typ Field Word          Key Typ Field Word          Key Typ Field Word
 1   a    2    1             2                           3
 4                           5                           6
 7                           8                           9
Select
key1=april

Action                      Order                       Type
Select and sort             Ascending                   Line sort

+(OR), *(AND), =, <>, >, <, >=, <=;  Press Exit when done
```

Fig. 13.11. Setting a single-key select condition.

Step 7: Press Exit (F7) to restore the Sort menu and press **P**erform Action (**1**).

Note: Verify that only one record is extracted from the database, that of April Fox. In the selected record, `April` is the first name; records for which birth month is April are excluded.

Using Select with a Complex Formula

Setting multiple criteria in a Select operation requires that you specify additional keys, which are followed by a formula entry referring to those keys. Separate and conditions with an asterisk (*), and separate or conditions with a plus sign (+). Be sure to include a space on either side of the asterisk or plus sign when you enter a complex formula.

To select records from the BIRTH13.LST document in which last name is `Beckman` and the birth month is `March`, follow these steps:

Step 1: Clear the screen without saving the current document and retrieve BIRTH13.LST.

Step 2: Access the **T**ools pull-down menu and select **S**ort (or press Ctrl-F9,2).

Step 3: Press Enter twice to indicate input from the screen and output to the screen.

Step 4: Choose **Keys (3)** and type **1 1** in the Key 1 area to select alphanumeric records based on the first word in field 1 (LNAME).

Step 5: Position the cursor at Key 2 and type a **3 1** to select alphanumeric records based on the first word in field 3 (BMONTH).

Step 6: Press Exit (F7) to restore the Sort menu.

Step 7: Choose **Select (4)**, and type **key1=beckman * key2=march** to limit record extraction to only those records meeting both criteria of last name `Beckman` and birth month `March` (see fig. 13.12).

```
Birthday List

LNAME            FNAME            BMONTH        BDAY

Keller           Theresa          September       5
McClelland       Ryan             October         1
Beckman          Len              March          21
Fox              April            July           23
Clements         Donna            February       18
Robling          Linda            August         21
                                                       Doc 2 Pg 1 Ln 1" Pos 1"
-------------------------------- Sort by Line --------------------------------

Key Typ Field Word              Key Typ Field Word              Key Typ Field Word
 1   a    1    1                 2   a    3    1                 3
 4                               5                               6
 7                               8                               9
Select
key1=beckman * key2=march

Action                          Order                           Type
Select and sort                 Ascending                       Line sort

+(OR), *(AND), =, <>, >, <, >=, <=;  Press Exit when done
```

Fig. 13.12. Setting multiple-key select criteria.

Step 8: Press Exit (F7) to restore the Sort menu and choose **Perform Action (1)**.

Note: Verify that three records are extracted, as shown in figure 13.13. Notice that the fields are no longer aligned. The tab code, which is part of the database, is lost during the search. You can correct this problem by repeating the selection process after blocking the database records.

```
Beckman   Marie     March      10
Beckman   Richard   March      29
Beckman   Len  March      21
```

Fig. 13.13. The initial display of records extracted through the use of multiple-key criteria.

Selecting Records from a Block

Limiting your Select operation to a block is as simple as block- marking the text to be searched and then executing the steps you already learned. In the previous exercise, you selected three records from an entire database. When the records were selected, the rejected portions of the database were deleted, including the tab format line. A return to the default format code caused the data fields in the selected records to appear out of alignment. You can correct this problem by limiting the selection process to only the record area, thus protecting the tab format code.

To repeat the preceding Select exercise, using Block mode, follow these steps:

Step 1: Clear the screen without saving the current document and retrieve BIRTH13.LST.

Step 2: Position the cursor at the beginning of the first record; press Alt-F4 (or F12); and press Home, Home, down arrow to highlight the database.

Step 3: Access the **T**ools pull-down menu and select **S**ort (or press Ctrl-F9).

Note: If database contents are blocked (highlighted) before you initiate a Select operation, you do not see prompts to direct input and output to the screen.

Step 4: Be sure that the following specifications are set from the preceding exercise: the Select formula entered as **key1=beckman** * **key2=march**, Key 1 defined as **a 1 1**, and Key 2 defined as a **3 1** (see fig. 13.12).

Step 5: Press **P**erform Action (**1**).

Note: Three records should again be extracted, as shown in figure 13.14. Notice that the fields are now aligned. The Tab code, which is part of the database, is protected because the selection is limited to the record area.

Keep the results on-screen, because the next exercise illustrates sorting the results of this most recent Select operation through the use of a numeric field.

```
Birthday List

LNAME          FNAME          BMONTH     BDAY

Beckman        Marie          March        10
Beckman        Richard        March        29
Beckman        Len            March        21
```

Fig. 13.14. *Using Block to improve the display of extracted records.*

Sorting Selected Records

After you reduce the display of database contents to only those records meeting your select criteria, you can sort (reorder) the records according to alphanumeric or numeric contents.

You can sort numbers of equal length, such as phone numbers, correctly as alphanumerics or numerics. But you should reorder numbers of unequal length (such as those in the BDAY field of the BIRTH13.LST database) through a numeric sort. To sort the three records extracted in the preceding Select operation in ascending order as the month progresses, follow these steps:

Step 1: Position the cursor at the front of the first record, press Block (Alt-F4 or F12), and highlight the three records.

Step 2: Access the **T**ools pull-down menu and select **S**ort (or press Ctrl-F9,2).

Step 3: Choose **K**eys (3) and enter **n 4 1** in the Key 1 area to select numeric records based on the first word in field 4 (BDAY).

Step 4: Position the cursor at the front of the Key 2 area and press Ctrl-End to delete the entries used in the previous Select operation.

Step 5: Choose **S**elect (4) and press Ctrl-End to erase the formula used in the previous Select operation (see fig. 13.15).

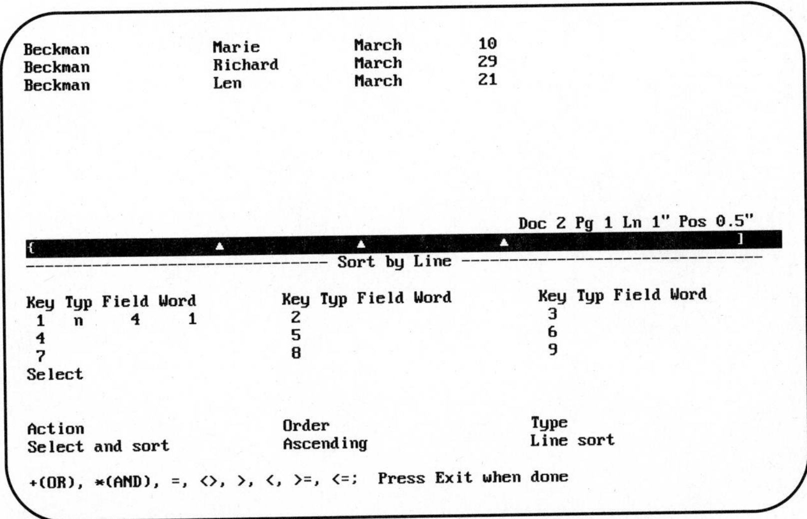

***Fig. 13.15.** Applying a numeric sort condition to selected records.*

Step 6: Press Exit (F7) to restore the Sort menu and choose **P**erform Action (**1**).

Note: The three records should appear in ascending order, according to the day within the month of March.

For Further Reference

If you would like additional information on database setup and variations of the Sort and Select operations, consult *Using WordPerfect 5.1*, Special Edition, (Que Corporation, Carmel, IN, 1989), Chapter 14.

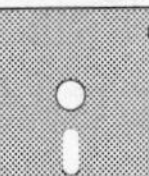

Summary of Concepts

Lesson 13 explains these concepts:

- ❑ WordPerfect's Sort and Select features can sort the contents of a database and select records from the database, according to specified criteria.
- ❑ You can apply Sort and Select operations to databases organized in any of three ways: those in which a record is a line, those in which a record is a paragraph, and those that are secondary merge files.
- ❑ Follow identical procedures to initiate Sort or Select operations.
- ❑ You can sort on up to nine keys after specifying the type of data (alphanumeric or numeric) and data locations (field and word within field).
- ❑ Select records by entering a formula containing field content specifications for one or more fields.
- ❑ A formula can contain more than one select condition if conditions with one or more math operators are joined.
- ❑ Set up limited search criteria by first setting the appropriate keys and then entering the applicable formula.
- ❑ A global select criterion ignores specifications for individual keys; enter a global selection criterion by typing a formula **keyg=(search condition)**.
- ❑ You can limit sorting and selection to a part of a database by first blocking the data to be sorted or selected.

Review Exercises

1. Clear the screen without saving the current document and retrieve BIRTH13.LST.
2. Set up and execute a one-key sort on the birth month (field 3, BMONTH) for all birthdays in January.
3. Use the Block command and sort all records in the database by last name. **Caution:** Block entire records, not just sections of records, to keep related information together.
4. Clear the screen without saving the current document, retrieve BIRTH13.LST, and set up and execute a two-key sort on last name (field 1, LNAME) and then first name (field 2, FNAME).
5. Execute a global select of those records in which `fox` appears in any field.
6. Clear the screen without saving the current document, retrieve BIRTH13.LST, and select those records in which the last name is `fox` or `beckman`. (**Hint:** Join *or* conditions with a plus sign; include a space on either side of the plus sign in the formula.)
7. Clear the screen without saving the current document, retrieve BIRTH13.LST, and select those records in which the birthday is `March 6`.
8. Clear the screen without saving the current document, retrieve PRES13.MRG, and sort the records on `city` (first word in the third field).

Creating Document References

14

In this lesson, you practice these activities:

- ❑ Creating a list
  Marking text for a list
  Defining a list
  Generating a list
- ❑ Creating an index
  Marking text for an index
  Defining an index
  Generating an index
- ❑ Creating a table of contents
  Marking text for a table of contents
  Defining a table of contents
  Generating a table of contents
- ❑ Using Reveal Codes to look at list, index, and table of contents codes

Many documents include a table of contents, an index, and one or more lists of information. Preparing these reference sections of the document used to be a time-consuming task, subject to human error. WordPerfect 5.1 offers easy-to-use features for assembling these and other document references. Simply follow a three-step process: mark applicable items, define the location of each reference in the document, and generate the references.

In this lesson, you create three familiar document references: a table of contents, a list, and an index.

Creating a List

Lists are easy to create. Simply mark text sections for a list as you type, indicate where you want to place the list within the document after you have marked all entries, and generate the list of the marked items.

WordPerfect 5.1 supports up to 10 lists in a document, each list numbered 1 through 10. Lists 1 through 5 can contain items that you block-mark and designate for a particular list. In the following exercises, you create a list of places to visit (List 1) and a list of states (List 2).

Lists 6 through 10 are dedicated to displaying captions for graphic boxes. You cannot mark and assign graphic box captions to a list. Instead, WordPerfect 5.1 automatically places graphic box captions (if any) in the following lists: figure box captions (List 6), table box captions (List 7), text box captions (List 8), user-defined box captions (List 9), and equation box captions (List 10). To display these lists, you need only define and generate the list. If list numbers 6 through 10 are not used to display graphic box captions, you can use them to display other information.

As you mark an item, WordPerfect prompts you to assign a list number. Once you determine the content of each list, you must define the location of each list with the Mark Text: Define command (Alt-F5, 5). Once all lists (and other references such as table of contents and index) are defined, generate the references with the Mark Text: Generate command (Alt-F5,6).

In this lesson, you mark lists manually. WordPerfect's powerful macro and style features can, however, make the job easier.

Marking Text for a List

To demonstrate WordPerfect's list-keeping capability, use the LIST14.DOC workbook lesson-disk file (see fig. 14.1) to create two lists: the first list will contain places of interest; the second list will contain states.

First, mark each item to be listed, identifying it as belonging to one of 10 lists. If you mark each item as you type, you do not forget entries. If this method interferes with writing, mark the list after you write the document, as illustrated later in this chapter.

To mark text, complete these steps:

Step 1: Position the cursor at the text to be marked and press Block (Alt-F4 or F12).

Step 2: Highlight text to be marked.

Step 3: Access the **M**ark pull-down menu or press Mark Text (Alt-F5).

Step 4: Choose **L**ist (**2**).

Step 5: Type the number of the list where the text should appear.

```
                    TRAVEL LOG

Illinois.  You will want to visit Abraham Lincoln's boyhood home in
Springfield.  Then travel north to Chicago.  Visit the Shedd
Aquarium and the Museum of Science and Industry.  While in the
Loop, get a bird's eye view of the city and Lake Michigan from the
top of the Sears Tower.

Tennessee.  Of course, you will want to visit Nashville, the
country music capital. Gatlinburg and the Smoky Mountain National
Park should also be on your list.

New Mexico.  Schedule your trip to visit Santa Fe during one of the
craft festivals.  Artists from all over the Southwest have their
works on exhibit.  Arrive at Carlsbad Caverns shortly before sunset
to witness the mass exodus of bats from the depths of the caverns.



C:\ATIWP\LIST14.DOC                          Doc 1 Pg 1 Ln 1" Pos 1"
```

Fig. 14.1. *The LIST14.DOC document.*

You can work through the document, marking text for only one list at a time. Or you can work through the document once, creating all lists. Because the workbook document is short, create both lists at one time.

To mark the first list entry, perform these steps:

Step 1: Clear the screen without saving the current document and retrieve the LIST14.DOC document.

Note: The instruction to clear the screen without saving the current document is used many times throughout the workbook. It means to access the **F**ile pull-down menu and select E**x**it (or press F7); when you are prompted `Save Document? Yes (No)`, press **N**; and when you are prompted `Exit WP? No (Yes)`, press **N**.

Step 2: Place the cursor on the first letter of `Illinois`.

Step 3: Access the **E**dit pull-down menu and select **B**lock (or press Alt-F4 or F12); highlight `Illinois`. Do not include the period.

Step 4: Access the **M**ark pull-down menu (or press Alt-F5).

Note: Figure 14.2 illustrates the **M**ark pull-down menu. If instead of accessing the pull-down menu you press Mark Text (Alt-F5), you see the following message and options across the bottom of the screen:

`Mark for: 1 ToC; 2 List; 3 Index; 4 ToA`

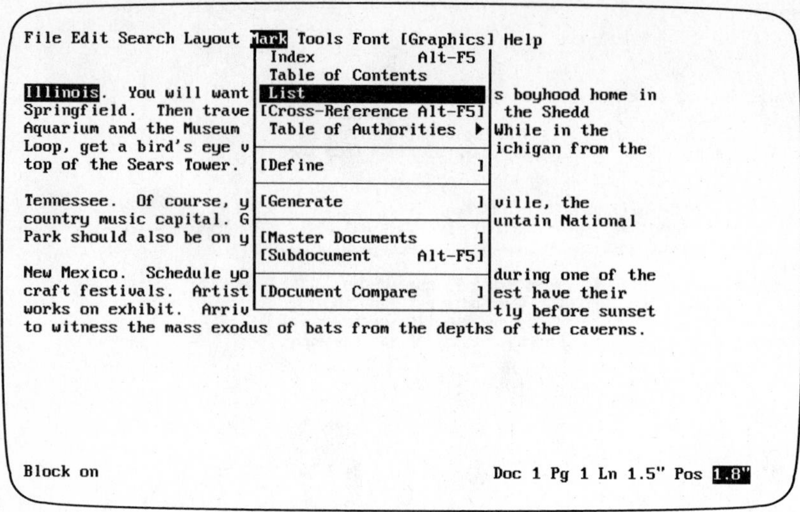

***Fig. 14.2.** The Mark pull-down menu, containing the List option.*

Step 5: Choose **List** (**2**).

Step 6: At the prompt `List Number:`, type **2** and press Enter.

Note: The name `Illinois` is marked for List 2 (states). The Mark Text feature (see fig. 14.2) is a dynamic menu. The menu content changes according to the text that is block-marked when Mark is activated.

To mark `Abraham Lincoln's boyhood home` for List 1 (places of interest), follow these steps:

Step 1: Place the cursor on the first letter of `Abraham`.

Step 2: Access the **E**dit pull-down menu and select **B**lock (or press Alt-F4 or F12); highlight the phrase `Abraham Lincoln's boyhood home`.

Step 3: Access the **M**ark pull-down menu and choose **L**ist (or press Alt-F5,2).

Step 4: When you are prompted `List number:`, type **1** and press Enter.

Viewing Marked Text with Reveal Codes

Each item for each list is marked in the document with paired codes, shown here as

```
[Mark:List,listnumber] marked text[End Mark:List:listnumber]
```

To see the two items you just marked and make additional entries for each list, perform these steps:

Step 1: Press Home, Home, up arrow to position the cursor in the upper left corner of the screen.

Step 2: Access the **E**dit pull-down menu and select **R**eveal Codes (or press Alt-F3 or F11).

Step 3: Make sure that the first line in the Reveal Codes section (bottom half) of the screen contains `[Mark:List...]` codes for the two items you highlighted, as shown in figure 14.3.

```
                         TRAVEL LOG

Illinois.  You will want to visit Abraham Lincoln's boyhood home in
Springfield.  Then travel north to Chicago.  Visit the Shedd
Aquarium and the Museum of Science and Industry.  While in the
Loop, get a bird's eye view of the city and Lake Michigan from the
top of the Sears Tower.

Tennessee.  Of course, you will want to visit Nashville, the
country music capital. Gatlinburg and the Smoky Mountain National
C:\ATIWP\LIST14.DOC                              Doc 1 Pg 1 Ln 1" Pos 1"
[Center]TRAVEL LOG[HRt]
[HRt]
[HRt]
[Mark:List,2]Illinois[End Mark:List,2].  You will want to visit [Mark:List,1]Abr
aham Lincoln's boyhood home[End Mark:List,1] in[SRt]
Springfield.  Then travel north to Chicago.  Visit the Shedd[SRt]
Aquarium and the Museum of Science and Industry.  While in the[SRt]
Loop, get a bird's eye view of the city and Lake Michigan from the[SRt]
top of the Sears Tower.  [HRt]
[HRt]

Press Reveal Codes to restore screen
```

Fig. 14.3. *Using Reveal Codes mode to view Mark:List codes.*

Step 4: Access the **E**dit pull-down menu and select **R**eveal Codes (or press Alt-F3 or F11) to restore full- screen display.

Step 5: Mark three additional entries for list one: `Shedd Aquarium`, `Museum of Science and Industry`, and `Sears Tower`.

If you want more practice in marking text, mark these items:

- ❑ List 1: `Nashville`, `Gatlinburg`, `Smoky Mountain National Park`, and `Carlsbad Caverns`.
- ❑ List 2: `Tennessee` and `New Mexico`.

If, however, you are comfortable marking text and ready to move to the next subject, go to the next section, "Defining a List." You can access a previously marked document for the next illustration.

Defining a List

Once you mark text and edit the document, tell WordPerfect where to put the list (or lists) and what page-numbering format to use. To place the list of states at the bottom of the document, follow these steps:

Step 1: Clear the screen without saving the current document and retrieve the LIST14.MRK document (a version of the original LIST14.DOC that is already marked for entries to two lists).

Step 2: Press Reveal Codes (Alt-F3 or F11), scroll through the document, and note that all `[Mark:List...]` codes are in place for states (List 2) and places of interest (List 1).

Step 3: Press Reveal Codes (Alt-F3 or F11) to return to the full-screen display.

Step 4: Position the cursor two lines below the last line of text in the document.

Step 5: Access the **L**ayout pull-down menu, select **A**lign, and choose **C**enter (or press Shift-F6).

Step 6: Type **LIST OF STATES** and press Enter three times.

Step 7: Access the **M**ark pull-down menu, choose **D**efine, and choose **L**ist (or press Alt-F5,5,2).

Note: Mark Text (Alt-F5) is a dynamic menu. The displayed options vary according to whether a block of text is highlighted. If a block is highlighted, you are presented with a menu from which you select the type of reference for marking the block of text. If no text is highlighted, you see a different menu.

Step 8: When you are prompted `List Number (1-10):`, type **2** and press Enter. A menu for selecting page number location appears.

Step 9: Choose **N**o Page Numbers (**1**).

Note: Although you do not see a change on-screen in full document display, the list is now defined by a `[Def Mark:List,2:1]` code that defines the beginning of marked List 2 with page option number 1 (no page numbers).

To position the list of places to see (List 1) under the list of states, perform these steps:

Step 1: Press Home, Home, down arrow and then press Enter four times to position the cursor for the next list.

Step 2: Press Center (Shift-F6), type **List of Places To Visit**, and press Enter three times.

Step 3: Access the **Mark** pull-down menu, choose **Define**, and choose **List** (or press Alt-F5,5,2).

Step 4: When you are prompted `List Number (1-10):`, type **1** and press Enter.

Step 5: Choose **No** Page Numbers (**1**).

You can use Reveal Codes (Alt-F3 or F11) to make sure that both definitions are in the document (see fig. 14.4). The code `[Def Mark:List,2:1]` defines the beginning of marked List 2 (states) with page option number 1 (no page numbers). The code `[Def Mark:List,1:1]` defines the beginning of marked List 1 (places to visit) with page option number 1 (no page numbers). Notice that you can place lists in any sequence and location in a document. In this exercise, List 2 is located before List 1.

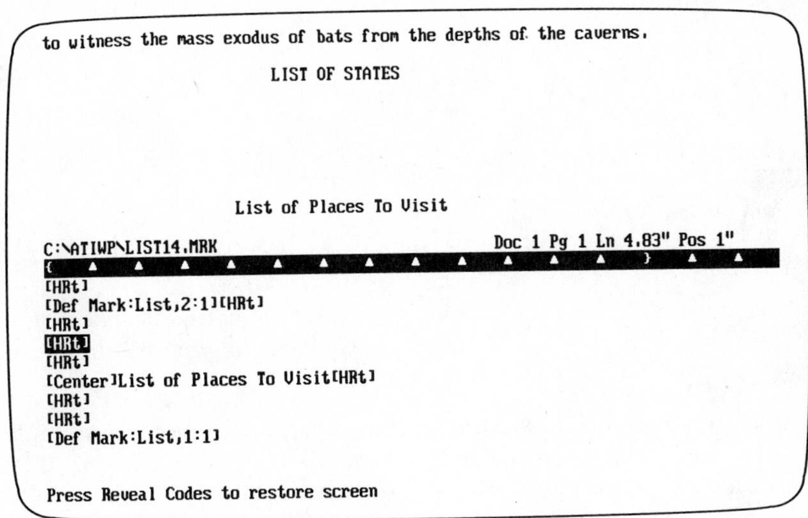

Fig. 14.4. *Using Reveal Codes mode to view Def Mark:List codes.*

Now that text is marked for lists and both lists are defined, the final step in the three-step process is generating the lists.

Generating a List

WordPerfect generates all document references at the same time, using the Mark Text: Generate menu (see fig. 14.5). You should therefore edit the document and define all lists before you generate document references. You can regenerate document references (and you may need to) after you see the first lists.

```
Mark Text: Generate

     1 - Remove Redline Markings and Strikeout Text from Document

     2 - Compare Screen and Disk Documents and Add Redline and Strikeout

     3 - Expand Master Document

     4 - Condense Master Document

     5 - Generate Tables, Indexes, Cross-References, etc.











Selection: 0
```

Fig. 14.5. *The Mark Text: Generate menu.*

A few words of caution: Save your document before you generate references. For added protection, save the document under a separate name so that you have two working copies.

Saving your work is particularly important if you have a large document or multiple documents. Generating references in large documents can take a lot of time, depending on the length and complexity of your document. The amount of unused RAM you have when WordPerfect generates references affects the generation time. Before generating references, you can remove any document from the second window and detach keyboard macros to free RAM.

During reference generation, you are most vulnerable to data loss from power failure, bad spots on a hard disk, and other disasters. If a problem occurs, the document in memory and on disk can be destroyed. A little insurance, such as a second copy, protects you from losing hours of work.

The generation phase of list development places the `[End Def]` code at the end of every list it generates. Do not delete this code. WordPerfect uses it to determine what code to delete when it regenerates a document reference. Although WordPerfect does not delete text if it cannot find the `[End Def]` code, it generates another list—and two lists result.

To make a backup copy of the current file and generate the two lists previously defined, perform these steps:

Step 1: Access the **F**ile pull-down menu and select **S**ave (or press F10); store the current document under the name LIST.TMP.

Note: You should now have three versions of the document on disk: the original unmarked document (LIST14.DOC); the version marked for two lists (LIST14.MRK)—both files provided on the lesson disk; and the current document you saved after defining two lists (LIST.TMP).

Step 2: Access the **M**ark pull-down menu and choose **G**enerate (or press Alt-F5,6).

Step 3: Choose **G**enerate Tables, Indexes, Cross-References, etc. (**5**).

Step 4: When you are prompted `Existing tables, lists, and indexes will be replaced. Continue? Yes (No)`, press **Y**.

Step 5: Scroll through the current document and make sure that the generation of the States list, followed by the Places to Visit list, is similar to that shown in figure 14.6.

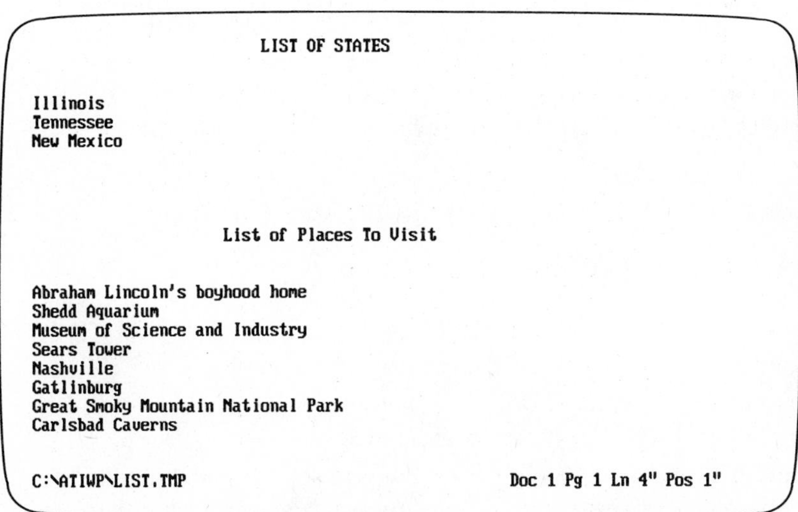

LIST OF STATES
Illinois
Tennessee
New Mexico
List of Places To Visit
Abraham Lincoln's boyhood home
Shedd Aquarium
Museum of Science and Industry
Sears Tower
Nashville
Gatlinburg
Great Smoky Mountain National Park
Carlsbad Caverns
C:\ATIWP\LIST.TMP
Doc 1 Pg 1 Ln 4" Pos 1"

Fig. 14.6. *The results of generating two lists.*

You just created two lists by marking text, defining locations of lists, and generating lists. If for some reason the lists do not generate, clear the screen without saving the current document and take one of these actions:

- ❑ Retrieve the LIST.TMP document and repeat the steps to generate a list.
- ❑ Retrieve the LIST14.MRK document and repeat the steps to define and generate a list.
- ❑ Retrieve the LIST14.DOC document and repeat the steps to mark, define, and generate a list.

Remember: Always have several copies of your documents on disk before you run the often lengthy routine of generating references.

Sorting a Generated List

Chapter 25 in *Using WordPerfect 5.1*, Special Edition, discusses the problems of sorting a generated list and refers to a macro, LSTRT.ARC, in DL0 of CompuServe's WordPerfect Support Group forum. If you have access to CompuServe, use the macro. It leaves the list definition in place so that you can regenerate the list without redefining it.

An alternative solution is to generate the list and use Reveal Codes to block the text between the `[Def Mark:List... ]` and `[End Def]` list definition codes found at the beginning and end of the list.

You can now use WordPerfect's Block Sort feature (see Lesson 13) to put the list in order. Each list entry is preceded by `[→Indent←]` and `[←Mar Rel]`. The Sort feature treats these codes as fields. Therefore, in the Sort key, you should specify field 3—for example, a **1 3 1**.

Creating an Index

Marking index entries is similar to marking list entries, with a few minor exceptions. Follow these simple procedures:

- ❑ If you are marking a single word to be included in the index, access the **M**ark pull-down menu (or press Alt-F5) and select **I**ndex.
- ❑ If you are marking more than one word (a phrase) to be included in the index, turn Block on, highlight the text, then access the **M**ark pull-down menu (or press Alt- F5) and select **I**ndex.
- ❑ Press Enter to accept `Index heading:` followed by the highlighted entry.
- ❑ At the prompt `Subheading:`, press Enter to bypass the entry; or type a subheading and press Enter.

Marking Text for an Index

Create an index based on the INDEX14.DOC document, which is similar to the document used to create lists, except that the information for each state is on a separate page. To practice marking a single word of text to be included in an index, perform these steps:

Step 1: Clear the screen without saving the current document and retrieve the INDEX14.DOC document.

Step 2: Position the cursor anywhere in `Illinois`.

Step 3: Access the **M**ark pull-down menu and choose **I**ndex (or press Alt-F5,3).

Step 4: When you are prompted `Index heading: Illinois.`, delete the period at the end of the prompt and press Enter.

Step 5: When you are prompted `Subheading:`, type **State of** and press Enter.

Note: The one-word heading is accepted into the index. Notice that you positioned the cursor in the middle of `Illinois` and pressed Mark Text.

Indexing a phrase is different. You must tell WordPerfect where the phrase begins and ends. The Block command does this.

To practice marking a text phrase to be included in an index and view the index codes, perform these steps:

Step 1: Position the cursor at the beginning of the phrase `Abraham Lincoln's boyhood home.`

Step 2: Access the **E**dit pull-down menu and select **B**lock (or press Alt-F4 or F12); highlight `Abraham Lincoln's boyhood home.`

Step 3: Access the **M**ark pull-down menu and choose **I**ndex (or press Alt-F5,3).

Step 4: At the prompt `Index heading: Abraham Lincoln's boyhood home`, press Enter to accept the entry.

Step 5: Press Enter to bypass the `Subheading:` prompt.

Step 6: Position the cursor in the upper left corner of the screen.

Step 7: Access the **E**dit pull-down menu and select **R**eveal Codes (or press Alt-F3 or F11).

Note: Each indexed item is marked with a code containing the word `Index:` followed by the marked text. Figure 14.7 illustrates `[Index:Illinois;State of]` and `[Index:Abraham Lincoln's boyhood home]` codes.

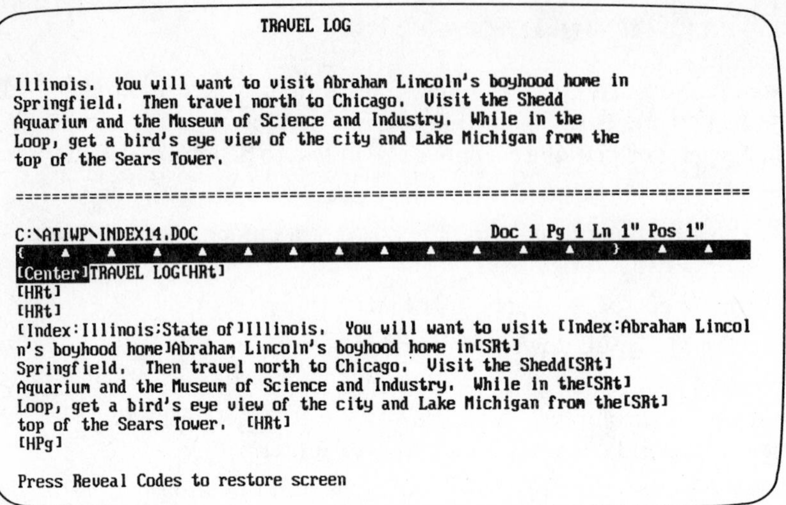

TRAVEL LOG
Illinois. You will want to visit Abraham Lincoln's boyhood home in
Springfield. Then travel north to Chicago. Visit the Shedd
Aquarium and the Museum of Science and Industry. While in the
Loop, get a bird's eye view of the city and Lake Michigan from the
top of the Sears Tower.
C:\ATIWP\INDEX14.DOC
Doc 1 Pg 1 Ln 1" Pos 1"
[Center]TRAVEL LOG[HRt]
[HRt]
[HRt]
[Index:Illinois;State of]Illinois. You will want to visit [Index:Abraham Lincol
n's boyhood home]Abraham Lincoln's boyhood home in[SRt]
Springfield. Then travel north to Chicago. Visit the Shedd[SRt]
Aquarium and the Museum of Science and Industry. While in the[SRt]
Loop, get a bird's eye view of the city and Lake Michigan from the[SRt]
top of the Sears Tower. [HRt]
[HPg]
Press Reveal Codes to restore screen

***Fig. 14.7.** Using Reveal Codes mode to view Index codes.*

Step 8: Access the **E**dit pull-down menu and select **R**eveal Codes (or press Alt-F3 or F11) to restore full document display.

To mark additional entries for an index, follow these steps:

Step 1: Repeat Steps 1 through 5 in the previous exercise and mark `Shedd Aquarium`.

Step 2: Repeat Steps 1 through 5 and mark `Museum of Science and Industry`.

Step 3: Repeat Steps 1 through 5 and mark `Sears Tower`.

If you want more practice marking text, mark these items: `Tennessee`, `Nashville`, `Gatlinburg`, `Smoky Mountain National Park`, `New Mexico`, and `Carlsbad Caverns`. Remember to put the subheading **State of** after `Tennessee` and `New Mexico`.

If you are confident about marking text for an index and ready to practice defining an index, continue with the next section (text marked for an index is provided on a lesson-disk file).

Defining the Index

Defining an index is similar to defining a list. Position the cursor at the location for the index, access menu options to define the index, bypass the concordance file prompt, and select the page number format.

To define the index for the current document and view the index definition code, perform these steps:

Step 1: Clear the screen without saving the current document and retrieve the INDEX14.MRK document.

Step 2: Access the **E**dit pull-down menu and select **R**eveal Codes (or press Alt-F3 or F11), scroll through the document, and make sure that all `[Index:]` codes are in place.

Step 3: Press Reveal Codes again (Alt-F3 or F11) and position the cursor two lines below the bottom of the document.

Step 4: Access the **L**ayout pull-down menu, select **A**lign, and then choose Hard **P**age (or press Ctrl-Enter).

Step 5: Access the **L**ayout pull-down menu, select **A**lign, and then choose **C**enter (or press Shift-F6).

Step 6: Type **INDEX** and press Enter three times.

Step 7: Access the **M**ark pull-down menu, choose **D**efine, and choose **I**ndex (or press Alt-F5,5,3).

Step 8: When you are prompted `Concordance Filename (Enter=none):`, press Enter to bypass this feature.

Step 9: Choose **P**age Numbers Follow Entries (**2**).

Step 10: Position the cursor in the upper left corner of the screen.

Step 11: Access the **E**dit pull-down menu and select **R**eveal Codes (or press Alt-F3 or F11).

Note: Figure 14.8 illustrates the `[Def Mark:Index,2]` code, which positions the index in the document and sets the second page numbering option (pages numbers follow entries).

Step 12: Access the **E**dit pull-down menu and select **R**eveal Codes (or press Alt-F3 or F11) to restore full document display.

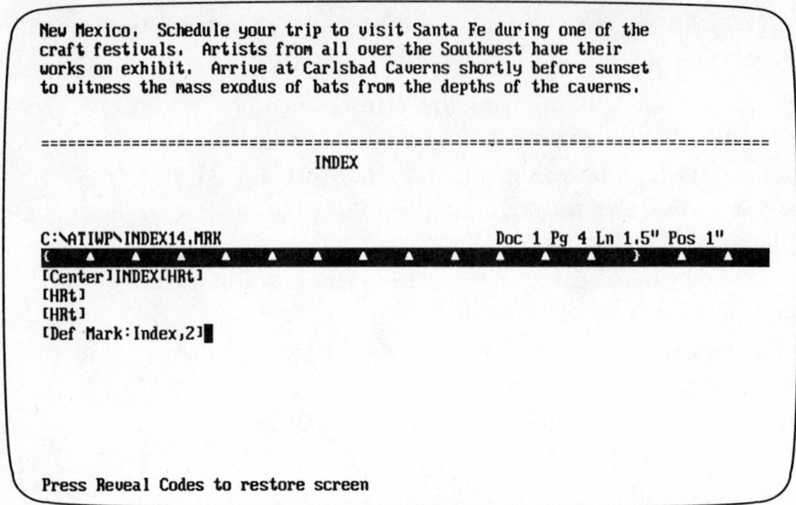

Fig. 14.8. *Using Reveal Codes mode to view the Def Mark:Index code.*

Generating the Index

To generate the index, follow the same procedure as you did for generating lists. Be sure to save one or more copies of your document before you run the often-lengthy generation routine. All document references are generated each time you execute this procedure.

To generate the index you defined, perform these steps:

Step 1: Access the **File** pull-down menu and select **Save** (or press F10); store the current document under the name INDEX.TMP.

Note: You should now have three versions of the document on disk: the original unmarked document (INDEX14.DOC); the version marked for the index (INDEX14.MRK); and the current document marked and defined for the index (INDEX.TMP).

Step 2: Access the **Mark** pull-down menu and choose **Generate** (or press Alt-F5,6).

Step 3: Choose **Generate** Tables, Indexes, Cross-References, etc. (**5**).

Step 4: When you are prompted `Existing tables, lists, and indexes will be replaced. Continue? Yes (No)`, press **Y**.

You just created the index by marking the items to go in the index, defining the location of the index, and generating the index (see fig. 14.9).

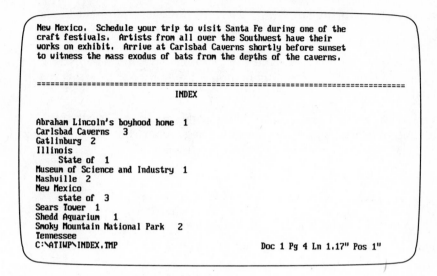

```
New Mexico. Schedule your trip to visit Santa Fe during one of the
craft festivals. Artists from all over the Southwest have their
works on exhibit. Arrive at Carlsbad Caverns shortly before sunset
to witness the mass exodus of bats from the depths of the caverns.

==================================================================================
                                 INDEX


Abraham Lincoln's boyhood home  1
Carlsbad Caverns   3
Gatlinburg  2
Illinois
    State of  1
Museum of Science and Industry  1
Nashville  2
New Mexico
    state of  3
Sears Tower  1
Shedd Aquarium   1
Smoky Mountain National Park   2
Tennessee
C:\ATIWP\INDEX.TMP                                  Doc 1 Pg 4 Ln 1.17" Pos 1"
```

Fig. 14.9. The results of generating the index.

If for some reason the index does not generate, clear the screen without saving the current document and take one of these actions:

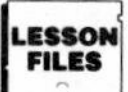

- ❑ Retrieve the INDEX.TMP document and repeat the steps to generate an index.
- ❑ Retrieve the INDEX14.MRK document and repeat the steps to define and generate an index.
- ❑ Retrieve the INDEX14.DOC document and repeat the steps to mark, define, and generate an index.

Remember: Always have backup copies of your documents on disk before you perform the often lengthy routine of generating references.

Creating a Table of Contents

Creating a table of contents is similar to creating lists and indexes. You will, however, find a few differences and potential problems.

When you add an item to the table of contents, you must specify which of the five levels within the table is appropriate for the new item. The level you choose affects the placement of the entry on the print line.

WordPerfect inserts one blank line before each level one line; all other levels are single-spaced. If you prefer having all lines in the table of contents double-spaced, mark the entry to include formatting codes such as carriage returns. As an alternative, you can make every entry level one and force double- spacing. When you force double-spacing, though, you lose all indentation caused by using levels. You must then insert codes to indent each line.

Implementing either method to force double-spacing can be very frustrating. The simplest method of handling most documents is to generate the table by using as many levels as necessary and add necessary spacing manually.

Marking Text for the Table of Contents

Use Block to highlight text for the table of contents. To mark text for inclusion in a table of contents for the TOC14.DOC document, and view the `[ToC]` codes, perform these steps:

Step 1: Clear the screen without saving the current document and retrieve the TOC14.DOC document.

Step 2: Position the cursor on the first letter of the heading `Introduction`.

Step 3: Access the **E**dit pull-down menu and select **B**lock (or press Alt-F4 or F12) and highlight the heading.

Step 4: Access the **M**ark pull-down menu and choose Table of **C**ontents (or press Alt-F5,1).

Step 5: When you are prompted `ToC Level:`, type **1** and press Enter.

Step 6: Position the cursor on the first letter of the heading `WordPerfect Features`, press Block (Alt-F4 or F12), and highlight the heading.

Step 7: Repeat Steps 4 and 5 to mark `WordPerfect Features` as a level one entry in the table of contents.

Step 8: Repeat Steps 4 and 5 four times to mark the subheadings `Speller`, `Thesaurus`, `Windows`, and `Graphics` , substituting level 2 for the numeral 1.

Step 9: Access the **E**dit pull-down menu and select **R**eveal Codes (or press Alt-F3 or F11); scroll through the document to view the `[ToC]` codes (see fig. 14.10).

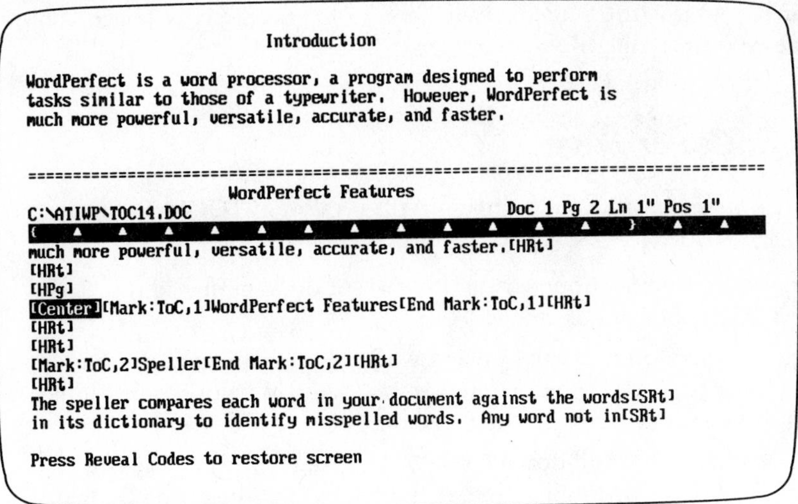

Introduction
WordPerfect is a word processor, a program designed to perform
tasks similar to those of a typewriter. However, WordPerfect is
much more powerful, versatile, accurate, and faster.
WordPerfect Features
C:\ATIWP\TOC14.DOC
Doc 1 Pg 2 Ln 1" Pos 1"
much more powerful, versatile, accurate, and faster.[HRt]
[HRt]
[HPg]
[Center][Mark:ToC,1]WordPerfect Features[End Mark:ToC,1][HRt]
[HRt]
[HRt]
[Mark:ToC,2]Speller[End Mark:ToC,2][HRt]
[HRt]
The speller compares each word in your document against the words[SRt]
in its dictionary to identify misspelled words. Any word not in[SRt]
Press Reveal Codes to restore screen

Fig. 14.10. *Using Reveal Codes mode to view Mark:ToC codes.*

Notice that the instructions have become less detailed. The marking process should be rather routine by now. If something does go wrong, go to the next section in the workbook where a correctly marked document is provided. As time permits, review the section on marking text.

Preparing To Define and Generate the Table of Contents

Before you define the table of contents, you usually complete some preliminary activities: inserting a page for the table of contents and redefining page numbering for both the table of contents and the document.

You can assemble documents in sections, using a WordPerfect feature called a Master Document. Or you can simply assemble the various parts into one document. Regardless of the method you use, you can put in your documents a cover page, the table of contents, the main document, and the index—as well as a bibliography and table of authorities. You can number the pages of each section differently, depending on the writing convention you follow.

In this exercise, you insert a cover page and table of contents page in front of the document contents in TOC14.MRK (a version of TOC14.DOC already marked for items to go in the table). You set New Page Numbering on the cover page, table of contents page, and first page of the document.

Inserting a Cover Page

To insert a cover page in front of the marked-up version of TOC14.DOC, perform these steps:

Step 1: Clear the screen without saving the current document and retrieve the TOC14.MRK document.

Step 2: Press Home, Home, Home, up arrow to position the cursor in the upper left corner of the document's first page, in front of any hidden codes (be sure to press Home three times).

Step 3: Access the **L**ayout pull-down menu, select **A**lign, and select Hard **P**age (or press Ctrl-Enter) to create a new page by inserting the hard-page-break code **[HPg]**.

Step 4: Press PgUp to move the cursor to the top of a new page.

Step 5: Access the **L**ayout pull-down menu and select **P**age (or press Shift-F8,2); choose **C**enter Page (top to bottom) (**1**) and press **Y**.

Step 6: Select S**u**ppress (this page only) (**8**).

Step 7: Choose Suppress **A**ll Page Numbering, Headers, and Footers (**1**).

Step 8: Press Exit (F7) to restore the current document display.

Step 9: Access the **L**ayout pull-down menu, select **A**lign, and choose **C**enter (or press Shift-F6). Type **THE ELEMENTS OF WORD PROCESSING** and press Enter three times.

Step 10: Press Center (Shift-F6), type **by**, and press Enter twice.

Step 11: Press Center (Shift-F6), type **Your Name** (use your real name), and press Enter twice.

Step 12: Access the **F**ile pull-down menu and select **P**rint (or press Shift-F7). Select **V**iew Document (**6**) and choose **F**ull Page (**3**) to see the cover page.

Step 13: Press Exit (F7) enough times to restore the current document display.

Step 14: Access the **F**ile pull-down menu and select **S**ave (or press F10); then save the file as TOC.TMP.

In the preceding steps, you created the extra page for a cover page (Steps 2–4); centered the contents of the new page top to bottom (Step 5); suppressed page numbering for the cover page only (Steps 6–7); entered the cover page text (Steps

9–11); and viewed and saved your work (Steps 12–14). If a problem arises as you work through the next few exercises, using the document you created and saved as TOC.TMP, you can retrieve a backup version called COVER14.MRK and continue with the next section.

Setting a New Page Number for the Document

The first page of the document is now no longer page 1 because you inserted the cover page. Before you print the document, you must tell WordPerfect to renumber pages of the main document.

To set New Page Numbering, perform these steps:

Step 1: Move the cursor to the first page after the cover page.

Step 2: Press Ctrl-Home, up arrow to position the cursor in the upper left corner of the page before any text on the page.

Step 3: Access the **L**ayout pull-down menu and select **P**age (or Shift-F8,2).

Step 4: Choose Page **N**umbering (**6**), choose Page Number **P**osition (**4**), and choose (**6**) to place page numbers bottom center.

Step 5: Choose **N**ew Page Number (**1**), type **1**, and press Enter.

Step 6: Press Exit (F7) to restore the current document display.

You positioned the cursor in the upper left corner of the first page containing document contents (Steps 1–2); directed WordPerfect to place page numbers in the bottom center of the page (Steps 3–4); and set page numbering to begin with one (Step 5). Now create the table of contents page.

Inserting and Numbering the Table of Contents Page

The document now has a cover page followed by the main portion of the document. Insert a table of contents page between the cover and the rest of the document, numbering this front matter with Roman numerals.

To insert the table of contents page and set a numbering scheme different from that used in the body of the document, perform these steps:

Step 1: Position the cursor underneath your name on the cover page.

Step 2: Access the **L**ayout pull-down menu, select **A**lign, and select Hard **P**age (or press Ctrl-Enter) to create a new page for the table of contents.

Step 3: Position the cursor on the newly created page and press Ctrl-Home, up arrow.

Step 4: Access the **L**ayout pull-down menu and select **P**age (or press Shift-F8,2).

Step 5: Choose Page **N**umbering (**6**), choose Page Number **P**osition (**4**), and choose (**6**) to place page numbers bottom center.

Step 6: Choose **N**ew Page Number (**1**), type **i** for Roman numeral one, and press Enter.

Step 7: Press Exit (F7) until the current document appears on-screen.

Step 8: Access the **L**ayout pull-down menu, select **A**lign, and choose **C**enter (or press Shift-F3,F6).

Step 9: Type **TABLE OF CONTENTS** and press Enter three times to insert three blank lines.

You inserted a new page (Steps 1–3), set page numbering beginning with Roman numeral one in the bottom center of the new page (Steps 4–7), and centered a title on the new page (Steps 8–9).

Now that you marked document contents for the table of contents and established appearance characteristics (cover page, separate table of contents page, and page number settings), you can position the index definition code on the table of contents page.

Defining the Table of Contents

To define the table of contents, move the cursor to where you want the table to appear. Use Mark menu selections to set the number of levels used and to determine how the page number appears (see fig. 14.11).

If you encounter any problems in preparing the document to this point, you can continue to work the following exercises by retrieving the lesson-disk file TOC14.DEF instead of using your own work.

To define the table of contents and save your work before generating the table, perform these steps:

Step 1: Position the cursor on the table of contents page three lines below the title `TABLE OF CONTENTS`.

Step 2: Access the **M**ark pull-down menu, select **D**efine, and select Table of Contents (or press Alt-F5,5,1).

Step 3: Choose **N**umber of Levels (**1**) and type **2** for two ToC levels.

Note: The option `Flush right with leader` appears next to the level numbers 1 and 2 (see fig 14.11). This message means that WordPerfect 5.1 places page numbers at the right margin with dot leaders as a visual aid. If you use a proportional print font, these dots may not align properly. If this happens, change the definition to eliminate the dot leaders or position the page numbers immediately following the table of contents entry.

```
Table of Contents Definition

     1 - Number of Levels          2

     2 - Display Last Level in     No
           Wrapped Format

     3 - Page Numbering - Level 1  Flush right with leader
                          Level 2  Flush right with leader
                          Level 3
                          Level 4
                          Level 5









Selection: 0
```

***Fig. 14.11.** The Table of Contents Definition screen.*

Step 4: Press Exit (F7) to restore the current document display.

Step 5: Access the **F**ile pull-down menu and select **S**ave (or press F10). Save the current document as TOC.TMP, replacing the earlier version.

Note: The table definition is inserted in the document. You can use Reveal Codes (Alt-F3 or F11) to verify that the code `[Def Mark:ToC,2:5,5]` is in the table of contents page, three lines below the title.

Generating the Table of Contents

To generate the table of contents, follow these familiar steps:

Step 1: Access the **M**ark pull-down menu and select **G**enerate (or press Alt-F5,6).

Step 2: Choose Generate Tables, Indexes, Cross-References, etc. (**5**).

Step 3: When you are prompted `Existing tables, lists, and indexes will be replaced. Continue? Yes (No)`, **press Y.**

Note: The table of contents you just created should appear on the page after the cover page, as shown in figure 14.12.

```
                THE ELEMENTS OF WORD PROCESSING

                              by

                          Linda Weist

================================================================================
                       TABLE OF CONTENTS


Introduction . . . . . . . . . . . . . . . . . . . . . . . . . . 1

WordPerfect Features . . . . . . . . . . . . . . . . . . . . . . 2
     Speller . . . . . . . . . . . . . . . . . . . . . . . . . . 2
     Thesaurus . . . . . . . . . . . . . . . . . . . . . . . . . 2
     Windows . . . . . . . . . . . . . . . . . . . . . . . . . . 2
     Graphics. . . . . . . . . . . . . . . . . . . . . . . . . . 3



C:\ATIWP\TOC.TMP                          Doc 1 Pg 2 Ln 1.5" Pos 1"
```

***Fig. 14.12.** The results of generating the table of contents.*

If for some reason the table of contents does not generate—or you just want to review the table of contents guided exercises—clear the screen without saving the current document and take one of these actions:

- ❑ Retrieve the TOC14.DEF document and repeat the steps to define and generate the table of contents.
- ❑ Retrieve the TOC14.MRK document and repeat the steps to insert a cover page, set a New Page Number, insert and number a table of contents page, and define and generate the table of contents.
- ❑ Retrieve the TOC14.DOC document and repeat all steps associated with creating a table of contents.

Remember: Always have several copies of your documents on disk before you run the often lengthy routine of generating references. Although WordPerfect's document references facility is far more sophisticated than the few exercises in this lesson demonstrate, you have actually used the skills needed for most documents you prepare. You can enhance your documents by inserting lists, creating indexes, and generating a table of contents. The summary exercises tie together all these three features. Do not hesitate to reinforce your skills by doing this important lesson again—as well as using these references in your documents.

For Further Reference

If you would like to know more about assembling document references, consult *Using WordPerfect 5.1*, Special Edition (Que Corporation, Carmel, IN, 1989), Chapter 25.

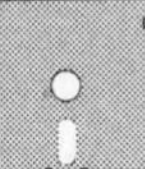

Summary of Concepts

Lesson 14 explains these concepts:

- ❑ Using WordPerfect, you can create a variety of references within a document, including lists, an index, and a table of contents, as illustrated in this workbook.
- ❑ You can create and maintain up to 10 lists per document.
- ❑ List numbers 6 through 10 are used to display graphic box captions but can be used for other information if graphic box captions are not in use.
- ❑ An index can include subheadings.
- ❑ You can use up to five levels of headings and subheadings in a table of contents.
- ❑ Creating references is a three-step process: mark text to be included, define location of references within the document, and generate references.
- ❑ Use Reveal Codes (Alt-F3 or F11) to see the codes for marking and defining references.
- ❑ After you mark and define a document, you should save a backup copy in case a problem develops when you generate references.

Review Exercises

Use the DOCREF14.EX file to create one document containing a cover page, table of contents, lists, and an index.

1. Retrieve the DOCREF14.EX document.
2. Insert a cover page (page 1) with title information centered left to right and top to bottom:

   ASSEMBLING DOCUMENT REFERENCES
   Index, List, Table of Contents
   Your Name
   The current date

3. Mark these items for a table of contents page as page 2. Use two TOC levels and the page-numbering format **P**age Numbers Follow Entries (**2**):

   Introduction
   WordPerfect Features
      Speller
      Thesaurus
      Windows
      Graphics

   Note: The indenting above indicates TOC levels.

4. Mark the following words for a list:

   Word processor
   Speller
   dictionary
   Thesaurus
   synonyms
   headwords
   antonyms
   Windows
   Panes

5. Mark these items for an index:

   Word processor
   Speller
   Dictionary
   Thesaurus
   synonyms

headwords
antonyms
Windows
panes
second window

6. Insert a table of contents page and define the table of contents as containing the list in exercise 3. Title it TABLE OF CONTENTS.
7. Create a list definition at the end of the original document (below the merge codes) but on the same page. Title it SUMMARY OF KEY WORDS.
8. Create an index definition on a separate last page. Title it INDEX.
9. Save a backup file on disk and generate all references. Add spacing to the lists to make them readable.
10. Print (Shift-F7,1) or View (Shift-F7,6) the results.

Using Footnotes, Endnotes, Outlines, and Line Numbers

15

In this lesson, you practice these tasks:

- ❏ Creating, viewing, and printing footnotes
- ❏ Revealing hidden footnote codes
- ❏ Adding, deleting, and editing footnotes
- ❏ Creating, editing, and printing endnotes
- ❏ Using the Outline feature
- ❏ Numbering lines within a page

WordPerfect includes a variety of features that make complex tasks easy to handle in a long document. Lesson 14 illustrates creating lists, indexes, and tables of content. This lesson presents generating an outline, creating footnotes or endnotes, and adding line numbers.

Using Footnotes and Endnotes

When you enter text that does not represent your original work, you may need to cite the sources of selected information within the document. On occasion, you may provide explanatory material that you do not want included in the body of the document. Notes provide a means to reference content sources and add additional information. Footnotes appear at the bottom of the page, and endnotes are grouped at the end of the document or in another position of your choice.

The processes of creating a footnote and creating an endnote are similar:

- ❑ Point, with the cursor, to the text where the number of the note should appear.
- ❑ Access the **L**ayout pull-down menu (or press Ctrl-F7), choose either **F**ootnote or **E**ndnote, and then choose **C**reate.
- ❑ Type the note onto the blank WordPerfect screen, using complete full-screen editing and all WordPerfect features, including the Speller and Thesaurus.
- ❑ Press Exit (F7) to leave the note facility.

WordPerfect automatically numbers notes for you in the text and on the editing screen that appears when you create the note. Follow nearly the same procedures to edit an existing footnote or endnote, except select **E**dit instead of **C**reate and specify the number of the note. If you add or delete a note, all succeeding notes are renumbered automatically.

No special techniques are required to print footnotes and endnotes. Simply print the document, and WordPerfect plans all the pages. Of course, WordPerfect provides the options to make aesthetic changes to the appearance and location of notes.

Creating a Footnote

You can create notes as you enter new text or add notes to existing text. To retrieve a workbook lesson-disk file and create an initial footnote, perform these steps:

Step 1: Clear the screen without saving the current document and retrieve the FOOTNO15.DOC document.

Note: The instruction to clear the screen without saving the current document is used many times throughout the workbook. It means to access the **F**ile pull-down menu and select E**x**it (or press F7); when prompted `Save Document? Yes (No)`, press **N**; when prompted `Exit WP? No (Yes)`, press **N**.

Step 2: Position the cursor immediately after the first occurrence of `dictionary` in the paragraph titled `Speller`.

Step 3: Access the **L**ayout pull-down menu, choose **F**ootnote, and select **C**reate (or press Ctrl-F7,1,1).

Note: Figure 15.1 illustrates the pull-down menu sequence.

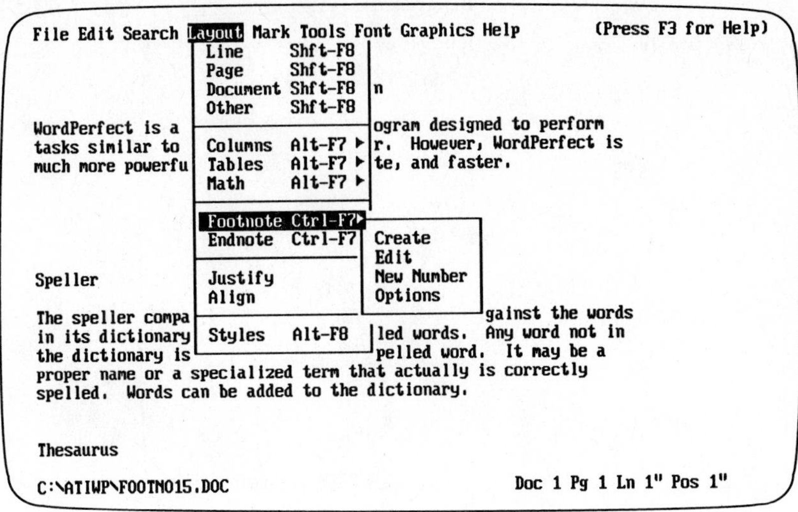

Fig. 15.1. Footnote options on the Layout pull-down menu.

Step 4: At the blank Footnote screen, next to the number 1, type **The WordPerfect Speller contains over 100,000 words in the original dictionary** (see fig. 15.2).

Step 5: Press Exit (F7) to restore the current document and notice the appearance of the footnote number 1 after the first occurrence of `dictionary` in the paragraph titled `Speller`.

You created the first footnote by positioning the cursor (Step 2), accessing the Create Footnote feature (Step 3), and entering the footnote (Steps 4–5). Before entering additional footnotes, see what one looks like in WordPerfect.

Viewing Footnote Contents

As you create and edit a document, you may want to look at the contents of a footnote. The footnote is not, however, in the document. You can see only the footnote number; the text associated with the note is filed on disk for use when the document is printed. You can use several methods to see a footnote by itself or in the document.

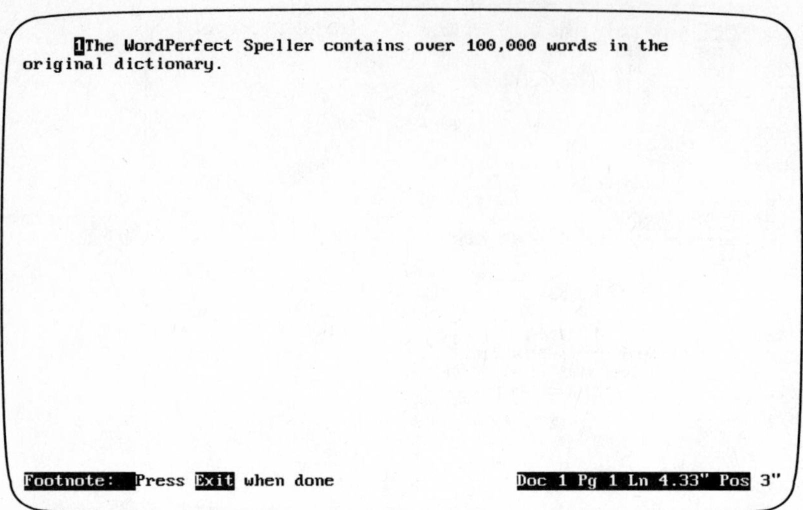

Fig. 15.2. The Footnote Create screen.

Using View Document To View a Footnote

Access the View Document option on the Print menu to see footnotes without printing them. You can, of course, view footnotes by actually printing the page (or pages) containing footnotes.

To view in View Document mode the footnote you just created, follow these steps:

Step 1: Access the **F**ile pull-down menu and select **P**rint (or press Shift-F7) and select **V**iew Document (**6**).

Step 2: Press Home, down arrow to see footnote 1.

Step 3: Press Exit (F7) enough times to restore the current document.

Using Reveal Codes To View a Footnote

Display the document in Reveal Codes mode to see the footnote hidden code and a part of the footnote. To reveal the initial footnote code you entered in FOOTNO15.DOC, follow these steps:

Step 1: Position the cursor on the line where footnote 1 is marked.

Step 2: Access the **E**dit pull-down menu and select **R**eveal Codes (or press Alt-F3 or F11).

Note: You can see the footnote code [Footnote:1;[Note Num] in the bottom half of the screen. The footnote text follows the code. Overlong notes are ended with ellipses (. . .).

Step 3: Position the cursor on the code [Footnote:1;[Note Num] and notice the expanded footnote content displayed in figure 15.3.

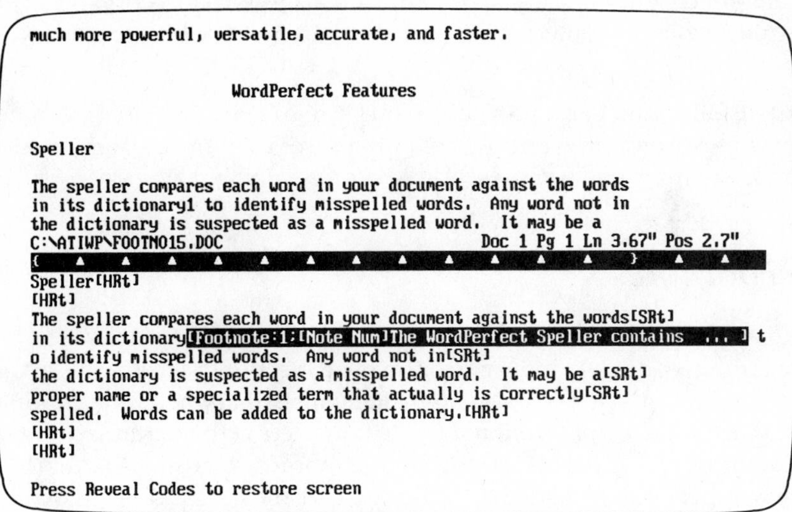

```
much more powerful, versatile, accurate, and faster.

                    WordPerfect Features

Speller

The speller compares each word in your document against the words
in its dictionary1 to identify misspelled words.  Any word not in
the dictionary is suspected as a misspelled word.  It may be a
C:\ATIWP\FOOTNO15.DOC                      Doc 1 Pg 1 Ln 3.67" Pos 2.7"
Speller[HRt]
[HRt]
The speller compares each word in your document against the words[SRt]
in its dictionary[Footnote:1;[Note Num]The WordPerfect Speller contains   ... ] t
o identify misspelled words.  Any word not in[SRt]
the dictionary is suspected as a misspelled word.  It may be a[SRt]
proper name or a specialized term that actually is correctly[SRt]
spelled.  Words can be added to the dictionary.[HRt]
[HRt]
[HRt]

Press Reveal Codes to restore screen
```

Fig. 15.3. *Using Reveal Codes to view a footnote code.*

Step 4: Access the **E**dit pull-down menu and select **R**eveal Codes (or press Alt-F3 or F11) to restore full screen display.

Using Footnote Edit To View a Footnote

Use the Footnote Edit option to see the entire footnote, but not the surrounding text. You also can use Edit to change the footnote, an action illustrated in a later section. To use Edit to look at a footnote, perform these steps:

Step 1: Access the **L**ayout pull-down menu, choose **F**ootnote, and choose **E**dit (or press Ctrl-F7,1,2).

Step 2: When prompted Footnote Number?, type **1**, press Enter, and view the footnote on the same screen that you used to create the footnote.

Step 3: Press Exit (F7) to restore the current document.

Managing Footnotes

Once footnotes are created, it is usually necessary to add more footnotes or delete, move, and edit the existing footnotes. WordPerfect 5.1's footnote feature makes it easy to perform these tasks without major revisions to your paper. For example, when you add, delete, and move footnotes, all footnotes that appear after the altered one are renumbered automatically. Text on each page is also reorganized to accommodate the increased (or decreased) space requirements for the footnotes on that page.

Adding a footnote follows the same procedure you used to create the initial footnote. In the next exercises, you retrieve files containing several footnotes and practice deleting, editing, and moving footnotes.

Deleting Footnotes

A footnote and its associated text are stored as one code, which can be deleted in the same manner as other codes. Place the cursor on the code, press Del, and press **Y** at the prompt `Delete[Footnote:number]? No (Yes)`. Remember that when you edit while using Reveal Codes, you are not prompted to verify a delete action because you can see the codes. If you make a mistake, undelete the footnote by using Cancel (F1). Numbering may appear out of sequence until you move the cursor or press Screen (Ctrl-F3), **R**ewrite (**0**). To practice deleting and restoring a footnote, perform these steps:

Step 1: Clear the screen without saving the current document and retrieve DELNO15.DOC.

Step 2: Scroll through the document, notice the appearance of four footnote numbers, and place the cursor on footnote 1.

Step 3: Press Del(ete), and when prompted `Delete [Footnote:1]? No (Yes)`, press **Y**.

Note: The footnote number after the first appearance of the word `dictionary` in the `Speller` paragraph disappears. The remaining footnotes are renumbered 1, 2, and 3.

Step 4: Access the **E**dit pull-down menu and choose **U**ndelete (or press F1).

Step 5: Choose **R**estore (**1**) to undelete the footnote and notice again that subsequent footnotes are renumbered.

You also can use a combination of deleting a footnote and then restoring the footnote in another location to accomplish a move.

Editing Footnotes

Like other text, footnotes may require editing. Simply follow the procedure to access Footnote menu choices, select the **E**dit option, specify the footnote number, make the appropriate revision, and press Exit (F7). To change footnote 2 by adding a sentence to the end of the footnote, perform these steps:

Step 1: Clear the screen without saving the current document and retrieve EDFOOT15.DOC.

Step 2: Access the **L**ayout pull-down menu, choose **F**ootnote, and choose **E**dit (or press Ctrl-F7,1,2).

Step 3: When prompted `Footnote Number?`, type **2** and press Enter.

Step 4: Position the cursor at the end of the footnote 2 text and type **Unlike the Speller, the Thesaurus cannot have words added to it**.

Step 5: Press Exit (F7) to restore the current document.

Moving Footnotes

Footnotes, like other text, may need to be moved elsewhere in the document. The moves may require moving only the footnote or the footnote and its surrounding text. Moving footnotes is similar to moving any other text. You can use WordPerfect 5.1's Move command to move a footnote. You also can accomplish a move by deleting the footnote, repositioning the cursor to the new location, pressing Cancel (F1), and restoring the previous deletion.

To move the first sentence in the paragraph under the title `Speller` (including footnote 1), perform these steps:

Step 1: Position the cursor at the beginning of the first sentence in the paragraph titled `Speller`.

Step 2: Access the **E**dit pull-down menu, choose Se**l**ect, and choose **S**entence (or press Ctrl-F4,1).

Step 3: Select **M**ove (**1**).

Step 4: Move the cursor to the end of the paragraph under the title `Thesaurus`, press Enter, and notice that footnotes 1 and 2 are renumbered to reflect the shift in position.

In other situations, you may need to move only the footnote, not the footnote and surrounding text. To move footnote 1 by using the Move command, perform these steps:

Step 1: Clear the screen without saving the current document and retrieve the MVFOOT15.DOC document.

Step 2: Position the cursor on footnote number 1.

Step 3: Access the **E**dit pull-down menu and select **B**lock (or press Alt-F4 or F12); then press the right arrow one time to highlight the footnote number.

Step 4: Access the **E**dit pull-down menu and select **M**ove (or press Ctrl-Del).

Step 5: Move the cursor to the end of the paragraph immediately following the last word, `dictionary`. The cursor should rest on the period.

Step 6: Press Enter.

To move the footnote number by using a combination of Delete and Cancel commands, perform these steps:

Step 1: Position the cursor on footnote number 1.

Step 2: Press Del, and when prompted `Delete Block? No (Yes)`, press **Y**.

Step 3: Move the cursor to the end of the first occurrence of `dictionary` in the first sentence of the `Speller` paragraph.

Step 4: Access the **E**dit pull-down menu and choose **U**ndelete (or press F1); then choose **R**estore (**1**).

Practice moving footnotes alone or footnotes including surrounding text until you are comfortable with the variety of ways you can accomplish the task.

Managing Endnotes

Creating and managing endnotes varies little from creating and managing footnotes. You will find differences in menu choices and in the positioning of endnotes. To create an endnote, select the menu item **E**ndnote (**2**) instead of **F**ootnote (**1**). Positioning endnotes in the document, as with other document references, is a matter of pointing to the location.

To retrieve a document in which four endnotes have been created and to instruct WordPerfect where to place the endnotes in the document, perform these steps:

Step 1: Clear the screen without saving the current document and retrieve ENDNO15.DOC.

Step 2: Position the cursor on the endnote number 1.

Step 3: Access the **E**dit pull-down menu and select **R**eveal Codes (or press Alt-F3 or F11).

Note: Figure 15.4 illustrates the `[Endnote:1;[Note Num]` code for the first endnote.

```
tasks similar to those of a typewriter. However, WordPerfect is
much more powerful, versatile, accurate, and faster.

                    WordPerfect Features

Speller

The speller compares each word in your document against the words
in its dictionary1 to identify misspelled words. Any word not in
C:\ATIWP\EDNO15.DOC                          Doc 1 Pg 1 Ln 3.67" Pos 2.7"
{  ▲  ▲  ▲  ▲  ▲  ▲  ▲  ▲  ▲  ▲  ▲  ▲  ▲  }  ▲  ▲
Speller[HRt]
[HRt]
The speller compares each word in your document against the words[SRt]
in its dictionary[Endnote:1;[Note Num]The WordPerfect Speller contains ... ] to
identify misspelled words. Any word not in[SRt]
the dictionary is suspected as a misspelled word. It may be a[SRt]
proper name or a specialized term that actually is correctly[SRt]
spelled. Words can be added to the dictionary.[HRt]
[HRt]
[HRt]

Press Reveal Codes to restore screen
```

Fig. 15.4. Using Reveal Codes to view an endnote code.

Step 4: Access the **E**dit pull-down menu and select **R**eveal Codes (or press Alt-F3 or F11) to restore full document display.

Step 5: Press Home, Home, down arrow and then adjust the cursor to four lines below the last line of the document.

Step 6: Access the **L**ayout pull-down menu, choose **E**ndnote, and choose **P**lacement (or press Ctrl-F7,3).

Step 7: When prompted `Restart endnote numbering? Yes (No)`, press **Y**.

Steps 6 and 7 inserted the hidden code **[Endnote Placement][HPg]** into the text. A message (see fig. 15.5.) indicating that WordPerfect cannot determine how much space is needed for endnotes appears on the screen.

WordPerfect does not maintain a running count of the space endnotes occupy. Instead, the status line reflects the space endnotes will occupy after you generate the endnotes. Remember: Save your file before executing the often lengthy Generate command. To save the current document under the name ENDNOTES.DOC, generate the endnotes, and view the endnotes, perform these steps:

Step 1: Access the **F**ile pull-down menu and select **S**ave (or press F10); save the document under the name ENDNOTES.DOC.

Step 2: Access the **M**ark pull-down menu and choose **G**enerate (or press Alt-F5,6).

Step 3: Select **G**enerate Tables, Indexes, Cross-References, etc. (**5**).

```
elements4.

As you plan your document, decide in advance the use of each of the
different types of boxes and how each is to look.  For example, in
a newsletter, you may decide to use figure boxes to hold graphics
created in another program.  In this case, define the figure box
with single borders.  You may decide to use table boxes to call out
important text in your document.  In this case, define the table
box with thick top and bottom borders and no side borders.  You may
want to put the nameplate in a text box defined with thick top and
bottom borders and 10% gray shading.  You may decide to use user-
defined boxes for major headlines, defined with no borders or
shading.


 Endnote Placement
 It is not known how much space endnotes will occupy here.
 Generate to determine.

==============================================================================
C:\ATIWP\EDN015.DOC                                Doc 1 Pg 3 Ln 1" Pos 1"
```

Fig. 15.5. *An endnote placement message.*

Step 4: When prompted `Existing tables, lists, and indexes will be replaced. Continue? Yes (No)`, press **Y**.

Step 5: Press Home, Home, down arrow.

Note: The message in the box changes to only `Endnote Placement`.

Step 6: Move the cursor to just below the box and note the line count in the lower right corner of the screen (`Ln 5.5"`).

Step 7: Move the cursor to just above the box and note the line count (`Ln 3.5"`).

Note: Your line counts may vary depending on the number of blank lines prior to endnote placement. WordPerfect computes the space required for the endnotes—in this case, two inches.

Step 8: Access the **F**ile pull-down menu and select **P**rint (or press Shift-F7); select **V**iew Document (**6**) to verify that the endnotes appear at the end of the document.

Step 9: Press Exit (F7) enough times to restore the current document.

If you do not like the way WordPerfect displays footnotes and endnotes, you may change styles. For example, you can change from single to double line spacing within a footnote. Consult *Using WordPerfect 5.1*, Special Edition, for a discussion of available options.

Converting Footnotes and Endnotes

If your document's style requirements change after you have inserted the footnotes or endnotes, you may be forced to convert your notes. WordPerfect 5.1 includes two macros to convert notes: one converts footnote codes to endnote codes (FOOTEND.WPM), and the other converts endnote codes to footnote codes (ENDFOOT.WPM). Once the footnotes are converted, you must place the footnotes at the end of the document and then generate the endnotes before they can be viewed or printed.

In the next exercise, the assumption is that the two conversion macros are stored in your default macro library. To convert footnotes in the FOOTEN15.DOC file to endnotes, perform these steps:

Step 1: Clear the screen without saving the current document and retrieve FOOTEN15.DOC.

Step 2: Scroll through the document in Reveal Codes mode, note the appearance of footnote codes, and restore full document display.

Step 3: Access the **T**ools pull-down menu and select M**a**cro (or press Alt-F10).

Step 4: When prompted `Macro:`, type **FOOTEND** and press Enter.

Note: After a short delay, the footnote codes are converted to endnote codes. It is still necessary to generate the endnotes.

Step 5: Scroll through the document in Reveal Codes mode, note the appearance of endnote codes, and restore full document display.

Step 6: Access the **M**ark pull-down menu and choose **G**enerate (or press Alt-F5,6).

Step 7: Select **G**enerate Tables, Indexes, Cross-References, etc. (**5**).

Step 8: When prompted `Existing tables, lists, and indexes will be replaced. Continue? Yes (No)`, press **Y**.

Step 9: Access the **F**ile pull-down menu and select **P**rint (or press Shift-F7); select **V**iew Document (**6**) to verify that the endnotes appear at the end of the document.

Step 10: Press Exit (F7) until the current document appears on the screen.

The preceding exercises illustrate the basic procedures for establishing, editing, and converting footnotes and endnotes. For additional assistance in managing long documents, WordPerfect offers three methods of organizing your written work: outlining, paragraph numbering, and line numbering. Outlining and paragraph numbering create typical outlines. Line numbering numbers every line on a page (or portion of a page) as it prints.

Using Automatic Outlining

Outlines can be wonderful organizing tools. If, however, you want to change numbering, insert or delete an outline topic, or move part of an outline, you can be frustrated by making changes unless numbering is automatically adjusted—as it is in WordPerfect.

With the aid of the Enter and Tab keys, WordPerfect's automatic outlining organizes "paragraphs," using up to eight levels of indentation. In an outline, `paragraph` means a phrase, a sentence, or a paragraph constituting a separate level in the outline. Add, change, or delete a paragraph, and the outline is rewritten with new numbers. You can even design a personal numbering scheme.

The text in an outline looks like any other text in a document but contains `[Par Num]` hidden codes to mark where paragraph numbers should appear. You can see a sample outline format in figure 15.6.

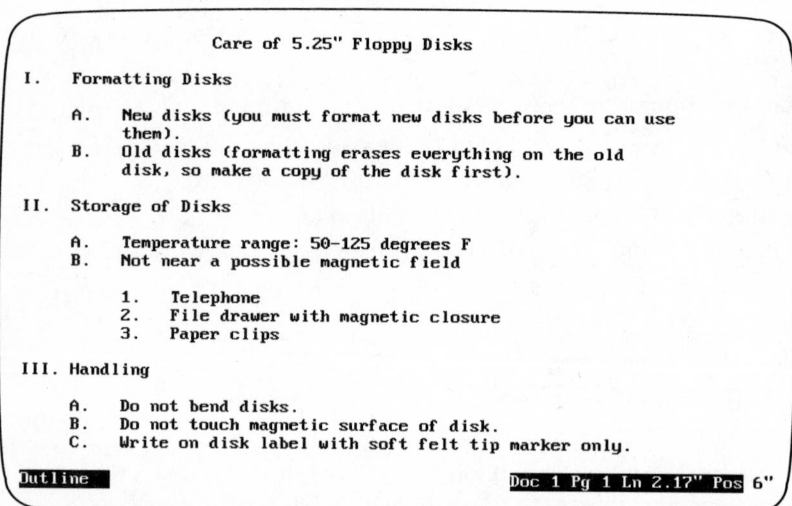

***Fig. 15.6.** A sample outline format.*

The outlining process requires these few simple steps:

❑ Access the **T**ools pull-down menu and select **O**utline (or press Shift-F5,4); select **D**efine (**6**) before you start the outline. This step is necessary only if you want to use a paragraph number style other than the default style.

- ❑ Access the **T**ools pull-down menu and select **O**utline (or press Shift-F5,4); select **O**n (**1**) to turn on outlining.
- ❑ Press Enter. A paragraph number is inserted at the same level as the last level entered in the outline.
- ❑ Press Tab, and the cursor moves right one tab stop—to the next paragraph level—and the paragraph number moves right, changing to the next lower level number (for example, A. in fig. 15.6).
- ❑ Press Indent (F4) and type the paragraph text.
- ❑ To add more paragraphs, press Enter and then use Tab to move to the appropriate level number for each paragraph.

Reveal Codes mode illustrates the hidden codes used in the outlining process (see fig. 15.7).

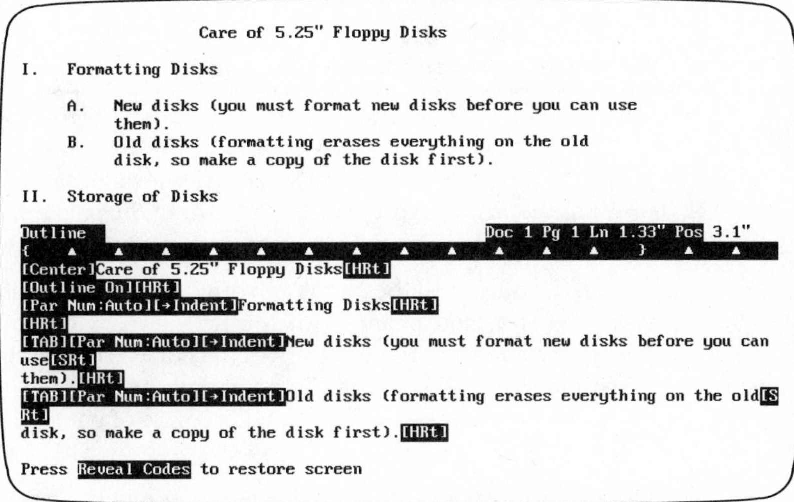

Fig. 15.7. *Using Reveal Codes to view outlining codes.*

Notice the hidden codes `[Outline On]` in the Reveal Codes section (bottom half of screen). This code, inserted when you turn on the outline feature, marks the beginning of the outline. Outline numbers start at this point. A corresponding `[Outline Off]` code appears at the end of the outline.

The Outline On and Off codes are new with WordPerfect 5.1. When the cursor is located between the On and Off hidden codes, you are in the Outline mode, and the word `Outline` appears in the lower left corner of the screen. During this time the Enter, Tab, and Insert keys function as described in table 15.1. Once you have finished the outline, if you delete the hidden Outline On/Off codes, you can edit the contents as if they were regular text. Of course, any paragraphs automatically numbered retain those numbers. Also, if an automatic paragraph number is changed or deleted, the others continue to be renumbered appropriately.

The code `[Par Num:Auto]` indicates that the paragraph is automatically numbered with a level-one number. `[Par Num:Auto]` preceded by a `[Tab]` code indicates a second-level paragraph number. Count the number of `[Tab]` codes that appear before the `[Par Num:Auto]`, and you can tell what paragraph level number is being used.

The functions of the Enter, Tab, and Indent keys are described in table 15.1. Refer to this table, if necessary, as you create outlines in this lesson.

Table 15.1
Key and Associated Actions in Outlining

Enter	Press Enter once, and a paragraph number—consistent with the last level number—is inserted in the outline at the left margin. Press Enter a second time, without using Indent, and a blank line is inserted without the paragraph number's being changed.
Tab	Press Tab once, and the paragraph number is moved right one tab stop and changed to the next-level paragraph number. Pressing Tab again moves the cursor right to the next tab stop and changes the paragraph number again. You can repeat this process for eight levels of paragraph numbers.
Shift-Tab	Press Shift-Tab once, and the paragraph number is moved left one tab stop and changed to the previous-level paragraph number.
Indent	Press Indent (F4) when line spacing and the paragraph number are set. Doing so creates a traditional indentation one tab stop from the paragraph number.

Creating an Outline

To create the outline, simply turn on Outline, type the text—including tabs—to establish paragraph numbers, and turn off Outline when you finish. The default numbering style uses Roman numerals for level one and capital letters for level two (the I. A. style shown in fig. 15.6). Follow these steps to turn on outlining:

Step 1: Clear the screen without saving the current document and position the cursor at the top left corner.

Step 2: Access the **L**ayout pull-down menu, select **A**lign, and then choose **C**enter (or press Shift-F6).

Step 3: Type **Care of 5.25" Floppy Disks** and press Enter once.

Step 4: Access the **T**ools pull-down menu and select **O**utline (or press Shift-F5,4).

Step 5: Select **On** (**1**) but do not press Enter.

Step 6: Access the **E**dit pull-down menu and select **R**eveal Codes (or press Alt-F3 or F11) to see the `[Outline On]` code; then press Reveal Codes (Alt-F3 or F11) to restore full document display.

The word `Outline` appears in the lower left corner of the screen.

This message appears when automatic outlining is active. Generating the indentation and outline numbering is now a matter of pressing Enter and Tab and then typing text. If you accidentally press Enter at the end of Step 3, you see the Roman numeral one (I.). If so, skip Step 1 of the next set of instructions. To begin entering the outline in figure 15.6, follow these steps:

Step 1: Press Enter to generate automatically `I.`, the initial paragraph number.

Step 2: Press Enter again to insert a blank line.

Step 3: Press Indent (F4) to anchor the paragraph number I.

Note: If you accidentally press Tab instead of indent (F4), the cursor moves to the right one tab stop and changes to the next-level lower number. To move the paragraph number back one level, press Shift-Tab, and the paragraph number will move to the correct level and be renumbered. Finally, move the cursor to the right of the paragraph number and press Indent (F4).

Step 4: Type **Formatting Disks**.

Step 5: Press Enter to create a paragraph number.

Step 6: Press Enter to insert a blank line.

Step 7: Press Tab to move right one level.

Step 8: Press Indent (F4) to anchor A., the level-two paragraph number.

Step 9: Type **New Disks (you must format new disks before you can use them)**.

Step 10: Enter a portion or all of the remaining outline, using the text in figure 15.6 (later exercises use a lesson-disk file).

It takes some practice to become comfortable using Tab, Shift-Tab, Indent, and Enter to produce the outlining results you want. To return to entering text normally, you must turn off Outline. `[Outline On]` and `[Outline Off]` are open codes. Once invoked, they remain in effect until the other code is encountered. To turn off Outline, follow these steps:

Step 1: Access the **T**ools pull-down menu and select **O**utline (or press Shift-F5,4).

Step 2: Choose O**f**f (**2**).

You can turn Outline off and on repeatedly if you want to mix text and outline. Once you define an outline, WordPerfect remembers the paragraph number last used and begins with the next number when you turn the feature on again.

Defining a Paragraph Number Style

WordPerfect offers four numbering styles and a "user-defined" option for numbering (see fig. 15.8).

The `Current Definition` line displays the numbering style currently selected. Outline is the default style. To change numbering style, simply choose one of the four styles or create a new style by pressing the number for that style (the numbers 2 through 6 appear to the left of their respective styles). Press Exit (F7) to begin your outline, using the new style.

WordPerfect 5.1 includes a new option, Outline Style **N**ame (**9**). If you create an Outline Style (Lesson 10 discusses the Style feature), you can reference or invoke it through the Paragraph Number Definition Screen. For a detailed discussion of this feature, consult *Using WordPerfect 5.1*, Special Edition, or your WordPerfect 5.1 reference manual.

The process of outlining is the same, regardless of the numbering style you choose. To see a different number style without keying the text again, simply change the definition. When Outline is turned on, a `[Par Num:Auto]` code is inserted in the text every time Enter is pressed. To change the numbering style of the existing outline, simply select a different style by inserting a `[Par Num Def]` code ahead of the text of the outline.

```
Paragraph Number Definition

     1 - Starting Paragraph Number              1
          (in legal style)
                                                 Levels
                                      1     2     3     4     5     6     7     8
     2 - Paragraph                    1.    a.    i.   (1)   (a)   (i)    1)    a)
     3 - Outline                      I.    A.    1.    a.   (1)   (a)    i)    a)
     4 - Legal (1.1.1)                1     .1    .1    .1    .1    .1    .1    .1
     5 - Bullets                      •     o     -     ■     *     +     ·     x
     6 - User-defined

     Current Definition               I.    A.    1.    a.   (1)   (a)    i)    a)
     Attach Previous Level                  No    No    No    No    No    No    No

     7 - Enter Inserts Paragraph Number         Yes

     8 - Automatically Adjust to Current Level  Yes

     9 - Outline Style Name



Selection: 0
```

Fig. 15.8. *The Paragraph Number Definition screen.*

To insert a paragraph number definition code in an outline already stored on disk, perform these steps:

Step 1: Clear the screen without saving the current document and retrieve the OUTL15A.DOC document.

Step 2: Move the cursor to the second line between the title and the I. line.

Step 3: Access the **T**ools pull-down menu and select **D**efine (or press Shift-F5,6).

Step 4: Choose **B**ullets (**5**) and press Exit (F7) until the current document appears on the screen.

Step 5: Press PgDn and note the switch to bullets designating the outline levels (see fig. 15.9).

WordPerfect also makes it easy to change paragraph numbers and to add, change, delete, or move paragraphs.

```
                  Care of 5.25" Floppy Disks

•     Formatting Disks

      o     New disks (you must format new disks before you can use
            them).
      o     Old disks (formatting erases everything on the old
            disk, so make a copy of the disk first).

•     Storage of Disks

      o     Temperature range: 50-125 degrees F
      o     Not near a possible magnetic field

            -     Telephone
            -     File drawer with magnetic closure
            -     Paper clips

•     Handling

      o     Do not bend disks.
      o     Do not touch magnetic surface of disk.
      o     Write on disk label with soft felt tip marker only.

C:\ATIWP\OUTL15A.DOC                       Doc 1 Pg 1 Ln 1" Pos 1"
```

Fig. 15.9. A bullets paragraph number definition.

Editing an Outline

Outline is a powerful feature that does not interfere with the creative process. Paragraph numbers can be added, changed, or deleted, and the remaining affected paragraph numbers change immediately. Similarly, entire paragraphs may be added, deleted, or moved. Type the text as it comes to mind. You can clean up and reorganize the outline with little effort.

Deleting a Paragraph Number

Paragraph numbers are not visible on-screen. You can, though, activate Reveal Codes, place the cursor on the paragraph number code, and delete it. You do not have to turn on Outline to delete a paragraph number.

To illustrate the process to delete a paragraph number, follow these steps:

Step 1: Clear the screen without saving the current document and retrieve the OUTL15B.DOC document.

Step 2: Move the cursor to the II. paragraph number (`Outline` should appear in the lower left corner of the screen, indicating the Outline feature is on).

Step 3: Access the **E**dit pull-down menu and select **R**eveal Codes (or press Alt-F3 or F11).

Step 4: Position the cursor on the `[Par Num:Auto]` code and press Del.

Step 5: Access the **E**dit pull-down menu and select **R**eveal Codes (or press Alt-F3 or F11) to restore full document display.

Figure 15.10 illustrates the results of deleting the II. paragraph number. Subsequent levels of paragraph numbers adjust. For example, the first two items under `Storage of Disks` renumber to `C.` and `D.`; items under `D.` display the next level of numbering.

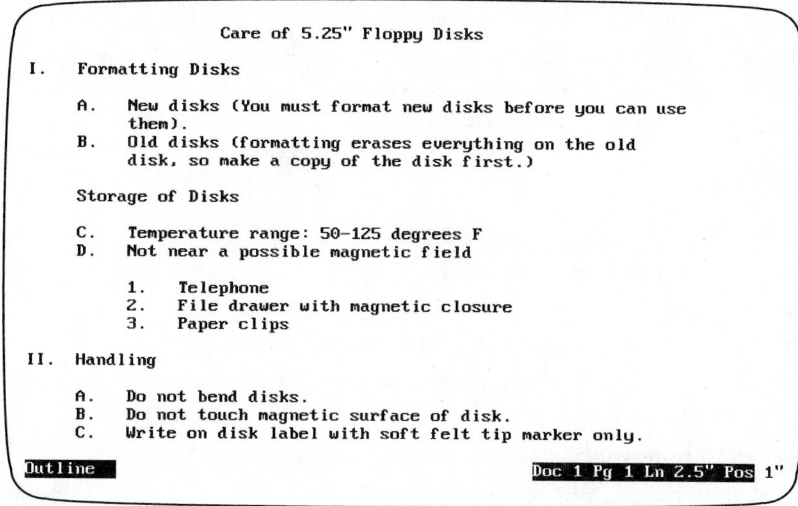

Fig. 15.10. *An outline reflecting a deleted paragraph number.*

Adding a Paragraph Number

To add a paragraph number, turn on Outline, position the cursor, press Enter, use Tab to set the level number, turn Outline off, and adjust line spacing if necessary. You may need to add paragraph numbers to replace an accidentally deleted number or to add a number to previously unnumbered text.

Step 1: Move the cursor to the left margin of the line `Storage of Disks`. (Outline is already turned on, as shown by the `Outline` message in the lower left corner of the screen.)

Step 2: Press Enter.

Note: Since the last paragraph number level used was `B.`, the letter `C.` is inserted. This problem is easily corrected with Outline turned on or off.

Step 3: Position the cursor on the `C.` (next to `Storage of Disks`) and press Shift-Tab.

Step 4: Adjust spacing as required to restore the outline to its initial appearance (see fig 15.6).

Changing a Paragraph Number

You can change paragraph numbers to the next higher (left) or lower (right) level number. The process is as easy as inserting or removing `[Tab]` codes on the line to be changed. Remember that changing numbers sometimes requires that some screen activity be performed to sequence the remaining numbers. To change a paragraph number, follow these steps:

Step 1: Position the cursor on paragraph number `II.`

Step 2: Press Tab and then press the down arrow.

Note: The former `II. Storage of Disks` is shifted right as `C.`, and all items below paragraph number `C.` are similarly renumbered.

Step 3: Position the cursor at the left margin on the line containing `Storage of Disks.`

Step 4: Press Del to remove the `[Tab]` code and restore the original outline.

Step 4 illustrates that you do not have to be in Reveal Codes mode to delete an outline code. However, you may prefer to activate Reveal Codes mode (Alt-F3 or F11) to verify a code (or codes) before executing any delete activity.

Moving a Numbered Paragraph

You can move a numbered paragraph the same way that you move any other text. Block the text to be moved, select Move, position the cursor where the text should be placed, and press Enter. Paragraph numbers will change appropriately. You may need to adjust spacing of the text.

As an alternative, WordPerfect 5.1 provides three commands that act on all paragraphs within a group: **M**ove Family, **C**opy Family, and **D**elete Family. These commands perform the tasks that their names imply. To access the OUTL15C.DOC document and switch the family of paragraphs under `I.` with the family of paragraphs under `II.`, follow these steps:

Step 1: Clear the screen without saving the current document and retrieve the OUTL15C.DOC document.

Note: The `I.` section Storage of Disks has been the `II.` section in previous illustrations.

Step 2: Position the cursor on the first character of `II. Formatting Disks`.

Step 3: Access the **T**ools pull-down menu and select **O**utline (or press Shift-F5,4).

Note: Figure 15.11 illustrates the pull-down menu sequence.

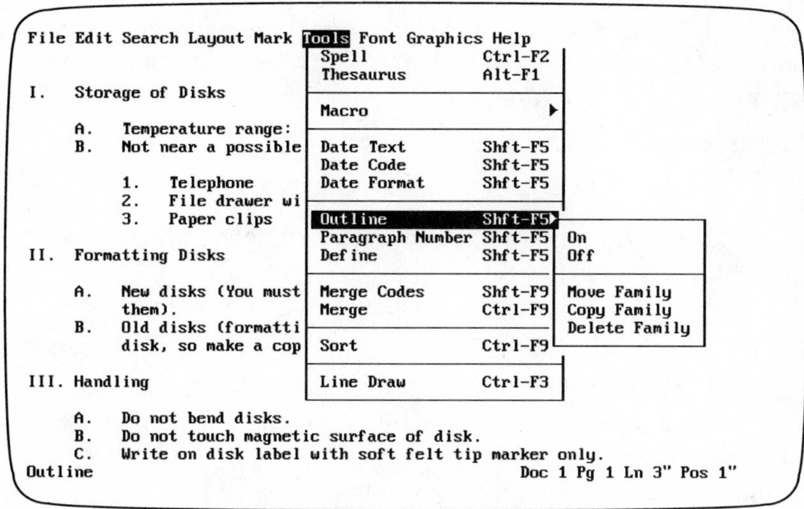

Fig. 15.11. *Menu options applying to outline families.*

Step 4: Choose **M**ove Family (**3**).

Step 5: Press the up arrow once and press Enter.

When you press the up arrow, paragraph II. immediately changes places with paragraph I. above it. The outline displays the original order (see fig 15.6). **C**opy Family and **D**elete Family work in a similar manner, although you do not press arrow keys to issue the latter command.

WordPerfect makes outlining so simple that it aids, rather than hinders, the writing process. You can request that WordPerfect insert the numbering of "paragraphs" one at a time as you type an outline, and produce the same results as if the numbering is totally automated by pressing Tab and Enter. This procedure makes it easier to create outlines containing many unnumbered paragraphs.

Using Line Numbers

Occasionally it is necessary to have line numbers printed in the left margin next to each line in a document. Some legal documents, computer program lists, and documents for editing are candidates for line numbering.

Once line numbering is activated, the WordPerfect code **[Ln Num:On]** is inserted into the document, and each line below the code is numbered. WordPerfect also offers a number of options such as numbering at intervals (every third line, for instance), starting with a certain number, or numbering blank lines.

WordPerfect 5.1's line numbering feature makes it easy to number items in a list. Turn on line numbering at the first line of the list, and turn off line numbering at the last line of the list.

To number the list of birthdays in the NUMBER15.LST document, follow these steps:

Step 1: Clear the screen without saving the current document and retrieve the NUMBER15.LST document.

Step 2: Position cursor on the `K` in `Keller` on line one of the list of names.

Step 3: Access the **Layout** menu and select **Line** (or press Shift-F8,1); choose Line **N**umbering (**5**) and press **Y**.

Step 4: View the Format: Line Numbering menu options and then press Exit (F7) to accept the default settings and restore the current document.

Step 5: Position the cursor at the end of the last line of the text.

Step 6: Access the **Layout** menu and select **Line** (or press Shift-F8,1), choose Line **N**umbering (**5**), and press **N** to turn off line numbering.

Line numbers do not appear on-screen. Use Reveal Codes (Alt-F3 or F11) to see the `[Ln Num:On]` hidden code. You can see the line numbers, though, if you use View Document or print the document. To view the numbered list on-screen, perform these steps:

Step 1: Access the **File** pull-down menu and select **Print** (or press Shift-F7); select **V**iew Document (**6**).

Step 2: Choose 100% (**1**) for the best view.

Step 3: Press Exit (F7) to restore the current document.

Figure 15.12 reproduces a printout of the document containing line numbers for the list of names. In Lesson 18 you combine graphics and line numbering to produce continuous line numbers with a vertically ruled left margin.

Birthday List

	LNAME	FNAME	BMONTH	BDAY
1	Keller	Theresa	September	5
2	McClelland	Ryan	October	1
3	Beckman	Len	March	21
4	Fox	April	July	23
5	Clements	Donna	February	18
6	Robling	Linda	August	21
7	Beckman	Mary	June	30
8	Fox	Tim	January	2
9	Beckman	Richard	March	29
10	Fox	Bonnie	January	11
11	Clements	Kasey	July	9
12	Strauss	Judy	April	15
13	Jackson	Ann	December	10
14	Weist	Linda	June	17
15	Love	Linda	May	14
16	Enloe	James	November	11
17	Enloe	Ree	September	21
18	Fox	Amy	October	1
19	Beckman	Marie	March	10
20	Beckman	Steve	November	21

Fig. 15.12. *Using line numbers in a document.*

For Further Reference

If you would like more information on endnotes, outlines, and line numbers, refer to *Using WordPerfect 5.1*, Special Edition (Que Corporation, Carmel, IN, 1989), Chapters 23 and 24.

Summary of Concepts

Lesson 15 explains these concepts:

- ❑ WordPerfect 5.1 provides footnote, endnote, outline, and line numbering features.
- ❑ Footnotes appear at the bottom of a page; endnotes are grouped in one location.
- ❑ You can look at the contents of a footnote or endnote as it appears in the finished document in one of two ways: print the document, or use the print option View Document to see the text with footnotes/endnotes on the screen.
- ❑ Delete a footnote or endnote by accessing Reveal Codes (Alt-F3 or F11) and positioning the cursor on the hidden code before pressing Del.
- ❑ Edit a footnote or endnote by accessing the Footnote command (Ctrl-F7), selecting Footnote (**1**) or Endnote (**2**), and typing the changes to the text after choosing Edit.
- ❑ You can move a footnote/endnote with its associated text or move only the footnote/endnote number.
- ❑ Move a footnote or endnote in one of two ways: highlight the block to be moved and execute the Move command (Ctrl-F4); or highlight the block to be moved, press Del, move the cursor to the new location, and press Cancel (F1) Restore (**1**).
- ❑ You must specify the location of endnotes and generate the endnotes.
- ❑ WordPerfect supports automatic outlining with up to eight levels of indentation.
- ❑ Outline is an open code: press Date/Outline (Shift-F5) and then select Outline (**4**) to turn Outline on; press the same key combination to turn Outline off.
- ❑ Outline numbering is controlled with hidden codes that you can view and edit through Reveal Codes.
- ❑ You can choose from one of four predetermined outline numbering displays—outline (the default), paragraph, legal, and bullets—or you can create your personal outline numbering system.
- ❑ Tabs control the outline levels: insert a Tab to move an outline item one level to the right; delete a Tab to move an outline item one level to the left.

- All edit capabilities available for a regular document can be used to alter an outline: you can add or delete a paragraph number or an entire paragraph, move a paragraph number, and so forth.
- WordPerfect provides a feature to add line numbers in the left margin of a document.
- View line numbers in one of two ways: press Print (Shift-F7) and select Full Document (**1**) to print the document; press Print (Shift-F7) and select View Document (**6**) to see the line numbering on-screen.

Review Exercises

Practice using the WordPerfect features in this lesson by completing the following exercises. If you do not remember how to do something, review the explanation and practice steps given earlier.

1. Clear the screen without saving the current document and retrieve the EXERCISE.15 document.
2. Move the cursor just after the second occurrence of the phrase `WordPerfect 5.1` in paragraph one. Enter the footnote **WordPerfect 5.1 replaces WordPerfect 5.0.**
3. Move only the footnote number created in Step 2 to just after the first occurrence of WordPerfect 5.1 in paragraph one.
4. Edit the footnote to read `WordPerfect 5.1 replaces WordPerfect 5.0 and 4.2.`
5. Use Reveal Codes (Alt-F3 or F11) to see the footnote hidden code.
6. Use the print command View Document at Full Page to see the footnote text displayed as part of the document.
7. Delete the footnote moved in Step 3.
8. Move the cursor just after the second occurrence of the phrase `WordPerfect 5.1` in paragraph one; enter the endnote **WordPerfect 5.1 replaces WordPerfect 5.0 and 4.2.**
9. Move the cursor just after the phrase The Cancel command in the first line of the paragraph below the Cancel heading. Enter the endnote **Press (F1) to activate the cancel operation.**
10. Position the endnotes at the end of the document, and determine the number of lines the endnotes will use.
11. Clear the screen without saving the current document.
12. Create the outline (or a part of it) of the Lesson 15 content as shown in figure 15.13, editing as necessary.
13. Change the numbering style to legal.
14. Reverse the paragraph families `I.` and `II.` and then return them to their original order.
15. Add line numbering to the document and View (Shift-F7, 6) or Print (Shift-F7, 1) the results.

```
                    Lesson 15
  Using Footnotes, Endnotes, Outlines, and Line Numbers

I.   Using Footnotes and Endnotes

     A.   Creating a Footnote
     B.   Viewing Footnote Contents
          1.   Using View Document To View a Footnote
          2.   Using Reveal Codes To View a Footnote
          3.   Using Footnote Edit To View a Footnote
     C.   Managing Footnotes
          1.   Deleting Footnotes
          2.   Editing Footnotes
          3.   Moving Footnotes
     D.   Managing Endnotes
     E.   Converting Footnotes and Endnotes

II.  Using Automatic Outlining

     A.   Creating an Outline
     B.   Defining a Paragraph Number Style
     C.   Editing an Outline
          1.   Deleting a Paragraph Number
          2.   Adding a Paragraph Number
          3.   Changing a Paragraph Number
          4.   Moving a Numbered Paragraph

III.      Using Line Numbers
```

Fig. 15.13. Outline of Lesson 15.

Working with Text Columns

16

In this lesson, you practice these tasks:

- ❑ Define newspaper columns and create them from regular text
- ❑ Define, edit, and move parallel columns
- ❑ Type columnar text
- ❑ Combine columns with regular text
- ❑ Change spacing in columns

Using WordPerfect's powerful Columns feature, you can divide the page into as many as 24 columns. You can enter text in Newspaper mode or in Parallel mode. The text in newspaper columns (sometimes referred to as *snaked* columns) fills the first column and then starts at the top of the next column in the same way that newspapers are printed. Parallel columns more closely resemble a script with the text read horizontally across columns. You determine which column mode you use when you define columns.

You can use the Columns feature many ways. You may need to write a newsletter or create other documentation. You can use Columns to compose easy-to-read tables of information and instructions. Columnar text is much easier and faster to read than text typed the width of the paper.

Creating Newspaper Columns

Figure 16.1 illustrates a newspaper column application.

VACATION IDEAS

Illinois

You'll want to visit Abraham Lincoln's boyhood home in Springfield. Then travel north to Chicago. Visit the Shedd Aquarium and the Museum of Science and Industry. While in the Loop, get a bird's eye view of the city and Lake Michigan from the top of the Sears Tower.

Tennessee

Of course, you'll want to visit Nashville, the country music capital. Gatlinburg and the Great Smoky Mountain National Park should also be on your list.

New Mexico

Schedule your trip to visit Santa Fe during one of the craft festivals. Artists from all over the Southwest have their works on exhibit. Arrive at Carlsbad Caverns shortly before sunset to witness the mass exodus of bats from the depths of the caverns.

Arizona

In the northern part of the state you'll want to see the Grand Canyon, Monument Valley, the Painted Desert, and the Meteor Crater. Drive through scenic Oak Creek Canyon and enjoy the natural red hues around Sedona. You'll also want to see the Sonoran desert in the southern part of the state and the unique Saguaro cacti.

Colorado

A summer visit to the state's majestic Rocky Mountains will be a cool treat. Come back in the winter for some of the country's finest skiing. You'll want to include tourist havens like Telluride and Silverton as well and Colorado Springs with its Garden of the Gods on your agenda.

Kansas

Although not traditionally a state high on the tourist's list, Kansas boasts several significant historical sights. Plan to visit Dwight Eisenhower's boyhood home in Abilene, an authentic restored adobe house and museum in Hillsboro, and recreated historic sites in Dodge City.

Fig. 16.1. An example of newspaper columns.

Creating the document in figure 16.1 requires placing the title at the top of the page, defining the column style, turning on Columns, entering text, and turning off Columns. Enter and edit text in columns the same way you enter regular text. This consistency of procedures with all of WordPerfect's features makes WordPerfect easy to use—and learning a new feature is relatively painless.

Defining Newspaper Columns

WordPerfect allows up to 24 columns per page. You must define the number and type of columns before you turn on Columns (see fig. 16.2).

```
Text Column Definition

     1 - Type                                          Newspaper

     2 - Number of Columns                             2

     3 - Distance Between Columns

     4 - Margins

     Column     Left        Right      Column      Left        Right
      1:        1"          4"         13:
      2:        4.5"        7.5"       14:
      3:                               15:
      4:                               16:
      5:                               17:
      6:                               18:
      7:                               19:
      8:                               20:
      9:                               21:
     10:                               22:
     11:                               23:
     12:                               24:

Selection: 0
```

Fig. 16.2. *The Text Column Definition screen.*

To set up the document and define columns, perform these steps:

Step 1: Clear the screen without saving the current document (the cursor should be on line one).

Note: The instruction to clear the screen without saving the current document is used many times throughout the workbook. It means to access the **F**ile pull-down menu and select E**x**it (or press F7), press **N** when you are prompted `Save Document? Yes (No)`, and press **N** when you are prompted `Exit WP? No (Yes)`.

Step 2: Access the **L**ayout pull-down menu, select **A**lign, and choose **C**enter (or press Shift-F6).

Step 3: Type **VACATION IDEAS** and press Enter three times for spacing.

Step 4: Access the **L**ayout pull-down menu, select **C**olumns, and select **D**efine (or press Alt-F7,1,3).

Step 5: Notice the default text column definitions for Type, Number of Columns, Distance Between Columns, and Margins (see fig. 16.2).

Step 6: Press Exit (F7) to accept the column-definition defaults and return to the Columns menu at the bottom of the screen.

Step 7: Choose **O**n (**1**).

Step 8: Access the **E**dit pull-down menu and select **R**eveal Codes (or press Alt-F3 or F11) to see the column-definition code as shown in figure 16.3.

Note: Your defined settings may vary somewhat from those shown in figure 16.3, depending on previous WordPerfect settings.

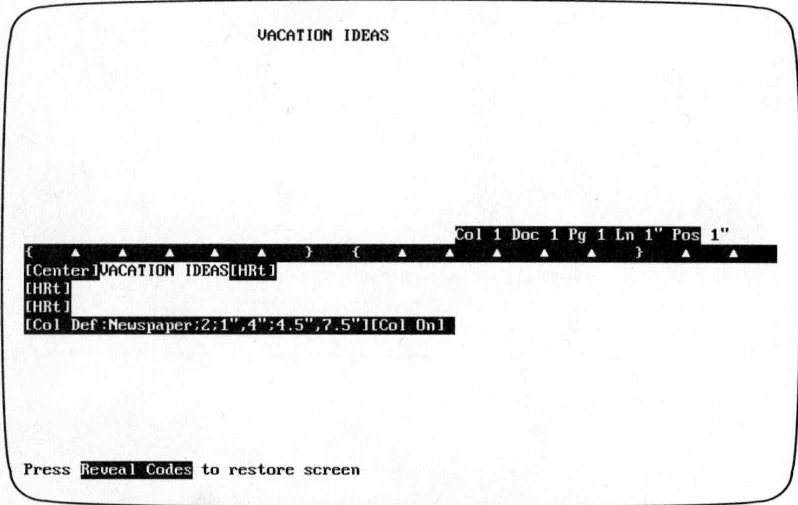

Fig. 16.3. *Hidden codes for the default column definitions.*

Step 9: Access the **E**dit pull-down menu and select **R**eveal Codes (or press Alt-F3 or F11) to restore full document display.

The column-definition code appears (see fig. 16.3) as `[Col Def: Newspaper; 2;1",4";4.5",7.5"][Col On]`. If you read the code from left to right, you can see that two columns are created, one at print positions 1" to 4" and the other at print positions 4.5" to 7.5".

On-screen prompts indicate that Columns is turned on. The [Col On] code actually reorganizes the page into two columns, and the status line now displays the prompt Col 1. As you type, the cursor moves through column one and then, at the bottom of the page, snakes up to the top of column two. As your typed text fills column two, the cursor moves to column one of the next page.

When you are in Reveal Codes mode, notice that the tab bar in the center of the screen actually displays two sets of margin braces { } to further illustrate the columns. If you do not see these indicators, be sure that the cursor is below the [Col On] code.

Typing Text into Newspaper Columns

Although you type text in columns the same way you type regular text, you may find a few differences in the way the cursor moves. Some differences are described in Table 16.1.

Table 16.1
Editing Keys in Columns

Keys	*Function*
Ctrl-End	Erases to the end of the line in the column you are editing
Ctrl-PgDn	Erases to the end of the column, starting at the cursor
Up arrow (↑)or down arrow (↓)	Scrolls up or down all columns together
Left arrow (←) or right arrow (→)	Moves cursor right or left within the column
Ctrl-Home, left arrow (←)	Moves the cursor to the previous column
Ctrl-Home, right arrow (→)	Moves the cursor to the next column

To see columns on-screen better, place a tab ruler at the bottom of the screen (see Lesson 5). Follow these steps to establish a tab ruler, enter text, and practice moving the cursor within and between columns:

Step 1: Access the **E**dit pull-down menu and select **W**indow (or press Ctrl-F3,1).

Step 2: When you are prompted `Number of lines in this window`, type **23** and press Enter.

Step 3: Press Home, Home, down arrow to position the cursor to the right of the `[Col On]` code.

Step 4: Access the **L**ayout pull-down menu, select **A**lign, and then choose **C**enter (or press Shift-F6).

Step 5: Type **Illinois** and press Enter twice.

Step 6: Type the description of Illinois, starting with **You'll want to visit. . .**, as shown in figure 16.1.

Step 7: Continue to type the document in figure 16.1 until you feel comfortable using newspaper columns.

Step 8: Use the cursor-movement keys listed in table 16.1 to practice moving the cursor within and between columns.

Mixing Regular Text with Columns

Mixing regular text with columns (see fig. 16.4) is as easy as turning Columns off and on. When you are in Columns mode and you want to switch to regular text, simply turn off Columns where you want regular text to begin. You can now type text that spans the page. To return to columns, position the cursor where columns should begin again and turn on Columns.

Creating Newspaper Columns from Existing Text

You can easily convert an existing document to newspaper columns. The process is so simple that you may prefer to create the document by using regular text and then convert it to columns. The document "Vacation Ideas" in figure 16.1 was created that way. To practice converting a document from regular to columnar text, follow these steps:

Step 1: Clear the screen without saving the current document and retrieve the NEWS16.001 document (see fig. 16.5).

VACATION IDEAS

Illinois

You'll want to visit Abraham Lincoln's boyhood home in Springfield. Then travel north to Chicago. Visit the Shedd Aquarium and the Museum of Science and Industry. While in the Loop, get a bird's eye view of the city and Lake Michigan from the top of the Sears Tower.

Tennessee

Of course, you'll want to visit Nashville, the country music capital. Gatlinburg and the Great Smoky Mountain National Park should also be on your list. For those of you who thrive on shopping, Pigeon Forge has plenty for quaint shops, and a theme park for the children.

When making reservations in any of the locations in these vacation areas, always inquire about seasonal discounts and family rates. You will be surprised at the bargains you will find. Merchants will often not mention discounts unless you ask.

New Mexico

Schedule your trip to visit Santa Fe during one of the craft festivals. Artists from all over the Southwest have their works on exhibit. Arrive at Carlsbad Caverns shortly before sunset to witness the mass exodus of bats from the depths of the caverns.

Colorado

A summer visit to the state's majestic Rocky Mountains will be a cool treat. Come back in the winter for some of the country's finest skiing. You'll want to include tourist havens like Telluride and Silverton as well and Colorado Springs with its Garden of the Gods on your agenda.

Arizona

In the northern part of the state you'll want to see the Grand Canyon, Monument Valley, the Painted Desert, and the Meteor Crater. Drive through scenic Oak Creek Canyon and enjoy the natural red hues around Sedona. You'll also want to see the Sonoran desert in the southern part of the state and the unique Saguaro cacti.

Kansas

Although not traditionally a state high on the tourist's list, Kansas boasts several significant historical sights. Plan to visit Dwight Eisenhower's boyhood home in Abilene, an authentic restored adobe house and museum in Hillsboro, and recreated historic sites in Dodge City.

Fig. 16.4. Combining newspaper columns with regular text.

```
                    VACATION IDEAS

                       Illinois

You'll want to visit Abraham Lincoln's boyhood home in
Springfield.  Then travel north to Chicago.  Visit the Shedd
Aquarium and the Museum of Science and Industry.  While in the
Loop, get a bird's eye view of the city and Lake Michigan from
the top of the Sears Tower.


                      Tennessee

Of course, you'll want to visit Nashville, the country music
capital. Gatlinburg and the Great Smoky Mountain National Park
should also be on your list.


                      New Mexico

Schedule your trip to visit Santa Fe during one of the craft
festivals.  Artists from all over the Southwest have their works
on exhibit.  Arrive at Carlsbad Caverns shortly before sunset to
witness the mass exodus of bats from the depths of the caverns.


                       Arizona

In the northern part of the state you'll want to see the Grand
Canyon, Monument Valley, the Painted Desert, and the Meteor
Crater.  Drive through scenic Oak Creek Canyon and enjoy the
natural red hues around Sedona.  You'll also want to see the
Sonoran desert in the southern part of the state and the unique
Saguaro cacti.


                       Colorado

A summer visit to the state's majestic Rocky Mountains will be a
cool treat.  Come back in the winter for some of the country's
finest skiing.  You'll want to include tourist havens like
Telluride and Silverton as well and Colorado Springs with its
Garden of the Gods on your agenda.


                        Kansas

Although not traditionally a state high on the tourist's list,
Kansas boasts several significant historical sights.  Plan to
visit Dwight Eisenhower's boyhood home in Abilene, an authentic
restored adobe house and museum in Hillsboro, and recreated
historic sites in Dodge City.
```

Fig. 16.5. *An example of regular (one-column) text display.*

Step 2: Position the cursor at the beginning of the blank line before the paragraph title `Illinois`.

Step 3: Access the **L**ayout pull-down menu, select **C**olumns, and choose **D**efine (or press Alt-F7,1,3).

Step 4: Press Exit (F7) to accept the defaults and return to the Columns menu.

Step 5: Choose **O**n (**1**).

Step 6: Press PgDn to rewrite the screen.

Step 7: Press PgUp to view the top of the two-column display.

Editing Newspaper Columns

Edit columns in the same way you edit regular text. You can use the Add, Change, Delete, Move, and Copy features to develop the final document. To make editing easier, use two features: displaying one column at a time and viewing columns.

Displaying One Column at a Time

If editing seems difficult with two or more columns on-screen, use Setup to switch the display to one column at a time. The column is, however, positioned with its normal offset, as seen in figure 16.6.

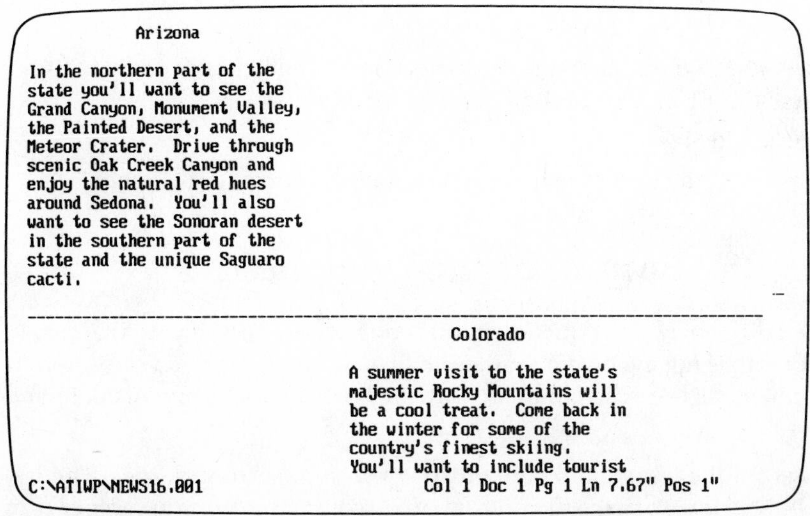

Fig. 16.6. *Side-by-side columns display turned off.*

To change the column display, follow these steps:

Step 1: Access the **F**ile pull-down menu, select Se**t**up, and choose **D**isplay (or press Shift-F1,2); choose **E**dit—Screen Options (**6**).

Step 2: Choose **S**ide-by-side Columns Display (**7**).

Step 3: Press **N** and press Exit (F7) enough times to restore the current document display.

Step 4: Press the down arrow or up arrow to scroll through the document.

Note: When side-by-side display is turned off, column widths are maintained. The left column is, however, displayed first; then the right column is displayed (see fig. 16.6). You may find it easier to move and copy text when columns are displayed in this manner.

Viewing Newspaper Columns

Viewing column displays can be helpful in planning document layout. If you turn off side-by-side display, you can still see columns side by side, using the Print: View Document feature. To view side-by-side columns (even though side-by-side display is turned off) and restore side-by-side display, follow these steps:

Step 1: Access the **F**ile pull-down menu and select **P**rint (or press Shift-F7); select **V**iew Document (**6**).

Step 2: Select Full Page (**3**) and view the side-by-side display.

Step 3: Press Exit (F7) enough times to restore the current document.

Step 4: Access the **F**ile pull-down menu, select Se**t**up, and choose **D**isplay (or press Shift-F1,2); choose **E**dit-Screen Options (**6**).

Step 5: Choose **S**ide-by-side Columns Display (**7**).

Step 6: Press **Y** and then press Exit (F7) to restore the current document.

Trimming the Bottom of the Document

Look at figure 16.1 or view your document on-screen again. You can see that text in the second column is not even with that in the first column. This uneven bottom is a common problem that you can eliminate with the Print: View Document command and some planning.

All columns except the last should contain an equal number of text lines. The last column may be shorter. To make the bottom of the columns even, you can perform the following actions:

- ❑ Divide the total number of printed lines in all columns on the page by the total number of columns on the page to obtain the average number of lines per column.
- ❑ Beginning at the left column, position the cursor at the average line number (which you just computed) and press Hard Page Break (Ctrl-Enter). Repeat this step for each full column.
- ❑ Use the Print: View Document command to see the rearranged columns. You may need to make some adjustments manually.

To see how this idea works, adjust the "Vacation Ideas" document. The first column of "Vacation Ideas" is full, containing 54 lines. There are 32 lines in the second, or last, column (use the cursor and the `Ln` number to do the counting). Divide 86 total lines (54 plus 32) by two columns. If the columns are equal, each has 43 lines.

If your display is set to inches, follow these same steps. If you have invoked a standard 10-pitch print font, your page is formatted six lines per inch; thinking in lines per inch is easy. To equalize text between two columns, follow these steps:

Step 1: Clear the screen without saving the current document and retrieve the LEVEL16.DOC document.

Step 2: Position the cursor at the left margin of the centered heading `Arizona` (in column 1, line 43 or 7.83").

Step 3: Access the **L**ayout pull-down menu, select **A**lign, and choose Hard **P**age (or press Ctrl-Enter).

Step 4: Press Home, Home, down arrow to move to the end of the document.

This technique of adjusting lines between columns works; column one, however, looks shorter. Both are actually 43 lines long, but column one contains blank lines at the end—and this makes it look shorter. To make the displayed lines look more even by removing the hard page break and inserting it down about four lines, follow these steps:

Step 1: Press Home, Home, up arrow.

Step 2: Access the **E**dit pull-down menu and select **R**eveal Codes (or press Alt-F3 or F11).

Step 3: Press Forward Search (F2), press Hard Page Break (Ctrl-Enter), and press Forward Search (F2) again.

Step 4: Press the left arrow once to position the cursor on the code `[HPg]`, and press Del to remove the unwanted hard page break.

Step 5: Access the **E**dit pull-down menu and select **R**eveal Codes (or press Alt-F3 or F11) to restore full document display.

Step 6: Move the cursor to the beginning of the second line under the title `Arizona (state you'll want. . .)`.

Step 7: Access the **Layout** pull-down menu, select **Align**, and choose Hard **Page** (or press Ctrl-Enter).

Step 8: Access the **File** pull-down menu and select **Print** (or press Shift-F7); select **View** Document (**6**).

Step 9: Choose Full Page (**3**) and view the improved distribution of text between columns one and two.

Step 10: Press Exit (F7) enough times to restore full document display.

The two columns still look uneven, but the column with fewer lines is the last column (this is a more acceptable display). Use the same technique to equalize the number of lines in three or more columns.

Creating Parallel Columns

Although parallel columns look much like newspaper columns, they are read differently. Text in parallel columns usually has a horizontal relationship. Figure 16.7 shows a table of information arranged in parallel columns. KEYS TO PRESS in column one is related to the FUNCTION in column two and the corresponding EXPLANATION in column three.

Planning and Defining Parallel Columns

Defining parallel columns is similar to defining newspaper columns. Parallel columns do, however, require more planning because the columns are usually not the same width.

With the Text Column Definition screen (see fig. 16.2) you can define the margins (width) of each column and the distance between columns. Plan the use of each column and estimate the width you need before you define columns. If columns are not the right size, you can insert a new definition and delete the old one without losing any text.

Cursor Movement and Parallel Columns

KEYS TO PRESS	FUNCTION	EXPLANATION
Ctrl-Home (GoTo), right/left arrow	Switch columns	Moves cursor left or right one column.
Home, up/down arrow	Column top or bottom	Moves cursor to the top or bottom of the column.
Up or down arrow	Scroll up/down	Moves cursor up/down one line but scrolls all columns.
Left or right arrow	Character left/right	Works normally within the column but moves from the bottom of one column to the top of the next.
Gray plus or minus keys	Up/down one screen	Moves cursor to top or bottom of the column on the screen.

Fig. *16.7. A table with parallel columns.*

To define parallel columns and create the table in figure 16.7, follow these steps:

Step 1: Clear the screen without saving the current document.

Step 2: Access the **L**ayout pull-down menu, select **A**lign, and choose **C**enter (or press Shift-F6).

Step 3: Type **Cursor Movement and Parallel Columns** and press Enter twice.

Step 4: Access the **L**ayout pull-down menu, select **C**olumns, and select **D**efine (or press Alt-F7,1,3).

Step 5: Choose **T**ype (**1**) and choose **P**arallel (**2**).

Step 6: Choose **N**umber of Columns (**2**), type **3** for three columns, and press Enter (see fig. 16.8).

```
Text Column Definition

     1 - Type                                      Parallel

     2 - Number of Columns                         3

     3 - Distance Between Columns

     4 - Margins

     Column     Left       Right      Column     Left       Right
       1:       1"         2.83"      13:
       2:       3.33"      5.17"      14:
       3:       5.67"      7.5"       15:
       4:                             16:
       5:                             17:
       6:                             18:
       7:                             19:
       8:                             20:
       9:                             21:
      10:                             22:
      11:                             23:
      12:                             24:

Selection: 0
```

Fig. 16.8. Settings for a three-column parallel column definition.

Step 7: Press Exit (F7) once to leave the Text Column Definition screen and access the Columns menu at the bottom of the screen.

Step 8: Choose **On** (**1**).

Typing Text in Parallel Columns

Typing text in a parallel column is very similar to typing regular text.

Caution: Because text in parallel columns is usually read left to right, it may become out of alignment horizontally with related text in other columns if text is edited in one column.

To enter the column titles shown in figure 16.7, follow these steps:

Step 1: Position the cursor two lines below the title, at the far left edge of the screen.

Step 2: Press Underline (F8), type **KEYS TO PRESS**, press Underline (F8), and press Hard Page Break (Ctrl- Enter) to move the cursor to column two.

Note: Use Ctrl-Enter to move to a column that does not yet contain text. Once text exists in a column, you can use Ctrl-Home (GoTo), left/right arrow to move between columns, as shown in table 16.1.

Step 3: Press Underline (F8), type **FUNCTION**, press Underline (F8), and press Ctrl-Enter to move the cursor to column three.

Step 4: Press Underline (F8), type **EXPLANATION**, press Underline (F8), and press Ctrl-Enter to return the cursor to the first column.

Note: If you have the Enhanced Keyboard (12 function keys) and if you installed the ENHANCED.WPK keyboard macro by using Setup: Keyboard Layout and choosing ENHANCED.WPK, you have several keys useful for working with columns. You can switch columns by pressing Alt-left arrow and Alt-right arrow.

The cursor should be in column one below the heading `KEYS TO PRESS`. You can enter text across columns or in one column at a time. Enter and edit text in a column just as you do regular text.

To enter the remaining information shown in figure 16.7, follow these steps:

Step 1: With the cursor positioned under the heading in column one, type **Ctrl-Home (GoTo), right/left arrow**; then press Ctrl-Enter to move the cursor to column two.

Step 2: With the cursor positioned under the heading in column two, type **Switch columns** and press Ctrl-Enter to move the cursor to column three.

Step 3: With the cursor positioned under the heading in column three, type **Moves cursor left or right one column**. Press Ctrl-Enter to move the cursor back to column one.

Practice entering all or a part of the text shown in figure 15.7 until you feel comfortable entering text in parallel columns. A copy of the table is available as a lesson-disk file if you do not want to enter the entire table.

Moving the Contents of Parallel Columns

You can move one section of parallel-column text to another location, but you must take care to include the `[Col On]` and `[Col Off]` codes. Before you move text, save the document under a backup name in case a problem occurs during the move.

Imagine that the table you just created is part of a larger document and that the table can be used in other documents as well. You can block just the table and store it as a separate document.

To save the Cursor Movement table on disk before you practice moving some of the parallel-column text within the table, follow these steps:

Step 1: Clear the screen without saving the current document and retrieve the COL316.DOC document. The order of information matches that shown in figure 16.7.

Step 2: Access the **E**dit pull-down menu and select **B**lock (or press Alt-F4 or F12); press Home, Home, down arrow to highlight the entire parallel-column text.

Step 3: Access the **F**ile pull-down menu and select **S**ave (or press F10).

Step 4: In response to the prompt `Block name:`, type **CURSOR.TBL** and press Enter.

When you move parallel-column text, be careful to move the `[Col On]` and `[Col Off]` codes with the text. To move the complete descriptions of the `Up or down arrow` and `Left or right arrow` sections to the top of the table from their current position in the middle of the table, follow these steps:

Step 1: Position the cursor on the `U` in `Up or down arrow` and press the left arrow once to include the `[Col On]` code.

Step 2: Access the **E**dit pull-down menu and select **B**lock (or press Alt-F4 or F12); press the down arrow to position the cursor on the blank line above `Gray plus or minus keys` (see fig. 16.9).

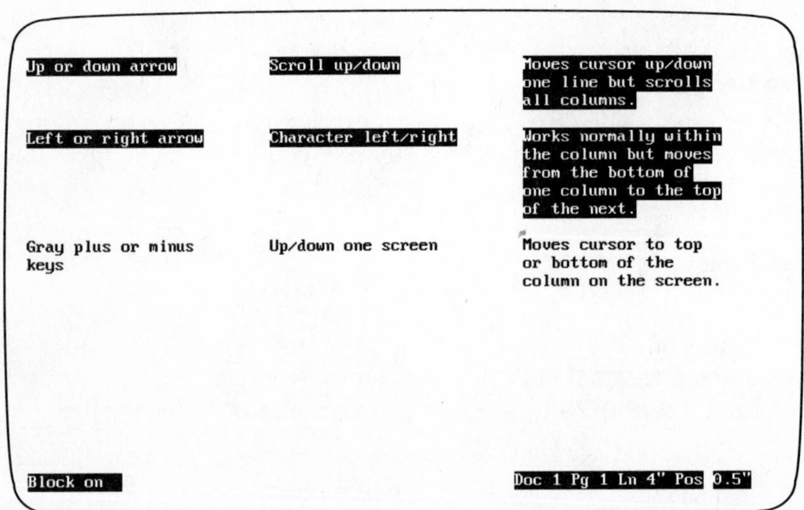

Fig. 16.9. *Highlighting parallel-column text before a move.*

Step 3: Press Move (Ctrl-F4), select **B**lock (**1**), and select **M**ove (**1**).

Step 4: Move the cursor to the blank line under KEYS TO PRESS at the top of the table and press Enter.

Step 5: Insert or delete blank lines to adjust spacing.

Figure 16.10 illustrates the successful results of moving two sections of the Cursor Movement table to a different location in the document. If your move does not produce the appropriate results, clear the screen without saving the document and retrieve your backup file CURSOR.TBL. Repeat the steps for the move and use Reveal Codes to check that [Col On] and [Col Off] codes surrounding the text to be moved are included in the highlighted text.

Cursor Movement and Parallel Columns

KEYS TO PRESS	FUNCTION	EXPLANATION
Up or down arrow	Scroll up/down	Moves cursor up/down one line but scrolls all columns.
Left or right arrow	Character left/right	Works normally within the column but moves from the bottom of one column to the top of the next.
Ctrl-Home (GoTo), right/left arrow	Switch columns	Moves cursor left or right one column.
Home, up/down arrow	Column top or bottom	Moves cursor to the top or bottom of the column.
Gray plus or minus keys	Up/down one screen	Moves cursor to top or bottom of the

C:\WP51\QUEDISK\COL3-15.DOC Doc 1 Pg 1 Ln 0.5" Pos 0.5"

Fig. 16.10. *Results of moving parallel-column text.*

If this lesson on using text columns seems complicated, practice it again. Once you are accustomed to working with columns, you will find it a very useful WordPerfect feature.

For Further Reference

If you would like to know more about text columns and special keyboard functions, consult *Using WordPerfect 5.1*, Special Edition, (Que Corporation, Carmel, IN, 1989), Chapters 17 and 18.

Summary of Concepts

- ❑ WordPerfect supports two types of columns: newspaper columns and parallel columns.
- ❑ Text in newspaper columns fills one column before continuing in the next column.
- ❑ Convert an existing document to newspaper columns by preceding the text with a column definition and turning on Columns.
- ❑ Text in parallel columns is read from left to right across the page.
- ❑ Parallel columns require more planning because the text in adjacent cells is usually related.
- ❑ You must first define columns and turn Columns on before you can use them.
- ❑ The default column definition includes newspaper type, two columns per page, and five characters (0.5") between columns.
- ❑ You can change default column settings for each column.
- ❑ You can mix columns and regular text by turning Columns on, typing in column mode, and then turning Columns off to type regular text.
- ❑ When Columns is active, you can move along columns and edit text with a variety of cursor-movement keys.

Review Exercises

Practice using the WordPerfect features in this lesson by completing the following exercises. If you do not remember how to use a feature, review the explanation and practice the steps presented in this lesson.

1. Clear the screen without saving the current document and retrieve GETTY16.ADD.
2. Position the cursor at the top of the document and insert a Column Definition for newspaper columns, three columns per page, with a distance of three (0.5") characters between columns. Accept the margins that WordPerfect specifies.
3. Turn on Columns. If the document does not reformat into columns, remember to move the cursor to the bottom of the document or to press Screen (Ctrl-F3) and choose Rewrite (**3**).
4. Print the document.
5. Clear the screen without saving the current document.
6. Center the heading `INVENTORY OF INSURABLE HOUSEHOLD PROPERTY`, followed by two blank lines.
7. Insert a column definition for parallel columns, three columns across. Accept the margins and distance between columns that WordPerfect specifies.
8. Turn on Columns.
9. Enter these headings in each of the columns:

   `ITEM VALUE DATE PURCHASED`
10. Enter at least five items of related information. Make sure that the information aligns across the page; then print the document. Enter more information until you feel comfortable working with parallel columns.

Working with Math Columns

17

In this lesson, you practice these tasks:

- ❑ Turn Math on and off
- ❑ Specify a math definition
- ❑ Create a simple column of numbers with a total
- ❑ Create a column of numbers with subtotals
- ❑ Create number and total columns that work together
- ❑ Create number and calculation columns that work together

One of the most tiring, tedious jobs is typing numbers. The task becomes more difficult when you make calculations and verify them manually. WordPerfect's Math feature simplifies entering numbers and making basic calculations. You can add numbers in vertical columns and add, subtract, multiply, or divide numbers horizontally. You can use the Math feature with many applications—number tables, invoices, financial statements, budgets, and automated forms, for example.

Learning the Steps for Creating Math Columns

WordPerfect offers two types of Math operations: simple column totals and more complex computations that use numbers in other columns on the same line. Performing any Math operation requires the same six steps:

- ❑ Set tab stops for each column.
- ❑ Create a math definition.
- ❑ Turn on Math.
- ❑ Enter text, numbers, and math operators.
- ❑ Calculate the results of the Math setup.
- ❑ Turn off Math.

Creating Number Columns

A number column with a total, such as the application illustrated in figure 17.1, is the simplest and most common number column. Simply typing all the numbers on the list may seem the easiest way to create the data. If, however, you use Math to generate any calculated amounts, you can later change numbers or expand the lists, and the totals recalculate. Creating the application in figure 17.1 should clarify the uses and procedures for math columns.

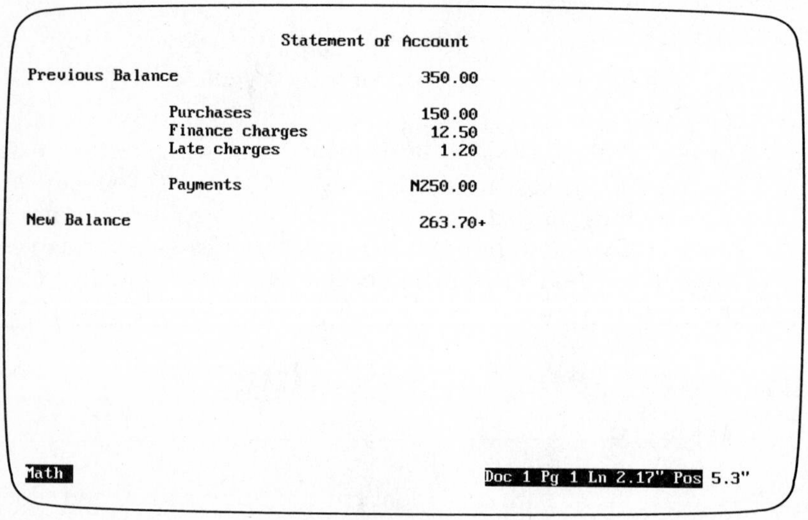

```
                    Statement of Account
Previous Balance                             350.00

             Purchases                       150.00
             Finance charges                  12.50
             Late charges                      1.20

             Payments                       N250.00

New Balance                                  263.70+










Math                          Doc 1 Pg 1 Ln 2.17" Pos 5.3"
```

Fig. 17.1. A number column application.

Setting Tab Stops

Each tab stop is considered a column. When you create a math column application, insert a tab line between the headings and the first row of column data and establish tab stops for each column. The list you develop first should have two tab stops—one at position 15 (for typing text) and one at position 45 (for entering the column of numbers).

To set up the application shown in figure 17.1, follow these steps:

Step 1: Clear the screen without saving the current document.

Note: The instruction to clear the screen without saving the current document is used many times throughout the workbook. It means to access the **F**ile pull-down menu and select E**x**it (or press F7), press **N** when you are prompted `Save Document? Yes (No)`, and press **N** when you are prompted `Exit WP? No (Yes)`.

Step 2: Access the **L**ayout pull-down menu, select **A**lign, and then choose **C**enter (or press Shift-F6).

Step 3: Type **Statement of Account** and press Enter twice to insert spacing after the heading.

Step 4: Access the **L**ayout pull-down menu and select **L**ine (or press Shift-F8,1); then choose **T**ab Set (**8**).

Step 5: Press Ctrl-End to delete the default tab stops.

Step 6: Move the cursor to position 15 (1.5") and press **L**; move the cursor to position 45 (4.5") and press **L**.

Step 7: Press Exit (F7) enough times to restore the display of the current document.

In Steps 4 through 7, you completed the first of six steps to perform a math operation—setting appropriate tab stops.

Setting Math Definition and Turning On Math

Like other WordPerfect defining operations, math definition specifies options associated with that feature. You do not have to insert a math definition to accept the defaults; just turn on Math columns and develop the document. If you use a math definition, specify it before you turn on Math columns. Figure 17.2 shows the default Math Definition screen.

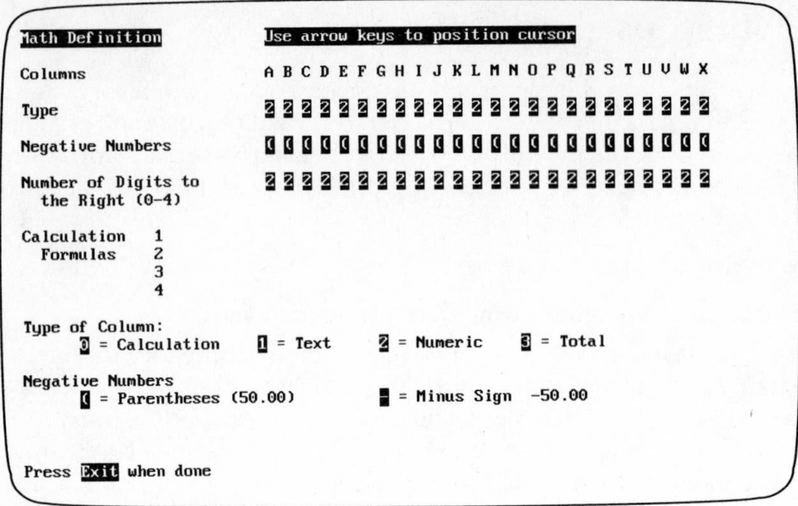

Fig. 17.2. The default Math Definition screen.

The following are some options on the Math Definition menu:

- ❑ `Columns`. WordPerfect supports up to 24 columns. Each column corresponds to a tab stop: A is the first tab stop, B the second, and so on. Set three options for each column: Type, Negative Numbers, and Number of Digits to the Right.
- ❑ `Type`. This option, for type of column, may be 0=Calculation; 1=Text; 2=Numeric (the default); and 3=Total.
- ❑ `Negative Numbers`. This option defines how negative numbers are displayed—with parentheses or with a minus sign (–).
- ❑ `Calculation Formulas`. When you designate a column type as Calculation (0), the cursor moves to the first empty Calculation Formulas line. You can enter an algebraic formula by using addition (+), subtraction (–), multiplication (*), and division (/). Use parentheses to change the order of calculations. Four calculation columns may be active in a math definition.

To access the Math Definition screen and change the first column (column A) to text instead of numeric (the default), follow these steps:

Step 1: Access the **Layout** pull-down menu and select **Math** (or press Alt-F7,3).

> **Note:** Figure 17.3 illustrates the pull-down menu sequence for accessing the Math feature.

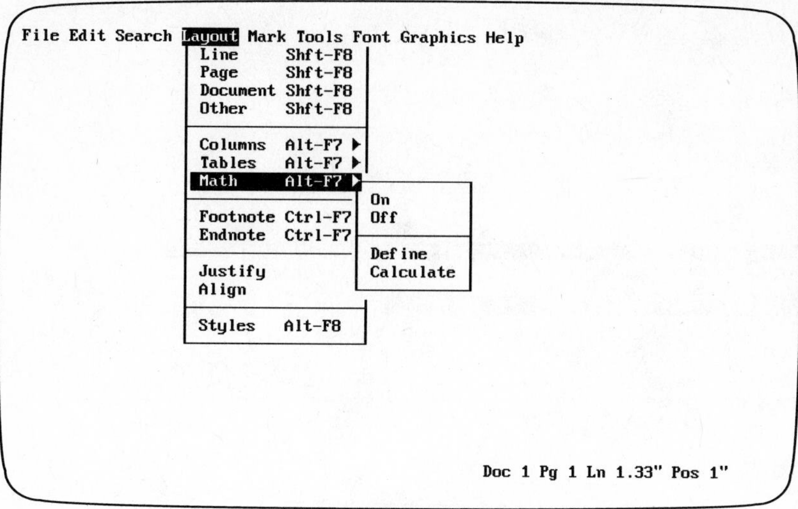

Fig. 17.3. *Accessing Math menu options.*

Step 2: Choose **D**efine (**3**).

Step 3: Move the cursor to column A and change `Type` to `Text` by typing **1**.

Step 4: Press Exit (F7) once to return to the Math menu at the bottom of the screen and choose **O**n (**1**).

Note: The word `Math` appears in the lower left corner of the screen to indicate that Math is active.

Step 5: Access the **E**dit pull-down menu and select **R**eveal Codes (or press Alt-F3 or F11) to view the WordPerfect math codes inserted into the document (see fig. 17.4).

Step 6: Access the **E**dit pull-down menu and select **R**eveal Codes (or press Alt-F3 or F11) to restore full document display.

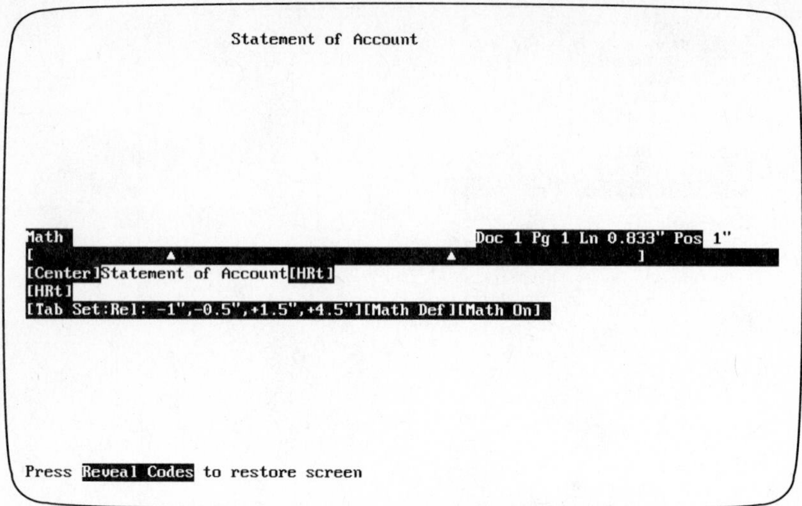

Fig. 17.4. Using Reveal Codes to view Math column codes.

You defined a Math code for the first column, A (Steps 1–3), and turned on Math columns (Step 4). You can now begin to enter text, numbers, and math operators by using Math.

Entering Text, Numbers, and Math Operators

To enter information into the Math columns, position the cursor on the first line and type the text or number, press Tab to move the cursor to the next field, and enter text or numbers. To end a line, press Enter.

When the cursor is at a tab representing a numeric, total, or calculation column, you see the prompt `Align char = . Math` in the lower left corner. Alignment on the decimal point occurs automatically at any kind of tab stop (L, R, decimal) if the associated column is any type other than text.

To execute math functions, type math operators (or symbols) with numbers. These operators, explained in table 17.1, control the math exercises in this lesson.

Table 17.1
The Function of Math Operators

Symbol	*Function*	*Explanation*	*Hierarchy Level*
+	Subtotal	Add all numbers in the column above the + since the last total or subtotal was taken (or from the beginning of the column).	2
t	Extra subtotal	Treat the number immediately following this operator as a subtotal.	2
=	Total	Add all subtotals (+) and extra subtotals (numbers preceded by t operators) since the last total.	3
T	Extra subtotal	Treat the number immediately after this operator as a total.	3
.	Grand total	Add all totals (=) and extra totals (numbers preceded by T operators) since the last grand total.	4
N	Negate	Reverses the sign of the result or number immediately following this operator for use in further calculations.	1, 2, or 3

To enter the data in figure 17.1, follow these steps:

Step 1: Position the cursor at the left margin of the third line and type **Previous Balance**.

Step 2: Press Tab, type **350.00**, and press Enter twice.

Step 3: Press Tab, type **Purchases**, press Tab, type **150.00**, and press Enter.

Step 4: Press Tab, type **Finance charges**, press Tab, type **12.50**, and press Enter.

Step 5: Press Tab, type **Late charges**, press Tab, type **1.20**, and press Enter twice.

Step 6: Press Tab, type **Payments**, press Tab, type **N250.00**, and press Enter twice.

Step 7: Type **New Balance** and press Tab twice. The message `Align char = . Math` appears in the status line.

Step 8: Type + and press Enter.

Step 9: Access the **F**ile pull-down menu and select **S**ave (or press F10). Type **NUMBER.COL** to save the single-column model.

The Statement of Account is entered. Notice the `N` next to the payment amount. This `N` tells WordPerfect to treat the number as negative. When that amount is added into the statement, WordPerfect actually subtracts the payment from the amount owed. The plus sign (+) tells WordPerfect to total all numbers above and place the sum where the + sign appears. The `N` and + appear on-screen but not in print.

Calculating the Number Column Model and Turning Math Off

You must calculate Math Columns to force all nontext fields to be computed. If you change any nontext columns, you must recalculate the model. To calculate the number column model and then turn Math off, follow these steps:

Step 1: Access the **L**ayout pull-down menu and select **M**ath (or press Alt-F7,3).

Step 2: Choose **C**alculate (**4**). All totals are calculated, as shown in figure 17.1.

Step 3: Access the **L**ayout pull-down menu and select **M**ath (or press Alt-F7,3).

Step 4: Choose **O**ff (**1**) to turn Math off.

Creating Total Columns

Number columns are suitable for simple columns of numbers requiring a total. When several subtotals are involved, however, the document is more easily read if subtotals are moved into a separate column (see fig. 17.5).

The document in figure 17.5 is created through the use of the same technique outlined in the preceding number column example: setting tab stops, setting math definition, entering data, and calculating the model.

```
                    Regional Sales - June

West Coast
              Region I           280,000
              Region II          390,000
                Total                        670,000+

Midwest
              Region III         850,000
              Region IV          450,450
              Region V         1,000,000
                Total                      2,300,450+

East Coast
              Region VI        1,200,500
              Region VII         480,000
                Total                      1,680,500+

U. S. Totals                               4,650,950=



C:\WP51\QUEDISK\TOTAL.COL                Doc 1 Pg 1 Ln 0.5" Pos 1"
```

Fig. 17.5. *A total column application.*

Setting Tab Stops and Math Definition for a Total Column

To set up the tab stops for a text column at position 15, a number column at position 45, and a total column at position 60, follow these steps:

Step 1: Clear the screen without saving the current document.

Step 2: Access the **L**ayout pull-down menu, select **A**lign, and then choose **C**enter (or press Shift-F6).

Step 3: Type **Regional Sales—June** and press Enter twice to insert spacing after the heading.

Step 4: Access the **L**ayout menu and select **L**ine (or press Shift-F8,1); choose **T**ab Set (**8**).

Step 5: Press Ctrl-End to delete the default tab settings.

Step 6: Set left tab stops at positions 15, 45, and 60 (if your screen displays in inches, set these tabs at 1.5", 4.5", and 6.0").

Step 7: Press Exit (F7) to restore the current document display.

After you create a title line and establish three tab stops, you are ready to enter the text shown in figure 16.5. First access the Math Definition screen and set up the math definition shown in figure 17.6 for the Regional Sales—June document. Follow these steps:

Step 1: Access the **L**ayout pull-down menu and select **M**ath (or press Alt-F7,3).

Step 2: Choose **D**efine (**3**).

Step 3: Move the cursor to column A and change `Type` to `Text` by typing **1**.

Step 4: Move the cursor to column B and change `Number of Digits to the Right` to zero by typing **0**.

Step 5: Move the cursor to column C, change `Type` to `Total` by typing **3** and then change `Number of Digits to the Right` to zero by typing **0**.

Note: Always verify the specifications in the Math Definition screen, because it is easy to place a specification in the wrong column. For example, as soon as you enter a column setting, the cursor moves to the next column. If you have more than one setting to change in a single column, such as in column C in the previous example, you must carefully reposition the cursor in the proper column for the second setting.

Step 6: Make any changes necessary to reproduce on your screen the setting shown in figure 17.6.

Step 7: Press Exit (F7) once to return to the Math menu at the bottom of the screen; choose **O**n (**1**).

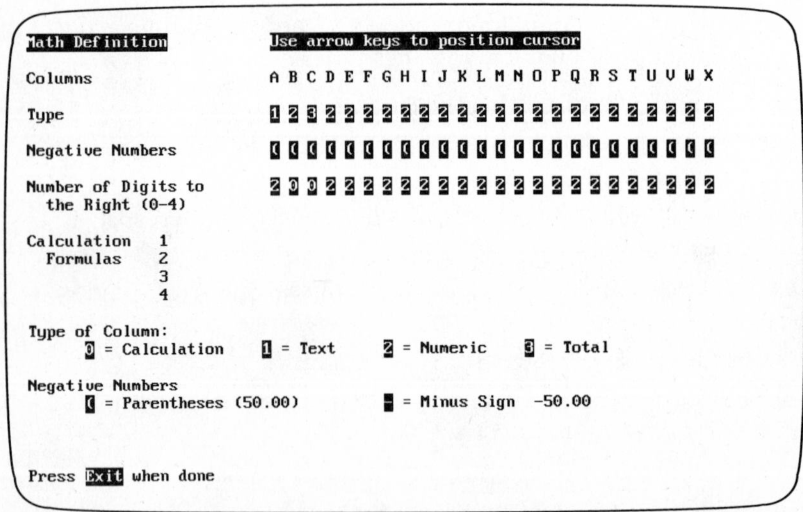

Fig. 17.6. The Math Definition screen for a total column application.

Entering Total Column Data and Setting Up Math Operations

The next step in creating a document with a separate subtotal column is to enter text, numbers, and math operators. Before you enter the data shown in figure 17.5, make sure that `Math` appears on the status line in the lower left corner of the screen. To enter the text, follow these steps:

Step 1: Position the cursor at the left margin of the third line, type **West Coast**, and press Enter.

Step 2: Press Tab, type **Region I**, press Tab, type **280,000**, and press Enter.

Step 3: Press Tab, type **Region II**, press Tab, type **390,000**, and press Enter.

Step 4: Press Tab, press the space bar twice, type **Total**, and press Tab twice.

Note: You should see the cursor in position 70 (7.0") and the message `Align char = . Math` in the status line. Your cursor position may vary, according to your margin and print style settings.

Step 5: Type **+** (a plus sign) and press Enter twice.

Step 6: Type **Midwest** and press Enter to move to the next line.

Step 7: Press Tab, type **Region III**, press Tab, type **850,000**, and press Enter.

Step 8: Press Tab, type **Region IV**, press Tab, type **450,450**, and press Enter.

Step 9: Press Tab, type **Region V**, press Tab, type **1,000,000**, and press Enter.

Step 10: Press Tab, press the space bar twice, type **Total**, press Tab twice, type **+** (a plus sign), and press Enter twice.

Step 11: Type **East Coast** and press Enter to move to the next line.

Step 12: Press Tab, type **Region VI**, press Tab, type **1,200,500**, and press Enter.

Step 13: Press Tab, type **Region VII**, press Tab, type **480,000**, and press Enter.

Step 14: Press Tab, press the space bar twice, type **Total**, press Tab twice, type **+** (a plus sign), and then press Enter twice.

Step 15: Type **U. S. Totals**, press Tab three times, type **=** (equal sign), and then press Enter.

Step 16: Access the **F**ile pull-down menu and select **S**ave (or press F10). Type **TOTAL.COL** to save the total column model.

You just entered the "Regional Sales" document including text, numbers, and math operators. The plus and equal signs tell WordPerfect what to total.

Calculating the Total Column Model and Turning Math Off

To calculate the document with a separate column for subtotals and turn Math off, follow these steps:

Step 1: Access the **L**ayout pull-down menu and select **M**ath (or press Alt-F7,3).

Step 2: Choose **C**alculate (**4**) and scroll through the document.

Note: Calculated results appear as shown in figure 17.5.

Step 3: Press Home, Home, down arrow.

Step 4: Access the **L**ayout pull-down menu and select **M**ath (or press Alt-F7,3).

Step 5: Choose **O**ff (**2**).

Creating Calculation Columns

Use number and total columns to solve applications with vertical totals. But if you need horizontal calculations, use calculation columns—for a third dimension of math capability. Calculations include adding, subtracting, multiplying, dividing, and reordering the sequence of calculations with parentheses. Put together a calculation column much the same way you create a number column or a total column.

Figure 17.7 illustrates a calculation column. The first and second columns, QUANTITY and UNIT PRICE, are number columns without subtotals or totals. TOTAL COST is a calculation column that results from multiplying QUANTITY by UNIT PRICE. TOTAL COST includes a column total. SALES TAX is a calculation column that results from multiplying TOTAL COST by 5.5 percent; this last column also includes a column total.

Creating a calculation column within a document follows many of the same procedures used to create number and total columns. You do, however, need to enter one or more formulas in a calculation column application.

Defining a Calculation Column

To set up a calculation column, follow these steps:

Step 1: Clear the screen without saving the current document.

Step 2: Access the **L**ayout pull-down menu, select **A**lign, and choose **C**enter (or press Shift-F6).

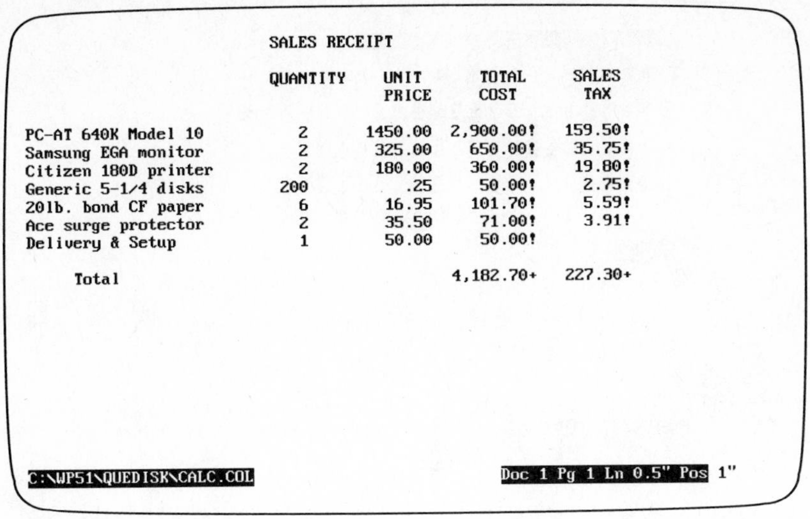

	SALES RECEIPT			
	QUANTITY	UNIT PRICE	TOTAL COST	SALES TAX
PC-AT 640K Model 10	2	1450.00	2,900.00!	159.50!
Samsung EGA monitor	2	325.00	650.00!	35.75!
Citizen 180D printer	2	180.00	360.00!	19.80!
Generic 5-1/4 disks	200	.25	50.00!	2.75!
20lb. bond CF paper	6	16.95	101.70!	5.59!
Ace surge protector	2	35.50	71.00!	3.91!
Delivery & Setup	1	50.00	50.00!	
Total			4,182.70+	227.30+

C:\WP51\QUEDISK\CALC.COL Doc 1 Pg 1 Ln 0.5" Pos 1"

Fig. 17.7. *Calculation column application.*

Step 3: Type **SALES RECEIPT** and press Enter twice to insert spacing after the heading.

Step 4: Access the **L**ayout pull-menu and select **L**ine (or press Shift-F8,1); choose **T**ab Set (**8**).

Step 5: Press Ctrl-End to delete the default tab settings.

Step 6: Set Center tab stops (type the letter **C**) at positions 30, 40, 50, and 60 (3.0", 4.0", 5.0", and 6.0" if your display is in inches); then press Exit (F7) to restore the current document display.

When Math is on, WordPerfect treats all tab stops as decimal tabs. If Math is off, the center, right, and left tab indicators position text accordingly. Figure 17.8 shows the completed Math Definition screen set up to produce the calculation column result displayed in figure 17.7.

To access the Math Definition screen and set up a math definition according to figure 17.8, follow these steps:

Step 1: Access the **L**ayout pull-down menu and select **M**ath (or press Alt-F7,3).

Step 2: Choose **D**efine (**3**).

Step 3: Move the cursor to column A and change `Number of Digits to the Right` to zero by typing **0**.

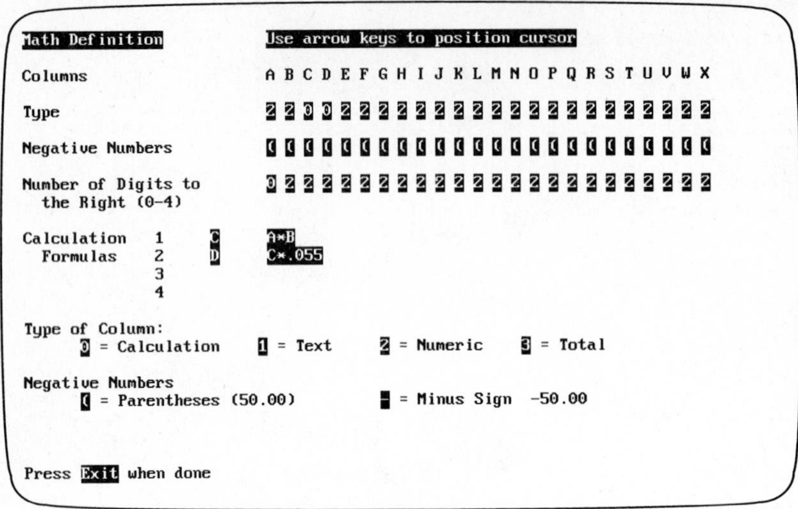

Fig. 17.8. The Math Definition screen for a calculation column application.

Step 4: Move the cursor to column C and change `Type` to `Calculation` by typing **0**. The cursor moves to the Calculation Formulas area.

Step 5: Type the formula **A*B** and press Enter.

Step 6: Move the cursor to column D, change `Type` to `Calculation` by typing **0**, type the formula **C*.055**, and press Enter.

Step 7: Compare the specifications on your screen to those in figure 17.8 and make corrections as necessary.

Step 8: Press Exit (F7) enough times to restore the current document display.

Entering Calculation Column Data and Setting Up Math Operations

The next steps include those for setting up column headings; turning Math on; and entering text, numbers, and math operators. To enter the data shown in figure 17.7, follow these steps:

Step 1: Position the cursor at the left margin of the third line, press Tab, and type **QUANTITY**. Press Tab and type **UNIT**. Press Tab and type **TOTAL**. Press Tab and type **SALES**. Press Enter to move to the next line.

Step 2: Press Tab twice. Type **PRICE**, press Tab, and type **COST**. Press Tab and type **TAX**. Then press Enter twice to end the column headings and insert a blank line.

Step 3: Access the **L**ayout pull-down menu and select **M**ath (or press Alt-F7,3); choose **On** (**1**).

Step 4: Type **PC-AT 640K Model 10**. Press Tab and type **2**. Press Tab and type **1450.00**. Press Tab twice and press Enter to move the cursor to the next line.

Note: An exclamation point (!) appears automatically in any field awaiting calculation by a formula.

Step 5: Type **Samsung EGA monitor**. Press Tab and type **2**. Press Tab and type **325.00**. Press Tab twice and press Enter to move the cursor to the next line.

Step 6: Type **Citizen 180D printer**. Press Tab and type **2**. Press Tab and type **180.00**. Press Tab twice; then press Enter.

Step 7: Type **Generic 5-1/4 disks**. Press Tab and type **200**. Press Tab and type **.25**. Press Tab twice and press Enter to move the cursor to the next line.

Step 8: Type **20lb. bond CF paper**. Press Tab and type **6**. Press Tab and type **16.95**. Press Tab twice and press Enter to move the cursor to the next line.

Step 9: Type **Ace surge protector**. Press Tab and type **2**. Press Tab and type **35.50**. Press Tab twice and then press Enter to move the cursor to the next line.

Step 10: Type **Delivery & Setup**. Press Tab and type **1**. Press Tab and type **50.00**. Press Tab once and press Enter twice to move the cursor to the next line and insert a line for spacing.

Step 11: Press the space bar five times. Type **Total** and press Tab three times.

Step 12: Press Backspace to remove the ! symbol (showing a defined calculation), type **+**, press Tab, press Backspace, type **+**, and press Enter.

Step 13: Access the **F**ile pull-down menu and select **S**ave (or press F10); then save the calculation column model as CALC.COL.

Text, numbers, and formulas are entered in the SALES RECEIPT document. Notice that the right two columns have the symbol ! where calculations should appear. After calculations are made, these positions display the calculated results. No ! is entered in the sales tax column for Delivery & Setup because services do not require a charge for sales tax. The absence of a ! suppresses the calculation.

Calculating the Calculation Column Model and Turning Math Off

To perform both horizontal and vertical calculations and turn Math off, follow these steps:

Step 1: Access the **L**ayout pull-down menu and select **M**ath (or press Alt-F7,3).

Step 2: Choose **C**alculate (**4**), scroll through the document, and note that calculated results appear as shown in figure 17.7.

Step 3: Press Home, Home, down arrow.

Step 4: Access the **L**ayout pull-down menu and select **M**ath (or press Alt-F7,3).

Step 5: Choose **O**ff (**2**).

If you change any numbers in a calculated document, you must repeat Steps 1 and 2 above to recalculate. The ! and + appear only on the display. These symbols disappear when the document is printed.

For Further Reference

For further information about the Math Definition menu and the differences between the plus and equal operators, consult *Using WordPerfect*, Special Edition (Que Corporation, Carmel, IN, 1989), Chapter 18.

Summary of Concepts

Lesson 17 explains these concepts:

- ❑ Using WordPerfect's Columns/Table (Alt-F7) feature, you can perform vertical and/or horizontal math within a document.
- ❑ Executing a math operation requires a standard six-step process: set tab stops for each column, create a math definition for the columns, turn on Math, enter data, calculate results, and turn off Math.
- ❑ WordPerfect supports up to 24 columns, each column corresponding to a tab stop.
- ❑ Once Math is turned on, all tab stops (such as L, R, and C) are considered decimal tabs until Math is turned off.
- ❑ Use the Math Definition screen to set the type of column, the display of negative numbers, and the calculation formulas.
- ❑ Each column must be designated as one of four types: text, numeric (the default), total, or calculation.
- ❑ Use the "toggle" key combination (Alt-F7,1) to turn Math on or off.
- ❑ Use Tab to move from column to column when you enter text, numbers, and math operators.
- ❑ Recalculate the model after any change in the numbers feeding the formulas.

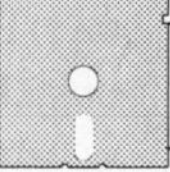

Review Exercises

Three summary exercises reinforce the tasks involved in creating the three types of math columns: number, total, and calculation. When a question mark (?) appears in the model, a formula should calculate results.

1. Set up and calculate the following number-column application:

Budgeted Monthly Income Statement

Revenues	5,000
Expenses:	
Cost of Goods Sold (COGS)	2,800
Selling	300
Administrative	700
Net Income	?

2. Set up and calculate the following total-column application:

Budgeted Monthly Income Statement

Revenues:	
Sales	4,500
Rental Fees	500
Total Revenues	?
Expenses:	
COGS	2,800
Selling	300
Administrative	700
Total Expenses	?
Net Income	?

3. Set up and calculate the following calculation-column application:

1st Quarter Expense Budget

Expense Item	Prior Jan	Prior Feb	Prior Mar	Prior Qtr 1	% Change	Revised Qtr 1
COGS	2,600	2,200	2,500	?	3%	?
Selling	200	500	350	?	(1%)	?
Admin	650	725	760	?	4%	?

Working with Tables

18

In this lesson, you practice these tasks:

- ❑ Create a table
- ❑ Move the cursor inside the table
- ❑ Change the table column width
- ❑ Enter and edit table data
- ❑ Sort the table
- ❑ Change the alignment of data within table columns
- ❑ Insert headings into the table
- ❑ Create and copy formulas in table cells
- ❑ Create subtotals and totals in the table
- ❑ Enhance the appearance of the table

The table feature, new with WordPerfect 5.1, is perhaps the most powerful feature of the new version. If you are familiar with one of the spreadsheet packages, such as Lotus 1-2-3, learning to use the table feature will be simple. If you are not familiar with spreadsheets, this feature is still easy to use.

This lesson presents a single project instead of a number of independent exercises. You create a table—composed of 17 rows and 5 columns—that contains a bid to provide computer equipment and services (see fig.18.1). The application integrates the features of math and text columns, the features of electronic spreadsheets, and the editing capability of a powerful word processor. Lesson-disk files are provided at various stages of the table-building project.

MICROCOMPUTER SYSTEM BID				
CAT	ITEM/SERVICE	QTY/HOURS	UNIT PRICE	TOTAL COST
HW	80mb hard disk	3	650.00	1,950.00
HW	IBM PS/2 Model 70	3	2,800.00	8,400.00
HW	HP LaserJet III	3	2,150.00	6,450.00
HW	Color VGA monitor	3	500.00	1,500.00
	TOTAL HARDWARE COST			18,300.00
SVS	General training	6	00.00	0.00
SVS	Delivery and setup	5	45.00	225.00
SVS	Software training	12	45.00	540.00
	TOTAL SERVICES COST			765.00
SW	dBASE IV	3	396.75	1,190.25
SW	WordPerfect 5.1	3	210.00	630.00
SW	DOS 4.01	3	75.00	225.00
SW	Lotus 1-2-3 R2.2	3	410.00	1,230.00
	TOTAL SOFTWARE COST			3,275.25
			TOTAL BID->	22,340.25

Fig. 18.1. *A WordPerfect 5.1 table.*

Creating a Table

Take a minute to analyze the organization of the table in figure 18.1. The table is formed by a matrix of cells, of varying sizes, arranged in rows and columns. When you work with a WordPerfect table, rows are referenced by numbers from top to bottom, and columns are referenced by letters from left to right. Each cell has a unique location identified by the column letter and row number that correspond to column and row whose intersection forms that cell. For example, the cell in the lower right corner of the table (containing the number 22,340.25) is called E17. You determine the E17 cell location by noting that the cell is located in the fifth column from the left and is in row 17 (counting from the top down).

The cells in one column may vary in width from cells in another column. Notice in figure 18.1 that the entries in the first column, titled CAT (category), are short codes (HW for `hardware`, SVS for `services`, and SW for `software`). Column A is therefore narrower than the second column, B, which contains a description of the item or service.

Row 1 in figure 18.1 illustrates a special situation because it contains only one cell. You will learn, later in this lesson, that a Join command was used to combine the five columns in row 1 into one cell. Therefore row 1 has only one cell, whose name is A1.

Plan the layout of your table in advance, including setting margins to accommodate the size of the table. A table can be as small as a single cell or as large as 32 columns wide by 32,765 rows high. An individual cell can be as small as a single letter or as large as a single page of the document.

The steps to create a table can be summarized as follows:

- ❑ Access the Columns/Table feature and create an empty table by defining its dimensions.
- ❑ Adjust the size of each column in the new table to the width necessary to hold the data and provide spacing between columns.
- ❑ Exit from the table editor and enter data in the appropriate cells.

You can create a table in an existing document or on a blank screen, as illustrated in the Lesson 18 exercises.

Defining Table Dimensions

To create the table, define its dimensions in a manner similar to that for creating math (see Lesson 17) and text (see Lesson 16) columns. Access the Columns/Table feature, select **T**ables, and select **C**reate. You will be prompted for the number of columns and rows your table is to contain. To define the initial table dimensions for creating the table shown in figure 18.1, follow these steps:

Step 1: Clear the screen without saving the current document.

Note: The instruction to clear the screen without saving the current document is used many times throughout the workbook. It means to access the **F**ile pull-down menu and select E**x**it (or press F7), press **N** when prompted `Save Document? Yes (No)`, and press **N** when prompted `Exit WP? No (Yes)`.

Step 2: Access the **L**ayout pull-down menu and select **L**ine (or press Shift-F8,1).

Step 3: Select **M**argins Left/Right (7), specify .5 as the left margin, specify .5 as the right margin, and press Exit (F7) enough times to restore the document screen.

Step 4: Access the **L**ayout pull-down menu, select **T**ables, and choose **C**reate (or press Alt-F7,2,1).

Step 5: When prompted `Number of Columns: 3`, type **5** and press Enter.

Step 6: When prompted `Number of Rows: 1`, type **12** and press Enter.

In Steps 5 and 6 you created 5 columns and 12 rows (all but 2 rows appear in fig. 18.2). However, the model shown in figure 18.1 contains 17 rows. You could create all 17 rows now, if you like. However, later in this lesson, you will add the missing rows to practice using the insert command.

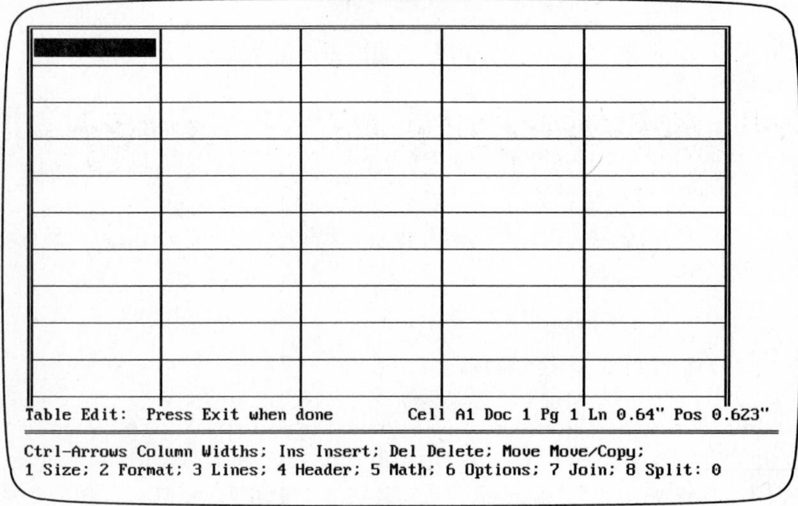

Fig. 18.2. *An empty table: 5 columns by 12 rows.*

The table structure appears on the screen, and the table editor is active. The main table-editor menu options appear in the last line at the bottom of the screen. A message line appears above the menu options, providing directions on which keys to press for various actions. The status line appears above the message line and includes a reference to the cell marked by the current cursor position (cell A1 in fig. 18.2).

Understanding Table Hidden Codes

When you defined table dimensions in the previous exercise, WordPerfect inserted the table definition code `[Tbl Def:I;5,1.5",1.5",1.5",1.5",1.5"]` at the beginning of the table (see fig. 18.3). This code indicates that there are 5 columns and that each column is one and one-half inches wide. Each row in the table is defined with the code `[Row][Cell][Cell][Cell][Cell][Cell]`. The end of the table is marked with the `[Tbl Off][HRt]` code. If you block-move a table within a document, be sure to include the `[Tbl Def: . . .]` and `[Tbl off][HRt]` codes.

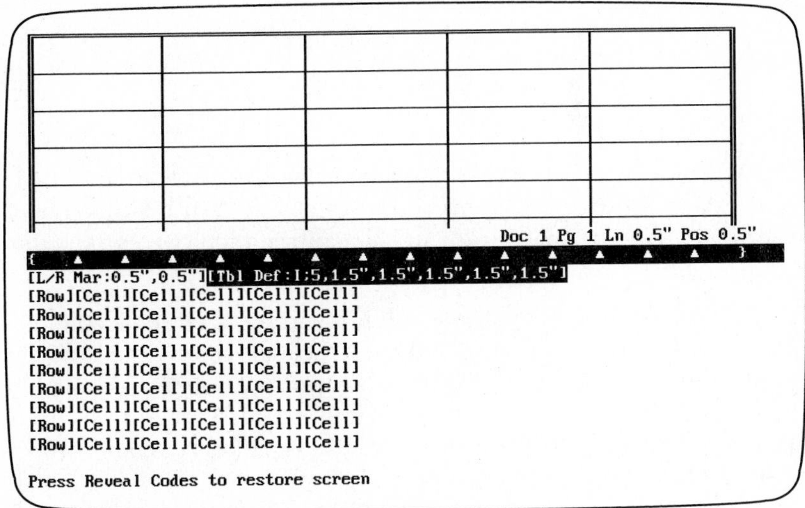

Fig. 18.3. *Using Reveal Codes to view table codes.*

Reveal Codes mode does not work from within the table editor. To see the hidden table codes, follow these steps:

Step 1: Press Exit (F7) to leave the table editor.

Note: You can exit from the table editor only by pressing Exit (F7). Pressing either Esc or Cancel (F1) will not work.

Step 2: Access the **E**dit pull-down menu and select **R**eveal Codes (or press Alt-F3 or F11); examine the table's hidden codes.

Step 3: Access the **E**dit pull-down menu and select **R**eveal Codes (or press Alt-F3 or F11) to restore full screen display.

If you attempt to delete one of the [Cell] codes while in Reveal Codes mode, the cursor simply moves to the next cell without deleting the cell code. WordPerfect provides protection from the accidental removal of a table code by forcing table modifications to be done through the table editor.

You can, however, delete the table definition code [Tbl Def:...] without accessing the table editor. WordPerfect 5.1 removes all hidden table codes but retains the data from each cell, separated by [Tab] codes. To delete the entire table, including data, block (highlight) the table—including the [Tbl Def:...] and [Table Off] codes—press Del, and press **Y**.

Changing Column Width

Before entering data in an empty table, adjust the width of each column to accommodate the data. WordPerfect permits tables larger than a single sheet. However, a table larger than a page of the document may be difficult to read and thus may lessen the impact the information has on the reader.

You must be in table-editor mode to change column width. To adjust a column's width, position the cursor in that column and press Ctrl-left arrow to reduce the column width one character each time the key combination is pressed. Or widen the column by pressing Ctrl-right arrow. Move the cursor from cell to cell in table-editor mode by pressing the up-, down-, left-, and right-arrow keys. Other key combinations for movement within the table editor are available as well.

You can change table display characteristics (column size, lines, shadings, and so on) in table-editor mode; you cannot enter or edit table data while in table-editor mode. Actions for moving the cursor outside the table editor include these:

- ❑ Press Tab to move the cursor right one cell; press Shift-Tab to move the cursor left one cell.
- ❑ Press the up arrow to move the cursor up one row; press the down arrow to move the cursor down one row.
- ❑ Press the left arrow and right arrow to move the cursor within a cell. (If the cursor reaches the end of data in that cell, pressing the left arrow or right arrow moves the cursor to the next cell in the direction indicated.)
- ❑ Press Ctrl-Home to move the cursor to a user-specified cell. When prompted Go to, type the cell reference (such as B5) and press Enter.

A variety of other key combinations is available for movement within a table, both inside and outside the table editor, including Alt-key combinations if you use an Enhanced Keyboard.

As you increase or decrease the size of a column, notice that the remaining columns on the screen adjust to divide the remaining space equally. To adjust the column sizes in your table, follow these steps:

Step 1: Position the cursor at cell A1.

Step 2: Access the **L**ayout pull-down menu, select **T**ables, and choose **E**dit (or press Alt-F7) to enter table-editor mode.

Note: If you choose the shorter method within parentheses to activate the table editor, notice that you press only Alt-F7 (not Alt-F7,2,2). If the cursor is positioned within an existing table at the time you press Alt-F7, WordPerfect immediately activates the table editor. Otherwise, pressing Alt-F7 presents the Columns/Table menu.

Step 3: Press Ctrl-left arrow four times to narrow column A by four characters.

Step 4: Position the cursor in any cell in column B.

Step 5: Press Ctrl-right arrow 10 times to widen column B.

The columns on your screen should be the same width as those in figure 18.1. You are now ready to enter data.

Entering and Editing Data

Recall that you cannot enter or edit data while in table-editor mode. To enter data into the first row of the table, follow these steps:

Step 1: Press Exit (F7) to exit from the table editor.

Step 2: Position the cursor at cell A1.

Step 3: Type **HW** and press Tab (the cursor shifts to cell B1).

Step 4: Type **IBM PS/2 Model 70** and press Tab (the cursor shifts to cell C1).

Step 5: Type **3** and press Tab (the cursor shifts to cell D1).

Step 6: Type **2,800.00** and press Tab.

The numeric data in the QTY/HOURS and UNIT PRICE columns (columns C and D, respectively, in fig. 18.4) appears left-justified. Numeric data should more properly be aligned to the right side of the column. Continue to enter the data left-justified. Later in this lesson you will center the QTY/HOURS data and right-justify the UNIT PRICE data. When you design your own tables, you may prefer to change the format of the cells before you enter data.

HW	IBM PS/2 Model 70	3	2,800.00	

Fig. 18.4. A table with one row of data.

To enter another row of data, follow these steps:

Step 1: Position the cursor at cell A2.

Step 2: Type **HW** and press Tab.

Step 3: Type **Color VGA monitor** in cell B2 and press Tab.

Step 4: Type **3** in cell C2 and press Tab.

Step 5: Type **500.00** in cell D2 and press Tab.

Figure 18.5 illustrates 11 rows of data to enter in the table. The bid items are not in the same order as those shown in figure 18.1; you learn to sort table contents in a subsequent exercise.

You have already entered the first two rows of data. On your own, continue to enter data from figure 18.5 until you feel comfortable with the process. It is not necessary to enter all rows to continue developing the table; a lesson-disk file provided for the next exercise contains all the data.

At Col A	At Col B	At Col C	At Col D
HW	IBM PS/2 Model 70	3	2,800.00
HW	Color VGA monitor	3	500.00
SVS	Software training	12	45.00
SW	Lotus 1-2-3 R2.2	3	410.00
HW	80mb hard disk	3	650.00
SW	DOS 4.01	3	75.00
SW	WordPerfect 5.1	3	210.00
SVS	Delivery and setup	5	45.00
HW	HP LaserJet III	3	2,150.00
SVS	General training	6	00.00
SW	dBASE IV	3	396.75

Fig. 18.5. Data to enter in a table.

Expanding and Organizing Table Contents

Once basic information is entered into the table, the data can be organized and expanded. The next steps in developing your table involve sorting the information into a meaningful sequence, changing the alignment of cell contents, and adding rows for headings.

Use the WordPerfect 5.1 Sort feature, presented in Lesson 13, to sort the table contents into three categories: HW (hardware), SVS (services), and SW (software). Improve the appearance of data within the table by centering amounts in the QTY/HOURS column (column C) and right-justifying entries in the UNIT PRICE column (column D) and the TOTAL COST column (column E). Finally, add two rows at the top of the table and enter the headings shown in figure 18.1.

Sorting the Table

WordPerfect 5.1's Sort facility allows you to sort on more than one table column. However, setting more than one sort key (column) may produce inaccurate results even if the table is small and simple. In this lesson you will sort the table contents by category of goods and services, located in column A (cell 1). Once the rows are sorted by category, you can insert subtotals and totals.

Caution: Always save a file to disk under a backup name before you sort. If the sort does not produce the results you expect, you can clear the screen without saving the unsatisfactory results and retrieve the backup copy of the file.

To perform an initial sort on an entire table saved on disk, follow these steps:

Step 1: Clear the screen without saving the current document and retrieve TBL18A.DOC.

Step 2: Press PgDn to view the blank row at the bottom (recall that table specifications established 12 rows in the table; 11 items are entered).

Step 3: Press PgUp and position the cursor in cell A1.

Step 4: Access the **T**ools pull-down menu and select **S**ort (or press Ctrl-F9,2).

Note: The sort key information (see fig. 18.6) now displays `Cell` as its second parameter. The default sort key 1 indicates that word 1, in line 1, of cell (column) 1 will be sorted in ascending sequence. These default settings reflect the desired sort sequence on the first column in the table.

HW	IBM PS/2 Model 70	3	2,800.00	
HW	Color VGA monitor	3	500.00	
SVS	Software training	12	45.00	
SW	Lotus 1-2-3 R2.2	3	410.00	
HW	80mb hard disk	3	650.00	

```
                                             Doc 2 Pg 1 Ln 1" Pos 0.5"
---------------------------------- Sort Table --------------------------------

Key Typ Cell  Line Word    Key Typ Cell  Line Word    Key Typ Cell  Line Word
 1   a    1     1    1      2                          3
 4                          5                          6
 7                          8                          9
Select

Action                     Order                     Type
Sort                       Ascending                 Table sort

1 Perform Action; 2 View; 3 Keys; 4 Select; 5 Action; 6 Order; 7 Type: 0
```

Fig. 18.6. *A Sort Table screen.*

Step 5: Choose **P**erform Action (**1**) and notice the blank row followed by a double line that appears at the top of the sorted table.

You may often have blank rows in a table, allowing for additional entries as necessary. By not blocking the rows to be sorted, you allow blank fields included in the table to sort to the top. The double line at the bottom of the file also moved and appears out of place at the top of the table. Do not be concerned at this point about the lack of uniformity in the lines. You correct line display problems in a later section.

By blocking only rows containing entries, you can avoid the problem of erroneously sorting blank rows. Perform these steps to repeat the sort with improved results:

Step 1: Clear the screen without saving the current document and retrieve TBL18A.DOC.

Step 2: Press the down arrow to position the cursor at cell A1.

Step 3: Access the **E**dit pull-down menu and select **B**lock (or press Alt-F4 or F12).

Step 4: Highlight cells A1 through E11 (the flashing cursor should be at the end of the last entry: 396.75).

Step 5: Access the **T**ools pull-down menu and select **S**ort (or press Ctrl-F9,2).

Step 6: Choose **P**erform Actions (**1**).

Check your results with figure 18.7 to see that all rows in the table are sorted, in ascending sequence, by the data in column A (cell 1). Notice that the blank line remains at the bottom of the table.

HW	80mb hard disk	3	650.00	
HW	IBM PS/2 Model 70	3	2,800.00	
HW	HP LaserJet III	3	2,150.00	
HW	Color VGA Monitor	3	500.00	
SVS	General Training	6	00.00	
SVS	Delivery and setup	5	45.00	
SVS	Software training	12	45.00	
SW	dBASE IV	3	396.75	
SW	WordPerfect 5.1	3	210.00	
SW	DOS 4.01	3	75.00	
SW	Lotus 1-2-3 R2.2	3	410.00	

Fig. 18.7. *The table sorted on column A.*

Changing the Alignment of Numeric Data

Recall that the data in the QTY/HOURS (C) and UNIT PRICE (D) columns is aligned at the left side of the respective columns. The default justification of data in a column is to the left, which is appropriate for text data. However, data to be added is normally justified to the right.

Using the table editor, you can assign an alignment characteristic to the data in one or more cells. When you assign an alignment characteristic to a cell, that characteristic remains in effect until changed. Justification options include left, right, center, full, and decimal alignment. You have used these enhancement features in other lessons. For example, right justification functions in the same manner as Flush Right (Alt-F6). Similarly, specifying center justification is the same as pressing Shift-F6.

If you prefer not to assign a justification attribute to a cell permanently, you can assign the justification to the data. In the next exercise, you assign center justification to all cells in the QTY/HOURS column and right justification to all cells in the UNIT

PRICE and TOTAL COST columns. Later, when entering headings in newly inserted rows 1 and 2, you simply include justification with the data.

To center the contents of the QTY/HOURS column (column C), perform these steps:

Step 1: If your current document does not match the one shown in figure 18.7, clear the screen without saving the current document and retrieve TBL18B.DOC.

Step 2: Press the down arrow once and press Tab twice to position the cursor in cell C1.

Step 3: Access the **L**ayout pull-down menu, select **T**ables, and choose **E**dit (or press Alt-F7).

Step 4: Select **F**ormat (**2**) and choose **C**olumn (**2**).

Step 5: Select **J**ustify (**3**) and choose **C**enter (**2**).

To right-justify the contents of the UNIT PRICE and TOTAL COST columns (D and E, respectively), perform these steps:

Step 1: Position the cursor in cell D1.

Step 2: Select **F**ormat (**2**), select **C**olumn (**2**), select **J**ustify (**3**), and choose **R**ight (**3**).

Step 3: Position the cursor in cell E1.

Step 4: Select **F**ormat (**2**), select **C**olumn (**2**), select **J**ustify (**3**), and choose **R**ight (**3**).

Step 5: Press Exit (F7) to exit from the table editor; check your results with those shown in figure 18.8.

HW	80mb hard disk	3	650.00	
HW	IBM PS/2 Model 70	3	2,800.00	
HW	HP LaserJet III	3	2,150.00	
HW	Color VGA monitor	3	500.00	
SVS	General training	6	00.00	
SVS	Delivery and setup	5	45.00	
SVS	Software training	12	45.00	
SW	dBASE IV	3	396.75	
SW	WordPerfect 5.1	3	210.00	
SW	DOS 4.01	3	75.00	
SW	Lotus 1-2-3 R2.2	3	410.00	

Fig. 18.8. *Column contents aligned left, center, and right.*

Another way to perform Steps 1 through 4 is to block the cells in both columns. Then, instead of selecting **C**olumn (**2**), select **C**ell (**1**). The results are the same as those produced by performing two individual column alignments.

Inserting Headings

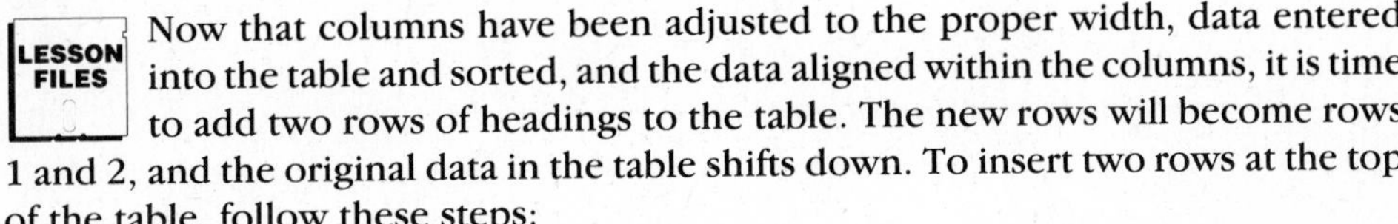

Now that columns have been adjusted to the proper width, data entered into the table and sorted, and the data aligned within the columns, it is time to add two rows of headings to the table. The new rows will become rows 1 and 2, and the original data in the table shifts down. To insert two rows at the top of the table, follow these steps:

Step 1: If your current document does not match the one shown in figure 18.8, clear the screen without saving the current document and retrieve TBL18C.DOC.

Step 2: Position the cursor in cell A1.

Step 3: Access the **L**ayout pull-down menu, select **T**ables, and choose **E**dit (or press Alt-F7).

Step 4: Notice the messages in the line just above menu choices at the bottom of the screen; follow the screen instructions and press Ins.

Step 5: Select **R**ows (**1**).

Step 6: When prompted `Number of Rows: 1`, type **2** and press Enter.

Two blank rows are inserted at the top of the table. Both rows contain the same number and size of columns as specified in the table definition code. The first row, however, should not contain any columns (see fig. 18.1). Use the Join command to join all columns in row 1 into one large cell with the address A1. Follow these steps:

Step 1: Position the cursor in cell A1.

Step 2: Access the **E**dit pull-down menu and select **B**lock (or press Alt-F4 or F12); then highlight cells A1 through E1.

Step 3: Select **J**oin (**7**), and when prompted `Join cells? No (Yes)`, press **Y**.

Notice that two rows have been added to the table and that the column barriers are removed from row 1, as shown in figure 18.9.

HW	80mb hard disk	3	650.00	
HW	IBM PS/2 Model 70	3	2,800.00	
HW	HP LaserJet III	3	2,150.00	

Fig. 18.9. *Two rows inserted for headings.*

To enter headings in the first two rows of the table, follow these steps:

Step 1: Press Exit (F7) to exit from the table editor.

Step 2: Position the cursor in cell A1, press Center (Shift-F6), type **MICROCOMPUTER SYSTEM BID**, and press the down arrow to position the cursor in cell A2.

Step 3: Press Center (Shift-F6), type **CAT**, and press Tab to position the cursor in cell B2.

Step 4: Press Center (Shift-F6), type **ITEM/SERVICE**, and press Tab to position the cursor in cell C2.

Step 5: Type **QTY/HOURS** and press Tab to position the cursor in cell D2 (recall that column C was previously set to center alignment).

Note: The cursor is positioned flush right in column D because you changed the alignment for all cells in column D and E to right-justification in a previous exercise. Only the cells D2 and E2 should be changed to center alignment.

Step 6: Access the **L**ayout pull-down menu, choose **T**ables, and select **E**dit (or press Alt-F7).

Step 7: Access the **E**dit pull-down menu and select **B**lock (or press Alt-F4 or F12); highlight cells D2 and E2.

Step 8: Select **F**ormat (**2**), select **C**ell (**1**), select **J**ustify (**3**), and choose **C**enter (**2**).

Step 9: Press Exit (F7) to exit from the table editor.

Step 10: Position the cursor in cell D2, type **UNIT PRICE**, and press Tab to position the cursor in cell E2.

Step 11: Type **TOTAL COST** and press Tab.

The cursor is now positioned in cell A3. Your headings should appear identical to those shown in figure 18.1.

Using Math Features in a Table

WordPerfect 5.1 supports basic math operations—addition (+), subtraction (–), multiplication (*), and division (/)—in its table feature. In the table you can include formulas that contain math operators and references to cells. For example, you can create the TOTAL COST data in column E by using formulas that multiply QTY/HOURS by UNIT PRICE. You can also create subtotals, totals, and grand totals.

Formulas and totals commands must be entered through the table editor. Data, however, is entered and edited only outside the table editor. If you enter multiple numbers by using math operators (+, –, *, /, and =) in a cell outside the table editor, WordPerfect ignores all but the last number. For example, if you type **13+12** into a cell, only the 12 is used as the value in the cell. In this section of the table-building project, you enter formulas to generate line item totals, subtotals by category, and a grand total for the microcomputer bid.

Entering Formulas That Create Line Item Totals

At this point in the table-building project, the cells in column E represent line item totals, computed by multiplying QTY/HOURS times UNIT PRICE. Use formulas to create the information in this column. You can enter into cell E3 a single formula for the first line item total and copy the formula to the remaining cells in the column. Recall that you must enter formulas through the table editor.

To enter the first formula in cell E3 and copy the formula to other cells in the column, follow these steps:

Step 1: If your current document does not match the layout shown in figure 18.9 and include headings in the first two rows, clear the screen without saving the current document and retrieve TBL18D.DOC.

Step 2: Position the cursor in cell E3.

Step 3: Access the **L**ayout pull-down menu, select **T**ables, and choose **E**dit (or press Alt-F7).

Step 4: Select **M**ath (**5**) and notice the appearance of the Math menu at the bottom of the screen (see fig. 18.10).

Note: The Math menu (see fig. 18.10) appears at the bottom of the screen. Using this menu you can calculate the table; enter or edit a formula in a cell; and copy a formula in a cell throughout a column or row, or to a specific cell.

```
Table Edit:  Press Exit when done          Cell E3 Doc 1 Pg 1 Ln 1.17" Pos 7.88"

Math: 1 Calculate; 2 Formula; 3 Copy Formula; 4 +; 5 =; 6 *: 0
```

Fig. 18.10. *The Math menu in the table editor.*

Step 5: Select **F**ormula (**2**), type **C3*D3**, and press Enter. The formula result `1,950.00` appears in cell E3; the formula appears near the lower left corner of the screen.

Step 6: Check that the cursor is positioned in cell E3.

Step 7: Select **M**ath (**5**) and choose Co**p**y Formula (**3**).

Step 8: When prompted `Copy formula to:`, select **D**own (**2**).

Step 9: When prompted `Number of times to copy formula: 1`, type **10** and press Enter.

Step 10: Press Exit (F7) to exit the table editor.

You copied the formula C3*D3 10 times because you have 11 line items in the table. When the formula copied, cell references changed relative to each new position. For example, if a formula C3*D3 is copied down, WordPerfect places the formula `C4*D4` in the first cell receiving a copied formula, places `C5*D5` in the next cell receiving a copied formula, and so forth. To view the copied formulas and formula results, perform these steps:

Step 1: Position the cursor on cell E4. The formula result `8,400.00` appears in cell E4; the formula `C4*D4` appears near the lower left corner of the screen.

Step 2: Position the cursor on cell E5. The formula result `6,450.00` appears in cell E5; the formula `C5*D5` appears near the lower left corner of the screen.

Entering Formulas That Calculate Subtotals and Grand Totals

The model in figure 18.1 subtotals the total cost of categories HW, SVS, and SW. To create the subtotals, first access the table editor; then insert rows at the appropriate places in the table and enter the subtotal operator (+). To create a total calculation on the last line, follow the same procedures as you do when creating a subtotal, except place an equal sign (=) in the cell instead of a plus (+) sign. To create an initial subtotal line and enter the appropriate math operator, follow these steps:

Step 1: Access the **L**ayout pull-down menu, select **T**ables, and choose **E**dit (or press Alt-F7).

Step 2: Position the cursor at cell E7.

Step 3: Press Ins and then select **R**ow (**1**).

Step 4: When prompted `Number of Rows: 1`, press Enter to accept 1.

Step 5: Check that the cursor position is cell E7.

Step 6: Select **M**ath (**5**) and choose **+** (**4**).

The subtotal operator plus (+) calculates a total of all cells in the same column between the cell containing the subtotal operator and the last subtotal operator (or in this case, the top of the table). To create a second subtotal line and enter the appropriate math operator, follow these steps:

Step 1: Position the cursor at cell E11.

Step 2: Press Ins and select **R**ow (**1**).

Step 3: When prompted `Number of Rows: 1`, press Enter to accept 1.

Step 4: Check that the cursor position is cell E11.

Step 5: Select **M**ath (**5**) and choose **+** (**4**).

To create a third subtotal line and a grand total line, and to enter the appropriate math operators, follow these steps:

Step 1: Position the cursor at cell E16.

Step 2: Press Ins and select **R**ow (**1**).

Step 3: When prompted `Number of Rows: 1`, press Enter to accept 1.

Step 4: Check that the cursor position is cell E16.

Step 5: Select **M**ath (**5**) and choose **+** (**4**).

Step 6: Position the cursor at cell E17.

Step 7: Select **M**ath (**5**) and choose **=** (**5**).

The table displays all calculated values, as shown in figure 18.11. If you exit from the table editor and change any figures that are used in formulas—such as those in columns C and D in the current table—you must reenter the table editor, select **M**ath (**5**), and select **C**alculate (**1**) to update the table results.

MICROCOMPUTER SYSTEM BID				
CAT	ITEM/SERVICE	QTY/HOURS	UNIT PRICE	TOTAL COST
HW	80mb hard disk	3	650.00	1,950.00
HW	IBM PS/2 Model 70	3	2,800.00	8,400.00
HW	HP LaserJet III	3	2,150.00	6,450.00
HW	Color VGA monitor	3	500.00	1,500.00
				18,300.00
SVS	General training	6	00.00	0.00
SVS	Delivery and setup	5	45.00	225.00
SVS	Software training	12	45.00	540.00
				765.00
SW	dBASE IV	3	396.75	1,190.25
SW	WordPerfect 5.1	3	210.00	630.00
SW	DOS 4.01	3	75.00	225.00
SW	Lotus 1-2-3 R2.2	3	410.00	1,230.00
				3,275.25
				22,340.25

***Fig. 18.11.** The table with line items totals, subtotals, and a grand total.*

To finish entering data in the newly created total lines, follow these steps:

Step 1: Press Exit (F7) to exit from the table editor.

Step 2: Position the cursor at B7.

Step 3: Press the space bar three times and type **TOTAL HARDWARE COST** (do not press Enter).

Note: Recall that WordPerfect inserts a hard return code ([HRt]) code when you press Enter. If you inadvertently press Enter and insert an unwanted line in the table, access Reveal Codes mode and delete the [HRt] code.

Step 4: Position the cursor at B11.

Step 5: Press the space bar three times and type **TOTAL SERVICES COST.**

Step 6: Position the cursor at B16.

Step 7: Press the space bar three times and type **TOTAL SOFTWARE COST.**

Step 8: Position the cursor at D17.

Step 9: Type **TOTAL BID->**.

Review the data in your table for accuracy and spelling. Compare your data with that in figure 18.1. Make any changes that are necessary.

Enhancing Table Appearance

The table is now complete with respect to the text, organization, formulas, and totals. Refer to figure 18.1; the only action needed to complete the microcomputer system bid table involves enhancing the table's appearance with lines and shading. The effective use of line variations and shadings can draw a reader's attention to important items.

Changing the Appearance of Lines

Grid lines in a table may become disorganized as a result of sorting data and adding lines. The easiest way to fix the appearance of lines is to change all lines to single lines and then begin changing the appearance of specific lines.

Access the table editor and select **Lines** (**3**) to change the appearance of lines in a table. The Lines menu at the bottom of the screen (see fig. 18.12) displays a list of the line settings for the four borders of the table. Options 1 through 6 refer to the border lines around the blocked cells. The **All** (**7**) option refers to the border and internal lines within the block. Select **Shade** (**8**) to add highlighting to blocked cells.

```
Top=Single; Left=Double; Bottom=Double; Right=None
Lines: 1 Left; 2 Right; 3 Top; 4 Bottom; 5 Inside; 6 Outside; 7 All; 8 Shade: 0
```

***Fig. 18.12.** The initial Lines menu in the table editor.*

To change the lines in your table, follow these steps:

Step 1: If your current document does not match figure 18.1 (with the exception of line widths and cell shadings), clear the screen without saving the current document and retrieve TBL18E.DOC.

Step 2: Position the cursor at cell A1.

Step 3: Access the **Layout** pull-down menu, select **Tables**, and choose **Edit** (or press Alt-F7).

Step 4: Access the **Edit** pull-down menu and select **Block** (or press Alt-F4 or F12); then highlight cells A1 through E17.

Step 5: Select **Lines** (**3**) and note the appearance of the initial Lines menu at the bottom of the screen (see fig. 17.12).

Step 6: Select **All** (**7**).

Note: Once you select which lines you want to change, the menu displays choices appropriate for the type of lines you selected (see fig. 18.13).

```
Top=Single; Left=Double; Bottom=Double; Right=None
1 None; 2 Single; 3 Double; 4 Dashed; 5 Dotted; 6 Thick; 7 Extra Thick: 0
```

Fig. 18.13. *Menu options suitable for all lines.*

Step 7: Select **Single** (**2**).

Step 8: Position the cursor at cell A1.

Step 9: Access the **Edit** pull-down menu and select **Block** (or press Alt-F4 or F12); then highlight cells A1 through E17.

Step 10: Select **Lines** (**3**), choose **Outside** (**6**), and then choose **Double** (**3**).

You reset all lines in the table to single lines and then changed the border lines around the table to double lines. To provide some variation in lines within the table, add double lines to separate the heading from the data at the top of the table and separate data from the final total line at the bottom of the table. Follow these steps:

Step 1: Position the cursor at cell A3.

Step 2: Access the **Edit** pull-down menu and select **Block** (or press Alt-F4 or F12); then highlight cells A3 through E3.

Step 3: Select **Lines** (**3**), choose **Top** (**3**), and then choose **Double** (**3**).

Step 4: Position the cursor at cell A16.

Step 5: Access the **E**dit pull-down menu and select **B**lock (or press Alt-F4 or F12); then highlight cells A16 through E16.

Step 6: Select **L**ines (**3**), choose **B**ottom (**4**), and then choose **D**ouble (**3**).

Step 7: Press Exit (F7) to exit from the table editor.

Step 8: Access the **F**ile pull-down menu and select **S**ave (or press F10). Save the table under the file name MODELBID.

Step 8 provided the first instruction to save the microcomputer bid table. You were not instructed to save the table earlier because lesson files captured the table at various stages of construction. When you create your own tables, be sure to save your work frequently. If at any point in table development you do not get the results you want, exit without saving the current display and retrieve the most recent correct version from disk.

Shading Cells

Add shading to cells in order to focus readers' attention on specific table contents. For example, in figure 18.1, each of the subtotals and the total line at the bottom of the table are shaded. To apply shading to row 7 in your table, follow these steps:

Step 1: Position the cursor at cell A7; access the **L**ayout pull-down menu, select **T**ables, and choose **E**dit (or press Alt-F7).

Step 2: Access the **E**dit pull-down menu and select **B**lock (or press Alt-F4 or F12); then highlight cells A7 through E7.

Step 3: Select **L**ines (**3**).

Step 4: Select **S**hade (**8**), and when prompted `Shading:`, choose **O**n (**1**).

To apply shading to row 11, row 16, and cells D17 through E17 in your table, follow these steps:

Step 1: Position the cursor at cell A11, access the **E**dit pull-down menu and select **B**lock (or press Alt-F4 or F12), and then highlight cells A11 through E11.

Step 2: Select **L**ines (**3**).

Step 3: Select **S**hade (**8**), and when prompted `Shading:`, choose **O**n (**1**).

Step 4: Position the cursor at cell A16, access the **E**dit pull-down menu and select **B**lock (or press Alt-F4 or F12), and then highlight cells A16 through E16.

Step 5: Select **L**ines (**3**).

Step 6: Select **S**hade (**8**), and when prompted `Shading:`, choose **O**n (**1**).

Step 7: Position the cursor at cell D17, access the **Edit** pull-down menu and select **Block** (or press Alt-F4 or F12), and then highlight cells D17 through E17.

Step 8: Select **Lines** (**3**).

Step 9: Select **Shade** (**8**), and when prompted `Shading:`, choose **On** (**1**).

Step 10: Press Exit (F7) to exit from the table editor.

Viewing and Printing a Table

Text and lines appear on the WordPerfect editing screen as you see them in print. However, you cannot see the shading unless you access the print facility and take one of two actions: select **View** Document (**6**) to view the table on the screen, or select **Full** Document (**1**) or **Page** (**2**) to print.

To view and then print the completed table, follow these steps:

Step 1: Access the **File** pull-down menu and select **Print** (or press Shift-F7).

Step 2: Select **View** Document (**6**) and select Full **Page** (**3**).

Note: Depending on the resolution of your monitor, the shading should be obvious in View Document mode. The shading may appear as small dots.

Step 3: Press Exit (F7) to restore the Print menu.

Step 4: Select **Page** (**2**).

Step 5: After the table prints, press Exit (F7) enough times to restore the current document display.

Note: Because the table contains graphics (the lines), the table may take several minutes to print. Check that your shaded lines are the same as those in figure 18.1.

Step 6: If shading from the previous exercise is not correct, clear the screen without saving the current document, retrieve your disk file MODELBID, and repeat the shading and printing exercises.

Step 7: Make any other necessary modifications and save the file.

In this lesson you created only one table, but in completing that project you practiced the basic actions required to use the new WordPerfect 5.1 table-building capability. Once you become familiar with the steps, it won't take you long at all to develop your own table applications.

For Further Reference

For more information on the cursor-movement keys and creating tables, consult *Using WordPerfect 5.1*, Special Edition (Que Corporation, Carmel, IN, 1989), Chapters 14 and 19.

Summary of Concepts

Lesson 18 explains these concepts:

- ❑ WordPerfect 5.1's table feature is similar to that of an electronic spreadsheet.
- ❑ A table is a combination of graphics grid lines that form a matrix of cells in which you can enter text, numbers, and formulas.
- ❑ To define a table, access the Columns/Table feature and specify the number of rows and columns to create.
- ❑ WordPerfect 5.1 provides a table editor to modify column size, insert or delete rows and columns, create formulas, change the position of data, add shading, and alter the style of the grid lines.
- ❑ You cannot enter or edit data while the table editor is active.
- ❑ Use the WordPerfect 5.1 Merge/Sort feature to organize data in a table, being careful to omit headings and subtotal rows from the block marked for sorting.
- ❑ When data referenced by formulas changes, access the math feature of the table editor and calculate the table in order to update the table results.
- ❑ Print a document containing a table the same way you would print a document without a table; however, printing the graphics lines adds considerable time to the task.
- ❑ Execute frequent save commands as you build tables.

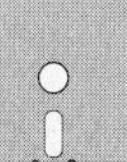

Review Exercises

Practice using the WordPerfect features in this lesson by completing these exercises. If you do not remember how to do something, review the preceding explanations and practice steps.

1. Access a blank document screen, set one-inch margins, and then create a table containing 10 rows and 4 columns.
2. Make the first 3 columns at least one inch wide and the fourth column three and one-half inches wide. You can adjust these widths later if you need more room in a column.
3. Access row 1 and join the four columns into one long cell (A1).
4. Center the heading **SUMMARY OF SERVICES** in cell A1.
5. At row 2 type and center the following headings:

   A2: TIME

   B2: RATE

   C2: AMOUNT

   D2: SERVICES

6. In columns A, B, and C, change the justification to right-align all numbers. Do not adjust the alignment in column D.
7. Enter the following data in row 3:

   A3: 16.0

   B3: 45.00

   D5.1 training—May 1990

8. Enter at least three more rows (4, 5, and 6) of data. Do not enter data in column C or in row 10. Assume that you provide training in WordPerfect 5.1 and other software.
9. At cell D10 type **AMOUNT DUE**.
10. At cell C3 enter a formula that multiplies cell A3 by B3. Copy the formula to cells C4 through C9. Do not copy the formula to cell C10.

11. At cell C10 enter a subtotal math operator (+).
12. Set a double line border around the outside of the table, set a double line between rows 2 and 3, set a thick line between rows 9 and 10, and shade cells C10 and D10.
13. Access View Document to see the table on-screen. Make any changes required and save the file.
14. Clear the screen and create a form billing letter to a client. After the date and salutation lines, provide a few sentences that indicate that the document is a bill. Skip several lines and then provide a few closing comments and signature lines. Save the form billing letter under a name different from the table's.
15. Retrieve the statement of services table into the current billing form letter and print the result.

Integrating Text and Graphics

19

In this lesson, you practice these tasks:

- ❑ Create a figure box, table box, and text box
- ❑ Set options for each type of box
- ❑ Import a graphic into a defined box
- ❑ Block-move text into a defined box
- ❑ Draw lines and boxes

WordPerfect 5.1 is loaded with features that help you produce high-quality, professional-looking documents. The graphics capability is perhaps the most exciting feature of version 5.1. Graphics can make a good document even better; they help you communicate ideas to the reader and make documents look exciting. The old saying that a picture is worth a thousand words has never been more true than in today's world of word processing.

With WordPerfect 5.1's line- and box-drawing feature, you can create your own graphics or import graphics from other software programs such as PC Paintbrush, Microsoft Windows Paint, GEM Paint, and Dr. HALO. You can even import graphics from drafting programs like AutoCAD or from spreadsheet programs like 1-2-3.

Desktop publishing means creating a publication-quality document by using the computer on your desk. Many of WordPerfect's features—including graphics, formatting, font management, headers and footers, and document assembly—combine to offer desktop publishing capabilities. WordPerfect is not, however, a true desktop publishing program like PageMaker or Ventura Publisher. True desktop publishing programs produce a screen image nearly identical to the printed result. When you use WordPerfect, you see the final document only when you produce hard copy or select View Document from the Print menu.

Understanding Types of Graphic Boxes

WordPerfect 5.1 supports five types of boxes, which you can use to focus the reader's attention on different types of information. The five default box types are these:

- ❑ The figure box, used to present illustrations (see fig. 19.1)

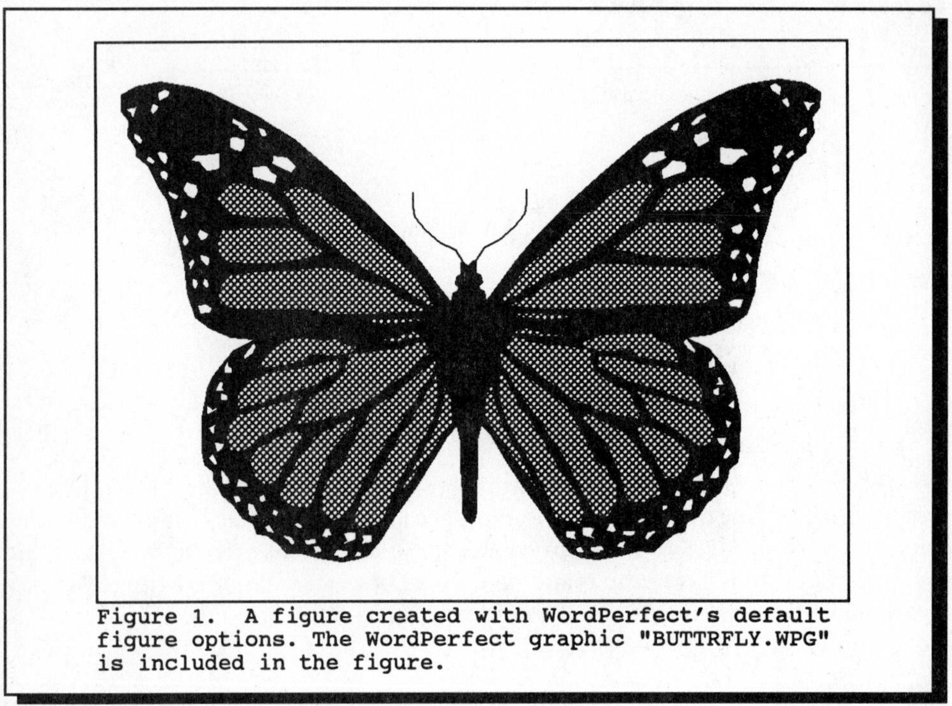

Figure 1. A figure created with WordPerfect's default figure options. The WordPerfect graphic "BUTTRFLY.WPG" is included in the figure.

Fig. 19.1. The default box for a figure.

- ❑ The table box, used to present tables of data (see fig. 19.2)

Table I. A WordPerfect table, using default options.

STAFF MEETING TIMES
July

	Dept. A	Dept. B	Dept. C
	(Mon)	(Tue)	(Wed)
Week 1	9:00am	10:00am	1:30pm
Week 2	10:00am	1:30am	3:00pm
Week 3	9:00am	10:00am	1:30pm
Week 4	10:00am	1:30pm	10:00am

Fig. 19.2. The default box for a table.

❑ The text box, used to set off quotations and excerpts from the text (see fig. 19.3)

Johannes Gutenburg, the fifteenth-century inventor of movable type, brought the written word to the public. Today, personal computers bring a new generation of publishing to the individual.

1. This is WordPerfect's text box, with a default options.

Fig. 19.3. The default box for text.

❑ The user-defined box, sometimes used to style text (see fig. 19.4)

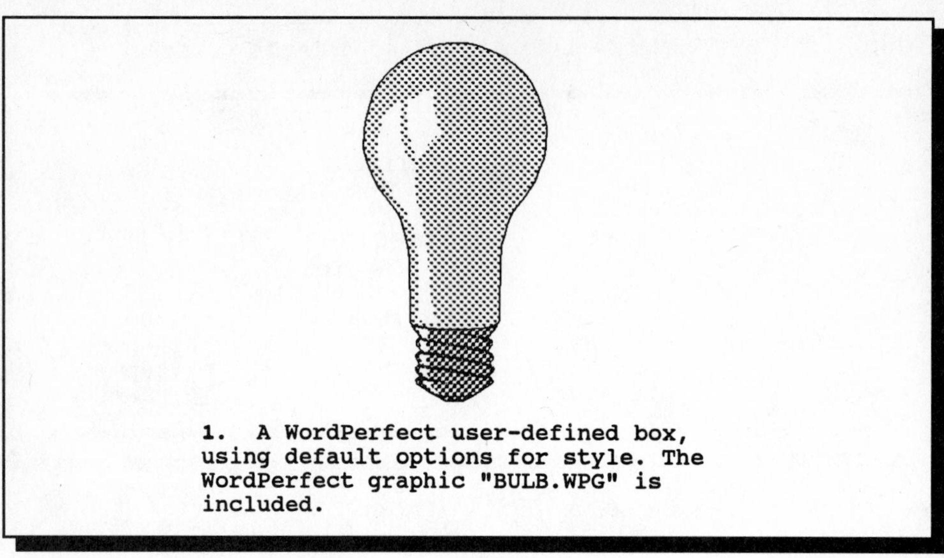

1. A WordPerfect user-defined box,
using default options for style. The
WordPerfect graphic "BULB.WPG" is
included.

Fig. 19.4. The default box for a user-defined box.

- ❑ The equation box, used to display equations created with the WordPerfect equation editor (see Chapters 22 and 27 in *Using WordPerfect 5.1*, Special Edition)

The default equation box is similar in style to the user-defined box. By default, WordPerfect centers the equation in the box. You can use many options to change each kind of box, but you create each box type by using the same steps and the same menus:

- ❑ Choose the box type, using the Graphics menu (Alt-F9).
- ❑ Choose the box options, using the Options menu (Alt-F9,4).
- ❑ Create and edit the box, using the Definition menu (Alt-F9,1).

All box types are interchangeable. You can use the figure box, for example, to display text, tables, or other user graphics. On the other hand, you can change the border style, caption, and shading of a text box to make it look like a table box. Selecting a box type simply brings to the screen a recognized or preferred "style" of borders, caption, and shading for the type of information in the box. Each box type is consecutively numbered for retrieval and caption-numbering purposes.

When you create a box, it is attached to the document. A box outline appears in the text (see fig. 19.5), but the contents of the box do not appear on-screen.

A WordPerfect Document with a Figure Attached

This is an example of what you see on the screen while editing a document with a figure attached. Notice only the outline is visible. The contents can only be seen if this document were viewed using View Document (Shift-F7, 6) or printed.

FIG 1

Doc 1 Pg 1 Ln 2" Pos 1.3"

Fig. 19.5. A screen display of a figure box.

To see the final product, access the **F**ile pull-down menu and select **P**rint (or press Shift-F7). You can then view the document by selecting **V**iew Document (**6**), print the **F**ull Document (**1**), or print the current **P**age (**2**). Figure 19.6 illustrates a printed display of a figure box.

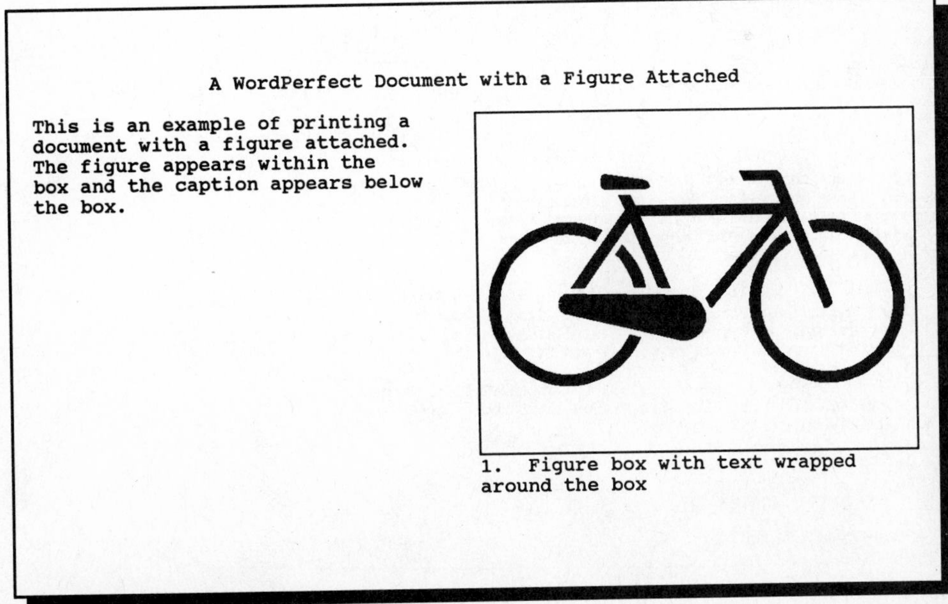

A WordPerfect Document with a Figure Attached

This is an example of printing a document with a figure attached. The figure appears within the box and the caption appears below the box.

1. Figure box with text wrapped around the box

Fig. 19.6. A printed display of a figure box.

Creating a Figure Box

You can use the figure box to dress up documents by adding one of the clip-art images on the WordPerfect Fonts/Graphics disk. For the exercises that follow, copy all files with the extension .WPG from the WordPerfect Fonts/Graphics disk to your data disk or the WordPerfect data directory on your hard disk.

Selecting the Figure Box Type

To practice adding a box to an existing document, follow these steps:

Step 1: Clear the screen without saving the current document and retrieve CLIP19A.DOC.

Note: The instruction to clear the screen without saving the current document is used many times throughout the workbook. It means to access the **File** pull-down menu and select Exit (or press F7), press **N** when prompted `Save Document? Yes (No)`, and press **N** when prompted `Exit WP?` **No (Yes)**.

Step 2: Position the cursor at the beginning of the third line in the first paragraph.

Step 3: Access the **Graphics** pull-down menu (see fig 19.7) and select **Figure** (or press Alt-F9,1).

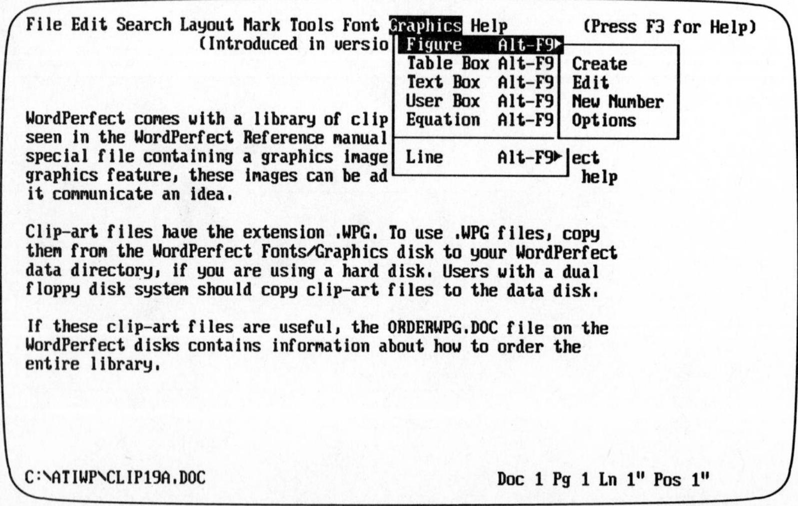

Fig. 19.7. *The Graphics pull-down menu.*

Step 4: Choose **C**reate (**1**) to access the Definition: Figure menu (see fig. 19.8).

```
Definition: Figure

     1 - Filename

     2 - Contents             Empty

     3 - Caption

     4 - Anchor Type          Paragraph

     5 - Vertical Position    0"

     6 - Horizontal Position  Right

     7 - Size                 3.25" wide x 3.25" (high)

     8 - Wrap Text Around Box Yes

     9 - Edit



Selection: 0
```

Fig. 19.8. *The Definition: Figure menu.*

The C**o**ntents (**2**) setting displays `Empty`, and several specifications have default entries such as Anchor **T**ype (Paragraph) and **H**orizontal Position (Right). You can add to, or alter, the current box definition.

Selecting the Figure Box Contents and Location

The Definition: Figure menu controls the content, position, and size of a figure with a variety of options. The following comments explain each menu selection.

To import text or a graphic image into the figure box, select **F**ilename (**1**) and enter the drive\path\filename. WordPerfect 5.1 has a setup option (see fig. 19.9) in the Setup: Location of Files menu that specifies the location of graphics files. If the graphic file you want to use is stored in this default directory, simply type the correct file name, and WordPerfect 5.1 will provide the drive/path. To check that a default directory has been specified and to change the directory if necessary, do the following:

- ❑ Access the **F**ile pull-down menu and select Set**u**p (or press Shift-F1).
- ❑ Choose **L**ocation of Files (**6**).

- ❑ Check the location of the graphic files. If no directory has been defined or the directory is incorrect, select **G**raphic Files (**6**) and type the correct directory information.
- ❑ Press Exit (F7) enough times to restore the current document.

```
Setup: Location of Files

     1 - Backup Files                    C:\WP51\BACKUP

     2 - Keyboard/Macro Files            C:\WP51\KBMAC

     3 - Thesaurus/Spell/Hyphenation
                        Main             C:\WP51\DIC51
                        Supplementary    C:\WP51\DIC51

     4 - Printer Files                   C:\WP51

     5 - Style Files                     C:\WP51\STYLES
              Library Filename           LIBRARY.STY

     6 - Graphic Files                   C:\WP51\GRAPH51

     7 - Documents                       C:\WP51\QUE51




Selection: 0
```

Fig. 19.9. *A sample display of the default graphic files directory.*

Select C**o**ntents (**2**) to specify that the figure will contain a graphic, a graphic on disk, text, or an equation.

Choose **C**aption (**3**) to specify a figure description, and select Anchor **T**ype (**4**) to attach the box to the document text. The default anchor type, Paragraph, indicates that the box remains with its associated paragraph, even if the paragraph is moved. A box may also be anchored to a page or character.

Vertical Position (**5**) and **H**orizontal Position (**6**) control the placement of the box on the page; select **S**ize (**6**) to adjust the width and height of the box.

Wrap Text Around Box (**8**) causes text outside the box to surround the box so that the box appears set in the text.

Edit (**9**) has two functions. If the figure is a graphic image, Edit permits you to move the image within the figure box, change the size of the figure, or rotate the image. If the figure is text or if the box is empty, a screen is presented so that you can enter and edit text.

To insert a picture of a computer (one of 30 images provided as .WPG files by WordPerfect) into existing text, follow these steps:

Step 1: Choose **F**ilename (**1**) from the Definition: Figure menu, and when prompted `Enter filename:`, type **PC-1.WPG** and press Enter. The **C**ontents (**2**) setting switches automatically to `Graphic`.

Note: If your .WPG files are not in the current graphics directory, precede PC-1.WPG with the disk drive and path where the .WPG files are located.

Step 2: Choose **C**aption (**3**) and notice the flashing cursor after `Figure 1` at the top of the screen and the prompt `Box Caption:` at the bottom of the screen.

Step 3: Type a period (.) followed by a space; then type **Clip-art for the PC**.

Step 4: Press Exit (F7) enough times to restore the current document.

Step 5: Press Screen (Ctrl-F3) and select **R**ewrite (**3**) or press Home, down arrow to view the outline of the figure box on the screen.

Step 6: Access the **F**ile pull-down menu and select **P**rint (or press Shift-F7); then select **P**age (**2**) to print the figure box and surrounding text. (If you do not want to print, you can view the figure by using the **V**iew Document option from the Print menu.)

The current document now has a picture of a microcomputer attached to the first paragraph. After the PC-1.WPG graphic image was imported into the figure box (Step 1), you specified the figure contents (Step 2), added a caption (Steps 3 and 4), and rewrote the screen to bring the figure outline onto the screen (Step 6). Figure 19.10 illustrates the integration of text and graphics in a figure box that you see after executing Step 7.

WORDPERFECT CLIP-ART LIBRARY

WordPerfect comes with a library of clip-art images which can be seen in the WordPerfect Reference manual. A clip-art image is a special file containing a graphics image. Using the WordPerfect graphics feature, these images can be added to a document to help it communicate an idea.

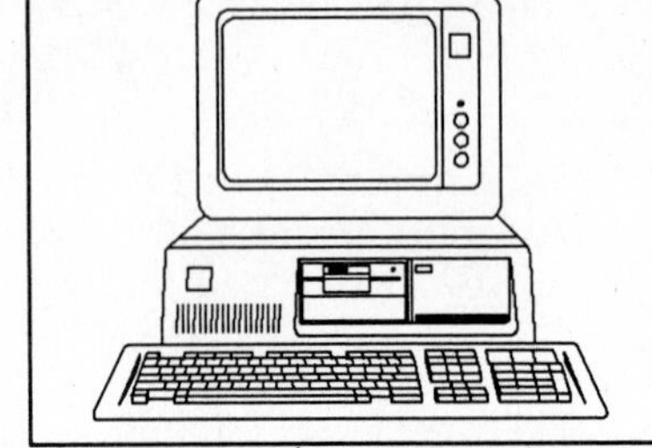

Figure 1. Clip-art for the PC

Clip-art files have the extension .WPG. To use .WPG files, copy them from the WordPerfect Fonts/Graphics disk to your WordPerfect graphics directory, if you are using a hard disk. Users with a dual floppy disk system should copy clip-art files to the data disk.

If these clip-art files are useful, an entire library of clip-art can be ordered. Ordering instructions should be included with your WordPerfect 5.1 software. If not, a call to WordPerfect's 800 number should get you information about how to order additional clip-art.

Fig. 19.10. The figure box in the default right-side position.

Changing the Figure Box Size

LESSON FILES

As you continue to enter text around a figure, you may need to change the size of the figure box. When you do, the figure inside the box is increased or decreased proportionately. You have the option of changing both width and height. Or you can change only the width or height, and the other will automatically be set. To change the width of the figure box in CLIP19B.DOC and let WordPerfect 5.1 change the height automatically, follow these steps:

Step 1: Clear the screen without saving the current document and retrieve CLIP19B.DOC.

Step 2: Access the **G**raphics pull-down menu, select **F**igure, and choose **E**dit (or press Alt-F9,1,2).

Step 3: When prompted `Figure number?`, type **1** and press Enter.

Step 4: Choose **S**ize (7) and notice the appearance of size menu options across the bottom of the screen (see fig. 19.11).

```
1 Set Width/Auto Height; 2 Set Height/Auto Width; 3 Set Both; 4 Auto Both: 0
```

Fig. 19.11. Menu options for setting the size of a graphics box.

Step 5: Choose Set **W**idth/Auto Height (**1**).

Step 6: When prompted `Width = 3.25"`, type **2.5** and press Enter.

Step 7: Press Exit (F7) enough times to restore the current document screen.

You can print or view the document to verify the change in figure size and the redistribution of text around the smaller figure.

Creating a Text Box

The text box (see fig. 19.3) usually contains excerpts from the typed text highlighted to emphasize a main point of the document. The contents of the box are usually shaded. The side borders are missing, but top and bottom borders are thick lines.

Creating a text box requires nearly the same process as creating a figure box. After you select the box type and attach it to the text, you can either type, retrieve, or move the contents into the box and then edit. You can type text into the box or retrieve it from an external file by using List Files (F5), **R**etrieve (**1**). You can also move or copy text into the box from elsewhere in the current document.

TEXTBX19.DOC contains a small left- and right-indented paragraph announcing a reception. In the next exercise, emphasize the indented paragraph by creating a text box and moving the reception information into the box.

Selecting and Positioning the Text Box Type

To create and position a text box, follow these steps:

Step 1: Clear the screen without saving the current document and retrieve TEXTBX19.DOC.

Step 2: Position the cursor on the line that precedes the announcement of a reception—the line beginning "`A reception will be held....`"

Step 3: Press Enter to insert eight blank lines to make room for the default text box size (six lines).

Step 4: Position the cursor two lines below the text describing Sam Weist, Director of Security..., in order to mark the location of a text box.

Step 5: Access the **G**raphics pull-down menu, select Text **B**ox, and choose **C**reate (or press Alt-F9,3,1).

Note: **F**ilename (**1**) and **C**aption (**3**) are left blank when you incorporate text from the current document in the text box. C**o**ntents (**2**) automatically displays Text.

Step 6: Choose Anchor **T**ype (**4**), choose **P**age (**2**) to anchor the box to the current page, and press Enter when prompted `Number of pages to skip: 0`.

Step 7: Choose **V**ertical Position (**5**), choose **S**et Position (**5**), and when prompted `Offset from top of page: 4.5"`, press Enter to accept the current cursor position.

Note: In Step 4 you moved the cursor to a position four and a half inches from the top of the page. WordPerfect displays the current cursor position (in this case, `4.5"`) as the suggested location (offset) for the text box. You can, of course, type a different location and then press Enter.

Step 8: Choose **H**orizontal Position (**6**); then choose **M**argins (**1**) and **C**enter (**3**).

Step 9: If necessary, set **W**rap Text Around Box (**8**) to **Y**es.

Step 10: Press Exit (F7) enough times to restore the current document display.

Step 11: Press Screen: Rewrite (Ctrl-F3,3).

The box outline appears on-screen. Here's what you did as you created the text box: you retrieved TEXTBX19.DOC, moved existing text to make room for the box, and positioned the cursor to mark the location of the box (Steps 1–4); next you chose the type of box (Step 5), anchored the text (Step 6), and fixed the exact location of the box (Steps 7–8); finally you turned on the wrap-text feature, exited the graphics feature, and rewrote the screen to produce the box outline (Steps 9–11).

Using Move and Edit To Enter Text Box Contents

Use Block Move with Text Box Edit to move into the box the text announcing the reception. At the prompt `Move cursor; press Enter to retrieve`, select Graphics, select the menu option to edit the text box, and press Enter to complete the move operation and place the blocked text with the text box. If you want to retain the blocked text in its original position in the document and also display the blocked text within a text box, use Copy instead of Move. To move blocked contents to the text box created in the preceding exercise, follow these steps:

Step 1: Move the cursor to the `A` of the indented reception invitation (`A reception will be held...`), access the **E**dit pull-down menu and select **B**lock (or press Alt-F4 or F12), and highlight the double-indented paragraph below the outline of the text box (the paragraph providing reception details).

Step 2: Press Ctrl-Del to "cut" the blocked text for a Move operation.

Step 3: When prompted `Move cursor; press Enter to retrieve`, access the **G**raphics pull-down menu, choose Text **B**ox, and then choose **E**dit (or press Alt-F9,3,2).

Step 4: When prompted `Text Box number?`, type **1** and press Enter to access the Definition: Text Box menu.

Step 5: Press **E**dit (**9**) to access the text box editing screen.

Step 6: Press Enter to complete the move and thus insert the text from the document into the text box.

Step 7: Exit (F7) enough times to restore the current document screen.

Step 8: Access the **F**ile pull-down menu and select **P**rint (or press Shift-F7); then select **P**age (**2**) to print the page (see fig. 19.12). As an alternative, you can select **V**iew Document (**6**) and then 100% (**1**) to adjust the screen and see the final document more clearly.

A shaded text box appears when you print or view the page containing the reception announcement. You just initiated a block move on the paragraph to be moved inside the text box (Steps 1–2), accessed the text box editing screen (Steps 3–5), completed the move (Steps 6–7), and printed or viewed the final document (Step 8).

```
                                              January 16, 1990

                          Announcement

     I am pleased to announce that we have hired several new
people to fill vacancies in the firm.  Please join me in
welcoming them to the company.


John Fox, Director of Marketing, West coast region.  John joins
     us from the Weber Corporation, where he was Assistant
     Marketing Director.

Linda Ann, Office Manager, Indianapolis office.   Linda joins us
     from a local firm where she was in charge of office
     administration and payroll.

Sam Weist, Director of Security, Midwest region. Sam joins us
     from a local security firm.


                  A reception will be held for
                  our new people in the
                  conference room, Friday,
                  January 19.  All employees
                  are invited.


L. C. Tyrant
Director of Personnel
```

Fig. 19.12. *An announcement with a text box.*

Creating a Table Box

LESSON FILES

Table boxes resemble text boxes in style and borders but differ in their shading and captions. A table of regional sales quotas, TBLBOX19.TBL, is prepared for you to integrate into a TBLBOX19.DOC memo to regional directors.

To incorporate TBLBOX19.TBL into TBLBOX19.DOC, retrieve the second of the two documents, position the cursor where the box is to be located, access Graphics, and select the type of box you want. Follow these steps:

Step 1: Clear the screen without saving the current document and retrieve TBLBOX19.DOC.

Step 2: Position the cursor two lines below the last line of the memo.

Step 3: Access the **G**raphics pull-down menu, choose **T**able Box, and then choose **C**reate (or press Alt-F9,2,1).

Step 4: Choose **F**ilename (**1**), type **TBLBOX19.TBL**, and press Enter.

Step 5: Choose **C**aption (**3**), type a period (.) followed by two spaces, type **Seasonally Adjusted Quotas**, and press Exit (F7) once.

Step 6: Choose Anchor **T**ype (**4**) and then choose **P**age (**2**) to anchor the box; when prompted `Number of Pages to skip:`, type **0** and press Enter.

Step 7: Choose **V**ertical Position (**5**), choose **S**et Position (**5**), and when prompted `Offset from top of page:`, press Enter to accept the current cursor position.

Step 8: Choose **H**orizontal Position (**6**), choose **M**argins (**1**), and choose **F**ull (**4**).

Step 9: Choose **W**rap Text Around Box (**8**) and press **N**.

Step 10: Press Exit (F7) enough times to restore the current document display.

Note: If **W**rap Text Around Box (**8**) is set to `No`, the outline of the box does not appear on the screen. Use Reveal Codes mode to view the code.

Step 11: Access the **F**ile pull-down menu and select **P**rint (or press Shift-F7); then select **P**age (**2**) to print the page illustrated in figure 19.13. As an alternative, select **V**iew Document (**6**) from the Print menu to view the table box on the screen.

Memorandum

To: All Regional Directors

From: Al Bottomline, Vice President, Finance

Subject: Quarterly Sales Targets

Quarterly sales targets by region are outlined below. Please review these figures and be prepared to discuss them at the directors' meeting next month.

Table I. Seasonally Adjusted Quotas

Regional Quarterly Sales Projections
in Units

Region	Qtr 1	Qtr 2	Qtr 3	Qtr 4
West	640	600	590	680
Midwest	820	790	810	940
East	580	560	560	610
Southwest	750	750	750	750
Southeast	540	590	610	700
U. S. Totals	3,330	3,290	3,320	3,680

Fig. 19.13. *A memorandum with a table box.*

Step 12: Press Exit (F7) enough times to restore the current document display.

You retrieved TBLBOX19.DOC and moved the cursor to your planned table box location (Steps 1–2); you chose the type of box (Step 3); you selected and integrated the file, wrote a caption, and anchored the text to the page (Steps 4–6); you fixed the exact location of the box, set Wrap Text Around Box off, exited from graphics mode, and printed or viewed the table box (Steps 7–12).

You just worked through brief exercises in creating three (of five) WordPerfect boxes: figure, text, and table. Once you create boxes, you can edit box contents and box display features.

Editing Boxes

You can change the display characteristics of boxes or change the content of boxes. Figure 19.14 illustrates the Options: Table screen that appears when you access the

Graphics pull-down menu, select **T**able Box, and select **O**ptions (or press Alt-F9,2,4). A similar screen appears if you select an alternative box type.

```
Options: Table Box

     1 - Border Style
              Left                       None
              Right                      None
              Top                        Thick
              Bottom                     Thick
     2 - Outside Border Space
              Left                       0.167"
              Right                      0.167"
              Top                        0.167"
              Bottom                     0.167"
     3 - Inside Border Space
              Left                       0.167"
              Right                      0.167"
              Top                        0.167"
              Bottom                     0.167"
     4 - First Level Numbering Method    Roman
     5 - Second Level Numbering Method   Off
     6 - Caption Number Style            [BOLD]Table 1[bold]
     7 - Position of Caption             Above box, Outside borders
     8 - Minimum Offset from Paragraph   0"
     9 - Gray Shading (% of black)       0%

Selection: 0
```

Fig. 19.14. *The Options: Table Box menu.*

Using the Options menu, you can change the style of border, change the distance between the border and text (the gutter), number captions, set a default value, and control box shading for the type of box selected. When you finish specifying your options, WordPerfect inserts an open code (for example, **[Tbl Opt]** for a table box), and the settings remain in effect until another box option code is encountered in the document.

The **E**dit (**9**) feature on the definition screen for a specific box allows you to change the text content of the box or alter the display of the graphic image in the box. If the box contains a graphic image, Edit lets you adjust the scale of a graphic image on both the X- and Y-axis, move the image within the box, and change the rotation of the image.

Changing the Display Characteristics for a Box Type

To change three display settings for all table box figures in the current document by accessing the Graphics Options screen for table boxes (see fig. 19.14), follow these steps:

Step 1: Clear the screen without saving the current document and retrieve EDIT19.TBL.

Step 2: Access the **G**raphics pull-down menu, choose **T**able Box, and then choose **O**ptions (or press Alt-F9,2,4).

Step 3: Select **F**irst Level Numbering Method (**4**) and choose **L**etters (**3**).

Step 4: Select **P**osition of Caption (**7**), choose **B**elow Box (**1**), and choose **O**utside of Border (**1**).

Step 5: Select **G**ray Shading (% of black) (**9**), type **5**, and press Enter.

Step 6: Press Exit (F7) enough times to restore the current document display.

Step 7: Access the **F**ile pull-down menu and select **P**rint (or press Shift-F7); then select **P**age (**2**) to print the table display revisions. As an alternative, select **V**iew Document (**6**) from the Print menu to view the table box on the screen.

Compare the results of your Step 7 to figure 19.13. The table caption appears below the table instead of above the table; the caption is labeled Table A. instead of Table I. In addition, the current version of the document appears lightly shaded.

Changing the Caption and Content of a Specific Box

In an earlier exercise in the figure box section, you changed the size of a specific figure box after accessing the Definition: Figure screen (see fig. 19.8) and selecting **S**ize (7) to display the size options (see fig. 19.11). Other choices on the definition screen affect display as well: including Anchor **T**ype, **V**ertical Position, **H**orizontal Position, and **W**rap Text Around Box. Two options apply to the text or graphics contents associated with the box: select **C**aption to edit a previously defined caption; select **E**dit to edit text content or alter a graphic image (move the image within the box, change the size of the image, or rotate the image).

To change the caption and content of the table box in the current document, follow these steps:

Step 1: Access the **G**raphics pull-down menu, choose **T**able Box, and then choose **E**dit (or press Alt-F9,2,2).

Step 2: In response to the prompt `Table Box number?`, type **A** and press Enter.

Step 3: Select **C**aption (**3**) and change the caption `Seasonally Adjusted Quotas` to **Seasonally Adjusted Goals**.

Step 4: Press Exit (F7) once to restore the Definition: Table Box screen.

Step 5: Select **Edit** (9), change `West` to **West Coast** and `East` to **East Coast.**

Step 6: Press Exit (F7) enough times to restore the current document screen.

Step 7: Access the **File** pull-down menu and select **Print** (or press Shift-F7); then select **Page** (2) to print the table caption and content revisions. As an alternative, select **View** Document (6) from the Print menu to view the table box on the screen.

Step 8: Press Exit (F7) enough times to restore the current document screen.

Using Line Draw To Create Lines and Boxes

WordPerfect's Line Draw feature (Ctrl-F3,2) provides a quick way to draw lines through the use of cursor arrows. You can specify single or double lines of various shadings and create a line composed of symbols, such as a dollar sign ($).

You can combine vertical and horizontal lines into shapes by using Line Draw. Exercise caution when you create a shape with arrow keys; you may accidentally type over it during later editing.

Drawing Lines

Because of its free-form capability, Line Draw is ideal for drawing organizational charts and other odd-shaped graphics. When you press Screen (Ctrl-F3), Line Draw (**2**), you see a menu on the status line. You may select one of three symbols for drawing lines. The next option, Change (**4**), opens another menu with even more graphics symbols that you can use for drawing. Use Erase (**5**) to draw over previously drawn lines and erase them. Move (**6**) turns off the current drawing symbol (without turning off Line Draw) so that the cursor can be moved.

The following exercise is not like previous exercises in which each step was a specific action to be taken. Several of the following steps instruct you to select a Line Draw option and then practice drawing lines until you are comfortable using the option.

To draw lines, perform these steps:

Step 1: Clear the screen without saving the current document.

Step 2: Access the **Tools** pull-down menu and choose **Line Draw** (or press Ctrl-F3,2).

Step 3: Press the right-, down-, left-, and up-arrow keys to practice drawing lines with the default single line character (**1**).

Step 4: Select **2** from the Line Draw menu at the bottom of the screen to produce a double line, or select **3** for a line composed of asterisks. Practice drawing lines and shapes.

Step 5: Select **M**ove (**6**) from the Line Draw menu, move the cursor to another location, select a drawing symbol, and practice drawing lines.

Step 6: Move the cursor onto a line that has been drawn, press **Erase** (**5**), and draw back over the line to erase it.

Step 7: Select **C**hange (**4**). Choose any of the eight graphics symbols and practice drawing lines.

Note: The option you choose becomes the third option on the main Line Draw menu.

Step 8: Select **C**hange (**4**) and then **O**ther (**9**); when prompted `Solid character`, type any keyboard character for drawing (the **$**, perhaps). Practice drawing lines.

Step 9: Press Exit (F7) to exit from Line Draw mode.

Using Macros To Draw Shapes

If you frequently use Line Draw mode to create the same shape, consider capturing the keystrokes in a macro (see Lesson 10). For example, if you develop an organizational chart, creating a box each time you need one is difficult and time-consuming. Quite often the boxes are different sizes. You can, however, simplify drawing charts by creating a macro to draw boxes.

Creating a Box Macro

To create a macro to draw a single box, follow these steps:

Step 1: Clear the screen without saving the current document.

Step 2: Access the **T**ools pull-down menu, choose M**a**cro, and then choose **D**efine (or press Ctrl-F10).

Step 3: When prompted `Define macro:`, type **box** and press Enter.

Step 4: When prompted `Description:`, type **rectangular shape** and press Enter.

Step 5: With `Macro def` blinking on the status line, press Screen (Ctrl-F3) and select **L**ine Draw (**2**).

Step 6: Choose (**1**) to create a single line.

Step 7: With the cursor in the upper left corner of the screen, press the following keys in sequence:

Right arrow 15 times

Down arrow 5 times

Left arrow 15 times

Up arrow 5 times

Exit (F7)

Home, Home, down arrow

Enter

Note: If all goes well, a rectangle appears in the upper left corner of the screen, with the cursor positioned at the left margin below the rectangle.

Step 8: Press Macro Define (Ctrl-F10) to turn macro off.

You just created a macro that draws a rectangle 15 characters wide and 5 lines high. You accessed a clear screen (Step 1); defined a macro called box (Steps 2–4); turned on Line Draw (Steps 5–6); drew a rectangle, terminated Line Draw, and positioned the cursor below the rectangle (Step 7); and turned off Macro Define (Step 8).

Drawing Boxes with a Macro

Drawing with the box macro is the easy (and fun) part. Simply place the cursor where you want the upper left corner of a rectangle to appear and press Macro. Follow these steps to create a single centered box on the first layer of an organizational chart and three more boxes on the second layer of the chart:

Step 1: Clear the screen without saving the current document.

Step 2: Access the **L**ayout pull-down menu and select **L**ine (or press Shift-F8,1), select **M**argins (7), type **.5** as the left margin and press Enter, and then type **.5** as the right margin and press Enter.

Step 3: With the cursor in the upper left corner of the screen, access the **L**ayout pull-down menu, select **A**lign, and then choose **C**enter (or press Shift-F6).

Step 4: Type **Organizational Chart**, press Enter three times, and press Center (Shift-F6).

Step 5: Access the **T**ools pull-down menu, select M**a**cro, and select E**x**ecute (or press Alt-F10).

Step 6: When prompted `Macro:`, type **box** and press Enter to produce a box centered on-screen.

Step 7: Move the cursor four lines below the bottom of the first box.

Step 8: Repeat Steps 5 and 6 to produce a second box at the left margin below the first box.

Step 9: Move the cursor to the top line of the box just drawn, press End, and press the space bar until the cursor lines up with the left edge of the box above.

Step 10: Repeat Steps 5 and 6 to produce a third box directly beneath the first box.

Step 11: Move the cursor to the top line of the box just drawn, press End, press the space bar 13 times, and repeat Steps 5 and 6 to produce a fourth box.

You have just drawn a blank organizational chart. Before you edit the chart to include titles and names, save the document to disk so that if anything goes wrong, you do not have to re-create the entire chart. If a problem occurs in the following set of steps, clear the screen and retrieve ORGCHART.DOC; begin again with Step 1.

Step 1: Press Save (F10), type the file name **ORGCHART.DOC**, and press Enter.

Step 2: Move the cursor into the top box by using the cursor-arrow keys and turn on typeover mode by pressing the Ins key until the `Typeover` prompt appears in the status line.

Step 3: Position the cursor near the inside left edge of the box and type **PRESIDENT**.

Step 4: Position the cursor on the next line inside the top box and type your own name.

Step 5: Type similar entries of your choice in the three boxes on the next level.

Step 6: Use Line Draw to draw connecting lines from the top box to the three boxes on the next level.

Line Draw is useful for creating odd graphics such as organizational charts. When you create tables, figures, and boxes of text, however, use Graphics (Alt-F9).

Creating a Graphics Line

The WordPerfect 5.1 Graphics feature provides a line option as well as five box options. Use the line option to create vertical and horizontal lines in a document. At the time you insert a graphics line in a document, you specify the length, width, and a percent of shading for the line. You can, for example, create a vertical line as a margin rule on note paper. Or you can create a horizontal line within a heading to separate clearly the heading from the remainder of the page.

Lesson 15 contains instructions to number items on a list within a document. Often business and legal documents require that each line be numbered. WordPerfect provides a line numbering format option that numbers blocked text or an entire document.

To create a page with all lines numbered and a vertical graphics line simulating a margin, perform the following steps:

Step 1: Clear the screen without saving the current document and retrieve the NUMBER19.DOC document.

Step 2: Press Home, Home, up arrow to position the cursor at the top of the page.

Step 3: Access the **L**ayout menu and select **L**ine (or press Shift-F8,1), choose Line **N**umbering (**5**), and press **Y**.

Step 4: At the Format: Line Numbering menu, press Exit (F7) to accept the default settings and restore the current document display.

Step 5: Access the **G**raphics pull-down menu, select **L**ine, and choose Create **V**ertical (or press Alt-F9,5,2).

Step 6: When prompted with the Graphics: Vertical Line menu, press Exit (F7) to accept the default settings and restore the current document display.

Step 7: Access the **F**ile pull-down menu and select **P**rint (or press Shift-F7); then select **P**age (**2**) to print the document containing a vertical graphics line and line numbering. As an alternative, select **V**iew Document (**6**) from the Print menu to view the vertical line and line numbering on the screen.

Step 8: Press Exit (F7) enough times to restore the current document display.

Figure 19.15 shows the resulting document.

January 16, 1990

Mr. Fred S. Gefeldt
Artesian Systems, Inc.
560 West Esteban Circle
Amazon, OK 78118

Dear Fred:

Crimson Travel & Tours is introducing a new corporate reservations department. We promise a prompt response to your questions about schedules and free delivery of tickets to your office or home.

The agents assigned to this department know that you have a very busy schedule. Their goal is to ensure that your trip is worry free and that you arrive on time at your destination. Our cruise specialists can assist with incentive as well as pleasure tours.

We guarantee you the best service. Call us the next time your itinerary takes you across the state or around the world.

Sincerely,

Aimee Lockyer
Senior Account Representative

Fig. 19.15. *Continuous line numbering and graphics vertical line.*

In this lesson you created three of five graphics boxes, made changes to a specific box by using three options on the box definition menu, made three changes to display characteristics for a specified box type, learned to use the Line Draw feature, and created a graphics line. Becoming comfortable with using the WordPerfect graphics and drawing features just requires practice.

For Further Reference

If you would like to know more about integrating text and graphics, consult *Using WordPerfect 5.1*, Special Edition (Que Corporation, Carmel, IN, 1989), Chapters 27 and 28.

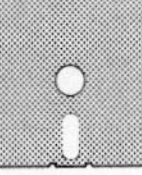

Summary of Concepts

Lesson 19 explains these concepts:

- ❑ Graphics and Line Draw are part of WordPerfect's desktop publishing capabilities.
- ❑ WordPerfect offers five types of graphics boxes that you may insert in a document to enhance information: figure, table, text, user-defined and equation.
- ❑ The five types of graphics boxes function in a similar manner. They differ only in their default border and shading styles and in their caption formats. Each is numbered separately by WordPerfect.
- ❑ A figure box is used primarily to hold graphics such as the clip-art images provided with WordPerfect or graphics images created by several popular software products such as 1-2-3.
- ❑ A table box accents a table of data. The default format for a table box is a box with thick lines on the top and bottom and no lines on the sides.
- ❑ A text box is generally used to accent an excerpt of text. The box format is similar to the table box except that the background is shaded.
- ❑ A user-defined box is not limited in its use and by default has no border or shading.
- ❑ An equation box is used to display equations created by the equation editor.
- ❑ Use Line Draw to produce straight-line graphics composed of single or double lines of varying widths and shadings or lines composed of keyboard symbols.

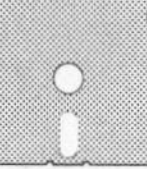

Review Exercises

LESSON FILES

Practice using the WordPerfect features in this lesson by completing these exercises. If you do not remember how to do something, review the preceding explanations and practice steps. Use View Document (Shift-F7,6) frequently to see how the final document is progressing. If your monitor does not, however, display a readable View Document, you may have to print the document.

1. Clear the screen without saving the current document and retrieve STATES19.LST.
2. Create a figure box and anchor it to the first paragraph. Use the default vertical and horizontal positions and make sure that word wrap is on. Exit to the current document.
3. Rewrite the screen to see an outline of the figure.
4. Access Graphics and edit the figure box just created to include the file name CLOCK.WPG and the caption "TIME TO TRAVEL."
5. Look at the document by using View Document; then print the document.
6. Clear the screen without saving the current document and create a short memo to employees about a vacation schedule. Create a table box at the bottom of the memo. Select **E**dit (**9**) from the Definition: Table Box menu and type a list of holidays. Type the name of the holiday in the first column and the date in a second column.
7. View the vacation-schedule document, make necessary changes, and then print a copy.
8. Using Line Draw, create a macro that draws a rectangle 10 characters wide and 3 lines high.
9. Start to create a "family tree" by typing your own name in a centered box drawn by the macro created in summary exercise 9. Save the partially completed document as FAMTREE.DOC.
10. Complete two more levels in the family tree to indicate your parents and grandparents, and print the result (remember to save your work frequently during the creation process).
11. Clear the screen without saving the current document, retrieve TBLBOX19.DOC, create a horizontal graphics line beneath the word Memorandum, and print or use View Document to see the results.

Appendix A

Installing the Disk Tutor and Lesson Files

WordPerfect PC Tutor includes a 5 1/4-inch, 360K diskette that contains the ATI Disk Tutor and the disk files that are used in the book lessons.

This disk, however, cannot be used "as is." To use the files on this disk, you must install them on either your hard disk or on two floppy disks (if you have a dual floppy disk system). This procedure is quite easy because the installation program is almost totally automatic.

Floppy Disk System Installation

If you have a dual floppy disk system, you first need to prepare two blank diskettes before the installation process. Follow these steps:

Step 1: Start your computer as usual.

Step 2: Format a blank diskette, label it "ATI Disk Tutor," and set it aside.

Step 3: Format another disk and label it "WordPerfect PC Tutor Lessons Disk."

Note: If you are using a computer system with two 3 1/2-inch, 720K diskette drives, you have the option of formatting only one disk; there is enough space on it for the Disk Tutor and the lesson files.

To install the Disk Tutor and lesson files using a dual floppy disk system, follow these steps:

Step 1: Replace the diskette in drive A that you used to boot your computer with the WordPerfect PC Tutor Disk that was supplied with this book.

Step 2: At the A> prompt, type **INSTALL** and press Enter. This will display a brief introduction screen.

Step 3: Press any key to go on to the next screen, which is the Installation Menu shown in Figure A-1.

```
*** INSTALLATION MENU ***

1 - Install to Hard Disk.
2 - Install to Floppy Disk.
3 - Quit Installation.

Select 1, 2, or 3
```

***Fig. A-1.** Installation Menu.*

If for any reason you do not wish to continue the installation program, just press **3** to abort.

Step 4: Because you are using a two floppy disk system, press **2**.

Step 5: The install program will now instruct you to place the formatted disk labeled "ATI Disk Tutor" into drive B and to press any key.

The install program will now decompress the Disk Tutor files and place them on drive B, so you can just sit back and relax.

Step 6: When prompted to do so, replace the disk in drive B with the WordPerfect PC Tutor Lessons Disk and press any key.

Note: If you are using a computer system with two 3 1/2-inch, 720K diskette drives, you have the option of simply leaving the ATI Disk Tutor disk in drive B; there is enough space on it for all the lesson files. The install program will now copy the lesson files that will be used throughout this book, so you can once again sit back and relax while the computer does the work.

Step 7: When the installation process is complete, you will see the screen displayed in Fig. A-2.

```
Floppy disk installation complete. If you
would like to start the ATI Disk Tutor,
put the disk labeled "ATI Disk Tutor" in
drive B, type ATI, and press Enter.
```

Fig. A-2. *Floppy disk installation complete message.*

Place the WordPerfect PC Tutor Disk into its sleeve and put it in a safe place. If you would like to start the ATI Disk Tutor, put the disk labeled "ATI Disk Tutor" back in drive B, type **ATI**, and press Enter. Follow the instructions in Lesson 1 to begin using the Disk Tutor.

Hard Disk System Installation

If you have a hard disk system, turn on your computer as you usually do. Then follow these steps to install the Disk Tutor and lesson files onto your hard disk:

Step 1: Place the WordPerfect PC Tutor Disk that was supplied with this book into drive A. Change to drive A by typing **A:** and pressing Enter.

Step 2: At the A> prompt, type **INSTALL** and press Enter. This will display a brief introduction screen.

Step 3: Press any key to go on to the next screen, which is the Installation Menu shown in Figure A-1.

If for any reason you do not wish to continue the installation program, just press **3** to abort.

Step 4: Because you are using a hard disk system, press **1**.

The Install program will tell you that it is creating a subdirectory and decompressing and copying files, so you can just sit back and relax.

Step 5: When the installation process is complete, you will see the screen displayed in Fig. A-3.

```
Hard disk installation complete. If you
would like to start the ATI Disk Tutor,
just type ATI and press Enter.
```

Fig. A-3. *Hard disk installation complete message.*

Place the WordPerfect PC Tutor Disk into its sleeve and put it in a safe place. You can go ahead and type **ATI** and press Enter to start the Disk Tutor. Follow the instructions in Lesson 1 to begin using the Disk Tutor.

Important Note:

If you accidentally delete material in a file, save a file when not directed to in a lesson, or delete a file entirely, you can restore the file by reinstalling the "WordPerfect PC Tutor Disk." To make the reinstallation quicker and easier, first delete all the Disk Tutor and lesson files from your "working" disks or hard drive subdirectory. Then follow the installation directions at the beginning of this appendix.

Appendix B

Lesson Files

The 76 lesson files are listed here in alphabetical order. Each file name contains the number of the lesson in which it is used. Files created by tutorial users are assigned names that do *not* contain the lesson number.

File Name	*Lesson*	*File Name*	*Lesson*
ANNOUNC6.DOC	Lesson 6	CRIMSON3.LTR	Lesson 3
ANNOUNC9.DOC	Lesson 9	CRIMSON3.TOP	Lesson 3
BIRTH13.LST	Lesson 13	CRIMSON4.LTR	Lesson 4
BLKSRT13.DOC	Lesson 13	CRIMSON5.LTR	Lesson 5
CLIP19A.DOC	Lesson 19	CRIMSON5.TOP	Lesson 5
CLIP19B.DOC	Lesson 19	CRIMSON6.LTR	Lesson 6
COL3-16.DOC	Lesson 16	CRIMSON6.TOP	Lesson 6
CONDEOP7.LST	Lesson 7	CRIMSON7.LTR	Lesson 7
COPYEX5	Lesson 5	CRIMSON9.LTR	Lesson 9
COVER14.MRK	Lesson 14	CRIMSO10.LTR	Lesson 10
COVER7.DOC	Lesson 7	DELNO15.DOC	Lesson 15
CRIM12A.PRI	Lesson 12	DOCREF14.EX	Lesson 14
CRIM12A.SEC	Lesson 12	EDFOOT15.DOC	Lesson 15
CRIMSO11.LTR	Lesson 11	EDIT19.TBL	Lesson 19
CRIMSO12.LTR	Lesson 12	ENDNO15.DOC	Lesson 15

File Name	Lesson	File Name	Lesson
EXRCIS10.DOC	Lesson 10	PAGES7.LST	Lesson 7
EXERCISE.15	Lesson 15	PAGES10.DOC	Lesson 10
FOOTEN15.DOC	Lesson 15	PAGESNR7.LST	Lesson 7
FOOTNO15.DOC	Lesson 15	PRES13.MRG	Lesson 13
GETTY16.ADD	Lesson 16	RATIFY13.LST	Lesson 13
INDEX14.DOC	Lesson 14	SEARCH4.DOC	Lesson 4
INDEX14.MRK	Lesson 14	SPELL8.CHK	Lesson 8
LEVEL16.DOC	Lesson 16	SPELL8.LTR	Lesson 8
LIST14.DOC	Lesson 14	STATES13.LST	Lesson 13
LIST14.MRK	Lesson 14	STATES19.LST	Lesson 19
MEMO8.THE	Lesson 8	STATES4.LST	Lesson 4
MOVING5.LTR	Lesson 5	TBL18A.DOC	Lesson 18
MULTIPG4.LST	Lesson 4	TBL18B.DOC	Lesson 18
MVFOOT15.DOC	Lesson 15	TBL18C.DOC	Lesson 18
NEWS16.001	Lesson 16	TBL18D.DOC	Lesson 18
NUMBER15.LST	Lesson 15	TBL18E.DOC	Lesson 18
NUMBER19.DOC	Lesson 19	TBLBOX19.DOC	Lesson 19
OFFICES5.LST	Lesson 5	TBLBOX19.TBL	Lesson 19
OFFICES7.LST	Lesson 7	TEXTBX19.DOC	Lesson 19
OUTL15A.DOC	Lesson 15	TOC14.DEF	Lesson 14
OUTL15B.DOC	Lesson 15	TOC14.DOC	Lesson 14
OUTL15C.DOC	Lesson 15	TOC14.MRK	Lesson 14
PAGES4.LST	Lesson 4	TRAVEL8.MEM	Lesson 8

Index

B

C

D

E

F

G

H

I

M

N

O

P

Q

R

S

T

U

V

W

Learn Your Favorite Applications Fast—On-Screen—With PC Tutors From Que!

Que makes it easy to learn new software applications with PC Tutors! Following a unique, on-screen teaching method, you learn by doing. Each PC Tutor offers step-by-step instructions and dozens of hands-on exercises. Best of all, these self-training tutorials get you started learning the application—without buying the software!

Personal computing is so easy with PC Tutors from Que!

MS-DOS PC Tutor

Que Development Group

Complete book-and-disk tutorial for hands-on learning of DOS! Users learn DOS basics quickly by following the disk tutorial developed by ATI. Then the text advances to more complex operations—when you're ready. Practical step-by-step exercises are ideal for quick and easy learning in an individual or group setting.

Book & Disk Set for DOS 3.X & 4.X

Order #1213 **$39.95 USA**

WordPerfect PC Tutor

Que Development Group

WordPerfect PC Tutor is the perfect learning tool for beginning users of WordPerfect 5.1! Practical hands-on exercises lead users through WordPerfect fundamentals and teach more advanced applications of WordPerfect.

Step-by-step examples teach you how to create, edit, and print WordPerfect documents.

Book & Disk Set for WordPerfect 5.1

Order #1214 **$39.95 USA**

1-2-3 Release 2.2 PC Tutor

Que Development Group

The quick learning guide to 1-2-3 spreadsheets! comes complete with tutorial disk so readers can quickly build 1-2-3 applications. Users complete the comprehensive disk tutorial and move on to logical book lessons and exercises for creating graphs, worksheets, databases, and printing reports.

Book & Disk Set for 1-2-3 Releases 2.01 & 2.2

Order #1232 **$39.95 USA**

To Order Call:

1-800-428-5331, ext. TUTR

dBASE IV PC Tutor

Que Development Group

Step-by-step introduction to dBASE IV! Readers use the easy-to-follow disk and tutorial lessons to create practical and dynamic databases. This book-and-disk set teaches you the basics of dBASE IV's newest release and leads you into complex customization techniques for dBASE applications. Packed with hands-on practice exercises and illustrations.

Book & Disk Set for dBASE IV 1.1

Order #1231 **$39.95 USA**

Computer Information From A-to-Z—Only From Que!

*"There are many on the market, but the choice is clear: **Que's Computer User's Dictionary**."*

Washington Post

"... the glossary contains most of the technical jargon an average user will encounter ... a focused reference."

PC Magazine

" ... a pocket dictionary of computer-related terms with several important differences from other similar books. First, it really is a user's dictionary ..."

New York Times

Que's Computer User's Dictionary *Que Development Group*

Que's Computer User's Dictionary is the critically acclaimed resource for everyone who uses a personal computer. Packed with definitions, illustrations, and examples, this handy reference is perfect for office, school, or home. Get yours today!

Covers IBM, Macintosh, Apple II, & Programming

Order #1086 **$9.95 USA**

To Order, Call

1-800-428-5331, ext. TUTR

If your computer uses 3 1/2-inch disks . . .

While most personal computers use 5 1/4-inch disks to store information, some newer computers are switching to 3 1/2-inch disks for information storage. If your computer uses 3 1/2-inch disks, you can return this form to Que to obtain a 3 1/2-inch disk to use with this book. Simply fill out the remainder of this form and mail to:

Disk Exchange
Que Corporation
11711 N. College
Carmel, IN 46032

We will send you, free of charge, the 3 1/2-inch version of the software.

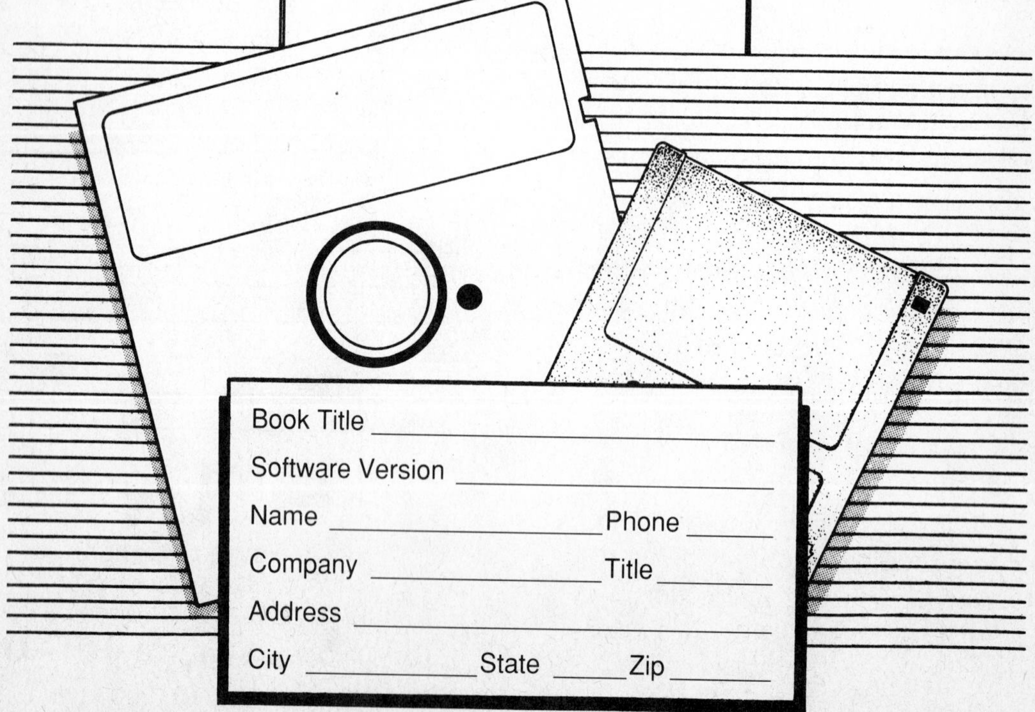
Book Title ______________________________
Software Version ________________________
Name ____________________ Phone ______
Company _________________ Title ______
Address _________________________________
City ______________ State _____ Zip _______

Free Catalog!

Mail us this registration form today, and we'll send you a free catalog featuring Que's complete line of best-selling books.

Name of Book ______________________

Name ______________________

Title ______________________

Phone ( ) ______________________

Company ______________________

Address ______________________

City ______________________

State ______ ZIP ______

Please check the appropriate answers:

1. Where did you buy your Que book?
   - ☐ Bookstore (name: ________)
   - ☐ Computer store (name: ______)
   - ☐ Catalog (name: ________)
   - ☐ Direct from Que
   - ☐ Other: ________

2. How many computer books do you buy a year?
   - ☐ 1 or less
   - ☐ 2-5
   - ☐ 6-10
   - ☐ More than 10

3. How many Que books do you own?
   - ☐ 1
   - ☐ 2-5
   - ☐ 6-10
   - ☐ More than 10

4. How long have you been using this software?
   - ☐ Less than 6 months
   - ☐ 6 months to 1 year
   - ☐ 1-3 years
   - ☐ More than 3 years

5. What influenced your purchase of this Que book?
   - ☐ Personal recommendation
   - ☐ Advertisement
   - ☐ In-store display
   - ☐ Price
   - ☐ Que catalog
   - ☐ Que mailing
   - ☐ Que's reputation
   - ☐ Other: ________

6. How would you rate the overall content of the book?
   - ☐ Very good
   - ☐ Good
   - ☐ Satisfactory
   - ☐ Poor

7. What do you like *best* about this Que book?

   ____

   ____

8. What do you like *least* about this Que book?

   ____

   ____

9. Did you buy this book with your personal funds?
   ☐ Yes ☐ No

10. Please feel free to list any other comments you may have about this Que book.

    ____

    ____

    ____

QUE

Order Your Que Books Today!

Name ______________________

Title ______________________

Company ______________________

City ______________________

State ______ ZIP ______

Phone No. ( ) ______________________

Method of Payment:

Check ☐ (Please enclose in envelope.)

Charge My: VISA ☐ MasterCard ☐

American Express ☐

Charge # ______________________

Expiration Date ______________________

Order No.	Title	Qty.	Price	Total

You can **FAX** your order to **1-317-573-2583.** Or call **1-800-428-5331, ext. ORDR** to order direct.

Please add $2.50 per title for shipping and handling.

Subtotal ______

Shipping & Handling ______

Total ______

QUE

NO POSTAGE
NECESSARY
IF MAILED
IN THE
UNITED STATES

BUSINESS REPLY MAIL
First Class Permit No. 9918 Indianapolis, IN

Postage will be paid by addressee

11711 N. College
Carmel, IN 46032

NO POSTAGE
NECESSARY
IF MAILED
IN THE
UNITED STATES

BUSINESS REPLY MAIL
First Class Permit No. 9918 Indianapolis, IN

Postage will be paid by addressee

11711 N. College
Carmel, IN 46032